The Certified
Pharmaceutical GMP
Professional Handbook

Also available from ASQ Quality Press:

The FDA and Worldwide Current Good Manufacturing Practices and Quality System Requirements for Finished Pharmaceuticals
José Rodríguez-Pérez

Statistical Process Control for the FDA-Regulated Industry
Manuel E. Peña-Rodríguez

Quality Risk Management in the FDA-Regulated Industry
José Rodríguez-Pérez

The FDA and Worldwide Quality System Requirements Guidebook for Medical Devices,
Second Edition
Amiram Daniel and Ed Kimmelman

CAPA for the FDA-Regulated Industry
José Rodríguez-Pérez

Development of FDA-Regulated Medical Products: A Translational Approach, Second
Edition
Elaine Whitmore

Medical Device Design and Regulation
Carl T. DeMarco

The Quality Toolbox, Second Edition
Nancy R. Tague

The Certified Manager of Quality/Organizational Excellence Handbook, Fourth Edition
Russell T. Westcott, editor

Root Cause Analysis: Simplified Tools and Techniques, Second Edition
Bjørn Andersen and Tom Fagerhaug

To request a complimentary catalog of ASQ Quality Press publications,
call 800-248-1946, or visit our website at http://www.asq.org/quality-press.

THE CERTIFIED PHARMACEUTICAL GMP PROFESSIONAL HANDBOOK

Mark Allen Durivage, Editor

ASQ Quality Press
Milwaukee, Wisconsin

American Society for Quality, Quality Press, Milwaukee 53203
© 2014 by ASQ
All rights reserved. Published 2014
Printed in the United States of America
20 19 18 17 16 15   5 4 3

Library of Congress Cataloging-in-Publication Data

Certified pharmaceutical GMP professional handbook / Mark Allen Durivage, editor.
   pages cm
  Includes bibliographical references and index.
  ISBN 978-0-87389-794-5 (hardcover : alk. paper)
  1. Pharmaceutical industry—Quality control. 2. Drug development. 3. Drugs—Standards.
 I. Durivage, Mark Allen.

  RM301.25C456 2014
  338.4'76151—dc23   2014011251

ISBN: 978-0-87389-794-5

Acquisitions Editor: Matt T. Meinholz
Managing Editor: Paul Daniel O'Mara
Production Administrator: Randall Benson

ASQ Mission: The American Society for Quality advances individual, organizational, and community excellence worldwide through learning, quality improvement, and knowledge exchange.

Attention Bookstores, Wholesalers, Schools, and Corporations: ASQ Quality Press books, video, audio, and software are available at quantity discounts with bulk purchases for business, educational, or instructional use. For information, please contact ASQ Quality Press at 800-248-1946, or write to ASQ Quality Press, P.O. Box 3005, Milwaukee, WI 53201-3005.

To place orders or to request ASQ membership information, call 800-248-1946. Visit our website at http://www.asq.org/quality-press.

 Printed on acid-free paper

Quality Press
600 N. Plankinton Ave.
Milwaukee, WI 53203-2914
E-mail: authors@asq.org

The Global Voice of Quality™

Table of Contents

List of Figures and Tables

Abbreviations and Acronyms

A

ACC—air chemical cleanliness

ACCME—Accreditation Council for Medical Education

ADE Report—Adverse Drug Experience Report

ADME—absorption, distribution, metabolism, and excretion

AE—adverse event

AHU—air-handling unit

AIP—Application Integrity Policy

ANDA—Abbreviated New Drug Application

AOAC—Association of Official Analytical Chemists

APA—Administrative Procedure Act *or* antiseptic processing area

APHIS—Animal and Plant Health Inspection Service

API—active pharmaceutical ingredient

APR—annual product review

AQL—acceptable quality level

ASQ—American Society for Quality

ASTM—American Society for Testing and Materials

B

BCMS—Business Continuity Management System

BET—bacterial endotoxin test

BIMO—Bioresearch Monitoring Program

BLA—Biological License Application

BoK—body of knowledge

BOM—bill of materials

BP—British Pharmacopeia

BSE—bovine spongiform encephalopathy

C

CANDA—Computer-Assisted New Drug Application

CAPA—corrective and preventive action

CBE-0—Supplement—Changes Being Effected

CBE-30—Supplement—Changes Being Effected in 30 Days

CBER—Center for Biologics Evaluation and Research

CCP—critical control point

CDC—Centers for Disease Control and Prevention

CDER—Center for Drug Evaluation and Research

CDRH—Center for Devices and Radiologic Health

CFR—Code of Federal Regulations

CFSAN—Center for Food Safety and Applied Nutrition

cfu—colony-forming unit

cGMP—current good manufacturing practices

CIMOS—Council for International Organizations of Medical Sciences

CIP—clean in place

CMC—chemistry, manufacturing, and controls

CME—continuing medical education

CMS—Centers for Medicare and Medicaid Services

COA—certificate of analysis

COC—certificate of compliance

COP—clean out of place

COTS—commercial off-the-shelf

CPG—Compliance Policy Guide

CPGP—certified pharmaceutical good manufacturing practices professional

C_{pk}—process capability index

CPP—critical process parameters

CPSC—Consumer Product Safety Commission

CQ—component qualification

CQA—critical quality attributes

CRA—clinical research associate

CRF—case report form

CRO—contract research organization

CSA—Controlled Substances Act

CTA—Clinical Trial Application

CTD—common technical document

CVM—Center for Veterinary Medicine

CVMP—cleaning validation master plan

D

DDMAC—Division of Drug Marketing, Advertising, and Communications

DEA—Drug Enforcement Agency

DESI—drug efficacy study implementation

DHR—device history record

DMF—drug master file

DOE—design of experiments

DOJ—Department of Justice

DOP—drop-off point

DQ—design qualification

DSHEA—Dietary Supplement Health and Education Act

DTC—direct to consumer

E

ECO—engineering change order

EDMS—electronic document management system

EDQM—European Directorate for the Quality of Medicines & HealthCare

EDR—electronic document room

EEA—European Economic Area

EIR—Establishment Inspection Report

EMA—European Medicines Evaluation Agency

EPA—Environmental Protection Agency

ERSR—electronic regulatory submission and review

ESM—electronic secure messaging

EU—European Union

F

FAERS—FDA Adverse Event Reporting System

FAP—food additive petition *or* filling assembly procedure

FAT—factory acceptance testing

FCR—facility change request

FDA—Food and Drug Administration

FDAAA—Food and Drug Administration Amendments Act

FDAMA—Food and Drug Administration Modernization Act

FDCA—Food, Drug, and Cosmetic Act

FMEA—failure mode and effects analysis

FMECA—failure mode, effects and criticality analysis

FOIA—Freedom of Information Act

FTA—fault tree analysis

FTC—Federal Trade Commission

G

GAMP—good automated manufacturing practices

GC—gas chromatography

GDP—good documentation practices

GEP—good engineering practices

GLP—good laboratory practices

GMP—good manufacturing practices

GRASE—generally recognized as safe and effective

H

HACCP—hazard analysis and critical control points

HAZOP—hazard operability analysis

HCFA—Healthcare Financing Administration

HEPA—high-efficiency particulate air (filter)

HHS—Department of Health and Human Services

HIC—hydrophobic interaction chromatography

HPFB—Health Products and Food Branch Inspectorate

HPKB—human pharmacokinetics and bioavailability

HPLC—high-performance (pressure) liquid chromatography

HVAC system—heating, ventilation, and air conditioning system

HW—Hardware

I

IB—investigator's brochure

ICDRA—International Conference of Drug Regulatory Authorities

ICF—informed consent form

ICH—International Conference on Harmonization

IDE—Investigational Device Exemption

IEC—ion-exchange chromatography

IFAP—Investigational Food Additive Petition

IMP—investigational medicinal product

INAD—investigational new animal drug

INAP—Investigational Food Additive Petition

IND—investigational new drug

INDA—Investigational New Drug Application

IPC—in-process control

IPEC—International Pharmaceutical Excipients Council

IQ—installation qualification

IR—infrared

IRB—Institutional Review Board

ISE—integrated summary of effectiveness

ISO—International Organization for Standardization

ISS—integrated summary of safety

J

JP—Japanese Pharmacopeia

L

LAL—limulus amebocyte lysate

LIMS—laboratory information management system

LOA—letter of authorization

M

MBR—master batch record

MDD—microbial data deviation

MDR—Medical Device Reporting

MDUFMA—Medical Device User Fee and Modernization Act

MHLW—Ministry of Health, Labour, and Welfare

MHRA—Medicines and Healthcare Products Regulatory Agency

MKT—mean kinetic temperature

MRA—mutual recognition agreement

MSDS—material safety data sheet

N

NAI—no action indicated

NCE—new chemical entity

NCR—nonconformance

NDA—New Drug Application

NDC—National Drug Code

NEPA—National Environmental Policy Act

NF—National Formulary

NIH—National Institutes of Health

NIST—National Institute of Standards and Technology

NMR—nuclear magnetic resonance

NMT—no more than

NOEL—no observable effect level

NOV—Notice of Violation

NSR—nonsignificant risk

O

OAI—official action indicated

ODA—Orphan Drug Act

ODE—Office of Device Evaluation

OECD—Organization for Economic Cooperation and Development

OOC—out of calibration

OOPD—Office of Orphan Products Development

OOS—out of specification

OOT—out of tolerance

OQ—operational qualification

OSHA—Occupational Safety and Health Administration

OTC—over the counter

P

PAS—Prior Approval Supplement

PAT—process analytical technology

PBR—production batch record

PDCA—plan–do–check–act

PDMA—Prescription Drug Marketing Act

PDUFA—Prescription Drug User Fee Act

PFDA—Pure Food and Drug Act

PFSB—Pharmaceutical and Food Safety Bureau

Ph Eur—European Pharmacopeia

PHA—preliminary hazard analysis

PhRMA—Pharmaceutical Research and Manufacturers of America

PHS—Public Health Service

PIC/S—Pharmaceutical Inspection Convention and Pharmaceutical Inspection Co-operation Scheme

PK—Pharmacokinetics

PL—Public Law

PMA—premarket approval

PPQ—process performance qualification

PQ—performance qualification

PQR—product quality review

PRO—patient-reported outcome

Q

QA—quality assurance

QAC—quaternary ammonium compounds

QbD—quality by design

QC—quality control

QCU—quality control unit

QMS—quality management system

QOL—quality of life

QP—qualified person

QSIT—quality system inspection technique

QU—quality unit

R

R&D—research and development

RAS—rapid alert system

RDP—regulatory development plan

REB—Research Ethics Board

RH—relative humidity

RODAC—replication organism detection and counting (plate)

RTD—resistance temperature detector

RTU—ready to use

S

SAT—site acceptance testing

SCHIP—State Children's Health Insurance Plan

SDA—Sabouraud dextrose agar

SDV—source document/data verification

SEC—Securities and Exchange Commission

SGE—special government employees

SMF—site master file

SNDA—Supplemental New Drug Application

SOP—standard operating procedure

SPC—statistical process control *or* surface particle cleanliness

T

TAMC—total aerobic microbial count

TGA—Therapeutic Goods Administration

TOC—total organic carbon

TRO—temporary restraining order

TSA—trypticase soy agar

TSE—transmission spongiform encephalopathy

U

UK—United Kingdom

ULPA—ultra-low penetration air (filter)

US—United States

USDA—United States Department of Agriculture

USP—United States Pharmacopeia

UV—ultraviolet

V

VAI—voluntary actions indicated

VMP—validation master plan

VNR—video news release

VSTA—Virus-Serum-Toxin Act

v/v—volume solute per volume solvent

W

WFI—water for injection

WHO—World Health Organization

WIP—work in progress

w/v—weight by volume

Preface

The purpose of this handbook is to highlight and partially annotate what the founders of the Certified Pharmaceutical Good Manufacturing Practices Professional (CPGP) examination believed to be the main topics comprising worldwide pharmaceutical *good manufacturing practices* (GMP). Logic and deduction aided the examination development volunteers and the professional staff of the Certification Offerings group at ASQ during their drafting and finalization of the inaugural version of the CPGP *body of knowledge* (BoK). The latter undergoes review and revision every five years per certification offerings and ASQ policy and procedures. Because each ASQ examination handbook must reflect the current BoK of its exam, this handbook will obligatorily undergo revision processes after all future CPGP BoK revisions. As the world becomes ever more paperless and electronically nimble and adaptive to changes, reference books such as the *CPGP Handbook* are obligated to provide as many means as possible of bridging, if not transcending, the predictable (and inevitable) changes to laws, regulations, guidelines/guidance documents, compendia, and consensus standards. This handbook inculcates the reader in where and how to tap appropriate URLs and other sources of the changing laws, regulations, guidelines, compendia, and consensus standards.

Acknowledgments

This first edition of *The Certified Pharmaceutical GMP Professional Handbook* is dedicated in memory of Martha Bennett. Martha had more than 30 years of experience in the area of US FDA law and regulations as an investigator, compliance officer, policy advisor to three commissioners, and consultant to companies worldwide regulated by the agency. She possessed strong analytical and communication skills, along with broad-based practical experience that she used to help clients develop sound regulatory and quality system programs. Martha provided litigation support as a consultant and expert witness. She was a Paul Harris Rotary Club Fellow and recipient of the Rotary Club Humanitarian Award. She was actively involved in the American Society for Quality, serving as the Education Chair for the Society's Food, Drug, and Cosmetic Division.

The following individuals are to be recognized as contributing chapter authors for this handbook: Bob Seltzer, John Lyall, Leann Christman, Mark Durivage, Scott Kochendoerfer, Kelli Turner, Bob Mehta, Elena Mack, Cathelene Compton, Mary Chris Easterly, Kanti Thirumoorthy, Jim Arnold, Carolina Valoyes, Nancy Van Gieson, Armand Niangara, Sofia Hernandez, Vidhya Sivakumar, Robert Johnson, Mary Kearnes, Yoko Doucette, and Frank Settineri. By using several individual subject matter experts, the overall quality and technical content of this handbook has been greatly enhanced.

Additionally, the following individuals are recognized for their contributions: Roland Bizanek, Jennifer Asleson, Ted Hilliard, David Schultenover, Rosemarie Christopher, Janet Rea, Martha Bennett, Richard Dolejan, Mairead Goetz, and Raj Rajamani.

I would also like to recognize the Food, Drug, and Cosmetic Division leadership committee. Without their combined vision, passion, and support, this project would not have been completed.

A special thanks to MaryAnn Foote, who provided technical editing services that helped harmonize the chapters by providing a unified writing style, and a "voice of reason" to bring this project to closure.

I would like to thank ASQ Quality Press, especially Matt Meinholz, Acquisitions Editor and Paul O'Mara, Managing Editor, for their expertise and technical competence that made this project a reality.

Lastly, I would like to acknowledge my wife Dawn and my boys, Jack and Sam, for being patient and allowing me the time to organize, write, and edit this handbook. Although it was stressful at times, I found the process to be very rewarding and fulfilling.

Mark Allen Durivage, ASQ Fellow
Editor and Project Leader
Lambertville, Michigan

Part I

Regulatory Agency Governance

Chapter 1

Global Regulatory Framework

UNITED STATES FEDERAL STATUTES RELEVANT TO PHARMACEUTICALS

The Administrative Procedure Act

The Administrative Procedure Act (APA) of 1946 is the United States federal law governing how administrative agencies (for example, the Food and Drug Administration [FDA]) within the federal government of the United States of America propose and establish regulation. The APA sets up a process for the United States federal courts to review directly (that is, judicial review) any agency decisions/regulations. The difference between *federal statutory law* and *federal administrative law* (agency regulation) is explained as follows: Congress finalizes the content and approves (legislates) a federal bill that, when signed by the president, becomes federal statutory law. Federal executive departments (that is, the president's cabinet) such as the Department of Health and Human Services (HHS) and subordinate administrative agencies (for example FDA, the National Institutes of Health [NIH]) declare and publish (promulgate) regulations/administrative law to codify and put into practical motion the governing federal statutory laws. The verb "promulgate" is interchangeable with the verb "codify," the verb associated with the Code (that is, collection) of Federal Regulations. The United States Justice Department indicts and prosecutes based on alleged violation of one or more specific regulations/administrative laws promulgated by a federal agency (which has its basis in a federal statutory law). A federal court verdict or injunction references the prevailing federal statutory law, while prosecutors present to the court evidence that is shown to violate one or more specific administrative laws/regulations.

United States Federal Food, Drug, and Cosmetic Act

The Food, Drug, and Cosmetic Act (FDCA) of 1938 is the United States federal statute governing the marketing, manufacture, and distribution of finished pharmaceuticals, medical devices, foods, dietary supplements, and cosmetics. It has never been replaced or renamed, but rather supplemented or amended through subsequent acts. The FDCA replaced the 1906 Federal Safe Food and Drugs Act after revelations in Upton Sinclair's book *The Jungle* of intentional inclusion of filth by the United States meat-packing industry. The 1938 FDCA improvements over the 1906 Act included the following:

- Extending control to cosmetics and therapeutic devices

- Requiring new drugs to be shown safe before marketing

- Providing that safe tolerances be set for unavoidable poisonous substances

- Authorizing standards of identity, quality, and fill-of-container for foods

- Authorizing factory inspections

- Adding the remedy of court injunctions (to the previous Act's seizures and prosecutions)

Table 1.1 provides some FDA website listings for amendments to the FDCA.

United States Public Health Service Act

The United States Public Health Service (PHS) originated in name in 1798; however, the PHS Act of 1944 consolidated many previous federal laws relating to public health services and newly mandated the licensing of human biologic products, or their suspension if they endangered public health. The PHS Act is codified and enforced by several federal agencies under the Department of HHS.

The Virus-Serum-Toxin Act

The Virus-Serum-Toxin Act (VSTA) (as amended) requires licensing of animal vaccine products and establishments, and requires permits for the importation of animal biologic products. The Veterinary Biologics Program of the United States Department of Agriculture's (USDA) Animal and Plant Health Inspection Service (APHIS) enforces the VSTA by codifying regulations in 9 CFR 101–118.

It should be noted that the term "pharmaceuticals" is interchangeable with "drugs" in the United States and with the term "medicinal products" in the rest of the world. It is an umbrella term that includes biologics (usually large-molecule therapeutic entities greater than 5 kDaltons) and nonbiologic drugs (usually small-molecule entities less than 5 kDaltons). Biologics, like other drugs, are used for the treatment, prevention, or cure of disease in humans; however, they are generally derived from living material and are complex in structure and often less definitively characterized than nonbiologic drugs. Biologics are not characterized down to every element, ionic state, water of hydration, three-dimensional structure, including disulfide bond, hydrogen bond, or protein quaternary subunit.

EUROPEAN UNION LEGAL SYSTEM RELEVANT TO PHARMACEUTICALS

Within the member countries of the European Union (EU), regulations, directives, and decisions are the principal forms of legislation governing pharmaceutical manufacturing and pharmaceutical marketing. Specifically, a "regulation" is a binding legislative act that must be applied in its entirety across the EU. A "directive" is a legislative act that sets out a goal that all EU countries must achieve;

Table 1.1   Food and Drug Administration amendments to the Food, Drug, and Cosmetic Act.

FDA history	Web links
Significant dates in U.S. food and drug law history	http://www.fda.gov/AboutFDA/WhatWe Do/History/Milestones/ucm128305.htm
Infant Formula Act of 1980 PL 96-359 (Oct 26, 1980)	http://thomas.loc.gov/cgi-bin/bdquery/ z?d096:HR06940:@@@L | TOM:/bss/ d096query.html | #summary
Orphan Drug Act PL 97-414 (Jan 4, 1983)	http://www.fda.gov/RegulatoryInformation/ Legislation/FederalFoodDrugandCosmeticAct FDCAct/SignificantAmendmentstotheFDCAct/ OrphanDrugAct/default.htm
Drug Price Competition and Patent Term Restoration Act of 1984 PL 98-417 (Sept 24, 1984)	http://thomas.loc.gov/cgi-bin/bdquery/ z?d098:SN01538:@@@D&summ2=m& | TOM:/ bss/d098query.html |
Prescription Drug Marketing Act of 1987 PL 100-293 (Apr 22, 1988)	http://www.fda.gov/RegulatoryInformation/ Legislation/FederalFoodDrugandCosmeticAct FDCAct/SignificantAmendmentstotheFDCAct/ PrescriptionDrugMarketingActof1987/default.htm
Generic Animal Drug and Patent Term Restoration Act of 1988 PL 100-670 (Nov 16, 1988)	http://www.fda.gov/RegulatoryInformation/ Legislation/FederalFoodDrugandCosmeticAct FDCAct/SignificantAmendmentstotheFDCAct/ ucm147135.htm
Nutrition Labeling and Education Act of 1990 PL 101-535 (Nov 8, 1990)	http://thomas.loc.gov/cgi-bin/bdquery/ z?d101:HR03562:@@@D&summ2=3& | TOM:/ bss/d101query.html |
Safe Medical Devices Act of 1990 PL 101-629 (Nov 28, 1990)	http://thomas.loc.gov/cgi-bin/bdquery/ z?d101:HR03095:@@@D&summ2=1& | TOM:/ bss/d101query.html |
Medical Device Amendments of 1992 PL 102-300 (June 16, 1992)	http://thomas.loc.gov/cgi-bin/bdquery/ z?d102:SN02783:@@@D&summ2=m& | TOM:/ bss/d102query.html |
Prescription Drug Amendments of 1992; Prescription Drug User Fee Act of 1992 PL 102-571 (Oct 29, 1992)	http://www.fda.gov/RegulatoryInformation/ Legislation/FederalFoodDrugandCosmeticAct FDCAct/SignificantAmendmentstotheFDCAct/ PrescriptionDrugAmendmentsof1992Prescription DrugUserFeeActof1992/default.htm
Animal Medicinal Drug Use Clarification Act (AMDUCA) of 1994 PL 103-396 (Oct 22, 1994)	http://www.fda.gov/RegulatoryInformation/ Legislation/FederalFoodDrugandCosmeticAct FDCAct/SignificantAmendmentstotheFDCAct/ AnimalMedicinalDrugUseClarificationAct AMDUCAof1994/default.htm

All websites active as of November 2013.
PL = Public law

Continued

Table 1.1   *Continued.*

FDA history	Web links
Dietary Supplement Health and Education Act of 1994 PL 103-417 (Oct 25, 1994)	http://www.fda.gov/RegulatoryInformation/ Legislation/FederalFoodDrugandCosmeticAct FDCAct/SignificantAmendmentstotheFDCAct/ ucm148003.htm
FDA Export Reform and Enhancement Act of 1996 PL 104-134 (Apr 26, 1996)	http://www.fda.gov/RegulatoryInformation/ Legislation/FederalFoodDrugandCosmeticAct FDCAct/SignificantAmendmentstotheFDCAct/ ucm148005.htm
Food Quality Protection Act of 1996 PL 104-170 (Aug 3, 1996)	http://www.fda.gov/RegulatoryInformation/ Legislation/FederalFoodDrugandCosmeticAct FDCAct/SignificantAmendmentstotheFDCAct/ ucm148008.htm
Animal Drug Availability Act of 1996 PL 104-250 (Oct 9, 1996)	http://www.gpo.gov/fdsys/pkg/PLAW-104 publ250/html/PLAW-104publ250.htm
Food and Drug Administration Modernization Act (FDAMA) of 1997 PL 105-115 (Nov 21, 1997)	http://www.fda.gov/RegulatoryInformation/ Legislation/FederalFoodDrugandCosmeticAct FDCAct/SignificantAmendmentstotheFDCAct/ FDAMA/default.htm
Best Pharmaceuticals for Children Act PL 107-109 (Jan 4, 2002)	http://www.fda.gov/RegulatoryInformation/ Legislation/FederalFoodDrugandCosmeticAct FDCAct/SignificantAmendmentstotheFDCAct/ ucm148011.htm
Medical Device User Fee and Modernization Act (MDUFMA) of 2002 PL 107-250 (Oct 26, 2002)	http://www.fda.gov/RegulatoryInformation/ Legislation/FederalFoodDrugandCosmeticAct FDCAct/SignificantAmendmentstotheFDCAct/ MedicalDeviceUserFeeandModernizationAct MDUFMAof2002/default.htm
Animal Drug User Fee Act of 2003 PL 108-130 (Nov 18, 2003)	http://www.fda.gov/RegulatoryInformation/ Legislation/FederalFoodDrugandCosmeticAct FDCAct/SignificantAmendmentstotheFDCAct/ AnimalDrugUserFeeActof2003/default.htm
Pediatric Research Equity Act of 2003 PL 108-155 (Dec 3, 2003)	http://www.gpo.gov/fdsys/pkg/PLAW-108 publ155/html/PLAW-108publ155.htm
Minor Use and Minor Species Animal Health Act of 2004 PL 108-282 (Aug 2, 2004)	http://www.fda.gov/RegulatoryInformation/ Legislation/FederalFoodDrugandCosmeticAct FDCAct/SignificantAmendmentstotheFDCAct/ MinorUseandMinorSpeciesAnimalHealthActof 2004/default.htm

Continued

Table 1.1   *Continued.*

FDA history	Web links
Dietary Supplement and Nonprescription Drug Consumer Protection Act PL 109-462 (Dec 22, 2006)	http://www.fda.gov/RegulatoryInformation/ Legislation/FederalFoodDrugandCosmeticAct FDCAct/SignificantAmendmentstotheFDCAct/ ucm148035.htm
Food and Drug Administration Amendments Act (FDAAA) of 2007 PL 110-85 (Sept 27, 2007)	http://www.fda.gov/RegulatoryInformation/ Legislation/FederalFoodDrugandCosmeticAct FDCAct/SignificantAmendmentstotheFDCAct/ FoodandDrugAdministrationAmendmentsActof 2007/default.htm
Family Smoking Prevention and Tobacco Control Act PL 111-31 (June 22, 2009)	http://www.fda.gov/tobaccoproducts/ guidancecomplianceregulatoryinformation/ ucm246129.htm
FDA Food Safety Modernization Act PL 111-353 (Jan 4, 2011)	http://www.fda.gov/RegulatoryInformation/ Legislation/FederalFoodDrugandCosmeticAct FDCAct/SignificantAmendmentstotheFDCAct/ ucm244718.htm
FDA Safety and Innovation Act (FDASIA) PL 112-144 (July 9, 2012)	http://www.fda.gov/regulatoryinformation/ legislation/federalfooddrugandcosmeticactfdcact/ significantamendmentstothefdcact/fdasia/ ucm20027187.htm

however, it is up to the individual countries to decide how to achieve that goal. A "decision" only deals with a particular issue and specifically mentioned persons or organizations.

Member states of the EU enact national laws to enforce the provisions of EU directives. Directive 2001/83/EC (similar to the United States FDCA) continues to be amended over time but maintains its original structure and general content (comprising Articles and Annexes). This directive requires each holder of a medicinal product manufacturing authorization to have "permanently and continuously at his disposal the services of at least one qualified person [QP]." The specific duties of the QP, as well as the guidelines for pharmaceutical *good manufacturing practices* (GMP), are detailed in the Eudralex Volume 4, Part I.

JAPAN LEGAL SYSTEM RELEVANT TO PHARMACEUTICALS

The Ministry of Health, Labour, and Welfare (MHLW) (the Koseirodosho) was established by a merger of the Ministry of Health and Welfare and the Ministry of Labour on January 6, 2001, as part of the government program for reorganizing government ministries. The MHLW, which was originally established in 1938, was in charge of the improvement and promotion of social welfare, social security, and public health, and the new organization has the same tasks. The department consists of the ministry proper, affiliated institutions, councils, local branches, and an external organization. The MHLW is in charge of pharmaceutical regulatory affairs in Japan (veterinary drugs are under the jurisdiction of the Ministry of Agriculture, Forestry and Fisheries). The Pharmaceutical and Food Safety Bureau (PFSB) undertakes the main duties and functions of the Ministry: it handles clinical studies, approval reviews, and post-marketing safety measures, that is, approvals and licensing for ensuring food and drug safety.

US - FDA
Eu - Eu
JA - PFSB

Chapter 2

Regulations and Guidances

It is necessary to possess the ability to interpret regulations and guidelines as published or administered by the Pharmaceutical Inspection Convention and Pharmaceutical Inspection Cooperation Scheme (PIC/S), Health Canada, the World Health Organization (WHO), the International Conference on Harmonization (ICH), the European Medicines Agency (EMA), the United States Food and Drug Administration (FDA), the Therapeutic Goods Administration (TGA), United States Department of Agriculture (USDA) 9 CFR (Code of Federal Regulations), USDA Veterinary Service, and the International Pharmaceutical Excipients Council (IPEC).

PHARMACEUTICAL INSPECTION CONVENTION AND PHARMACEUTICAL INSPECTION COOPERATION SCHEME

PIC/S are two authorities that provide guidance in the field of *good manufacturing practices* (GMP). The goal of PIC/S is to lead the international development, implementation, and maintenance of harmonized GMP standards and quality systems in the field of medicinal products. This goal is to be attained by developing and promoting harmonized GMP standards and guidance documents. Additionally, PIC/S promotes the training of authorities and inspectors to ensure competent GMP assessments. Currently, 44 regulatory bodies participate in PIC/S, including representatives from South America, Europe, Asia, Australia, and North America.

HEALTH CANADA

A federal department known as Health Canada is responsible for helping Canadians maintain and improve their health while respecting individual choices and circumstances. The goal of the department is to maintain a balance between the potential health benefits and risks posed by all drugs and health products.

Branch-wide compliance and enforcement activities are the responsibility of the Inspectorate, enabling consistency of approach across the spectrum of regulated products. Core functions include compliance monitoring, compliance verification and investigation—supported by establishment licensing of drugs and medical devices, and laboratory analysis.

Quality assurance (QA) that ensures that drugs are consistently produced and controlled in such a way as to meet the quality standards appropriate to their intended use, as required by the marketing authorization, includes GMP. Inspections are conducted to verify the compliance with GMP (Part C, Division 2 of the Food and Drugs Regulations), which is a requirement for the issuance of an establishment license. The Inspectorate has developed the GMP guidelines and a series of guides and other related documents to ensure a uniform application of the established requirements and to help the industry comply.

WORLD HEALTH ORGANIZATION

WHO is responsible for providing leadership on global health matters. Within the United Nations system, WHO is the directing and coordinating authority for health, working to shape the health research agenda, set norms and standards, articulate evidence-based policy options, provide technical support to countries, and monitor and assess health trends. WHO membership includes 194 countries and two associate members.

INTERNATIONAL CONFERENCE ON HARMONIZATION

In 1990 the pharmaceutical industries of Europe, Japan, and the United States began to work with drug regulatory authorities with the goal of harmonizing the interpretation and application of technical guidelines and requirements for product registration. Regulatory and pharmaceutical industries benefit from the harmonization as illustrated by the reduction of duplicate clinical trials and minimization of the use of animal testing without compromising safety and effectiveness for drug development. ICH Tripartite Guidelines were developed through scientific consensus with regulatory and industry experts to achieve harmonization.

EUROPEAN MEDICINES AGENCY

EMA is responsible for the scientific evaluation of medicines developed by pharmaceutical companies for use in the European Union (EU). This responsibility includes the scientific evaluation of applications for EU marketing authorizations for human and veterinary medicines. Pharmaceutical companies must submit a single marketing authorization application to the Agency and can only start to market a medicine after receiving marketing authorization.

Most of the Agency's scientific evaluation work is carried out by its scientific committees, which are made up of members from European Economic Area (EEA) countries, as well as representatives of patient, consumer, and healthcare-professional organizations. Committees are responsible for evaluating the development, assessment, and supervision of medicines in the EU. The Agency constantly monitors the safety of medicines and can take action if information indicates that the benefit–risk balance of a medicine has changed since authorization.

THE UNITED STATES FOOD AND DRUG ADMINISTRATION

The US FDA consists of four core functions of the agency: Medical Products and Tobacco, Foods and Veterinary Medicine, Global Regulatory Operations, and Policy and Operations. FDA is tasked with protecting the public health by assuring the safety, effectiveness, quality, and security of human and veterinary drugs, vaccines and other biologic products, medical devices, the nation's food supply, all cosmetics, dietary supplements, and products that give off radiation *Over-the-counter* (OTC) and prescription drugs, including generic drugs, are regulated by FDA's Center for Drug Evaluation and Research (CDER).

THERAPEUTIC GOODS ADMINISTRATION

The TGA is part of the Australian Government Department of Health. The TGA is responsible for ensuring that therapeutic goods available for supply in Australia are safe and fit for their intended purpose. The TGA's overall purpose is to protect public health and safety by regulating therapeutic goods that are either imported into Australia or are manufactured in Australia, or exported from Australia. TGA defines therapeutic goods to include medicines, medical devices, and human blood, blood products, and tissues. The goal of TGA is to ensure access, within a reasonable time frame, to new therapeutic goods. These include goods Australians rely on every day, such as vitamin tablets and sunscreens, as well as goods used to treat serious conditions, such as prescription medicines, vaccines, blood products, and surgical implants.

USDA 9 CFR ANIMALS AND ANIMAL PRODUCTS

The CFR annual edition is the codification of the general and permanent rules published in the *Federal Register* by the departments and agencies of the federal government. It is divided into 50 titles that represent broad areas subject to federal regulation. CFR Title 9 concerns animals and animal products.

USDA VETERINARY SERVICE MEMORANDUM NO. 800.65

This memorandum provides guidance on preparing veterinary biological products that use embryonated chicken eggs or chicken tissue as an ingredient. It is meant to assist licensees, permittees, and applicants in meeting the purity and quality requirements in 9 CFR 113.50.

INTERNATIONAL PHARMACEUTICAL EXCIPIENTS COUNCIL

The IPEC Federation is a source for regulatory and guidance documents critical to the excipient industry. The association serves the interests of producers, distributors, and users of pharmaceutical excipients. IPEC-Americas, composed of finished drug manufacturers, excipient producers, and distributors, is part of a global federation, the IPEC Federation, that brings together excipient manufacturers, distributors, and users from the United States, Europe, Japan, and China to set the bar on quality standards.

Chapter 3
Mutual Recognition Agreements

MUTUAL RECOGNITION AGREEMENTS

Mutual recognition agreements (MRA) are international agreements that specify the conditions under which the participating countries will accept or recognize one another's conformity assessments, and that identify how the parties will cooperate on other activities, as specified. The primary objective of MRA is to provide effective and efficient market access throughout the territories of the MRA parties.

MRA Established by the European Union and Partner Countries

The European Union (EU), Australia, Canada, New Zealand, and Switzerland are referred to as MRA *partner countries*, whereas other countries outside the European Economic Area (EEA) are referred to as *third countries*. Each agreement has slight differences in coverage; however, the broad general purpose of each MRA is fourfold:

- Facilitate market access while safeguarding consumer health

- Grant mutual acceptance of reports, certificates, and authorizations issued by the regulated authorities of the signatories, and provide certification of conformity to the requirements

- Exchange information concerning procedures used to ensure that the conformity bodies comply with the general principles of designation

- Encourage greater international harmonization

The premise of the MRA is that the MRA partner country and EU member states mutually recognize relevant manufacturing authorizations granted by the competent authorities of the other party, conclusions of inspections of manufacturers carried out by the relevant inspection services of the other party, and manufacturers' certification of the conformity of each batch to its specifications by the respective party without recontrol at import.

The scope of the agreements covers medicinal products that have undergone one or a series of manufacturing operations in the MRA partner country and/or the EU. For the purposes of these agreements, manufacturing operations include manufacturing, labeling, testing, and wholesaling activities.

Key Elements of Mutual Recognition Agreements

Issuance of Certificate of GMP Compliance of Manufacturers. The purpose of the certificate is to confirm that the manufacturer or laboratory is authorized to carry out activities and is regularly inspected and complies with national *good manufacturing practices* (GMP) requirements that are deemed equivalent to EU GMP. Authorities responsible for supervision of the entity issue the certificate. A manufacturer can request an inspection by the local competent authority to obtain a certificate.

Batch Certification. Each batch being transferred between MRA countries must be accompanied by a batch certificate issued by the manufacturer in the exporting country. The importer of the batch needs to receive and to maintain this certificate that attests that the batch has been manufactured in accordance with the requirements of the marketing authorization of the importing country and that it meets specifications. The certificate includes a statement that batch processing and packaging records have been reviewed and comply with GMP. The content of the batch certificate has been harmonized and agreed on by MRA partners.

Responsibilities of the Qualified Person. The *qualified person* (QP) may rely on the written confirmation of the manufacturer's batch certificate without further testing. Responsibilities of the various parties should, however, be clearly defined in a written agreement.

Pharmaceutical Inspection Cooperation Scheme

The Pharmaceutical Inspection Convention and the Pharmaceutical Inspection Co-operation Scheme (jointly referred to as PIC/S) provide a means for international cooperation in the field of GMP. PIC/S is a cooperation scheme. Membership, however, does not mean that an MRA exists. PIC/S's mission is to lead the international development, implementation, and maintenance of harmonized GMP standards and quality systems of inspectorates in the field of medicinal products. The purpose of the PIC/S scheme is to:

- Pursue and strengthen the cooperation established between the participating authorities in the field of inspection and related areas with a view to maintaining mutual confidence and promoting quality assurance of inspections

- Provide the framework for all necessary exchange of information and experience

- Coordinate mutual training for inspectors and for other technical experts in related fields

- Continue common efforts toward the improvement and harmonization of technical standards and procedures regarding the inspection of the manufacture of medicinal products and the testing of medicinal products by official control laboratories

- Continue common efforts for the development, harmonization, and maintenance of GMP

- Extend cooperation to other competent authorities having the national arrangements necessary to apply equivalent standards and procedures with a view to contributing to global harmonization.

Currently there are 44 member countries, including all EEA countries, Argentina, Australia, Canada, Israel, Malaysia, Singapore, South Africa, and Switzerland. The United States Food and Drug Administration (FDA) is also a participating authority.

Before a regulatory authority can become a member of the PIC/S, a detailed assessment is undertaken to determine whether the authority has the arrangements and competence necessary to apply an inspection system comparable to that of current PIC/S members. This assessment involves an examination of the authority's inspection and licensing system, quality system, legislative requirements, inspector training, and so on, and is followed by a visit from a PIC/S delegation to observe inspectors carrying out actual GMP inspections.

Chapter 4

Regulatory Inspections

INSPECTION AUTHORITY

The Food, Drug, and Cosmetic Act (FDCA) grants the United States Food and Drug Administration (FDA) the authority to conduct establishment inspections and collect samples to enforce the Act. FDA, in the Center for Biologics Evaluation and Research (CBER) Compliance Program Guidance Manual, Inspection of Biological Products, 7345.848, outlines three reasons for conducting inspections:

- To safeguard the public health by reducing the risk of adulterated or misbranded drugs reaching the marketplace

- To increase communication between the industry and FDA

- To provide timely input to firms during inspections to improve the firm's compliance with *current good manufacturing practices* (cGMP) requirements

Countries that import drugs manufactured in the United States can inspect drug manufacturing establishments in the United States. For example, Health Canada performs inspections for on-site monitoring and assessment of applicable requirements in the Canadian Food and Drugs Act and associated regulations. Health Canada inspections routinely are conducted on a predetermined cycle or as required to assess compliance.

TYPES OF INSPECTIONS

Regulatory inspections for GMP compliance in the pharmaceutical industry typically are categorized as preapproval inspection, routine surveillance (post-approval), and compliance (one of which is "for cause"). A *preapproval inspection* of a drug manufacturing facility is conducted as part of the evaluation of a new drug before it is approved for commercial sale by FDA. If an *active pharmaceutical ingredient* (API) or excipient is made by a facility other than the manufacturer of the drug product, these facilities may also be inspected. If major issues are observed during a preapproval inspection, a follow-up inspection may be required before drug approval to review corrective actions implemented by the firm.

Routine surveillance inspections, conducted after a drug product is approved by the FDA, are intended to be conducted every two years. The FDA uses a risk management approach to assess which products pose a high risk and, as a result, require more-frequent oversight. A firm is considered to be a higher risk if the company has a history of cGMP compliance issues or is closer to the end of the processing of a drug product, or issues have occurred with similar categories of products (for example, heparin API contamination).

A *compliance inspection* is conducted to examine the effectiveness of corrective actions implemented by a firm due to a regulatory action. A compliance inspection may be referred to as a "for cause" inspection when an issue has occurred, such as contamination, adverse events (for example, patient deaths or severe side effects), or lack of drug effectiveness (perhaps due to a counterfeit drug).

INSPECTIONS OF FOREIGN DRUG MANUFACTURERS

Part of FDA's mission is to assure that drug, medical device, biologic, and food products manufactured in foreign countries and intended for US distribution are in compliance with the law and regulations, that noncompliance is identified and corrected, and that any unsafe or unlawful products are removed from the marketplace. FDA performs inspections of products at the US border on a risk-based approach. Materials that do not meet requirements are destroyed or exported back to the source. FDA typically conducts inspections of foreign drug manufacturing firms when:

- The firm is identified in an application or submission as the main supplier or alternate supplier of materials, products, or services.

- The firm has had a violative inspectional history and/or problems.

- The firm was prioritized using a tiered approach based on factors such as risk, volume of products, or complexity of processes.

- The firm had problems related to adverse reactions or was involved in recalls.

INSPECTION TECHNIQUES

During a regulatory inspection, FDA may evaluate the systems in place to assess the firm's cGMP compliance. If the system is determined to be in a state of control for the product or products examined during the inspection, the system should be adequate for the same class of products made by that firm.

FDA can conduct a comprehensive inspection, often referred to as a *full inspection*, for a broad and deep evaluation of the firm's cGMP compliance. The full inspection covers every system at the facility subject to FDA jurisdiction to determine compliance status. A full inspection is required for a compliance inspection and for the initial FDA inspection of a facility.

Alternatively, FDA can conduct a *directed inspection*, also known as an *abbreviated inspection*, to provide an efficient update of the firm's cGMP compliance. The abbreviated inspection covers specific areas to the depth necessary to address the purpose of the inspection.

FDA evaluates an organization by inspecting its cGMP systems. The FDA review of a system includes the systems being used as well as specific examples that illustrate the effectiveness of system implementation. The systems and evidence of implementation are covered in sufficient detail so that FDA can determine whether the system is in a state of control. FDA divides systems into six categories: quality, facilities and equipment, materials, production, packaging and labeling, and laboratory control. Full inspections require assessment of a minimum of four systems, one of which must be the quality system. Abbreviated inspections require a minimum of two systems, one of which must be the quality system. During subsequent abbreviated inspections, the systems evaluated are rotated so that all six systems are periodically addressed. Depth of coverage of each system depends on the findings during an inspection.

INSPECTION PROCESS

Upon arrival at the facility being inspected, and regardless of the type of inspection conducted, the FDA investigator displays credentials and gives documentation of the inspection on form FDA 482, Notice of Inspection, to the top management official at the facility. The FDA 482 usually is presented during an opening meeting with the inspection team and company management.

Inspections can be conducted by one investigator or a team of experts from within the firm's FDA district, from other districts, and/or from FDA headquarters, with one member designated as team leader. The inspection may consist of any combination of observing processes and the facility, reviewing procedures and records, and asking employees of the firm questions about their responsibilities and the tasks they perform.

Frequently, the inspection begins with a walk through the facility while it is in operation. FDA investigators take notes during all parts of the inspection to document what they have seen, the personnel encountered, and any concerns they have. Daily debriefings may occur so that FDA can indicate their concerns as they are encountered.

At the close of the inspection, the investigator provides the top management official with any inspection findings on form FDA 483, Inspectional Observations, usually during a closing meeting with company management. Observations listed on the FDA 483 are cGMP deficiencies related to a requirement in the cGMP regulations. If no observations of significance were identified, no FDA 483 is issued. Form FDA 484, Receipt for Samples, is presented to top management if samples were taken during the inspection. Routine surveillance samples are often collected during regulatory inspections. Samples also may be collected as a result of enforcement action.

After the close of the on-site inspection, the FDA investigator(s) are obligated to complete an *establishment inspection report* (EIR). Once the inspection is considered closed, and the EIR is available, it is typically forwarded to the company for inclusion in their inspection files.

Chapter 5

Enforcement Actions

Pharmaceutical companies and the regulatory agencies that provide oversight for their activities share a responsibility for ensuring the manufacture and distribution of quality drug products and for ensuring compliance with *good manufacturing practices* (GMP) regulations. When these agencies identify areas of noncompliance within a company (for example, during a regulatory inspection or as a result of mandatory problem reporting), they have an obligation to the public to take appropriate enforcement action to remedy the situation. The agencies have a number of enforcement tools at their disposal and will take action consistent with the seriousness of the violation (or violations) and the risk of harm to the public.

The most common enforcement tool used to compel compliance with regulatory requirements is a notice of observations/violations (for example, form FDA 483) that is provided to a company after an on-site inspection by the applicable regulatory agency. If a company fails to adequately address all of the issues in the notice, or if the compliance issues identified during the inspection are more serious or widespread, the regulatory agency may issue a warning letter to the company. In more serious cases, where there is an immediate risk to patient health and safety, the regulatory agency may choose to seize impacted product (product seizure) or prevent its continued distribution (through an injunction). In the United States, a company may be compelled to enter into a consent decree that outlines, in specific detail, the steps required to bring the organization back into compliance, and the reporting and oversight obligations necessary to fulfill the requirements of the consent decree. Finally, in those instances where previous enforcement action has been unsuccessful in compelling compliance, or where there are indications that compliance will not be possible, the regulatory agency may choose to withdraw a marketing authorization (specific to a product) or withdraw an establishment license (applicable to the company as a whole). This stepwise approach allows the regulatory agency to use a risk-based methodology to determine where to focus its efforts toward ensuring compliance with applicable regulations while continuing to meet its obligation to protect the public health.

ENFORCEMENT ACTIONS

Notice of Observations/Violations

If, during an inspection by FDA, significant compliance issues are observed, the investigator may choose to document those observations on form FDA 483, Inspectional Observations. Form 483 is used to notify the inspected establishment's top management, in writing, of significant objectionable conditions that were observed during the course of the inspection. If an observation related to a previous inspection has not been corrected (FDA is very good about verifying commitments made to correct previous 483 items) or is a recurring observation, it may also be noted on the form 483 for the current inspection. It is important to note, however, that additional observations of questionable significance may be discussed verbally with a firm's top management at the inspection closeout meeting. FDA's intent in making top management aware of these issues is to let them know that, if left uncorrected or unaddressed, these issues could become a violation. The *establishment inspection report* (EIR) that is provided after the inspection is closed provides documentation of both the written (on form 483) and verbal observations documented during the inspection.

A similar process is used by Health Canada. The Health Products and Food Branch Inspectorate (HPFBI) will document GMP-related observations on the inspection exit notice that is shared with the firm's management at the formal exit meeting. Differently than in the United States, a specific rating is assigned to the firm at the end of the inspection. Either a "C" rating (firm is recommended for the continuation or issuance of the establishment license) or an "NC" rating (firm is not recommended for the continuation or issuance of the establishment license) is assigned based on the results of the inspection.

In the United Kingdom (UK), after an inspection by the Medicines and Healthcare Products Regulatory Agency (MHRA), a post-inspection letter, outlining the deficiencies noted during the inspection, is sent to the inspected firm to provide written confirmation of the deficiencies reported verbally during the closing meeting with management. In the case of the post-inspection letter, all deficiencies are classified as critical, major, or other.

In all cases where an inspection report is issued, or areas of noncompliance are discussed verbally with the firm, the expectation of the regulatory agency is that the firm will take the appropriate corrective and preventive action to prevent future noncompliance. A written response from the firm, outlining the planned or completed actions, is necessary to preclude further enforcement action and to close the inspection.

These enforcement actions might include warning letter or notice, caution, criminal prosecution, and asset confiscation and civil action (injunction). Application of a sanction is dependent on several factors, including the nature of the noncompliance (critical or major), duration of the noncompliance, and actual or potential impact on public health.

In Europe, serious deficiencies that potentially could result in risk to public health are typically discussed in the inspection closeout (final) meeting, and immediate action is taken, as necessary, before issuing an inspection report. After the inspection, a draft inspection report or post-inspection letter is sent to the company for its comments to allow the report to be finalized. Any response received from the manufacturing firm is considered in the final report. Issuance of the final report is needed for the issuance of a GMP certificate, where applicable.

Warning Letters

FDA may choose to issue a *warning letter* if a company fails to adequately address all of the issues in the form FDA 483, or if the compliance issues identified during the inspection are more serious or widespread. Warning letters typically are issued for violations of regulatory significance, that is, those that may lead to further enforcement action if not corrected promptly and adequately.

FDA will label the correspondence as a "warning letter." They generally are addressed both to the highest known official at the corporation and to the highest known official at the site that was inspected, and include the dates of the inspection, a brief description of the violations, and the specific sections of the law that are in violation. The correspondence also will acknowledge any corrections promised during the inspection or in the firm's written response, and the Agency's position related to those corrections. Finally, it will request a prompt response to the warning letter, typically within 15 working days.

Unlike form FDA 483, warning letters are posted publicly on the FDA website and can result in significant harm to the firm's reputation. It is in a firm's best interest to correct identified areas of noncompliance quickly and completely to preclude the issuance of a warning letter. A warning letter may include a recommendation to withhold approval for any pending applications, which could result in significant financial harm to the company. It is important to note, however, that FDA is under no legal obligation to issue such a letter before taking additional and more serious enforcement action.

FDA may issue a warning letter closeout letter once it has completed an assessment of the corrective actions taken in response to the warning letter. Closeout letters apply only to those warning letters issued after September 1, 2009. The closeout letter can only be issued after FDA has verified (typically through a follow-up inspection) that the corrective actions have been taken. If the letter contains GMP violations that can not be corrected, no closeout letter will be issued.

Product Seizures

A *product seizure* is a judicial (court-approved) action for removing violative products from the marketplace. Seizures generally fall into one of three categories:

- *Mass seizure.* The seizure of all FDA-regulated products at an establishment or facility. This type of seizure is indicated when all of the suspect products have been held in the same environment (for example, dirty warehouse) or were produced under the same conditions (for example, nonconformance with GMP requirements).

- *Open-ended seizure.* The seizure of all units of a specific product or products, regardless of lot or batch number, where the violation is anticipated to be continuous.

- *Batch-specific seizure.* The seizure of a batch or batches of a regulated product where the violation is limited to a period of time or unique to a specific set of batches.

Product seizures typically are initiated when a company has not voluntarily recalled product that the regulatory agency believes is in violation of the law and where there is a perceived or known health risk to the public.

Injunctions

An *injunction* is another type of judicial action and is initiated to stop or prevent a violation of the law. It is typically invoked to halt the flow of violative products and to correct the conditions that caused the violations to occur. An injunction is considered for any significant out-of-compliance circumstance, but particularly when a health hazard has been identified. When an injunction is granted, FDA has a duty to monitor the injunction and to advise the courts if the company fails to follow through on their obligations. The three most common types of injunctions are the temporary restraining order, the preliminary injunction, and the permanent injunction.

Temporary Restraining Order. A *temporary restraining order* (TRO) is a court-ordered cease-and-desist order that is used in emergency situations. FDA, for example, may recommend a TRO when the Agency believes that a serious violation has occurred and the situation must be controlled or the flow of product stopped immediately.

Preliminary Injunction. A motion for preliminary injunction is subject to a full hearing before a court. Once the motion is granted, the preliminary injunction is in effect. A preliminary injunction may stand indefinitely until the case is settled or a permanent injunction has been entered, after trial.

Permanent Injunction. A decree of permanent injunction may be entered at any time after the complaint is filed, either after a hearing or as a result of a negotiated settlement between the government and the defendant. A decree of permanent injunction remains in effect until it is dissolved by an order of the court.

Consent Decree of Permanent Injunction. In the United States, a consent decree is a court-ordered agreement between FDA and a company that outlines the steps that a company needs to take to resume normal operations. Although each situation is unique, the consent decree will likely include the need for changes within the company (for example, to bring the organization into compliance with applicable regulations) and a requirement to involve outside consultants to oversee the changes and ensure ongoing compliance. FDA will typically seek a consent decree only when serious issues have been identified with a drug product manufacturer and other enforcement mechanisms have been unsuccessful in encouraging the company to address the issues in a timely fashion.

Loss of Marketing License

Regulatory agencies including FDA, MHRA, and the European National Competent Authorities are charged with ensuring that the drugs that are marketed are safe for their intended use and that their benefits outweigh the risks involved with any drug product. As a result, regulatory agencies constantly monitor and evaluate the safety data that are transmitted to them, either through periodic safety reports (by the manufacturer) or spontaneous reports (by healthcare practitioners or consumers). They weigh the benefits of existing drugs against any new emerging drug products or treatment therapies to determine whether older drugs still provide a medical benefit to patients.

When the regulatory agencies identify serious safety issues with a drug product, or deem the safety risks to outweigh the benefits provided by the drug product, they may choose to suspend or revoke the existing marketing license.

According to the World Health Organization (WHO), a marketing authorization may be suspended or revoked in any of the following circumstances:

- The product has proved to be ineffective for the approved indication(s).

- It is strongly suspected that the product is unsafe in the normal conditions of use.

- The quantitative or qualitative composition is not as agreed on in the marketing authorization.

- The product is not in compliance with the conditions of the marketing authorization.

- The product is being promoted in an inappropriate or unethical manner.

The marketing authorization holder is typically notified of the suspension or revocation along with the reasons for the decision and any appeal mechanisms available to them.

Loss of Establishment License

In the most serious cases of noncompliance, a regulatory agency may choose to suspend or revoke a pharmaceutical company's establishment license. A firm's repeated failure and unwillingness to comply with cGMP requirements, or the submission of false data in support of an application, are instances where a regulatory agency may be compelled to take this type of enforcement action.

Debarment

FDA has the authority to prohibit specific individuals and companies from participating in certain aspects of the drug industry. If an individual is convicted of certain felonies or misdemeanors, such as those related to the drug approval process or FDA's regulation of drugs in general, FDA may debar that individual.

Debarment means that the individual may no longer work for a firm holding a pending or approved drug product application at FDA. Moreover, FDA will not accept or review abbreviated drug applications submitted by debarred individuals. Companies are subject to debarment for felonies and some misdemeanors if the offenses are related to the development or approval of an abbreviated drug product application, which are related to generic drugs. A debarred company can not submit, or assist others in submitting, future abbreviated drug product applications.

Voluntary Actions

Recalls. Under the Food, Drug, and Cosmetic Act, FDA does not have the statutory authority to mandate that a firm recall or remove drug products from distribution. In those cases where the Agency believes that the product may pose a threat to consumer health and safety, FDA may recommend or request a field action, but companies are under no regulatory obligation, in the United States, to comply. In reality, however, most companies recall or remove product voluntarily from the field, and it is only in rare situations that FDA is required to take more immediate and serious actions (for example, court-ordered recall or seizure).

Like warning letters, information related to the recall of drug products is made public. FDA publishes a weekly Enforcement Report that identifies product recalls across the industries that they oversee. For more serious recalls, a formal press release, either by the company or FDA, may be initiated to alert the public of the potential health hazard.

Pharmaceutical companies need to have a procedure in place to handle recalls, and should have systems in place that maintain traceability of product distributed to their customers. Procedures should identify the person or persons responsible for the recall decision and the individual or group that is responsible for carrying out the recall action. In the absence of an actual recall, it is recommended that a pharmaceutical company conduct mock recalls to exercise their procedures and ensure that their systems are adequate to reconcile 100% of their distributed product.

Field Corrections and Market Withdrawals. Field corrections and market withdrawals are another voluntary mechanism to repair or remove questionable product that has left the control of the pharmaceutical company. In the case of a field correction, the repair, modification, adjustment, relabeling, destruction, or inspection of a product is conducted without physically removing it to some other location. In the case of a market withdrawal, the company removes or corrects a distributed product that involves a minor violation that would not be subject to legal action by FDA.

Chapter 6

Regulatory Agency Reporting

Once a pharmaceutical product is introduced into commercial distribution, a number of changes or events can trigger a requirement to submit information to the applicable regulatory authorities. These events can be planned (for example, a predetermined change to the product or manufacturing process) or unplanned (for example, failure of a drug product on stability), but, in either case, the burden of responsibility for reporting these events falls to the pharmaceutical manufacturer. Professionals working in a *good manufacturing practices* (GMP) environment must have an understanding of the types of events (both planned and unplanned) that result in a regulatory reporting obligation and the specific requirements for submitting the required reports. Failure to submit the required reports can result in enforcement action against the firm.

PLANNED CHANGES

It is not uncommon for changes (or variations) to marketing applications/ authorizations to be necessary throughout the life cycle of the drug product. Changes resulting from increased technical or process knowledge or additional safety and quality information resulting from consumer experience or post-marketing studies need to be effectively assessed and communicated to the appropriate regulatory agencies for inclusion in the approved application.

In the United States, the Food and Drug Administration (FDA) seeks to provide clarity around the types of changes and the reporting requirements through their guidance document *Changes to an Approved NDA or ANDA*. In this guidance document, FDA outlines three categories of changes based on their potential to have an adverse effect on the identity, strength, quality, purity, or potency of a drug product (Table 6.1).

In Europe, the marketing authorization holder is required to take into account technical and scientific progress and to submit amendments that incorporate changes (variations) based on that progress. Additionally, marketing authorization holders may wish to alter or improve the drug product, and those changes or variations also require submission of supplements or amendments to their approved application. The regulations in Europe have classified these changes or variations into two categories:

Table 6.1   Three categories of changes based on potential for adverse effect on identity, strength, quality, purity, or potency of a drug product.

Category	Criteria
Major	Change has a substantial potential to have an adverse effect on the identity, strength, quality, safety, purity, or potency of a drug product. A submission to the Agency, and approval of the submission by the Agency, are required before distribution of the drug product made using the change.
Moderate	Change has a moderate potential to have an adverse effect on the identity, strength, quality, safety, purity, or potency of a drug product. A submission to the Agency before the distribution of the drug product made using the change is required. Two types of submissions have been identified for moderate changes.
Minor	Change has minimal potential to have an adverse effect on the identity, strength, quality, safety, purity, or potency of a drug product. A submission to the Agency before the distribution of the drug product made using the change is not required.

Agency = United States Food and Drug Administration

- *Minor variations.* Type IA (administrative changes or simple changes with no potential impact on the safety of the drug product) and Type IB (other minor changes as specified in Annex I to Commission Regulation 1085/2003)

- *Major variations.* All changes (other than Type IA or IB) that require approval before the marketing authorization holder can move forward with the change.

EVALUATING POST-MARKETING CHANGES

The holder of the marketing application or authorization is responsible for assessing the effects of any change before distributing a drug product made with the change in place. Drug manufacturers should have a formal change control process in place to identify what needs to be done to complete the assessment and to document the outcome of the assessment process. While the assessment may vary depending on the type of change, some of the typical steps that may be taken to evaluate the impact of a change on the drug product are standard.

Technical Assessment

It is important to evaluate the impact of the change on the manufacturing process, and any impact on the finished dosage form. This evaluation should pay close attention to the impact of the change on the *critical quality attributes* (CQA) of the product and the *critical processing parameters* (CPP) for the drug manufacturing process. The technical assessment should determine the impact on the validated state of the process and determine whether additional validation activities will be necessary to demonstrate that the process remains in a state of control.

Analytical Assessment

First, it is important to determine whether the change has an impact on the approved regulatory specifications. Changes to incoming raw materials or changes in the manufacturing process may have an impact on the ability of the finished product to meet the regulatory specifications identified in the application.

Depending on the type of change proposed, a change to the regulatory specifications might be necessary. A change that requires a change in the approved specifications will almost always require approval by the regulatory agency involved before product made with the change can be distributed.

Second, it may be important to perform additional analytical testing to demonstrate that the change has not, or will not, have an adverse effect on the bioavailability, stability, or any of the chemical, physical, microbiological, and biological properties of the drug product. Providing a scientific argument or data that demonstrate that the product manufactured with the change will maintain an appropriate level of quality over time is often required before making a change.

Equivalence Assessment

It may be prudent, depending on the type of change, to conduct an assessment of product manufactured before the change versus product manufactured after the change to demonstrate that they are equivalent. Simply stated, is the finished drug product made after the change equivalent to the drug product made before the change? Demonstrating in vitro equivalence may be necessary to preclude the need for in vivo studies.

Adverse Effect

The change needs to be evaluated to determine whether the particular change in question has an adverse effect on the identity, strength, quality, purity, or potency of the drug product. While it seems counterintuitive that a company would move forward with a change that has an adverse impact, an application holder may be forced to do so as a result of changes beyond their control. For example, a change made by an *active pharmaceutical ingredient* (API) supplier may result in a change in the impurity profile for the finished drug product. If the change is necessary for the API supplier, the pharmaceutical company may be forced to move forward with the change to be able to continue to market the product. While these types of situations are rare, they do occur, and the pharmaceutical company must have systems in place to effectively evaluate these types of changes.

Reporting Strategy

The required reporting strategy may differ depending on the type of change. It is critical that the group responsible for determining the regulatory strategy (typically Regulatory Affairs) is made aware of the change(s) early on so that the requirements for submitting the change to the regulatory agency can be evaluated, and the appropriate timing for implementing the change(s) can be determined. It is often through this assessment that the need for additional testing or manufacture of batches made with the change in place is identified.

REGULATORY REPORTING REQUIREMENTS

Planned Changes

Requirements in the United States. For drug products approved in the United States, FDA identifies four reporting categories depending on the classification of the change:

- *Prior Approval Supplement* (PAS). A PAS is recommended for anything classified as a major change. In the case of a PAS, the company must wait to distribute product made with the change until after they receive approval from FDA on the supplement.

- *Supplement—Changes Being Effected in 30 Days* (CBE-30). A CBE-30 is recommended for certain types of moderate changes. In the case of a CBE-30, the supplement needs to be submitted to FDA, and the application holder must wait at least 30 days before the distribution of the drug product. If FDA informs the applicant within 30 days of receipt of the supplement that information is missing, or that a PAS is required, distribution of product must be delayed until the missing information is provided or the PAS is approved. If, after review of the CBE-30, FDA disagrees with the change, they may request that the manufacturer cease distribution of the drug products made using the change.

- *Supplement—Changes Being Effected* (CBE-0). A CBE-0 is recommended for certain types of moderate changes. In the case of a CBE-0, distribution of product manufactured with the change can occur once FDA receives the supplement. Similarly to what can transpire with the CBE-30, if FDA disagrees with the change, they may request that the manufacturer cease distribution of the drug products made using the change.

- *Annual reports.* The submission of annual reports for marketed drug products covered by an approved application should include the description of minor changes made to the drug product over the time period covered by the annual report. As a reminder, these minor changes are those changes that have a minimal potential to have an adverse impact on the identity, strength, quality, safety, purity, or potency of the drug product. It is not appropriate to include changes with either a substantial potential or moderate potential for adverse impact in a drug product annual report.

It is important to note that a single change can require more than one change to the approved application. For example, a change in manufacturing site may involve a change in the equipment used to manufacture the product, or a change in the API may involve a change in the processing parameters for the manufacturing process, or necessitate a change in the approved regulatory specifications. For multiple related changes where the recommended reporting category for the individual changes differs, FDA recommends that the submission strategy use the most restrictive of the categories recommended for the individual changes. When the multiple related changes all have the same recommended reporting category, FDA recommends that the submission use the reporting category for the individual changes.

Requirements in Europe. For drug products approved in Europe, a reporting system similar to that of the FDA is used depending on the type of variation (change) to the marketing authorization being proposed. The submission requirements differ depending on the type of variation, as does the ability of the manufacturer to move forward with implementing the change on commercial product. Three types of variations are recognized:

- *Type IA variations.* The application holder should verify that all the conditions for a type IA notification are met and that all the documentation requirements are complete. Once the type IA notification is received by the applicable member state (reference member state), the clock is started. By day 14, the reference member state is required to notify the applicant regarding the status of the notification, that is, the notification is acknowledged (accepted) or it is not accepted along with the reason for nonacceptance. If it is acknowledged, or if the application holder has not received communication from the reference member state that the notification has not been approved, the application holder may move forward with the change and distribution of product manufactured with the change.

- *Type IB variations.* Similarly to a type IA notification, the application holder must ensure that all the conditions for the type IB notification are met and that all documentation requirements are complete and included with the notification. In the case of a type IB notification, the clock does not start immediately upon receipt. The reference member state has 10 working days to verify that the requirements for a type IB notification have been met and that all the supporting data are included. After that 10-day period, the reference member state will inform the applicant of the start date. By day 30, after the clock start date, the reference member state will communicate the status of the notification (approval or nonapproval). Again, similarly to type IA notifications, if it is acknowledged, or if the application holder has not received communication from the reference member state that the notification has not been approved, the application holder may move forward with the change and distribution of product manufactured with the change.

- *Type II variations.* These types of variations are typically processed within 60 days of the clock start date; however, the regulations do allow for a reduced or extended assessment period. As with the type

IB variations, the reference member state has 10 working days to validate the submission, and they must notify the application holder of the clock start date. Where there is agreement between member states regarding the outcome of the assessment, the reference member state will send a formal approval or refusal letter to the applicant. The application holder must wait until they receive a formal approval letter before implementing the change.

Unplanned Events

Most often, these events relate to product quality issues or failure of the drug product to meet regulatory specifications throughout its intended shelf life. In those situations where the event is unplanned, strict and very tight deadlines exist for providing the reports to the appropriate regulatory agencies. It is critical to understand the reporting requirements specific to the country or countries in which the products are marketed and the deadlines for submission of the initial reports. Once the issue or event is made known to the pharmaceutical manufacturer, the clock starts, and it is incumbent on the individuals responsible for the reporting to act quickly and to gather as much relevant information as possible in a short period of time.

FDA Field Alert Reports. The FDA Field Alert reporting requirements, as outlined in 21 CFR 314.81, first became effective in May 1985. This regulation requires holders of New Drug Applications (NDA) and Abbreviated New Drug Applications (ANDA) to submit information about distributed drug products to their jurisdictional FDA district office within three business days of receipt of the information by the application holder. These reports, unlike the Adverse Drug Experience (ADE) Reports required under 21 CFR 314.80, are required when a manufacturer is made aware of specific quality issues affecting batches of product that remain in commercial distribution.

For example, generation of an out-of-specification (OOS) result for a finished drug product would be considered the type of "information concerning any failure" described in this regulation. Unless the OOS result is found, through investigation, to be invalid within three days, an initial Field Alert Report should be submitted. Follow-up reports are submitted as new information is identified during the investigation; a final Field Alert Report is submitted once the investigation is finalized and closed.

Biologic Product Deviation Reports. Under 21 CFR 600.14, manufacturers of licensed biologic products are required to promptly notify FDA of deviations in the manufacturing of products that may affect their safety, purity, or potency. Manufacturers must report any event, as well as any information relevant to the event, associated with the manufacturing of the biologic product if that event:

- Represents a deviation from GMP, applicable regulations, applicable standards, or established specifications that may affect the safety, purity, or potency of that product or represents an unexpected or unforeseeable event that may affect the safety, purity, or potency of that product

- Occurs in the sponsor's facility or a facility under contract with the sponsor

- Involves a distributed biologic product

It is important to note that the expectation regarding the decision to report should be based on whether the event has the potential to affect the safety, purity, or potency of a product.

These reports should be submitted as soon as possible to the FDA but, in all cases, no more than 45 calendar days from the date the deviation was first discovered. Like the Field Alert Reports, follow-up reports are required to update the Agency on any actions taken since the initial report. A final report is also required to close these reports.

Rapid Alert Reports. The alert system agreed on in the framework of the mutual recognition agreement (MRA) ensures that batch recalls and other safety measures resulting from quality defects of medicinal products discovered by one party are transmitted to the MRA partner without delay. It is based on the current *rapid alert system* (RAS) operational in the European Economic Area (EEA) and in the respective MRA partner country (Australia, Canada, Switzerland, and New Zealand). The alert system provides for communication about counterfeiting and fraud. Suspension and withdrawals of manufacturing authorization are communicated through the alert system as well.

The alert is classified from 1 to 3 depending on the expected risk presented to the public or animal health by the defective product. This classification is internationally agreed on for medicinal product recalls (Table 6.2). In the case of class 1 recalls, a rapid alert notification must be sent to all European Economic Area member states, and the Pharmaceutical Inspection Convention and Pharmaceutical Inspection Co-operation Scheme (PIC/S), European Directorate for the Quality of Medicines & HealthCare (EDQM), World Health Organization (WHO), FDA, and MRA partners, irrespective of whether the batch was exported to that country. In most cases, class 1 recalls are to patient level; however, this action may not be appropriate if alternative medicines are not available, so that an assessment by the reporter of the overall risk to patients/animals must be conducted. Consideration must be given to the difficulties of communicating to patients since

Table 6.2   The rapid alert system alerts are classified from 1 to 3 depending on the expected risk presented to the public or animal health by the defective product. This classification is internationally agreed on for medicinal product recalls.

Class	Criteria
1	The defect presents a life-threatening or serious risk to health
2	The defect may cause mistreatment or harm to the patient or animal, but it is not life threatening or serious
3	The defect is unlikely to cause harm to the patient, and the recall is carried out for other reasons, such as noncompliance with the marketing application or specification

marketing authorization holders may need to arrange press releases and advertising campaigns.

Class 2 rapid alert notifications should be sent only to those EEA member states, and PIC/S, EDQM, WHO, and MRA partners to which it is known, or believed, that the batch has been distributed. In identifying those countries, due consideration should be given to parallel distribution and import arrangements and the free trade between wholesale distributors within the EEA. In the case of parallel imports where there is difficulty in establishing the traceability of batches, consideration should be given to notifying all member states through the RAS.

Class 3 recalls are not notified through the RAS. For class 2 and class 3 recalls, recall to patient level is rarely required as lack of the product may present a greater risk to the patient than continuing treatment. Occasionally, class 2 or class 3 recalls can be accomplished solely at the wholesale level in circumstances such as where stocks are unlikely to be found farther down the supply chain and the level of risk is sufficiently low.

Chapter 7

Site Master File (SMF) and Drug Master File (DMF)

SITE MASTER FILE

A *site master file* (SMF) is a succinct document that provides information about the control of pharmaceutical manufacturing operations for a production site. The document is prepared by the manufacturer and contains information about the specific *good manufacturing practices* (GMP) operations carried out at the named site and any closely integrated operations. If only part of a pharmaceutical operation is done at the site (for example, testing, packaging), the SMF describes only those operations performed at the site.

When submitted to a regulatory authority, the SMF provides information on the manufacturer's operations and procedures that can be useful in the efficient planning and undertaking of a GMP inspection. The GMP inspection report issued for inspections conducted by the European Medicines Agency (EMA) includes a notation on whether an SMF was available before the inspection, and the date of the SMF is included in the report.

SMFs are required by the European Union (EU), Medicines and Healthcare Products Regulatory Agency (MHRA), Pharmaceutical Inspection Convention and the Pharmaceutical Inspection Co-operation Scheme (PIC/S), and the World Health Organization (WHO). United States Food and Drug Administration (FDA) regulations currently do not require submission or maintenance of an SMF. The mutual recognition agreements (MRA) between the European Community (EC) and Canada, New Zealand, and Australia include the SMF as part of a full inspection report that may be shared upon request.

The structure, formatting, and length of the SMF are prescribed by several guidance documents, including those published by WHO (guidelines for drafting SMF), PIC/S (explanatory notes), and the MHRA (guidance notes) (Figure 7.1). The SMF should be succinct and, where possible, not more than 25 to 30 A4 pages. For small companies, particularly those with a small product range, the SMF may be fewer than 25 pages. It is expected that the SMF will be maintained and improved to facilitate inspections. The SMF contains nine chapters (Table 7.1).

CONTENT OF SITE MASTER FILES

Chapter 1. General Information

- *Name, address, and company description* (C.1.1): Includes a brief description of the company, relation to other sites, and any information relevant to understanding the manufacturing operations.

- Each page is a loose and individually numbered A4 sheet.

- Each page has an edition (revision) number and an effective date.

- Each chapter (1 to 9) starts on a new page so that updates can be provided and the relevant sheets replaced.

- The format and headings follow those given in the guidance notes.

- Wherever possible, simple plans, outline drawings, or schematic layouts are used instead of a narrative. These plans, drawings, or layouts must fit on A4 sheets of paper.

- If narrative or page limitations are not included in a section, information may be included in a table, tabular list, or bulleted format.

Figure 7.1   Formatting requirements for a site master file.

Table 7.1   Site master files contain nine chapters.

Chapter number	Title
1	General Information
2	Personnel
3	Premises and Equipment
4	Documentation
5	Production
6	Quality Control
7	Contract Manufacturing and Analysis
8	Distribution, Complaints, and Product Recall
9	Self-Inspection

- *Licensed pharmaceutical manufacturing activities* (C.1.2): Provides the relevant document issued by a national authority, and, if applicable, the period of validity for the manufacturing license. This section includes any conditions/restrictions of the manufacturing license and, where applicable, the *drug master file* (DMF) for each product.

- *Description of other pharmaceutical and nonpharmaceutical activities* (C.1.3).

- *Name and address of the site* (C.1.4): Includes the name of the site, the complete street address and postal address, the telephone number, fax number, and e-mail address of a contact person, and a 24-hour contact telephone number.

- *Products manufactured at the site* (C.1.5): Lists the types of products manufactured at the site and provides information about specific toxic or hazardous substances handled, including their manufacturing. This section provides information on whether the products are manufactured in a dedicated facility or on a campaign basis and states whether both human and veterinary products are manufactured on the site. For contract manufacturing or analytical sites, this section defines whether the firm is the contract giver or acceptor.

- *Description of the site* (C.1.6): Provides the location and immediate environment, and the size of the site, types of buildings, and their ages.

- *Number of employees engaged in production, quality control, storage, and distribution* (C.1.7): Provides the total number of employees and the number of employees engaged in production, quality control (QC), quality assurance (QA), storage and distribution, and technical and engineering support services.

- *Listing and description of outside scientific, analytical, or other technical assistance in relation to manufacture and analysis* (C.1.8): Provides the company name, address, telephone number, and fax number of each outside contractor, and includes a brief outline (not more than 100 words) of the activity being undertaken. Also includes the establishment license number, where applicable.

- *Description of the quality management system* (QMS) (C.1.9): Provides a short description (750 words or three A4 pages) of the QMS of the firm responsible for manufacture. Describes the quality policy and the responsibilities of the QA function, including audit programs, approval and starting, primary packaging material suppliers, batch release, and document control. The responsibilities specific to the head of quality, QA manager, and QC manager are included. Describes the elements of the QA system (for example, organizational structure, responsibilities, procedures, and processes, specifications, test methods, and other quality-related data collection). It is important to show that quality management is independent from production management. Briefly describes the self-inspections or audits undertaken by external organizations. A cross-reference to Chapter 9 can be added for additional details regarding the self-inspection program. Describes how quality system results are reviewed to demonstrate the adequacy of the quality system in relation to the objective. Identifies the standards used to assess or audit the company's quality system, or used by the company to assess suppliers, such as ISO 9001, 21 CFR 211, and EU GMP. When suppliers of critical materials and packing materials are assessed, this section details how this is done, and describes the supplier selection process.

Chapter 2. Personnel

- *Organization charts* (C.2.1): Organization charts define the overall organizational structure for QA, production, and QC, with detailed charts for each area, depicting senior managers and supervisors only. As this information also is included in section 2.1, a cross-reference to that section can be used.

- *Qualifications, experience, and responsibilities of key personnel* (C.2.2): Includes brief details of academic qualifications, work-related qualifications, and years of relevant experience since qualifying.

- *Training program* (C.2.3): Describes how training needs are identified and by whom. Gives details of training relative to GMP requirements, including new employee training and continuous GMP training. Describes job-related skills training and in-house and external training, and how practical experience is gained. Explains how retraining needs are identified and details how training is recorded and records are maintained.

- *Health requirements for production personnel* (C.2.4): Describes who is responsible for checking the health of employees. Describes requirements for preemployment medical examinations and how employees are checked depending on the nature of their work. Describes the system for reporting sickness or contact with sick people before working in a critical area. Provides information on any system of reporting back to work after illness, and the requirements for personnel who work in sterile areas and any additional monitoring to which they may be subjected.

- *Personnel hygiene and clothing requirements* (C.2.5): States the washing, changing, and rest areas and the clothing/gowning requirements for the production areas. Gives instructions on how clothing should be used and when it should be changed. Describes gowning room/change room procedures. States the rules on eating, drinking, smoking, and use of chewing gum or tobacco. It is helpful to inspectors to include references to the applicable procedures for hygiene and clothing requirements.

Chapter 3. Premises

- *Site plan and manufacturing areas* (C.3.1): Provides a site plan highlighting the production areas, and a simple plan of each production area with indication of scale. For sterile product areas, indicates room and area classification(s) and pressure differentials between adjoining areas of different classifications.

- *Nature of construction and finishes* (C.3.2): A narrative format is preferred for this section. To reduce the length of the narrative for a large, complex plant, the details should be limited to critical areas, including processing and packaging areas. Describes wall construction, nature of finishes, floors, ceilings, doors and windows, lighting, piping, and drainage system(s).

- *Brief description of ventilation system* (C.3.3): To reduce the length of the narrative, schematic drawings should be used where possible. Details should be given for critical areas with potential risks of airborne contamination, including sterile product areas and areas for processing powders, granulation, and tableting. For manufacture of sterile or aseptic products, classification of the rooms used for production should be mentioned. A summary of the results of the most recent qualification/requalification should also be included. The MHRA guidance specifies that room classification should be given in accordance with the grading system outlined in the *EC/PIC Guide to GMP*. Outlines the *heating, ventilation, and air conditioning* (HVAC) system, areas with different classes of air, pressure differential principles to prevent cross-contamination, dedicated *air handling units* (AHUs), and forced ventilation systems. The limits for changing the filters should be given. If a *drop-off point* (DOP) is introduced, the point must be shown.

- *Special areas for the handling of highly toxic, hazardous, and sensitizing materials* (C.3.4): This section is similar to section C.3.1, and includes information such as whether materials are handled only in the QC laboratory, whether solids or waste are neutralized and collected in separate containers, and whether extracted gases from the fume hood are neutralized and scrubbed before they are allowed to exit into the external environment.

- *Description of water and steam systems* (C.3.5): This section provides a schematic drawing back to the main city supply system or source of the raw water, and the capacity of the system (maximum quantity produced per hour). Construction materials of the vessels and distribution system (pipework) are provided, along with specification of any filters in the system. If water is stored and circulated, the temperature at the point of return is provided, and the specifications of the water produced (that is, chemical, conductivity, and microbiological descriptions) are provided. The sampling points and frequency of sampling should be included. If a steam system is needed, the same sort of information must be provided for the system.

- *Description of planned preventive maintenance program and recording system* (C.3.6): "Maintenance" is done by the manufacturer and "servicing" by an outside contractor. This section describes the planned preventive maintenance program, including written procedures and suitable reporting forms for maintenance and servicing.

- *Brief description of major production and control laboratories equipment* (C.3.7): This section provides a list of equipment. Although the make and model numbers of the equipment are not required, several points should be addressed, including appropriateness and validity of construction material and ease of cleaning. For specific pieces of machinery (for example, a rotary tablet press), only a general description is required. If the equipment has additional devices, however, these devices should be recorded (for example, automatic weighing machines with printer, a labeler incorporating a bar code reader for the label). Further information is required for QC laboratory and microbiology laboratory and for computers and microprocessors in the manufacturing facility.

- *Maintenance (description of planned preventive maintenance program and recording system)* (C.3.8): Identifies who is responsible for maintenance and servicing and whether there are written procedures and contractual details for servicing. Maintenance routines that could affect product quality must be identified, and annual planned preventive maintenance programs for equipment must be in accordance with machine/instrument manufacturers' requirements. Documentation must be provided that records are kept on the type and frequency of service or check, details of service repairs and modifications, and reports provided to the users.

- *Qualification, validation, and calibration, including recording system and arrangements for computerized systems validation* (C.3.9): This section briefly describes the company's general policy and protocols for qualification, prospective validation, and retrospective validation, and describes and outlines the essential steps of the manufacturing process validation and cleaning validation. Any revalidation policy must be described. An outline of process validation may be given here or cross-referenced to production paragraph 5.4. A description of the system for the release for sale or supply of development and validation batches should be provided, as well as the arrangements for computer validation, including software validation. The equipment calibration policy and how calibration records are kept should be included in this section.

- *Availability of written specifications and procedures for cleaning manufacturing areas and equipment* (C.3.10): This section summarizes the cleaning strategy, schedules, and documentation for manufacturing areas and equipment. If cleaning agents are changed periodically, it should be noted, along with any validation of cleaning processes, including the cleaning methods (and their frequency) for the water supply system, air handling system, and dust extraction system.

Chapter 4. Documentation

- *Arrangements for the preparation, revision, and distribution of necessary documentation for manufacture* (C.4.1): This section includes a description of the documentation system and who is responsible for the preparation, revision, and distribution of documents. The storage place for the master documents is described, as well as type of documents stored (that is, product/process specifications, raw material specifications, packaging component specifications, standard process instructions including packaging, batch records including packaging, analytical methods, and QA release procedures). Information on how documentation is prepared and controlled and retention policy is provided, as well as the arrangements for any electronic or microfilmed records.

- *Other documentation related to product quality* (C.4.2): This section includes any other relevant documentation related to product quality that is not described elsewhere (for example, microbiological controls on air and water). The section should list and briefly explain the use of any additional standard documentation used routinely, including documentation for equipment specifications, specifications for disposables, standard operating procedures (SOPs), QC procedures, training procedures, computer program specifications, documentation control of process deviations, other validation documents, and reconciliation of batches of raw materials, bulk product, and major packing components (for example, product-contact and printed materials).

Chapter 5. Production

- *Brief description of production operations using, wherever possible, flow sheets and charts specifying important parameters* (C.5.1): This section should describe the operations capable of being done at the site with the existing facilities, and specify the categories of medicinal products produced. In facilities where only packaging is undertaken, it is necessary only to provide a brief description of labeling and filling and the nature of the containers used (for example, tamper-evident glass containers). More information is required in this section if cytotoxic or radioactive substances are handled. Flowcharts are useful to describe the production operations; technical details are not required.

- *Arrangements for the handling of starting materials, packaging materials, bulk and finished products, including sampling, quarantine, release, and storage* (C.5.2): Purchasing procedures (approval of suppliers of active pharmaceutical ingredients, excipients, and primary packing materials), and material requisition procedures from stores to manufacturing plant and vice versa, including sampling, quarantine, release, and storage, are all described in this section. Identification of supplier's lot number with the company's lot number is provided, along with sampling plans. Other details to be included are status labeling (for example, by using labels or by computer), issue of materials to manufacture and package, control of weighing, checking methods, and how materials being used for manufacture are identified and confirmed. Information for the control of bulk manufacturing (that is, records of key parameters and in-process checks) and packing (that is, release of bulk, semifinished product, and packing materials, along with in-process checks) is provided.

- *Arrangements for the handling of rejected materials and products* (C.5.3): Information must be given to show that rejected materials are clearly labeled and that they are stored in a dedicated area. This section also describes the arrangements for sentencing the materials and their disposal.

- *Brief description of general policy for process validation* (C.5.4): An outline of process validation protocol only is required. An outline may be given here or cross-referenced to Chapter 3 (3.9).

Chapter 6. Quality Control

Chapter 6 provides a description of the QC system and activities, particularly the procedures for the release of finished products. The information includes a description of the analytical testing, packaging, component testing, and microbiological testing, and outlines the arrangements for the preparation, revision, and distribution of documents for specification test methods and release criteria, if not mentioned elsewhere (see also paragraph 1.9 and Chapter 4, Documentation).

Chapter 7. Contract Manufacture and Analysis

This chapter describes how GMP compliance of the contract acceptor is assessed, as well as the technical contract between the contract giver and acceptor, and the way in which the GMP compliance is assessed to ensure product compliance with the marketing authorization.

Chapter 8. Distribution, Complaints, and Product Recalls

- Arrangements and recording system for distribution (C.8.1): A description of the storage and distribution practices, ways of securing the warehouse, environmental controls of the warehouse, and how materials are stored is provided in this section. It is important to describe how the status of products is controlled (for example, by computer or by label), and how rejected materials are securely isolated. The authorities should be comfortable that the distribution records permit full batch traceability from the factory to the customer, in terms of the date of sale, customer details, and quantity dispatched, and that these records are readily available to permit an effective recall if required.

- *Arrangements for the handling of complaints and product recalls* (C.8.2): This section refers to the procedures for handling complaints and product recalls. Quality defects should be investigated and appropriate measures taken to prevent recurrence.

- *Complaints* (C.8.3): The person or persons responsible for logging, classifying, and investigating complaints is provided, along with information about written reports, their review and retention, and how causes of quality defects are investigated.

- *Product recalls* (C.8.4): Who is responsible for product recalls? Is there a written procedure that describes the sequence of actions to be followed (for example, retrieval of distribution data, notification to customers, receipt/segregation/inspection of returned product, investigation/reporting of cause, and reporting corrective action). Who notifies the authorities of complaints and recalls? Is the authority involved in complaints and the decision to recall? Can recalls be effective below wholesale level? List products recalled over the last two years. If none has been recalled, record "none."

Chapter 9. Self-Inspection

- Include references to documented procedures that describe the self-inspection program and follow-up activities to self-inspections.

- Describe how the self-inspection system verifies that activities that have a bearing on quality comply with planned arrangements (that is, are records reviewed and activities observed to verify compliance with documents, procedures, and regulations?).

- State whether the program assesses the effectiveness of the quality system.

- Describe how the results of the self-inspection system are documented and brought to the attention of the personnel having responsibility for the area and activities inspected.

- Describe how the system ensures that those responsible for the area or activity take timely corrective action on the deficiencies found.

DRUG MASTER FILE

A *drug master file* (DMF) is a submission to FDA of information, usually concerning the *chemistry, manufacturing, and controls* (CMC) of a component of a drug product, to permit FDA to review this information in support of a third party's submission. A DMF may be used to provide confidential, detailed information about facilities, processes, or articles used in the manufacturing, processing, packaging, and storing of one or more human drugs. Drug product information or other non-CMC information may be filed in a DMF.

The submission of a DMF is not required by law or FDA regulation. A DMF is submitted solely at the discretion of the holder to maintain confidentiality of proprietary information (for example, manufacturing procedures) and to permit access to information by reviewers in the Center for Drug Evaluation and Research (CDER) to support applications submitted by one or more applicants. The information contained in the DMF may be used to support an Investigational New Drug Application (IND), a New Drug Application (NDA), an Abbreviated New Drug Application (ANDA), another DMF, an export application, or amendments and supplements to any of these.

A DMF is not a substitute for an IND, NDA, ANDA, or export application. It is not approved or disapproved. Technical contents of a DMF are reviewed only in connection with the review of an IND, NDA, ANDA, or export application. The DMF is reviewed only when it is referenced in an application or another DMF. The DMF is reviewed using the same regulatory and scientific criteria as review of an application.

Inspections of drug substance manufacturers usually are triggered when there is an application under review that references a DMF for the manufacture of that drug substance.

Confidentiality of information in DMFs is assured through 21 CFR 314.420(e). As DMFs usually cover manufacturing information, they usually are not considered releasable under a Freedom of Information Act (FOIA) request. Applications and DMFs are different (Table 7.2).

Types of Drug Master Files

Four types of DMFs have been identified (Table 7.3). More information on the number, type of DMF, and holder of the DMF are listed on the FDA website. The FDA website also provides detailed instructions and guidance for DMF submissions.

Table 7.2   Differences between applications and drug master files.

Application	Drug master file
Submitted to a particular review division.	Submitted to Center for Drug Evaluation and Research
Each submission (including supplement) is entered into the application database and assigned to a reviewer, and an acknowledgment letter sent.	Each submission is entered into a database (different from application database) and no acknowledgment letter sent.
Each submission has a due date.	Reviewed only when referenced. No assignment to a reviewer, no due date.

Table 7.3   The four types of drug master files.

Type II	Drug substance, drug product, intermediates, and material used in their manufacture
Type III	Packaging
Type IV	Excipients
Type V	Other sterile manufacturing plants, biotech contract facilities, clinical, and toxicology

Note: Type I files are no longer used or recognized by the FDA.

Changes to Drug Master Files

The DMF holder is expected to submit all changes to the DMF as amendments, notify FDA of change in holder name or address, notify FDA of change in agent/representative, submit an annual report or update, submit *letter of authorization* (LOA) for each item referenced for each customer, and notify authorized parties of changes. While annual updates to a DMF are not required by regulation, section VII of the DMF Guidelines recommends reporting a list of authorized parties, what they are authorized to reference, the date of the LOA, and a list of changes reported during the past year (that is, not a list of changes made, but a list of changes already reported). Stability updates should be reported as amendments.

If the anniversary date is missed, FDA will not send a reminder (unlike applications). If no changes have been made, it is important to send an update with a statement to that effect. It should be remembered that an *amendment* is a report of a change or addition of technical or administrative information. A *supplement* is not an amendment but only applies to approved applications. Pages that replace an already numbered page from a previous submission should also contain the page number in the current submission (for example, a page replacing page 10 in the original submission may be page 14 in the new submission). Finally, no pages are ever physically replaced in a DMF.

Part II
Quality Systems

Chapter 8

Quality Management System

A *quality management system* (QMS) can be defined as a set of policies, processes, and procedures required for planning and execution (production/development/service) in the core business area of an organization. A QMS integrates the various internal processes within the organization and provides a process approach for project execution. The QMS enables organizations to identify, measure, control, and improve the various core business processes, which ultimately leads to improved business performance.

The design and implementation of a QMS will vary depending on the type, size, and products of the organization. Implementing a QMS within an organization needs to be a decision by top management. Continued support by top management is critical to the ongoing success of the QMS.

The objectives of the QMS need to be clearly defined so that the system can be effective. QMS objectives must be measurable and reflect the overall company objectives. The QMS must be managed properly, and adequate resources must be allocated. The system must be practical and accessible to all employees within the organization. The system also must be reviewed regularly and measured for effectiveness, and adjustments must be made to reflect major changes to the organization and business practices.

Each company will have its own objectives for implementing a QMS; however, enhancing company effectiveness and profitability are often cited as primary drivers for implementation. A QMS can assist a company by managing costs and risks, increasing effectiveness and productivity, identifying improvement opportunities, and increasing customer satisfaction. A well-managed QMS will have an impact on customer loyalty and repeat business, market share, operational efficiencies, and flexibility and the ability to respond to market opportunities. It also helps in the effective and efficient use of resources and reducing costs, provides competitive advantages, and can increase participation and motivation of human resources, industry reputation, and control on all processes.

ESTABLISHING A QUALITY MANAGEMENT SYSTEM

A QMS must ensure that the products/services conform to customer needs and expectations and, at the same time, meet the objectives of the organization. Factors to be considered when setting up a QMS include design and build, deployment and implementation, control, measurement, review, and improvement.

Design and build include the structure of the QMS, the process, and its implementation. The design should be led by senior managers and ideally is accomplished using a framework to lead the thinking. Design of the QMS should result from determining the organization's core processes and well-defined goals and strategies, and be linked to the needs of the stakeholders. The process for designing and building the QMS must be clear. The quality function plays a key role in the design and build of the QMS, but involvement and buy-in to the system must come from all other functions as well.

Deployment and implementation are best achieved using process packages, where each core process is broken down into subprocesses and described by a combination of documentation, education, training, tools, systems, and metrics.

Control of the QMS will depend on the size and complexity of the organization. Local control, where possible, is effective, and good practice is found where key stakeholders are documented within the process and where the process owner is allowed to control all of the process. Ideally, process owners/operators are involved in writing the procedures that document the QMS.

Measurement determines the effectiveness and efficiency of each process toward attaining its objectives. It should include the contribution of the QMS to the organization's goals, and could be achieved by measuring policy definition completeness, business coverage, reflection of policies, deployment, usage, opinion regarding helpfulness of the QMS by staff, speed of change of the QMS, and relevance of QMS architecture to the job at hand. A form of scorecard deployed throughout the organization down to the individual objective level can be used, and the setting of targets at all levels is vital.

Review of the effectiveness, efficiency, and capability of the QMS is vital, and the outcome of these reviews should be communicated to all employees, including senior management. Reviewing and monitoring should be conducted whether or not improvement activities have achieved their expected outcomes.

Improvement should follow as a result of the review process, with the aim of seeking internal best practice. It is part of the overall improvement activities and an integral part of managing change within the organization.

QUALITY MANAGEMENT SYSTEM PRINCIPLES

ISO 9001:2008 (*Quality management systems—Requirements*) is an internationally recognized standard that specifies the requirements for a QMS that may be used by organizations for internal application, certification, or contractual purposes. ISO 9001:2008 and ISO 9004:2009 (*Managing for the sustained success of an organization—A quality management approach*) are QMS standards that complement each other, but also may be used independently. ISO 9001 emphasizes a need for management commitment, customer focus, a quality policy, quality planning, communication of responsibility and authority, and the need for a review of the organization's QMS.

Monitoring of customer satisfaction is necessary to evaluate and validate whether customer requirements have been met. Reference is made in the standard to a methodology known as *plan–do–check–act* (PDCA) that can be applied to all processes.

The standard suggests that an effective QMS must be a strategic tool designed to deliver business objectives and must have, at its core, a process approach, with each process transforming one or more inputs to create an output of value to the customer. The key business processes may be supported by procedures and work instructions in those cases where it is judged necessary to rigidly define what rules are to be followed when undertaking a task. Most organizations will have core business processes that define those activities that directly add value to the product or service for the external customer, and supporting processes that are required to maintain the effectiveness of the core processes.

The understanding of the many interrelationships between these processes demands that a systems approach to management is adopted. The processes must be thoroughly understood and managed so that the most efficient use is made of available resources to ensure that the needs of all the stakeholders—customers, employees, shareholders, and the community—are met.

Customer satisfaction is a constantly moving target depending on changes in technology and the marketplace, so an effective QMS must be in a state of continual improvement. For this goal to be achieved, attention needs to be given to both the voice of the customer—through complaint analysis, opinion surveys, and regular contacts—and the voice of the processes—through measurement, monitoring, and analysis of both process and product data.

QUALITY MANAGEMENT SYSTEM PRACTICES

Audits, Reviews, and Assessments

A good QMS will not function or improve without adequate audits and reviews. Audits are done to ensure that actual practices adhere to documented procedures. System reviews should be done periodically and methodically to ensure that the system achieves the required effect.

A schedule for audits, with different activities requiring different frequencies, should be established. An audit should not be conducted solely for the purpose of revealing defects or irregularities; it should be conducted to establish the facts rather than to find fault. Audits may indicate necessary improvement and corrective actions, but also are intended to determine whether processes are effective and responsibilities have been correctly assigned. The emphasis on process improvement and enhancing customer satisfaction in the revised ISO 9001:2008 standard will require a more thoughtful approach to auditing. Typically, a QMS review should take place once a year, and should cover:

- Results of audits

- Customer feedback

- Process and product conformity

- Status of preventive and corrective actions

- Follow-up actions from previous management reviews

- Changes that could affect the QMS

- Recommendations for improvements

Outputs should include improvements to the QMS and processes, product improvements related to customer requirements, and identification of resource needs. In addition, the procedures for conducting audits and reviews, and the results from them, should be documented and be subject to review. Internal system audits and reviews should be positive and conducted as part of the preventive strategy, and not as a matter of expediency resulting from problems.

The assessment of a quality system against a standard or set of requirements by internal audit and review is known as a *first-party* assessment or approval scheme. If an external customer makes the assessment of a supplier against its own requirements, or a national or international standard, a *second-party* scheme is in operation. The assessment by an independent organization, not connected with any contract between the customer and supplier, but acceptable to them both, is an independent, *third-party* assessment scheme.

ICH Q10: *Pharmaceutical Quality System*

ICH Q10 describes one comprehensive model for an effective pharmaceutical quality management system that is based on International Organization for Standardization (ISO) quality concepts, includes applicable *good manufacturing practices* (GMP) regulations, and complements ICH Q8 *Pharmaceutical Development* and ICH Q9 *Quality Risk Management.*

ICH Q10 is a model for a pharmaceutical QMS that can be implemented throughout the different stages of a product life cycle. Much of the content of ICH Q10 applicable to manufacturing sites is currently specified by regional GMP requirements and ICH Q7 *Good Manufacturing Practice Guidance for Active Ingredients.*

ICH Q10 demonstrates industry and regulatory authorities' support of an effective pharmaceutical QMS to enhance the quality and availability of medicines globally in the interest of public health. Implementation of ICH Q10 throughout the product life cycle should facilitate innovation and continual improvement and strengthen the link between pharmaceutical development and commercial manufacturing activities. The elements of ICH Q10 should be applied in a manner that is appropriate and proportionate to each of the product life cycle stages, recognizing the differences between, and the different goals of, each stage (Table 8.1).

ICH Q10 provides a harmonized model for a pharmaceutical QMS throughout the life cycle of a product and is intended to be used together with regional GMP requirements. The QMS elements and management responsibilities described in this guideline encourage the use of science and risk-based approaches at each life cycle stage, thereby promoting continual improvement across the entire product life cycle.

ICH Q10 Objectives

Implementation of the Q10 model should result in achievement of three main objectives that complement or enhance regional GMP requirements:

- *Achieve product realization.* To establish, implement, and maintain a system that allows the delivery of products with the quality attributes appropriate to meet the needs of patients, healthcare professionals,

Table 8.1   Technical activities included in the product life cycle for new and existing products.

Pharmaceutical development	Drug substance development
	Formulation development, including container/closure system
	Manufacture of investigational products
	Delivery system development (where relevant)
	Manufacturing process development and scale-up
	Analytic method development
Technology transfer	New product transfers during the development to manufacturing stages
	Transfers within or between manufacturing and testing sites for marketed products
Commercial manufacturing	Acquisition and control of materials
	Provision of facilities, utilities, and equipment
	Production, including packaging and labeling
	Quality control and assurance
	Release
	Storage
	Distribution (excluding wholesaler activities)
Product discontinuation	Retention of documentation
	Sample retention
	Continued product assessment and reporting

regulatory authorities (including compliance with approved regulatory filings) and other internal and external customers.

- *Establish and maintain a state of control.* To develop and use effective monitoring and control systems for process performance and product quality, thereby providing assurance of continued suitability and capability of processes. Quality risk management can be useful in identifying monitoring and control systems.

- *Facilitate continual improvement.* To identify and implement appropriate product quality improvements, process improvements, variability reduction, innovations, and pharmaceutical quality system enhancements, thereby increasing the ability to fulfill quality needs consistently. Quality risk management can be useful for identifying and prioritizing areas for continual improvement.

Enablers: Knowledge Management and Quality Risk Management

Use of knowledge management and quality risk management enables a company to implement ICH Q10 effectively and successfully. These enablers facilitate achievement of the three regional GMP requirements objectives by providing the means for science- and risk-based decisions related to product quality.

Knowledge Management. *Knowledge management* is a systematic approach to acquiring, analyzing, storing, and disseminating information related to products, manufacturing processes, and components. Sources of knowledge include, but are not limited to, public domain or internally documented knowledge, pharmaceutical development studies, technology transfer activities, process validation studies over the product life cycle, manufacturing experience, innovation, continual improvement, and change management activities. Product and process knowledge should be managed from development through the commercial life of the product up to and including product discontinuation. For example, development activities using scientific approaches provide knowledge for product and process understanding.

Quality Risk Management. Quality risk management is integral to an effective pharmaceutical QMS. It can provide a proactive approach to identifying, scientifically evaluating, and controlling potential risks to quality. It facilitates continual improvement of process performance and product quality throughout the product life cycle. ICH Q9 provides principles and examples of tools for quality risk management that can be applied to different aspects of pharmaceutical quality.

Design and Content Considerations, Quality Manual

The design, organization, and documentation of the pharmaceutical QMS should be well structured and clear to facilitate common understanding and consistent application. The elements of ICH Q10 should be applied in a manner that is appropriate and proportionate to each of the product life cycle stages, recognizing the different goals and knowledge available for each stage. The size and complexity of the company's activities should be taken into consideration when developing a new pharmaceutical QMS or modifying an existing one.

The design of the pharmaceutical QMS should incorporate appropriate risk management principles. While some aspects of the pharmaceutical QMS can be companywide and others site specific, the effectiveness of the pharmaceutical QMS normally is demonstrated at the site level. The pharmaceutical QMS should include appropriate processes, resources, and responsibilities to provide assurance of the quality of outsourced activities and purchased materials. The pharmaceutical QMS should include process performance and product quality monitoring, corrective and preventive action, and change management and management review. Performance indicators should be identified and used to monitor the effectiveness of processes within the pharmaceutical QMS. Finally, management responsibilities should be identified within the pharmaceutical QMS. A quality manual or equivalent documentation approach should be established and should contain the description of the pharmaceutical QMS (Figure 8.1).

MANAGEMENT RESPONSIBILITY

Leadership is essential to establish and maintain a companywide commitment to quality and for the performance of the pharmaceutical QMS.

- Quality policy

- Scope of the pharmaceutical QMS

- Identification of the pharmaceutical QMS processes, including sequences, linkages, and interdependencies, as well as process maps and flow

- Management responsibilities within the pharmaceutical QMS

Figure 8.1   Components of a quality manual.

Management Commitment

Senior management holds the ultimate responsibility to ensure that an effective pharmaceutical QMS is in place to achieve the quality objectives. They are responsible for ensuring that the roles, responsibilities, and authorities are defined, communicated, and implemented throughout the company. Management should:

- Participate in the design, implementation, monitoring, and maintenance of an effective pharmaceutical QMS.

- Demonstrate strong and visible support for the pharmaceutical QMS and ensure its implementation throughout their organization.

- Ensure that a timely and effective communication and escalation process exists to raise quality issues to the appropriate levels of management.

- Define individual and collective roles, responsibilities, authorities, and interrelationships of all organizational units related to the pharmaceutical QMS.

- Ensure that these interactions are communicated and understood at all levels of the organization. An independent quality unit or structure with authority to fulfill certain pharmaceutical quality system responsibilities is required by regional regulations.

- Conduct management reviews of process performance and product quality, and of the pharmaceutical QMS.

- Advocate continual improvement.

- Commit appropriate resources.

Quality Policy

Senior management should establish a *quality policy* that describes the overall intentions and direction of the company related to quality. The quality policy should include an expectation to comply with applicable regulatory requirements and should facilitate continual improvement of the pharmaceutical QMS. The quality policy should be communicated to, and understood by, personnel at all levels in the company. The quality policy should be reviewed periodically to ensure continued effectiveness.

Quality Planning

Senior management should ensure that the quality objectives needed to implement the quality policy are defined and communicated. Quality objectives should be supported by all relevant levels of the company. Quality objectives should align with the company's strategies and be consistent with the quality policy. Management should provide the appropriate resources and training to achieve the quality objectives. Performance indicators that measure progress against quality objectives should be established, monitored, communicated regularly, and acted on as appropriate.

Resource Management

Management should determine and provide adequate and appropriate resources (human, financial, materials, facilities, and equipment) to implement and maintain the pharmaceutical quality system and continually improve its effectiveness. Management should ensure that resources are appropriately applied to a specific product, process, or site.

Internal Communication

Management should ensure that appropriate communication processes are established and implemented within the organization. Communication processes should ensure the flow of appropriate information between all levels of the company and should ensure the appropriate and timely escalation of certain product quality and pharmaceutical quality system issues.

Management Review

Senior management should be responsible for pharmaceutical QMS governance through management review to ensure its continued suitability and effectiveness. Management should assess the conclusions of periodic reviews of process performance and product quality, and of the pharmaceutical QMS.

Management of Outsourced Activities and Purchased Materials

The pharmaceutical QMS, including the management responsibilities, extends to the control and review of any outsourced activities and quality of purchased materials. The pharmaceutical company is responsible to ensure that processes are in place to assure the control of outsourced activities and quality of purchased materials (Figure 8.2).

Management of Change in Product Ownership

When product ownership changes (for example, through acquisitions or divestitures), management should consider the complexity of these events and ensure

---

- Assessing, before outsourcing operations or selecting material suppliers, the suitability and competence of the other party to carry out the activity or provide the material using a defined process (for example, audits, material evaluations, qualification).

- Defining the responsibilities and communication processes for quality-related activities of the involved parties. For outsourced activities, this information should be included in a written agreement between the contract giver and contract acceptor.

- Monitoring and review of the performance of the contract acceptor or the quality of the material from the provider, and the identification and implementation of any needed improvements.

- Monitoring incoming ingredients and materials to ensure they are from approved sources using the agreed-on supply chain.

Figure 8.2   Management of outsourced activities and purchased materials.

that ongoing responsibilities are defined for each company involved and the necessary information is shared or transferred.

CONTINUAL IMPROVEMENT OF PROCESS PERFORMANCE AND PRODUCT QUALITY

Life cycle stage goals and four specific pharmaceutical quality system elements augment regional requirements to achieve the ICH Q10 objectives.

Life Cycle Stage Goals

Pharmaceutical Development. The goal of pharmaceutical development activities is to design a product and its manufacturing process to consistently deliver intended performance and meet the needs of patients, healthcare professionals, and regulatory authorities, and internal customers' requirements. Approaches to pharmaceutical development are described in ICH Q8. The results of exploratory and clinical development studies, while outside the scope of this guidance, are inputs to pharmaceutical development.

Technology Transfer. The goal of technology transfer activities is to transfer product and process knowledge between development and manufacturing and within or between manufacturing sites to achieve product realization. This knowledge forms the basis for the manufacturing process, control strategy, process validation approach, and ongoing continual improvement.

Commercial Manufacturing. The goals of manufacturing activities include achieving product realization, establishing and maintaining a state of control, and facilitating continual improvement. The pharmaceutical quality system should assure that the desired product quality is routinely met, suitable process performance is achieved, the set of controls is appropriate, improvement opportunities are identified and evaluated, and the body of knowledge is continually expanded.

Product Discontinuation. The goal of product discontinuation activities is to manage the terminal stage of the product life cycle effectively. For product discontinuation, a predefined approach should be used to manage activities such as retention of documentation and samples and continued product assessment (for example, complaint handling, adverse event reporting, and stability) and reporting in accordance with regulatory requirements.

Pharmaceutical Quality Management System Elements

Four elements are required, in part, under regional GMP regulations; however, the Q10 model's intent is to enhance these elements to promote the life cycle approach to product quality. These four elements are process performance and product quality monitoring system, corrective action and preventive action (CAPA) system, change management system, and management review of process performance and product quality. These elements should be applied in a manner that is appropriate and proportionate to each of the product life cycle stages, recognizing the differences between, and the different goals of, each stage. Throughout the product life cycle, companies are encouraged to evaluate opportunities for innovative approaches to improve product quality.

Process Performance and Product Quality Monitoring System. Pharmaceutical companies should plan and execute a system for the monitoring of process performance and product quality to ensure that a state of control is maintained. An effective monitoring system provides assurance of the continued capability of processes and controls to produce a product of desired quality and to identify areas for continual improvement. The process performance and product quality monitoring system should:

- Use quality risk management to establish the control strategy, which can include parameters and attributes related to drug substance and drug product materials and components, facility and equipment operating conditions, in-process controls, finished product specifications, and the associated methods and frequency of monitoring and control. The control strategy should facilitate timely feedback/feed forward and appropriate corrective action and preventive action.

- Provide the tools for measurement and analysis of parameters and attributes identified in the control strategy (for example, data management and statistical tools).

- Analyze parameters and attributes identified in the control strategy to verify continued operation within a state of control.

- Identify sources of variation affecting process performance and product quality for potential continual improvement activities to reduce or control variation.

- Include feedback on product quality from both internal and external sources, for example, complaints, product rejections, nonconformances, recalls, deviations, audits, and regulatory inspections and findings.

- Provide knowledge to enhance process understanding, enrich the design space (where established), and enable innovative approaches to process validation.

Corrective Action and Preventive Action (CAPA) System. The pharmaceutical company should have a system for implementing corrective actions and preventive actions resulting from the investigation of complaints, product rejections, nonconformances, recalls, deviations, audits, regulatory inspections and findings, and trends from process performance and product quality monitoring. A structured approach to the investigation process should be used with the objective of determining the root cause. The level of effort, formality, and documentation of the investigation should be commensurate with the level of risk, in line with ICH Q9. CAPA methodology should result in product and process improvements and enhanced product and process understanding.

Change Management System. Innovation, continual improvement, the outputs of process performance and product quality monitoring, and CAPA drive change. To evaluate, approve, and implement these changes properly, a company should have an effective change management system. Generally, a difference in formality of change management processes exists before the initial regulatory submission and after submission, where changes to the regulatory submission might be required under regional requirements. The change management system ensures that continual improvement is undertaken in a timely and effective manner. It should provide a high degree of assurance that no unintended consequences will occur because of the change. As part of the change management system, as appropriate for the stage of the life cycle:

- Quality risk management should be used to evaluate proposed changes. The level of effort and formality of the evaluation should be commensurate with the level of risk.

- Proposed changes should be evaluated relative to the marketing authorization, including design space, where established, and/ or current product and process understanding. An assessment determines whether a change to the regulatory filing is required under regional requirements. As stated in ICH Q8, working within the design space is not considered a change (from a regulatory submission perspective); however, from a pharmaceutical QMS standpoint, all changes should be evaluated by a company's change management system.

- Proposed changes should be evaluated by subject matter expert teams contributing the appropriate expertise and knowledge from relevant areas (for example, Pharmaceutical Development, Manufacturing, Quality, Regulatory Affairs, and Medical) to ensure the change is technically justified. Prospective evaluation criteria for a proposed change should be set.

- After implementation, an evaluation of the change should be undertaken to confirm that the change objectives were achieved and that there was no deleterious impact on product quality.

Management Review of Process Performance and Product Quality. Management review should provide assurance that process performance and product quality are managed over the product life cycle. Depending on the size and complexity of the company, management review can be a series of reviews at various levels of management, and should include a timely and effective communication and escalation process to raise appropriate quality issues to senior levels of management for review. The management review system should include:

- The results of regulatory inspections and findings, audits and other assessments, and commitments made to regulatory authorities.

- Periodic quality reviews that can include measures of customer satisfaction such as product quality complaints and recalls, conclusions of process performance and product quality monitoring, and the effectiveness of process and product changes, including those arising from corrective action and preventive actions.

- Any follow-up actions from previous management reviews. The management review system should identify appropriate actions, such as improvements to manufacturing processes and products, provision, training, and/or realignment of resources, and capture and dissemination of knowledge.

CONTINUAL IMPROVEMENT OF THE PHARMACEUTICAL QUALITY SYSTEM

Management Review

Management should have a formal process for reviewing the pharmaceutical QMS on a periodic basis. The review should include measurement of achievement of pharmaceutical quality system objectives, and assessment of performance indicators that can be used to monitor the effectiveness of processes within the pharmaceutical quality system (that is, complaint, deviation, CAPA, and change management processes, feedback on outsourced activities, self-assessment processes, including risk assessments, trending, and audits, and external assessments such as regulatory inspections and findings and customer audits).

Monitoring of Internal and External Factors

Management can monitor several factors that impact the QMS, including emerging regulations, guidance, and quality issues, innovations, changes in business environment and objectives, and changes in product ownership.

Outcomes of Management Review and Monitoring

The outcome of management review of the pharmaceutical QMS and monitoring of internal and external factors can include improvements to the pharmaceutical quality system and related processes, allocation or reallocation of resources and/or personnel training, revisions to quality policy and quality objectives, and documentation and timely and effective communication of the results of the management review and actions, including escalation of appropriate issues to senior management.

Chapter 9

Quality Unit (Site) Management

egulations define the *quality unit* (QU) as the concept that is consistent with modern quality systems in ensuring that the various operations associated with all systems are appropriately planned, approved, conducted, and monitored. Assigned responsibilities for the QU include ensuring that controls are implemented and completed satisfactorily during manufacturing operations and that developed procedures and specifications are appropriate and followed; approving and rejecting incoming materials, in-process materials, and drug products; and reviewing production records and investigating any unexplained discrepancies.

Responsibilities are divided between *quality control* (QC) and *quality assurance* (QA) functions. QC typically assesses suitability of components and products, evaluates the performance of the manufacturing process with respect to specifications and limits, and determines the acceptability of each batch for release. QA typically reviews and approves procedures, reviews records, and performs audits and trend analyses.

The United States Food and Drug Administration (FDA) has not moved away from the term *quality control unit* (QCU), which is defined in 21 CFR 210.3(b)(15) and described in 211.22. According to 21 CFR 210.3, the QCU is responsible for the duties relating to QC, whereas according to 211.22, the QCU is an independent group with unique responsibilities and authority to manage product excellence, consumer safety, compliance, and company liability. The QU encompasses nearly all manufacturing processes, including setting ingredient standards to ensure they are met, qualifying third-party testing laboratories, packaging components and labeling, calculating practical cost considerations, and ensuring finished product quality.

QUALIFIED PERSON

The legal basis for the *qualified person* (QP) is defined in the European Directives. These Directives specify that European Union (EU) member states take all appropriate measures to ensure that the holder of the manufacturing authorization has permanently and continuously at its disposal the services of at least one QP. Additionally, member states must ensure that the QP fulfills the minimum conditions of qualification.

Qualifications for the role of QP include possession of a diploma, certificate, or other evidence of formal qualifications awarded on completion of a university course of study or a course recognized as equivalent by the member state concerned, obtained over a period of at least four years of theoretical and practical study in one of six scientific disciplines (pharmacy, medicine, veterinary medicine, chemistry, pharmaceutical chemistry and technology, or biology). Alternatively, the minimum duration of the university course may be 3.5 years where the course is followed by a period of theoretical and practical training for a minimum of one year, and must include a training period of at least six months in a pharmacy open to the public, corroborated by an examination at university level. The course of studies includes both theoretical and practical usage in a number of subjects, including applied physics, general and inorganic chemistry, organic chemistry, analytical chemistry, pharmaceutical chemistry, including analysis of medicinal products, general and applied biochemistry (medical), physiology, microbiology, pharmacology, pharmaceutical technology, toxicology, and pharmacognosy (study of the composition and effects of natural active substances of plant and animal origin).

In addition to the formal training, a QP must have acquired practical experience over at least two years, in one or more facilities that are authorized to manufacture medicinal products, in the activities of qualitative analysis of medicinal products, of quantitative analysis of active substances, and of the testing and checking necessary to ensure the quality of medicinal products. The duration of practical experience may be reduced by one year when a university course lasts for at least five years and by 1.5 years when the course lasts for at least six years.

Responsibilities of the Qualified Person

The QP has several important responsibilities. In the case of medicinal products, the QP must ensure that each batch of medicinal products has been manufactured and checked in compliance with the laws in force in the member state and in accordance with the requirements of the marketing authorization; and in the case of medicinal products coming from third countries, the QP must ensure that each production batch has undergone in the importing member state a full qualitative analysis, a quantitative analysis of at least all the active constituents, and all the other tests or checks necessary to ensure the quality of medicinal products in accordance with the requirements of the marketing authorization. The batches of medicinal products that have undergone such controls in a member state are exempt from the controls if they are marketed in another member state and are accompanied by the control reports signed by the QP. In the case of medicinal products imported from a third country, where appropriate arrangements have been made by the European Community (EC) with the exporting country, the QP must ensure that the manufacturer of the medicinal product applied standards of *good manufacturing practices* (GMP) at least equivalent to those of the EC, and must ensure that the controls have been carried out in the exporting country. The QP may be relieved of responsibility for carrying out those controls. In all cases, and particularly where the medicinal products are released for sale, the QP must certify in a register or equivalent document provided for that purpose that each production batch satisfies the provisions of the regulations, and that the register or equivalent document is kept current as operations are completed and remains at the disposal of the agents of the competent authority for the period specified in the provisions of the member state concerned, and in any event for at least five years.

Specific Requirements for the Qualified Person

Qualification of Suppliers of Active Pharmaceutical Ingredients. EU Directives require that *active pharmaceutical ingredients* (APIs) used for the manufacture of medicinal products have been manufactured according to the GMP for starting materials. The ICH Q7A Guide *Good Manufacturing Practice Guidance for Active Pharmaceutical Ingredients* has been transferred to Part II of the *EU Guide to GMP*. It is expected that these standards are implemented in API manufacturing.

The QP responsible for the final production batch must be satisfied that the provisions of the Directive(s) are met and that a systematic system of supplier qualification is in place to give the assurance that only GMP-compliant API will be used for the manufacture of medicinal products.

Contract Manufacture and Analysis. Chapter 7, "Contract Manufacture and Analysis," of Part 1 of the *EU Guide to GMP* states that the contract manufacture and analysis must be correctly defined, agreed on, and controlled to avoid misunderstandings that could result in a product or work of unsatisfactory quality. To realize this objective, the QP needs to have the assurance that a written contract is in place that clearly defines the duties of each party, and that the contract contains the requirements. Any proposed changes in technical or other arrangements should be in accordance with the marketing authorization for the product concerned. The QP must ensure that a system to assess the competence of the contract acceptor to fulfill the principles of GMP is in place, and the contract acceptor must be aware of any problems associated with the product or the work that might pose a hazard to the premises, equipment, personnel, other materials, or other products. All processed products and materials delivered by the contract acceptor comply with their specification or have been released by the responsible quality unit.

Manufacture of Investigational Medicinal Products. Annex 13 of the GMP guide *Manufacture of Investigational Products* defines in detail the requirements in the manufacture and testing of *investigational medical products* (IMP), as well as ordering, shipping, and returning clinical supplies. In the case of IMPs, the QP is specifically responsible for ensuring that systems are in place that meet the requirements of Annex 13. The QP must, therefore, have a broad knowledge of pharmaceutical development and clinical trial processes. The QP is charged with making sure that release of IMPs does not occur until after the QP has certified that relevant requirements have been met.

Shipping. Investigational medicinal products should remain under the control of the sponsor until completion of a two-step release procedure: certification by the QP and release after fulfillment of the requirements of Article 9 ("Commencement of a Clinical Trial") of Directive 2001/20/EC. The sponsor should ensure that these are consistent with the details actually considered by the QP. Both releases should be recorded and retained in the relevant trial files held by or on behalf of the sponsor. Transfers of IMPs from one trial site to another should be an exception to the process. Such transfers should be covered by *standard operating procedures* (SOPs). The product history while outside of the control of the manufacturer, through trial monitoring reports and records of storage conditions at the original trial site, should be reviewed as part of the assessment of the product's suitability for transfer, and the advice of the QP should be sought. The product should be returned to the manufacturer or another authorized manufacturer for relabeling, if necessary, and certification by a QP. Records should be retained and full traceability ensured.

Complaints. The conclusions of any investigation carried out in relation to a complaint that could arise from the quality of the product should be discussed between the manufacturer or importer and the sponsor (if different). This discussion should involve the QP and those personnel responsible for the relevant clinical trial to assess any potential impact on the trial, product development, or subjects.

Certification of Batch Release

The certification of batch release is defined in Annex 16 of the *EU Guide to GMP*. In addition, European Medicines Agency (EMA) published a paper on a proposed solution for dealing with minor deviations from the detail described in *Marketing Authorization for Human and Veterinary Medicinal Products* (including biological products).

MAINTENANCE OF A QUALITY MANAGEMENT SYSTEM

Chapter 1 of the *EU Guide to GMP* requires that a comprehensively designed and correctly implemented system of QA incorporating GMP, and thus QC, is in place. It should be fully documented and its effectiveness monitored. The key requirement for the QP (specific to Chapter 1) is to ensure that medicinal products are not sold or supplied before a QP has certified that the batch has been produced and tested in accordance with the requirements of the marketing authorization and any other regulations relevant to the production, control, and release of medicinal products. To realize this objective, a QP should be involved in the implementation and maintenance of the *quality management system* (QMS).

The Qualified Person and the Product Quality Review

The requirement of a *product quality review* (PQR) was introduced with the addition of article 1.5 in Chapter 1 ("Quality Management") of the *EU Guide to GMP*. The aim of this requirement is to verify the consistency and appropriateness of the existing process, the adequacy of current specifications for starting material and finished product, and the presence of product and process improvements.

The PQR should be conducted and documented annually and should cover all aspects of the supply chain: starting materials, the process, process environment, and the final product. The manufacturer and marketing authorization holder, where different, should evaluate the results of this review, and an assessment should be made as to whether corrective and preventive action or any revalidation should be undertaken.

The QP responsible for final batch certification, together with the marketing authorization holder, should ensure that the quality review is performed in a timely manner and is accurate. It is necessary to understand the aim and basic principles of the PQR to assume responsibility. The generation of the PQR can be done by any of the functions, but QA, in association with the QP, should lead the way to interpret data and define and follow up any consequences.

The Qualified Person and Reference and Retention Samples

The requirements on the taking and holding of reference samples of starting materials, packaging materials, or finished products, and retention samples of finished products, are defined and included in the EU GMP as Annex 19 to the *EU Guide to GMP* Part 1. Reference samples are samples of starting materials or finished products intended to be reanalyzed in case of any complaint, dispute, or discrepancy; retention samples are samples of a fully packaged unit from a batch of finished product stored for identification purposes.

According to the different purposes, the amounts to be stored are different: reference samples are usually in a sample size sufficient to allow at least two full analytical controls on the batch (with some dispute still ongoing whether this would include sterility testing if appropriate), and retention samples are usually only one package per packaging presentation.

Reference and retention samples from finished products must be retained for at least one year after the expiry date. If no longer period is required under national law, samples of starting materials (other than solvents, gases, or water used in the manufacturing process) must be retained for at least two years after the release of the product. Storage conditions must be in accordance with the conditions submitted in the marketing authorization. In case a product has been manufactured (partially) outside the EU, reference samples must be stored in the EU, unless there is an operational *mutual recognition agreement* (MRA) in place.

External Qualified Persons

Some companies may use an external QP who provides an independent service. The duties and responsibilities do not differ from the ones that are applicable to QPs that are full-time employees of a company. To fulfill the tasks, it is required to have a detailed contract to ensure that all duties and responsibilities are met.

Delegation of Tasks/Absence of a Qualified Person

In general, the task of a QP, especially the process of batch certification and release, can only be delegated to another QP who is registered with the responsible authority for supervision of the marketing authorization and/or supervision.

Organizational Duties to Be Established by the Company of the Qualified Person

To perform their duties and responsibilities, a QP needs support from the company and its senior management. Three organizational tasks should be implemented:

- Senior management should be actively involved in the implementation, maintenance, and further development of the QMS.

- A clear job description should be in place to define the responsibilities of the QP and their relationship to other departments, responsible managers, and especially to the head of production and the head of QC, and, if appropriate, the head of QA.

- The QP should at all times have access to the marketing authorization dossier and should be informed about all changes related to the dossier.

ANNEX 16 TO THE EU GUIDE TO GMP CERTIFICATION AND BATCH RELEASE

Annex 16 covers those cases where a batch has had different stages of production or testing conducted at different locations or by different manufacturers, and where an intermediate or bulk production batch is divided into more than one finished product batch. It also covers the release of batches that have been imported both when there is and is not an MRA between the EC and the third country.

Principle

Each batch of finished product must be certified by a QP before being released for sale or supply or for export. The purpose of controlling batch release in this way is to ensure that the batch has been manufactured and checked in accordance with the requirements of its marketing authorization, the principles and guidelines of EC GMP or the GMP of a third country recognized as equivalent under an MRA, and any other relevant legal requirement before it is placed on the market. In the event that a defect needs to be investigated or a batch recalled, this process ensures that the QP who certified the batch and the relevant records are readily identifiable.

Introduction

Manufacture, including QC testing, of a batch of medicinal products takes place in stages that may be conducted at different sites and by different manufacturers. Each stage should be conducted in accordance with the relevant marketing authorization, GMP, and the laws of the member state concerned, which should be taken into account by the QP who certifies the finished product batch before release to the market.

In an industrial situation, however, it is usually not possible for a single QP to be closely involved with every stage of manufacture. The QP who certifies a finished product batch may need therefore to rely in part on the advice and decisions of others. Before doing so, the QP should ensure that this reliance is well founded, either from personal knowledge or from the confirmation by other QPs within a quality system.

When some stages of manufacture occur in a third country, it is still a requirement that production and testing are in accordance with the marketing authorization, that the manufacturer is authorized according to the laws of the country concerned, and that manufacture follows GMP of the EC.

General

One batch of finished product may have different stages of manufacture, importation, testing, and storage before release conducted at different sites. Each site should be approved under one or more manufacturing authorizations and should have at its disposal the services of at least one QP. The correct manufacture of a particular batch of product, regardless of how many sites are involved, should be the overall concern of the QP who certifies that finished product batch before release.

Different batches of a product may be manufactured or imported and released at different sites in the EC/European Economic Area (EEA). For example, an EC marketing authorization may name batch release sites in more than one member state, and a national authorization may also name more than one release site. In this situation, the holder of the marketing authorization and each site authorized to release batches of the product should be able to identify the site at which any particular batch has been released and the QP who was responsible for certifying that batch.

The QP who certifies a finished product batch before release may do so based on personal knowledge of all the facilities and procedures employed, the expertise of the persons concerned, and of the quality system within which they operate. Alternatively, the QP may rely on the confirmation by one or more other QPs of the compliance of intermediate stages of manufacture within a quality system. This confirmation by other QPs should be documented and should identify clearly the matters that have been confirmed. The systematic arrangements to achieve this should be defined in a written agreement.

This agreement is required whenever a QP wishes to rely on a confirmation by another QP. The agreement should be in general accordance with Chapter 7. The QP who certifies the finished product batch should ensure that the arrangements in the agreement are verified. The form of such an agreement should be appropriate to the relationship between the parties, for example, an SOP within a company or a formal contract between different companies, even if within the same group.

The agreement should include an obligation on the part of the provider of a bulk or intermediate product to notify the recipient(s) of any deviations, out-of-specification (OOS) results, noncompliance with GMP, investigations, complaints, or other matters that should be taken into account by the QP who is responsible for certifying the finished product batch.

When a computerized system is used for recording certification and batch release, particular note should be taken of the guidance in Annex 11. Certification of a finished product batch against a relevant marketing authorization by a QP in the EC/EEA need not be repeated on the same batch provided the batch has remained within the EC/EEA.

Whatever particular arrangements are made for certification and release of batches, it should always be possible to identify and recall without delay all products that could be rendered hazardous by a quality defect in a batch.

Batch Testing and Release of Products Manufactured in the EC/EEA

All Manufacture Occurs at a Single Authorized Site. When all production and control stages are carried out at a single site, the conduct of certain checks and controls may be delegated to others, but the QP at this site who certifies the finished product batch normally retains personal responsibility for these within a defined quality system. However, he or she may, alternatively, take account of the confirmation of the intermediate stages by other QPs on the site that is responsible for those stages.

Different Stages of Manufacture Are Conducted at Different Sites within the Same Company. When different stages of the manufacture of a batch are done at different sites within the same company (which may or may not be covered by the same manufacturing authorization), a QP should be responsible for each stage. Certification of the finished product batch should be performed by a QP of the manufacturing authorization holder responsible for releasing the batch to the market, who may take personal responsibility for all stages or may take account of the confirmation of the earlier stages by the relevant QP responsible for those stages.

Some Intermediate Stages of Manufacture Are Contracted to a Different Company. One or more intermediate production and control stages may be contracted to a holder of a manufacturing authorization in another company. A QP of the contract giver may take account of the confirmation of the relevant stage by a QP of the contract acceptor but is responsible for ensuring that this work is conducted within the terms of a written agreement. The finished product batch should be certified by the QP of the manufacturing authorization holder responsible for releasing the batch to the market.

Bulk Production Batch Is Assembled at Different Sites into Several Finished Batches Released under Single Marketing Authorization. This situation could occur, for example, under a national marketing authorization when the assembly sites are all within one member state, or under an EC marketing authorization when the sites are in more than one member state. One alternative is for a QP of the manufacturing authorization holder making the bulk production batch to certify all the finished product batches before release to the market. In doing so, he or she may either take personal responsibility for all manufacturing stages or take account of the confirmation of assembly by the QPs of the assembly sites. Another alternative is for the certification of each finished product batch before release to the market to be performed by a QP of the manufacturer who has conducted the final assembly operation. In doing so, he or she may either take personal responsibility for all manufacturing stages or take account of the confirmation of the bulk production batch by a QP of the manufacturer of the bulk batch.

In all cases of assembly at different sites under a single marketing authorization, one person, normally a QP of the manufacturer of the bulk production batch, should have overall responsibility for all released finished product batches that are derived from one bulk production batch. The duty of this person is to be aware of any quality problems reported on any of the finished product batches and to coordinate any necessary action arising from a problem with the bulk batch. While the batch numbers of the bulk and finished product batches are not necessarily the same, there should be a documented link between the two numbers so that an audit trail can be established.

Bulk Production Batch Is Assembled at Different Sites into Several Finished Batches Released under Different Marketing Authorizations. This situation could occur, for example, when a multinational organization holds national marketing authorizations for a product in several member states or when a generic manufacturer purchases bulk products and assembles and releases them for sale under its own marketing authorization. A QP of the manufacturer doing the assembly who certifies the finished product batch may either take personal responsibility for all manufacturing stages or may take account of the confirmation of the bulk production batch by a QP of the bulk product manufacturer. Any problem identified in any of the finished product batches that may have arisen in the bulk production batch should be communicated to the QP responsible for confirming the bulk production batch, who should then take any necessary action with respect to all finished product batches produced from the suspected bulk production batch. This arrangement should be defined in a written agreement.

A finished product batch may be purchased and released to the market by a manufacturing authorization holder, which could occur, for example, when a company supplying generic products holds a marketing authorization for products made by another company, purchases finished products that have not been certified against its marketing authorization, and releases them under its own manufacturing authorization in accordance with its own marketing authorization. In this situation, a QP of the purchaser should certify the finished product batch before release. In doing so he or she may either take personal responsibility for all manufacturing stages or may take account of the confirmation of the batch by a QP of the vendor manufacturer.

Quality Control Laboratory and Production Site Are Authorized under Different Manufacturing Authorizations. A QP certifying a finished product batch may either take personal responsibility for the laboratory testing or may take account of the confirmation by another QP of the testing and results. The other laboratory and QP need not be in the same member state as the manufacturing authorization holder releasing the batch. In the absence of such confirmation, the QP should have personal knowledge of the laboratory and its procedures relevant to the finished product to be certified.

BATCH TESTING AND RELEASE OF PRODUCTS IMPORTED FROM A THIRD COUNTRY

General

Importation of finished products should be conducted by an importer. Each batch of imported finished product should be certified by a QP of the importer before release for sale in the EC/EEA. Unless an MRA is in operation between the EC and the third country, samples from each batch should be tested in the EC/EEA before certification of the finished product batch by a QP. Importation and testing need not necessarily be performed in the same member state. The guidance in this section should be applied as appropriate to the importation of partially manufactured products:

- A complete batch or the first part of a batch of a medicinal product is imported. The batch or part batch should be certified by a QP of the importer before release. This QP may take account of the confirmation of the checking, sampling, or testing of the imported batch by a QP of another manufacturing authorization holder (that is, within EC/EEA).

- Part of a finished product batch is imported after another part of the same batch has previously been imported to the same or a different site. A QP of the importer receiving a subsequent part of the batch may take account of the testing and certification by a QP of the first part of the batch. If this is done, the QP should ensure, based on evidence, that the two parts do come from the same batch, that the subsequent part has been transported under the same conditions as the first part, and that the samples that were tested are representative of the whole batch. The conditions are most likely to be met when the manufacturer in the third country and the importer(s) in the EC/EEA belong to the same organization operating under a corporate system of quality assurance. If the QP can not ensure that the conditions are met, each part of the batch should be treated as a separate batch. When different parts of the batch are released under the same marketing authorization, one person, normally a QP of the importer of the first part of a batch, should take overall responsibility for ensuring that records are kept of the importation of all parts of the batch and that the distribution of all parts of the batch is traceable within the EC/EEA. The QP should be made aware of any quality problems reported on any part of the batch and should coordinate any necessary action concerning these problems and their resolution. This should be ensured by a written agreement between all the importers concerned.

Location of Sampling for Testing in EC/EEA

Samples should be representative of the batch and be tested in the EC/EEA. To represent the batch, it may be preferable to take some samples during processing in the third country. For example, samples for sterility testing may best be taken throughout the filling operation; however, to represent the batch after storage and transportation, some samples should be taken after receipt of the batch in the EC/EEA.

When any samples are taken in a third country, they should either be shipped with and under the same conditions as the batch that they represent, or if sent separately, it should be demonstrated that the samples are still representative of the batch, for example, by defining and monitoring the conditions of storage and shipment. When the QP wishes to rely on testing of samples taken in a third country, this should be justified on technical grounds.

Batch Testing and Release of Products Imported from a Third Country with EC MRA

Unless otherwise specified in the agreement, an MRA does not remove the requirement for a QP within the EC/EEA to certify a batch before it is released for sale or supply within the EC/EEA. However, subject to details of the particular agreement, the QP of the importer may rely on the manufacturer's confirmation that the batch has been made and tested in accordance with its marketing authorization and the GMP of the third country and need not repeat the full testing. The QP may certify the batch for release when he or she is satisfied with this confirmation and that the batch has been transported under the required conditions and has been received and stored in the EC/EEA by an importer under defined conditions.

Routine Duties of a Qualified Person

Before certifying a batch for release, the QP doing so should ensure that at least the following requirements have been met:

- The batch and its manufacture comply with the provisions of the marketing authorization (including the authorization required for importation, where relevant).

- Manufacture has been done in accordance with GMP or, in the case of a batch imported from a third country, in accordance with GMP standards at least equivalent to EC GMP.

- The principal manufacturing and testing processes have been validated, and account has been taken of the actual production conditions and manufacturing records.

- Any deviations or planned changes in production or QC have been authorized by the persons responsible in accordance with a defined system. Any changes requiring variation to the marketing or manufacturing authorization have been reported to and authorized by the relevant authority.

- All the necessary checks and tests have been performed, including any additional sampling, inspection, tests, or checks initiated because of deviations or planned changes.

- All necessary production and QC documentation has been completed and endorsed by the staff authorized to do so.

- All audits have been carried out as required by the QA system.

- The QP should in addition take into account any other factors of which he or she is aware that are relevant to the quality of the batch.

A QP may have additional duties in accordance with national legislation or administrative procedures. A QP who confirms the compliance of an intermediate stage of manufacture has the same obligations in relation to that stage as there would be with final release. A QP should maintain his or her knowledge and experience up to date in the light of technical and scientific progress and changes in quality management relevant to the products that he or she is required to certify.

If a QP is called on to certify a batch of a product type with which they are unfamiliar, for example, because the manufacturer for whom they work introduces a new product range or because they start to work for a different manufacturer, they should first ensure that they have gained the relevant knowledge and experience necessary to fulfill this duty. In accordance with national requirements, the QP may be required to notify the authorities of such a change and may be subject to renewed authorization.

Chapter 10

Risk Management

Quality risk management is a systematic process for the assessment, control, communication, and review of risks to the quality of the product throughout its life cycle. ICH Q9, *Quality Risk Management*, provides the framework that may be applied to all aspects of pharmaceutical quality, including development, manufacturing, distribution, inspection, and submission/review processes across the life cycle of drug substances and drug products as well as biologic and biotechnological products. Quality risk management can be applied in the product life cycle to the use of raw materials, solvents, excipients, packaging, and labeling materials.

The two primary principles of quality risk management are that the evaluation of the quality risk should ultimately link back to the potential harm to the patient, and that the level of effort, formality, and documentation of the quality risk management process should be commensurate with the level of risk.

GENERAL QUALITY RISK MANAGEMENT PROCESS

Quality risk management should include systematic processes designed to coordinate, facilitate, and improve science-based decision making with respect to risk. Steps used to initiate and plan a quality risk management process include:

- Defining the process, which typically involves risk assessment, risk control, risk communication, and risk review elements at an appropriate level of detail

- Assembling background information and/or data on the potential hazard, harm, or human health impact relevant to the risk assessment

- Identifying a leader and critical resources

- Specifying a timeline, deliverables, and appropriate level of decision making for the risk management process

- Identifying the interrelationships of the elements of the quality risk management process

RISK ASSESSMENT

Risk assessment consists of the identification of hazards and the analysis and evaluation of risks associated with exposure to those hazards. Quality risk assessments begin with a well-defined problem description or risk question. When the risk in question is well defined, an appropriate risk management tool and the types of information required to address the risk question will be readily identifiable. As an aid to clearly defining the risk(s) for risk assessment purposes, three fundamental questions are often used:

- What might go wrong?

- What is the likelihood (probability) it will go wrong?

- What are the consequences (severity)?

The output of a risk assessment is either a quantitative estimate of risk or a qualitative description of a range of risk. When risk is expressed quantitatively, a numerical probability is used. In quantitative risk assessments, a risk estimate provides the likelihood of a specific consequence, given a set of risk-generating circumstances. Thus, quantitative risk estimation is useful for one particular consequence at a time. Alternatively, risk can be expressed using qualitative descriptors, such as "high," "medium," or "low," that should be defined in as much detail as possible. Sometimes a *risk score* is used to further define descriptors in risk ranking. In addition, some risk management tools use a relative risk measure to combine multiple levels of severity and probability into an overall estimate of relative risk. The intermediate steps within a scoring process can sometimes employ quantitative risk estimation.

Risk identification provides the basis for further steps in the quality risk management process. It systematically uses information to identify hazards associated with the risk question or problem description. Information can include historical data, theoretical analysis, informed opinions, and the concerns of stakeholders. It addresses the "What might go wrong?" question, including identifying the possible consequences. *Risk analysis* is the estimation of the risk associated with the identified hazards. It is a qualitative or quantitative process of linking the likelihood of occurrence with the severity of harms. The extent to which the harm can be detected also factors into the estimation of risk. *Risk evaluation* compares the identified risk against given risk criteria and considers the strength of evidence for the three fundamental questions.

RISK CONTROL

The purpose of *risk control* is to reduce the risk to an acceptable level. The amount of effort used for risk control should be proportional to the significance of the risk. Decision makers might use different processes, including benefit–cost analysis, for understanding the optimal level of risk control.

Risk control might focus on the following questions:

- Is the risk estimated in the risk assessment above an acceptable level?

- What can be done to reduce or eliminate risk(s)?

- What is the appropriate balance between benefits, risks, and resources?

- Are new risks introduced due to the identified risks being controlled?

Risk reduction focuses on mitigation and avoidance of quality risk when it exceeds a specified (acceptable) level. It includes actions taken to mitigate the severity, and reduce the probability, of harm. It may also identify processes that improve the detectability of hazards.

The implementation of risk reduction measures can introduce new risks into the system or increase the significance of other existing risks. Hence, it might be appropriate to revisit the risk assessment to identify and evaluate any possible change in risk after implementing a risk reduction process.

Risk acceptance is a decision to accept risk. It can be a formal decision to accept the residual risk, or it can be a passive decision in which residual risks are not specified. For some types of harms, even the best quality risk management practices might not entirely eliminate risk. In these circumstances, it might be agreed that an appropriate quality risk management strategy has been applied, and that quality risk is reduced to a specified (acceptable) level. This specified and acceptable level will depend on many parameters and should be decided on a case-by-case basis.

RISK COMMUNICATION AND RISK REVIEW

Risk communication is the exchange or sharing of information about risk and its management between the decision makers and others. Communication should include the existence, nature, form, probability, severity, and detectability of the risk. This process can sometimes be formal. It may be internal (that is, occur within the organization) or external (that is, occur with suppliers, customers, or regulators). Formal processes should be documented. *Risk review* is a process that allows for the review or monitoring of events. It should incorporate new knowledge and experience and may be used for planned or unplanned events, and it should be performed periodically.

RISK MANAGEMENT METHODOLOGY

Quality risk management supports a scientific and practical approach to decision making. It provides documented, transparent, and reproducible methods to accomplish steps of the quality risk management process based on current knowledge about assessing the probability, severity, and, sometimes, the detectability of the risk. Figure 10.1 lists some risk management tools. Combined use of these tools provides flexibility that can facilitate the application of quality risk management principles.

INTEGRATION INTO INDUSTRY AND REGULATORY OPERATIONS

Quality risk management is the foundation for science-based decisions when integrated into a *quality management system* (QMS). It does not obviate industry's obligations to comply with regulatory requirements. It can facilitate better and

- Traditional informal ways (empirical and/or internal procedures) based on compilation of observations, trends, and other information

- Failure mode, effects and criticality analysis (FMECA)

- Fault tree analysis (FTA)

- Hazard analysis and critical control points (HACCP)

- Hazard operability analysis (HAZOP)

- Risk ranking and filtering

- Preliminary hazard analysis (PHA)

- Supporting statistical tools

Figure 10.1   Some risk management tools.

more-informed decisions and may provide regulators with greater assurance of a company's ability to address potential risks. It may affect the extent and level of direct regulatory oversight.

The degree of rigor and formality used in quality risk management should be commensurate with the complexity and/or criticality of the issue. Quality risk management should be integrated into existing operations and documented appropriately. Finally, training of personnel provides for greater understanding of decision-making processes and builds confidence in quality risk management outcomes.

METHODS AND TOOLS

Basic Risk Management Facilitation Methods

Basic risk management facilitation methods include flowcharts, check sheets, process maps, and cause-and-effect diagrams (that is, the Ishikawa diagram, or fishbone diagram).

Failure Mode and Effects Analysis

Failure mode and effects analysis (FMEA) includes the evaluation of potential failure modes and their effect on outcomes. It methodically breaks down the analysis of complex processes into manageable steps; risk reduction can then be used to eliminate, contain, reduce, or control failures.

The potential areas of use for FMEA are to prioritize risks and monitor the effectiveness of risk control activities. It can be applied to equipment and facilities, and might be used to analyze a manufacturing operation and its effect on product or process. It identifies elements/operations within the system that render it vulnerable. The output or results of FMEA can be used as a basis for design or further analysis, or to guide resource deployment.

Failure Mode, Effects and Criticality Analysis

Failure mode, effects and criticality analysis (FMECA) is extended to investigate the degree of severity of the consequences, probabilities of occurrence, and detectability. It can identify places for additional preventive actions.

Potential areas of use for FMECA application in the pharmaceutical industry should be primarily for failures and risks associated with manufacturing processes; however, it is not limited to this application. The output of an FMECA is a relative risk score for each failure mode, which is used to rank the modes on a relative risk basis.

Fault Tree Analysis

Fault tree analysis (FTA) evaluates system (or subsystem) failures one at a time, represented pictorially in the form of a branching tree of fault modes. At each level in the tree, combinations of fault modes are described with logical operators (for example, AND, OR). FTA relies on experts' process understanding to find causes. A potential area of use for FTA can be to establish the pathway to the root cause of the failure. FTA can be used to investigate complaints or deviations to fully understand their root cause and to ensure that intended improvements will resolve the issue and not lead to other issues. FTA is an effective tool for evaluating how multiple factors affect a given issue. The output of an FTA includes a visual representation of failure modes. It is useful both for risk assessment and in developing monitoring programs

Hazard Analysis and Critical Control Points

Hazard analysis and critical control points (HACCP) is used to manage risks with physical, chemical, and biological hazards. HACCP has seven steps:

1. Conduct a hazard analysis and identify preventive measures for each step of the process.

2. Determine the critical control points.

3. Establish critical limits.

4. Establish a system to monitor the critical control points.

5. Establish the corrective actions to be taken when monitoring indicates that the critical control points are not in a state of control.

6. Establish a system to verify that the HACCP system is working effectively.

7. Establish a record-keeping system.

Potential areas of use for HACCP might be to identify and manage risks associated with physical, chemical, and biologic hazards (including microbiological contamination). HACCP is useful when product and process understanding is sufficiently comprehensive to support identification of critical control points. The output of a HACCP analysis is risk management information that facilitates monitoring of critical points not only in the manufacturing process but also in other life cycle phases.

Hazard Operability Analysis

Hazard operability analysis (HAZOP) is used primarily to evaluate process safety hazards. It is a systematic brainstorming technique for identifying hazards using guide words (for example, *no, more, other than, part of*). HAZOP is for risk events caused by design or operating deviations. Potential areas of use for HAZOP are manufacturing processes, including outsourced production and formulation, and the upstream suppliers, equipment, and facilities for drug substances and drug products. It has been used primarily in the pharmaceutical industry for evaluating process safety hazards. As is the case with HACCP, the output of a HAZOP analysis is a list of critical operations for risk management. This facilitates regular monitoring of critical points in the manufacturing process.

Preliminary Hazard Analysis

Preliminary hazard analysis (PHA) is the application of experience or knowledge of a hazard to identify future hazards. This tool consists of identification of the possibility that the risk event happens, qualitative evaluation of the extent of possible injury or damage to health that could result, relative ranking of the hazard using a combination of severity and likelihood of occurrence, and identification of possible remedial measures.

Potential areas of use for PHA might be analysis of existing systems or prioritizing hazards where circumstances prevent a more extensive technique from being used. It can be used for product, process, and facility design, as well as to evaluate the types of hazards for the general product type, then the product class, and finally the specific product. PHA is most commonly used early in the development of a project when little information on design details or operating procedures is available; thus, it will often be a precursor to further studies. Typically, hazards identified in the PHA are further assessed with other risk management tools.

Risk Ranking and Filtering

Risk ranking and filtering is a tool for comparing and ranking risks including filters (for example, cutoff scores). Potential areas of use include prioritizing manufacturing sites for inspection/audit by regulators or industry. Risk ranking methods are particularly helpful in situations in which the portfolio of risks and the underlying consequences to be managed are diverse and difficult to compare using a single tool. Risk ranking is useful to management in evaluating both quantitatively assessed and qualitatively assessed risks within the same organizational framework.

Supporting Statistical Tools

These tools support data assessment and facilitate decision making. The most common statistical tools are control charts, design of experiments (DOE), histograms, Pareto charts, process capability analysis, FTA, FMEA, and HACCP.

Chapter 11

Training and Personnel Qualifications

Good manufacturing practices (GMP) require that personnel have the education, training, and experience needed to perform their assigned responsibilities. Inadequate training can cause the United States Food and Drug Administration (FDA) to declare the product to be adulterated under the Food, Drug, and Cosmetic Act (FDCA), potentially preventing the product from being sold or distributed. Training on both specific job tasks and GMP is required.

JOB-SPECIFIC TRAINING

Managers (or supervisors) are responsible for defining the training needed for a specific position in a list of required documents and training courses such as a job curriculum. If retraining needs to be performed periodically, such as for aseptic practices, the curriculum can indicate this timing requirement. The curriculum should indicate what training is needed before specific tasks can be performed by the employee. Training is done and documented before an employee performs the task.

Training should not be considered a one-time exercise that is provided only when an employee is hired. Training related to job tasks is necessary when procedures, batch records, and/or test methods are revised or when a task has not been performed recently. Similarly, when an employee's job changes within an organization, his or her education, experience, and training should be reevaluated to determine what areas need to be addressed to perform the new job. Changes in work experience and education can be documented by maintaining an up-to-date resume or work history in the employee's training file.

Defect awareness training should make personnel aware of the need to understand that if they do not follow procedures, batch records, or test methods as written, an adverse impact to product quality may occur.

GOOD MANUFACTURING PRACTICES TRAINING

Many pharmaceutical companies provide annual GMP training courses. These courses may include topics such as recent trends in the GMP industry, new or newly revised GMP regulations, summary of deviations and internal audit observations that have occurred in the past year, or a review of GMP regulations that impact the organization. In addition, if a pharmaceutical manufacturer has been distributing its products solely within the United States and gains approval to sell its products in Canada, it would be beneficial to train employees on the Canadian GMP, although they closely resemble the FDA GMP. Pharmaceutical manufacturers also should train employees on the specific GMP related to their jobs.

FDA's *Quality Systems Approach to Pharmaceutical CGMP Regulations* guidance document indicates that *quality unit* (QU) personnel should have some understanding of scientific and technical topics, product and process knowledge, and the ability to assess risk. The QU has many responsibilities, the most important of which is releasing or rejecting product. For this responsibility, quality unit personnel should be trained to identify any deviations in manufacturing or testing processes that may not have been observed and addressed during manufacturing and testing, and to conduct effective investigations to determine whether product quality was impacted. If product quality was adversely impacted, or if the impact to product is unknown, the product should not be released.

European GMP regulations include specific requirements for training of personnel whose duties involve manufacturing or *quality control* (QC)–related activities. These are discussed in EudraLex, *Good Manufacturing Practice (GMP) Guidelines: The Rules Governing Medicinal Products in the European Union.* Training also applies to visitors or untrained personnel who must enter production or QC areas. These individuals must first receive information on personal hygiene and use of protective clothing, and should be closely supervised.

European training requirements include basic training on GMP as well as ongoing training. The concept of *quality assurance* (QA) and its implementation should be addressed in GMP training. Specific training should be given if personnel work in areas where contamination may be a hazard. EudraLex specifies that the training programs be approved, preferably by the head of production or quality control, as appropriate, and records of training must be maintained. Effectiveness of training should be assessed as well. World Health Organization (WHO) GMP training requirements are similar to those discussed in EudraLex and also include a requirement for contractors and consultants to receive training.

TRAINING EFFECTIVENESS

According to *Quality Systems Approach to Pharmaceutical GMP Regulations*, managers (supervisors) are responsible for ensuring that training is effective by verifying that the skills are learned and implemented in their employees' daily performance. Management is also responsible for communicating employee roles, responsibilities, and authorities within the quality system and ensuring that interactions between different roles are defined and understood.

Any evidence that indicates the employee's training was not effective, or that they do not have the appropriate experience or skills (for example, frequently occurring deviations when executing tasks), should trigger an evaluation of whether the employee is capable and/or whether additional training or retraining is needed. If the original training was not effective, simply retraining an employee may not be sufficient to resolve performance issues. The training may need to be redesigned to be effective.

EMPLOYEE QUALIFICATIONS

Managers need to define the qualifications for a position (which is usually defined by a job title). The responsibilities for a specific position are defined in a document such as a job description. In addition to responsibilities, the job description can include minimum education and experience requirements, skills, and required certifications. Certifications provide a good yardstick for knowledge of a topic because a *body of knowledge* (BoK) is measured by an examination, but they do not replace the experience and hands-on training provided by performance of a job or task. ASQ certification is peer recognition that an individual has proficiency with, and comprehension of, a specified BoK. A clear job description facilitates hiring the best person for the job.

Job descriptions for personnel who perform testing and/or calibration tasks have specific minimum requirements as outlined in ISO/IEC 17025:2005, *General requirements for the competence of testing and calibration laboratories*. These requirements include:

- Responsibilities for performing and planning tests and/or calibrations and evaluating the results, reporting opinions and interpretations, and modifying, developing, and validating new methods.

- Expertise and experience required includes qualification and training programs and managerial duties.

DOCUMENTATION OF TRAINING

All training should be documented by recording the topic and an overview of the content, the trainer, the date trained, and the trainee's name. Regulatory agencies expect to see documentation that trainers are qualified, as well. For example, a GMP trainer should have experience and training in GMP in addition to knowledge of the topic of the training program. It is important that training records be maintained, as well, to provide evidence of employee competency.

EMPLOYEE PROFICIENCY

Proficiency for a particular task should be documented before the employee performs the task independently. For critical tasks (those that could impact product quality), task training can be performed to ensure that the employee thoroughly understands the task. Task training consists of the trainee reading any related procedures, observing the task being performed by a qualified individual, performing the task under the supervision of a qualified individual with assistance and coaching, if needed, and performing the task independently. The trainer indicates on the training documentation that the trainee satisfactorily completed training, and the employee indicates that he or she understands the task and associated documentation.

Proficiency for gaining knowledge from training can be assessed by administration of a test after the training event. Verification that knowledge was gained during the training session can be accomplished by administering a pretest before the training event occurs and comparing the results to the post-training test. A minimum passing grade is typically defined for GMP tests. Retention of the knowledge gained by attending the training could be assessed by testing a trainee when time has elapsed after the training event occurs.

Chapter 12

Change Control and Management

The United States Food and Drug Administration (FDA) provides very specific requirements for change control and management, requiring written procedures for production and process controls to ensure that drug products have the identity, strength, quality, safety, and purity they purport or are represented to possess, and that medical devices are safe and effective. These requirements extend beyond procedures and work instructions to include changes to specifications, products, labels, methods of testing and production, packaging, equipment, and facilities.

21 CFR 211 and 820 provide the requirements for establishing and maintaining documents, including requirements for reviewing, for adequacy, and approval before issuance. The *quality unit* (QU) is ultimately responsible for the change control and management function. However, other functions usually participate in the process depending on the application and requirements, including engineering, production, manufacturing, distribution, regulatory affairs, and clinical.

Procedures for production and process controls are usually birthed or modified using a predetermined *engineering change control* (ECO) system. The ECO system usually includes a list of requirements and considerations, an evaluation checklist, and required signatures. The complexity of the change usually determines the level of control and authorization required. For example, to update a procedure that contains a grammatical error may be considered an administrative change and therefore allow for an abbreviated approval and signature process, whereas a procedural change that modifies a critical process parameter usually requires the full evaluation and approval process, including risk analysis and change effectiveness. Figure 12.1 depicts a typical change control process.

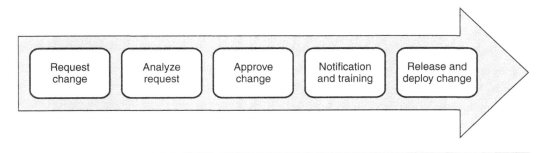

Figure 12.1 Typical change control process.
Source: Figure courtesy of the ASQ Food, Drug, and Cosmetic Division. Used with permission.

Changes to procedures for production and process controls include a description of the change, identification of the affected documents, the signature of the approving individual(s), the approval date, and when the change becomes effective. Obsolete documents are promptly removed from all points of use. This process is necessary to prevent unintended use of obsolete documents.

Written production and process control procedures are followed in the execution of the various production and process control functions, and are documented at the time of performance. Any deviation from the written procedures must be recorded and justified. Deviation should be reviewed by the quality unit to ensure no deleterious effect and that the drug products have the identity, strength, quality, safety, and purity they purport or are represented to possess. When deviations occur, it may necessitate the use of the *nonconformance* (NCR) and/or the *out-of-specification* (OOS) process as appropriate.

Another consideration when production and process control functions are birthed or changed is notification and training. It is required that approved changes be communicated to the appropriate personnel in a timely manner, and, where appropriate, the personnel are trained on the changes.

Chapter 13

Investigations and Corrective and Preventive Action (CAPA)

According to the United States Food and Drug Administration (FDA) guidance *Quality Systems Approach to Pharmaceutical CGMP Regulations*, "CAPA is the regulatory concept for investigating, understanding, and correcting discrepancies while attempting to prevent their recurrence." *Corrective and preventive action* (CAPA) is an absolute that defines the backbone of the *quality management system* (QMS). The systemic management of the CAPA program is an expectation of most standards and regulations (for example, FDA, European Medicines Agency [EMA], International Organization for Standardization [ISO]).

CAPA is essential throughout the life cycle of any product in the pharmaceutical drug and medical device industries; it is not a system used only during the production phase of a pharmaceutical product. ICH Q10 provides a table that allows insight into the various ways in which CAPA is relevant to each stage (Table 13.1). Regulatory agencies have a clear expectation that companies have a defined system in place for the documentation and implementation of corrective actions arising from "investigation of complaints, product rejections, nonconformances, recalls, deviations, audits, regulatory inspections and findings, and trends from process performance and product quality monitoring."

The term *CAPA* is used to define the program in quality manuals as well as in the *standard operating procedures* (SOPs) defining the quality system. Whether there is a single procedure that defines the process for CAPAs or whether there are separate procedures for CAPA is not important. What is important is that the process be clearly defined, that it is structured, and most critically, that the investigations have the objective of determining the root cause of the issue.

Table 13.1 Application of a corrective action and preventive action system throughout the product life cycle.

Pharmaceutical development	Technology transfer	Commercial manufacturing	Product discontinuation
Product or process variability is explored. CAPA methodology is useful where corrective actions and preventive actions are incorporated into the iterative design and development process.	CAPA can be used as an effective system for feedback, feed forward, and continual improvement.	CAPA should be used, and the effectiveness of the actions should be evaluated.	CAPA should continue after the product is discontinued. The impact on product remaining on the market should be considered, as well as other products that might be impacted.

FDA guidance *Quality Systems Approach to Pharmaceutical CGMP Regulations* states that there are three separate concepts used in the quality system model for CAPA (Figure 13.1): remedial corrective actions to correct the immediate problem identified, root cause analysis to determine and understand the actual cause of the deviation or issue and potentially provide guidance for the prevention of a future occurrence of a similar problem or issue, and preventive action, which includes those activities carried out as a result of the root cause analysis to prevent a recurrence of the same or similar issue.

Good manufacturing practices (GMP) requirements dictate that all of the manufacturing, packaging, testing, and holding of drug product must take place according to established and approved procedures. Once the situation is such that this condition is not met, it is necessary to investigate to determine the corrective action necessary. The level of investigation, the corrective action necessary, the formality with which it is documented, and the level of control extended should be based on the risks involved (in accordance with ICH Q9). Many firms have established "alert" and "action" limits on many of their processes to assist in defining the level of formality needed. Regardless of level of formality involved, specific needs for every investigation include:

- The individuals involved in the investigation, and the decision-making authority, must have sufficient education, experience, and knowledge to carry out their associated tasks, which usually means cross-functional multidisciplinary teams including Quality Assurance.

- The investigation must be thorough, timely, unbiased, well-documented, and scientifically sound.

- It must include sufficient information to stand on its own and allow an independent reviewer (possibly a regulator) to understand the logic, the rationale for decisions, and who the decision makers were.

- It must identify the appropriate corrective action, and to properly take preventive measures, it must identify the root cause of the problem.

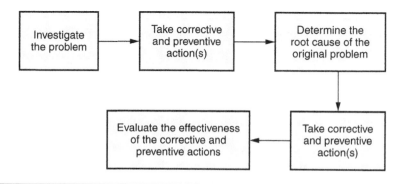

Figure 13.1   Flowchart of interactions of a quality system model.

Source: Figure courtesy of the ASQ Food, Drug, and Cosmetic Division. Used with permission.

An investigation is a process. While the individual situation and immediate players involved may change, the steps taken, the tools employed, and the key decision makers should be well defined and not decided ad hoc.

The initial investigation usually will not determine the root cause, but will usually provide guidance on immediate corrective actions necessary to prevent further nonconformity. The investigation is not over when the initial corrective action is taken; it must continue further to determine the root cause(s). Determining root cause can be arrived at by various methods: flowcharts, fishbone diagram, process mapping, checklists, fault tree analysis, and so on. FDA prefers, whenever feasible, that statistical and qualitative tools be used to find the most likely root cause(s) by identifying trends and patterns. Whichever method is used, the rationale and the data to support the decision for the preventive action(s) should be documented and should be approved by the proper authority (as defined by company policy). Preventive measures are taken to prevent nonconformance. They are meant to prevent recurrence, even if that recurrence is at another company location; preventive measures may not always be site specific.

Who is responsible for carrying out a corrective action and who must approve the activity are usually defined in a firm's policies and procedures. Because the need for corrective action must be determined taking into consideration the possible consequence or result of the action, the selection of who will carry out the action(s) should be based on the expertise required, the immediacy of need, and the level of risk to the product. The corrective actions taken must be documented (21 CFR 211.192) and are subject to review and approval by the quality unit. All corrective actions are expected to take place in a timely manner to prevent loss of data and loss of product integrity. Corrective actions that prompt change should go through the company's change management system.

Once the corrective action is complete, the preventive action is implemented; there should be a plan to follow up at a specified time to ensure that the CAPAs were effective. Once the results of CAPA have been reviewed and determined to have been effective, the evaluation should be documented.

Chapter 14

Audits and Self-Inspections

AUDIT TYPES

An *audit* is a "systematic, independent, and documented process for obtaining audit evidence and evaluating it objectively to determine the extent to which audit criteria are fulfilled." Audits can be categorized in different ways (Table 14.1). This chapter focuses on first-party audits in a *good manufacturing practices* (GMP) organization.

FIRST-PARTY AUDITS

Internal audits are performed according to a schedule to evaluate the quality system in order to determine if it is effectively implemented and maintained. In addition, they are performed to determine whether the organization's processes and products meet established parameters and specifications.

The organization performs *internal audits* to ensure that its systems are compliant by proactively evaluating them and addressing any gaps in compliance. This evaluation process increases the chance that the organization will produce goods and services that meet quality requirements, and help ensure that consumers can trust that their medications and medical devices are safe and effective. Internal audits can give early warning of a problem before it can impact product quality. Ensuring that quality systems are under control also maximizes the likelihood that a third-party audit of the organization will be successful.

Table 14.1 First-, second-, and third-party audits.

First party	Internal audit (self-inspection) is performed within an organization. A first-party audit could be performed within an organization's site by its own internal auditor, or could be conducted by a corporate auditor of one of the organization's sites.
Second party	Audit is performed by an organization of its supplier to ensure that contractual requirements are being met, or an audit is performed of a potential supplier to determine if it is capable of meeting specific requirements for a product or service. A manufacturer could perform a second-party audit of its raw material suppliers, contract laboratory, sterilization subcontractor, or packaging supplier.
Third party	An audit or inspection of an organization is performed by a regulator. In the United States, FDA performs inspections of companies that are subject to GMP to ensure compliance with these regulations.

Table 14.2   System, process, and product audits.

System	A system audit reviews a group of processes and controls, including activities crossing multiple organization, process, and product boundaries.
Process	A process audit examines the input, actions, and output of a single process to ensure that they meet requirements.
Product	A product audit examines a product or service to ensure that it meets requirements or specifications.

System, process, and product audits have different areas of focus that can be used for internal audits (and for second- or third-party audits, as well) (Table 14.2). The United States Food and Drug Administration (FDA) has identified six systems that they may review when conducting regulatory inspections: production, materials, laboratory controls, facilities and equipment, packaging and labeling, and quality. *Process audits* can address an aspect of a quality system, such as change control, product disposition, or validation. *Product audits* are usually narrower in scope than system or process audits and focus on a specific product or product family.

AUDIT PROCESS

Internal audits (also referred to as *self-inspections*) are conducted by GMP organizations to evaluate the effectiveness of their quality systems in complying with GMP. The generic steps involved in an audit are:

- Initiation (scope and frequency)
- Preparation (review of documentation, the program, and working documents)
- Execution (opening meeting, examination and evaluation, collecting evidence, observations, closing meeting with the auditee)
- Report (preparation, content, and distribution)
- Completion (report, submission, and retention)

GMP regulations and guidance documents from the US, Canada, European Union (EU), and Japan have similar requirements for an internal audit program:

- A written procedure to define the audit process
- A defined audit schedule covering all quality systems
- Qualified, independent, trained auditors
- Documentation of findings and corrective actions
- Management responsibility for timely implementation of effective corrective actions

Written Procedure

All of the steps necessary to conduct the audit should be defined in a written *standard operating procedure* (SOP). The written procedure should include how an auditor will be qualified. An auditor should be knowledgeable about the requirements against which he/she will be auditing (for example, GMP for pharmaceutical products) and the auditing process. The auditor should have experience in conducting audits.

The procedure should document which requirements are to be evaluated during the audit (for example, US GMP for finished pharmaceuticals, EU requirements for medicinal products for human use) and define how the audit schedule will be established. The frequency of audits and audit topics should be addressed in the written procedure.

The audit SOP includes requirements for the auditor to conduct an opening meeting with the auditee to explain the audit process and scope and to schedule the execution of the audit. The audit methodologies usually include observation of processes, facilities, and equipment, interviews with process participants, and review of procedures and records. At the closing meeting of the audit, the auditor addresses the draft observations with the auditees; in some cases, the auditee may provide missing information that indicates no gap in compliance exists, and the draft observation can be removed.

The procedure indicates that the auditor compiles the observations (gaps in compliance with requirements) in an audit report, which is provided to the auditee. The manager(s) responsible for the areas in which there are observations provide a response for each observation within a defined amount of time (for example, two weeks or one month after the completion of the audit). Finally, the procedure should include the methods used to monitor corrective actions to completion, and mechanisms to determine effectiveness of the corrective actions after they are implemented.

Audit Schedule

The audit schedule is often issued for a one-year period (for example, at the beginning of the calendar year) and indicates the areas and topics to be audited and when the audits will occur. Audits can be prioritized by evaluating the potential risk to product of various quality system elements, but the entire quality system should be evaluated on a periodic basis. The schedule is approved by management of the audit function. This document can be used to assign auditors to specific audits and to track the execution of audits as they are completed. When a regulatory agency conducts an inspection of an organization, this document can be used to provide evidence that the audits are being conducted as planned. Internal audit reports are not reviewed by FDA during the course of a routine inspection. FDA will only review internal audit reports in the following cases (*FDA Access to Results of Quality Assurance Program Audits and Inspections*):

- In directed or for-cause inspection and investigations of a sponsor or monitor of a clinical investigation

- In litigation (for example, grand jury subpoenas, discovery, or other agency or Department of Justice law enforcement activity, including administrative regulatory actions)

- During inspections made by inspection warrant where access to records is authorized by statute and when executing any judicial search warrant

Qualified, Independent Auditors

Auditors should be qualified to perform audits based on education, training, and experience. Education and training on GMP and the audit process can be obtained through courses and conferences provided by a variety of GMP consultants and organizations. An auditor's knowledge about current GMP can be increased by reading industry periodicals, regulations, and guidance documents from applicable countries for the type of products being manufactured, inspection results (for example, as summarized in GMP Trends [http://www.gmptrends.com/] or documented in warning letters), and books on GMP topics.

Auditors can become certified through organizations such as the American Society for Quality (ASQ), which has certified quality auditor, certified biomedical auditor, and certified hazard analysis and critical control points (HACCP) auditor designations.

The best way for a new auditor to learn about auditing is to work with an experienced (lead) auditor. First, the new auditor needs to be trained on the organization's procedure for internal audits. Once he or she is familiar with the organization's procedures, the new auditor can observe audits in process. Once he or she is comfortable with the process, the new auditor can assist a lead auditor in performing audits and writing observations and audit reports. As a final step, the new auditor can conduct an audit with oversight by an experienced lead auditor. When the new auditor has proven to the lead auditor that they can conduct an audit and write clear, objective audit reports, he or she is ready to perform audits independently. It is important to document the new auditor's education, training, and experience to demonstrate his or her qualifications to conduct audits.

Auditors must be independent of the areas that they audit. An auditor should be able to objectively assess compliance with requirements. Auditors are typically part of Quality Assurance, but it is not uncommon for individuals from a variety of departments to participate on audit teams.

Analyze Audit Results to Assess Conformance to Requirements

During the execution of the audit, the auditor needs to determine whether the procedures meet regulatory requirements, and whether actual practices follow the written procedures. Starting with regulatory requirements, the auditor confirms that written procedures exist to meet these requirements. Next, the auditor assesses whether actual practice is consistent with the company procedures by observing the execution of the procedures, interviewing process participants, and/or reviewing records. The auditor asks questions such as:

- Do procedures exist for each regulatory requirement?
- Is there evidence that each procedure is being followed as written?
- Are procedures and records clear and understandable?
- Are records legible?
- Are corrections to records clear and justified?
- Are deviations initiated when procedures are not followed?
- Is the change control process followed to evaluate potential impact of a change before it is implemented?
- Are training needs identified for each GMP employee for his or her assigned job?
- Is each GMP employee trained to perform a task before the task is performed?
- Do employees receive general GMP training periodically?

Documentation of Findings and Corrective Actions

Once the audit has been completed, a report is written by the auditor to serve as a record of the audit. The scope, purpose, and what was observed during the audit, both positive and negative (that is, gaps in compliance), should be documented. The observations of gaps in compliance should be written to clearly indicate which regulation, guidance, or procedural requirement was not met.

It is in the internal auditor's and the company's best interest for the internal auditor to maintain a positive relationship with coworkers. Even though a primary goal of auditing is to identify noncompliances, this process should be portrayed as an opportunity for continuous improvement. When an internal auditor conducts an audit, he or she can report on positive results observed (areas observed to be compliant) in addition to the gaps in compliance. It is important to write the observations to address the gaps with GMP and not to place blame on anyone for the gaps. Also, the auditor should not impose his or her solution to an observation; the people performing the process are the experts and owners of the process. The auditor may provide feedback about proposed corrective actions if requested by the auditee. In general, if the internal auditor (or audit team) treats the auditee with respect throughout the audit process, a positive relationship can be maintained.

Management Responsibility for Implementation of Corrective Actions

Manager(s) of the areas in which noncompliances were observed are responsible for providing responses to the observations. The responses should identify the corrective actions to be taken to close any gaps in compliance. Each corrective action should indicate specific action to be taken, who is responsible for implementing the action, and the date when the action will be implemented.

More than one corrective action may be needed to successfully address the observation. The timeliness of implementation of a corrective action should be based on the criticality of the observation. Noncompliant situations that have a high risk to product quality (for example, potential contamination of product) should be implemented immediately. Observations with a low risk to product quality can be implemented as soon as practical. At no time, however, should audit corrective actions languish; they should be given priority by management and implemented in a timely fashion.

After the responses are approved by audit management, responsible management ensures that the corrective actions are implemented by the date indicated in the corrective action plan. If for some reason the action can not be implemented as indicated in the response or by the date in the response, the area management should proactively contact audit management to communicate the change. If the scope of the corrective action or timeliness of implementation need to change, audit management should approve the change and document it in the audit records. If the noncompliance is critical to product quality, the necessary resources should be found to make it possible to meet the original corrective action plan.

Verification of Corrective Actions

The audit department tracks the corrective actions to ensure they are closed as indicated. The audit department may follow up on the dates when the actions were to be completed or check periodically (for example, monthly) to ensure that the actions were completed. The responsible managers provide objective evidence to the audit department to demonstrate that the corrective action was implemented. The objective evidence should be reviewed by the audit department to close the observation. Once the objective evidence is reviewed to confirm that the corrective action was implemented, the audit department can close the observation.

To ensure that the corrective actions effectively resolve the compliance gaps, the next time that an audit is conducted in the area where the observations were made, the auditor will review all previous observations within the scope of the current audit. During the current audit, the auditor reviews the previous noncompliances to make sure that they have been adequately addressed and that the compliance gaps no longer exist.

Another method that could be used to follow up on adequacy of corrective actions is to review the compliance gap after a fixed period of time has elapsed. For example, if an SOP was revised to clarify a process so that it is performed correctly, the audit department could check six months after the SOP is implemented to ensure that no further processing errors have been made as a result of following the revised procedure.

In some cases, a noncompliant observation written for one specific compliance gap may be a symptom of a systemwide gap. For example, an observation was listed regarding mechanics not being required to attend annual GMP training. It is possible that other departments who should attend annual GMP training were overlooked, but they do not have this requirement in their training curricula. Finance employees typically do not perform GMP tasks, but if they use the GMP inventory computer system to track product costs, they, at a minimum, need to be trained on GMP procedures for this computer system. When determining the corrective actions to be included in an audit observation response, responsible management should evaluate the potential for any systemwide gaps.

If the responsible area does not implement the corrective actions as indicated in the audit response, the audit department should determine why they were not implemented. If there are resource issues, the audit department should work with management to obtain the necessary resources, and adjust the due date for implementation if the risk assessment permits a delay. As a last resort, if the area management does not cooperate with the audit process, the audit department can escalate the issue with upper management or issue a nonconformance for not following the audit procedure.

If a corrective action was implemented but was found not to be effective, the organization needs to find the true root cause and address it with an appropriate corrective action. A follow-up audit could be performed to review more closely the context of the noncompliance, or the responsible area could investigate the root cause of the noncompliance again using more-rigorous problem-solving tools. The second round of corrective actions should be tracked by the audit department, and effectiveness of these corrective actions should be checked after implementation.

Chapter 15

Documents and Records Management

Documentation is an essential part of a *good manufacturing practices* (GMP) quality system. A well-written document ensures that responsibilities for GMP processes are known, and the steps to ensure quality and consistency in the output of the processes are clearly identified and can be followed. A well-documented quality system, combined with the records generated throughout GMP operations, go a long way toward ensuring that the pharmaceutical products manufactured have the high level of quality that regulators and patients demand.

DOCUMENTATION HIERARCHY

No single right answer exists when it comes to organizing documentation in a GMP environment. Figure 15.1 illustrates an example of how an organization may organize their documents. The external environment (for example, regulations and guidance documents) provide the overarching requirements that shape the documentation system. The regulatory requirements identify the minimum set of documents that must be in place to operate in compliance and to meet the expectations of the regulators. It is not atypical, however, for a firm to expand the scope of their documentation system to include information not required by regulation and to take advantage of the benefits that a document hierarchy brings to an organization.

At the highest level of the documentation hierarchy in most companies sits the *quality manual*, which defines the corporate objectives related to quality and compliance. It establishes a figurative road map including guiding principles (regulatory and internal) that employees and other users may refer to in meeting organizational objectives related to the quality system.

Just below the quality manual sit *corporate policies* that describe, in general terms, how the company intends to conduct their business in compliance with the requirements defined in the quality manual. A more detailed discussion of how the company will comply with individual aspects of the requirements in the quality manual is found in documents such as *standard operating procedures* (SOPs) and *validation master plans* (VMPs). SOPs describe, in detail, how firms will conduct operations related to each requirement in the GMP regulations, such as receipt of materials, operation of equipment, and handling of investigations. VMPs provide a detailed description of how a firm will qualify their facility or equipment and the governance program that will ensure that it remains in a qualified state. Additional detail, including step-by-step instructions on how to perform a specific task or activity within a GMP environment, can be found in

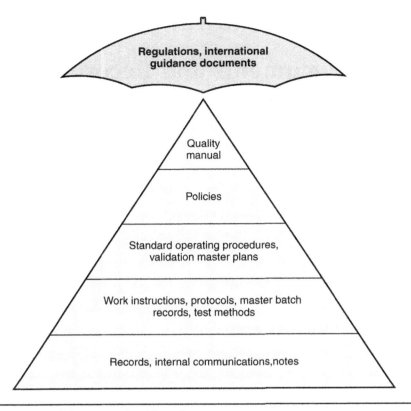

Figure 15.1   Typical documentation hierarchy.

Source: Figure courtesy of the ASQ Food, Drug, and Cosmetic Division. Used with permission.

documents such as *master batch records, test methods, protocols,* and *work instructions.* Master manufacturing and packaging batch records (sometimes referred to as manufacturing formulae, processing, and packaging instructions) detail each step of the processing and packaging of the drug product and are used by operations personnel to produce the finished drug product. Test methods provide the detailed steps for testing incoming materials and in-process or finished product. Protocols are often generated for special studies, such as validation studies or stability studies. Work instructions may provide even greater detail and are often used when step-by-step instruction is critical to ensure that processes are performed consistently and reliably. *Records, internal communications,* and *notes* represent the data that demonstrate that a company has operated in compliance with their own documentation and the regulations that govern their business.

DOCUMENTS AND RECORDS

It is important to distinguish between the concepts of *documents* and *records.* *Documents,* in a GMP environment, refer to the how-to instructions that outline what needs to be done to produce the product or operate in compliance with the regulations. *Records*, in a GMP environment, refer to the body of information (history) or data related to the manufacturing, packaging, testing, and holding of each batch of finished product. Once a document has data written on it, it becomes a record.

In 1997, the United States Food and Drug Administration (FDA) issued the Part 11 regulations to ensure the authenticity and integrity of documentation and records that are maintained in an electronic format. After much discussion with industry and contractors, FDA moderated their position related to Part 11 and narrowed the scope of the requirements. What did not change, however, was FDA's commitment to enforcement of all predicate rule requirements, including those that cover GMP records and record-keeping requirements. If a company chooses to use GMP documents or records in an electronic format in place of a paper format, the requirements of Part 11 apply.

GOOD DOCUMENTATION PRACTICES

Master Documents

GMP regulations require that master documents (for example, SOPs, master batch records, protocols, and specifications) be:

- Designed, prepared, and reviewed in accordance with the requirements in the regulations

- Clearly written and unambiguous

- Approved (signed and dated) by appropriate (that is, qualified by education and/or experienced) and authorized individuals

- Identified with a number or code that is unique to the document

- Regularly reviewed and maintained up to date

Executed Documents

GMP regulations specify several practices to be followed in the execution of GMP documents:

- Recording of information and data should be clear, legible, and indelible (typically recorded in ink; pencil and erasable forms of ink are not allowed).

- Information and data should be recorded at the time the activity or step is completed and in a manner that ensures that all of the significant activities associated with the manufacturing and packaging of the drug product are traceable.

- Any alteration or correction to information or data that were previously recorded should be crossed out with a single line, the new information recorded, and signed and dated by the individual making the correction (Figure 15.2).

467.4 NLVG 5/31/09

Record the weight of the final blend: 464.7 kg

Figure 15.2   Example of a correction done according to regulations. Note that the correction is done with a single line through the error, the correct information is added, and the person executing the correction provides their initials and date.

Source: Figure courtesy of the ASQ Food, Drug, and Cosmetic Division. Used with permission.

- Electronic capture of data and information is allowed once the electronic system has been qualified and secured. An audit trail, that is, a record of all data recording, changes, and deletions, must also be in place and secure.

- The executed documents are managed in a manner that allows for ease of retrieval and ensures that the documents are retained in compliance with regulatory requirements.

GMP RECORDS

Globally, GMP regulations mandate the recording of data and information about pharmaceutical products and the materials, equipment, processes, and people involved in their manufacture. It is through this recording of data that GMP records evolve. While some believe that this data recording is an onerous task, there is tremendous value in the data, and they can often be used to benefit the organization.

Training Records

GMP regulations require that personnel have the education, training, and experience needed to perform their assigned responsibilities. Training on both specific job tasks and GMP regulations is required. Training related to job tasks is necessary when a task is new to the employee, when procedures, batch records, and/or test methods are revised, or when a task has not been performed recently. Similarly, when an employee's job changes within an organization, his or her education, experience, and training should be reevaluated to determine what areas need to be addressed to perform the new job. Education and experience are typically documented in a resume or employee work history. Ongoing training is typically documented in separate training records for each training event. These training records can be used to:

- Demonstrate compliance with the personnel requirements in the GMP regulations

- Identify knowledge gaps within a functional area and support the justification for additional training

- Assess the needs for additional training after an investigation or product issue

- Assess the effectiveness of various training programs and methodologies

Facility Records

A considerable number of records need to be generated and maintained regarding the qualification and ongoing maintenance of the facilities used to manufacture pharmaceutical products. Some of the records (for example, qualification of utilities or equipment) are generated when the facilities or equipment are first commissioned for use. They may be amended or updated when changes to the facilities or equipment take place, but are relatively static in nature. They provide a snapshot in time of the particular utility or piece of equipment in question. Other records (for example, unscheduled maintenance, preventive maintenance, or calibration documentation) are updated regularly and provide a historical record of what has happened to a piece of equipment over time. These equipment records can be used to demonstrate compliance with the regulations covering the qualification, maintenance, and calibration of facilities and equipment, troubleshoot equipment failures and determine the impact of the failure on previously produced product, and investigate *out-of-specification* (OOS) test results to determine whether the equipment might have played a role in the product failure.

Material Receipts

GMP regulations require that materials are purchased from approved suppliers and that they are received, sampled, tested, and stored in such a manner as to prevent deterioration or contamination. When a material is first received into the pharmaceutical company's warehouse, a record of its receipt is generated. This initial step can verify that the material received matches the material requested (for example, on a company purchase order) and that it is from the approved supplier. The quantity of the material is typically recorded along with the number of containers and any supplier-specific batch or control number. The material typically moves on to a quarantine area (either physical or virtual) and waits to be sampled. Sampling is usually performed by the *quality unit* (QU), and the material is placed back into a quarantine status until testing is complete and the material has been released. After testing by the QU, the material may move to a different area of the warehouse or, in the case of an electronic quarantine system, have its status changed to "released," which allows it to be used in manufacturing. All of these steps are typically recorded on the material receipt record. This material receipt record can be used to:

- Demonstrate compliance with the GMP requirements for material receipt (that is, demonstrate to the regulators that the material was received appropriately, its identity was appropriately verified, and it was stored appropriately until use)

- Evaluate vendor performance (for example, determine whether the vendor met the required delivery date and supplied the requested quantity of material)

- Facilitate traceability to a specific batch of material in the event of a recall by the vendor

- Improve internal operations by evaluating metrics related to material processing time, number of material movements, testing time, and inventory turns.

Batch Records

Pharmaceutical companies are required to develop *batch processing records* (*master batch records* [MBR]) that outline the steps required to manufacture and package pharmaceutical products. Clearly written, detailed batch records are critical to ensuring product quality. The executed batch records provide a record of how the product was manufactured or packaged (for example, the materials and equipment used, the personnel involved). These records can be used to:

- Demonstrate compliance with the requirements for written batch-processing records

- Demonstrate compliance with the processes outlined in approved marketing authorizations

- Facilitate investigations into product problems

- Demonstrate employee proficiency through the lack of process problems or deviations

- Demonstrate that the product remains in a state of control (validated state)

- Identify areas for improvement

Log Books

Log books are typically used throughout a GMP facility to document the work that has been done in a particular area or to record the activities performed on individual pieces of equipment. Log books are generally assigned to an area or piece of equipment and provide a chronological history of the products that were produced in the area/equipment and any other work that has been conducted (for example, maintenance, calibration). Log books can be used to demonstrate compliance with the requirements for capturing equipment or area usage, facilitate investigations into product problems, demonstrate that appropriate cleaning procedures have been followed, and identify opportunities for improvements to equipment based on historical calibration or maintenance activities.

Complaint Records

GMP regulations, specifically in 21 CFR 211.198, require companies to maintain written records of each drug product complaint and the investigation conducted to determine the root cause of the complaint. These records demonstrate a company's commitment to its customers and compliance with the requirements for complaint handling, and identify product or process issues that require correction or improvement.

RECORDS MANAGEMENT

The ISO 15489-1: 2001 standard defines *records management* as "the field of management responsible for the efficient and systematic control of the creation, receipt, maintenance, use and disposition of records, including the processes for capturing and maintaining evidence for and information about business activities and transactions in the form of records." Records management is critical, not only from a GMP perspective, but from a company business perspective, as well. Company records provide the evidence that an organization has operated in a compliant and lawful manner. In addition, they provide the historical context in which business decisions were made and allow personnel to better understand the reasoning behind those decisions. Without good records management, a company runs the risk of repeating past mistakes.

Record Retention

A key component of any records management program is a documented *record retention* process. Records, and the information contained within those records, have a useful life during which they are an asset to the company. Beyond that useful life, records become an unnecessary expense and can be a corporate liability. It is important to define the retention requirements (or useful life) of each type of record and have a process in place for disposing of records once they have moved beyond their established retention period.

Throughout the GMP regulations, a number of record types have specified retention periods. These retention periods become the minimum requirements for record retention. A company may maintain these records for a period of time beyond the minimum requirements outlined in the regulations, but should do so only if business needs or litigation requirements dictate. Specific retention periods are identified in the GMP regulations (Figure 15.3).

Litigation Concerns

Properly maintained records can provide significant value to an organization. Unorganized, inaccessible records, or records that are retained after their useful life has passed, can become a corporate liability. While not a GMP concern per se, it is important for companies to have processes in place to notify employees regarding new and ongoing litigation matters. Many of these matters will require employees to maintain or produce, for the attorneys, the applicable documents that are the subject of the litigation. If a document is covered by a litigation matter, it can not be destroyed even if it has reached the end of its established retention period.

- Any production, control, or distribution record associated with a batch of a drug product must be retained for at least one year after the expiration date of the batch or, in the case of an over-the-counter (OTC) drug product that lacks an expiration date, for three years after the distribution of the batch.

- Records associated with all components, drug product containers or closures, and labeling must be retained for at least one year after the expiration date or, in the case of certain OTC drug products, for three years after distribution of the last lot of drug product incorporating the component or using the container/closure or labeling.

- Complaint records involving a drug product must be retained for at least one year after the expiration date of the drug product, or one year after the date that the complaint was received, whichever is longer. In the case of certain OTC products that lack an expiration date, complaint records must be retained for at least three years after the distribution of the drug product. While not specific to the GMP regulations, it is important to note that adverse event complaint records have a much longer retention requirement. Adverse event records must be retained for a minimum of 10 years from receipt.

Figure 15.3   Specific retention periods identified in the GMP regulations.

Chapter 16

Product Quality Complaints versus Adverse Event Reports

The United States Food and Drug Administration (FDA) places a significant amount of emphasis on the need for pharmaceutical companies to develop an effective approach to complaint management, including the establishment of well-written procedures. In fact, the Agency believes that complaint management is such a salient element for drug manufacturers that 21 CFR 211 has a dedicated section for the management and retention of complaint files, 21 CFR 211.198. Additionally, 21 CFR 314 expands on the post-market surveillance process under 21 CFR 314.80. Equally important is the reporting of adverse events through the use of the FDA Adverse Event Reporting System (FAERS). Although the management of complaint files and subsequent investigative process is distinctly different from the voluntary and in some cases mandatory reporting of adverse events through the use of FAERS, the two processes are linked.

Although FDA citation for failure to comply with 211.198 in a warning letter is a rare event, the Agency does occasionally cite such violations. More common is the citing of a failure to complete and/or document investigations pursued as a result of a complaint.

IMPORTANCE OF 21 CFR 314.80 AND 21 CFR 314.81

As part of the drug application process, FDA wants to reinforce the need for review and reporting of adverse drug experiences (that is, adverse drug event), post-marketing studies, periodic reporting requirements, annual reporting requirements, and the importance of record keeping. Similarly to medical devices, drug manufacturers are required to report adverse drug experiences through the use of form FDA 3500A. Once a drug manufacturer becomes aware of an adverse drug experience, the company is required to perform a thorough investigation followed by the completion and submission of form 3500A; however, an exemption is noted for post-marketing studies. A 15-calendar-day window must be adhered to when reporting an adverse drug experience. Within 15 calendar days of initial receipt of information, the drug applicant is required to report every serious adverse drug experience and every unexpected adverse drug experience. The best practice is to notify FDA has soon as possible when such adverse drug experiences occur. Additionally, drug manufacturers are required to script procedures that delineate their processes for managing surveillance, receipt, evaluation, and reporting of post-marketing adverse drug experiences to FDA, including record keeping (10 years).

Additional reporting requirements delineated within 21 CFR 314 include periodic adverse drug experience reports and annual reports. Periodic adverse drug experience reports are required to be filed quarterly with FDA for a period of three years from the date the initial drug application was approved. These quarterly reports are due within 30 days after close of the quarter. At the discretion of the Agency, the quarterly reporting requirement can be extended. Annual reports are due to the Agency within 60 days of the anniversary date of the application approval.

BUILDING AN EFFECTIVE COMPLAINT MANAGEMENT SYSTEM

The building of an effective complaint management system compliant with 21 CFR 211.198 commences with the establishment of written procedures. From a compliance perspective, FDA requires specific steps to be included in written procedures needed to support an effective complaint management system. When scripting procedures, a single well-written procedure delineating an organization's approach to complaint management should be the goal. That being said, as a minimum, the following components of complaint management should be included in the procedure:

- An applicability statement for oral and written complaints.

- A mandatory review of all complaints by the quality function.

- A discussion on the complaint investigation process; all decisions made in regard to not performing an investigation need to be documented and supported by written rationale.

- A provision for reporting a complaint as an adverse event when deemed necessary (recommend creating a decision tree to support the reporting process).

- The need to create and retain a complaint file for each complaint.

- Complaint files (record) retention time periods (one year after the expiration of the drug product or one year after the complaint was received, whichever is longer).

Additionally, the complaint record must include the name and strength of the drug product, the lot number in question, the name of the individual and/or organization filing the complaint, the nature of the complaint, and the pharmaceutical company's response to the complainant. Furthermore, if an investigation is performed, it is imperative that the result of the investigation be included in the complaint file. As previously stated, if the organization determines that a complaint investigation is not warranted, the decision not to investigate, including supporting rationale and the responsible person making the decision will need to be documented and retained in the complaint file. Finally, ensure that personnel tasked with complaint management duties are trained on the procedure and the training is documented.

ADVERSE EVENT REPORTING—FAERS

FAERS is simply a database that captures adverse events and medication error reports submitted to the Agency. The primary purpose of FAERS is as a tool to support the Agency's post-marketing safety and surveillance program. FDA uses the data to assess product safety concerns, and can use the data to drive regulatory actions necessary to protect the public health.

It should be noted that the reporting of adverse events and medication errors is considered voluntary for drug consumers and healthcare professionals; however, if a manufacturer of a drug product receives an adverse event report, the manufacturer is required by law to send the adverse event report to the agency.

SALIENT DIFFERENCES BETWEEN COMPLAINTS AND ADVERSE EVENTS

The first salient difference between complaints and adverse events is that not all complaints will result in the reporting of adverse events. Complaint files, however, must be opened and retained by drug manufacturers regardless of a report of an adverse event. A complaint that is identified as the cause of a serious and unexpected adverse drug experience is required to be reported to the Agency in accordance with 21 CFR 310.305.

The second salient difference between complaints and adverse events is that complaint files are managed by the drug manufacturer, and adverse events are entered into FAERS and tracked by FDA. The expectation is that the pharmaceutical companies perform a thorough review of all received complaints. The FDA is continuously monitoring FAERS for trends in adverse events as part of its post-market safety surveillance program. If the Agency determines that there are issues associated with a drug, it will take appropriate regulatory action. It is an immensely important task to keep accurate, current, and complete complaint file records.

The third salient difference between complaints and adverse events is that the reporting of adverse events is voluntary for healthcare providers and consumers; however, when complaints are reported to a drug manufacturer (verbal or written), entering the complaint into the complaint management system is not optional. It is strongly recommended that pharmaceutical manufacturers visit FAERS frequently to ensure that a negative trend pertaining to drug performance is not occurring.

KEYS TO COMPLIANCE

Drug manufacturers can pursue several steps to ensure that compliance issues never occur. To start, compliance is always rooted in a well-scripted procedure that complies with all 21 CFR 211.198 requirements. It is strongly recommended that complete and thorough complaint investigations occur for all reported complaints. If a decision is made not to investigate a complaint, the decision always needs to be documented and supported by a written rationale. Build an adverse event reporting decision tree into the procedure. It is always prudent to side with caution when it comes to reporting an adverse event. The data can be updated when the complaint investigation has been completed. Always take the position that FDA will review complaint files as part of any Agency inspection. Records must be complete, accurate, exhibit *good documentation practices* (GDP), and be available for review. Do not overlook the training piece. All individuals handling complaint calls, performing complaint investigations, or managing the complaint files must be adequately trained on the established procedure(s).

Chapter 17

Product Trend Requirements

Organizations, no matter what industry they're in, generate a significant amount of data as a result of running their business. This situation is certainly true of the pharmaceutical industry. *Good manufacturing practices* (GMP) regulations worldwide require pharmaceutical companies to generate a significant body of data related to all their activities, from the receipt of starting materials through the distribution (and return) of finished products. A large amount of data is generated around the quality of the finished product, both at release for distribution and throughout the established shelf life of the product.

Regulatory agencies around the world recognize that there is value in the data that are generated or obtained (for example, through receipt of returned goods or product complaints) as a result of complying with GMP regulations. It is this acknowledgment, as well as the recognition that it is important to critically assess the "health" of each pharmaceutical product, that resulted in the regulatory requirement for some form of annual assessment. The goals of the annual assessments are to:

- Confirm that the products and associated processes remain in a state of control

- Identify the need for changes to the products or processes

- Recognize opportunities for continuous improvement

Companies that undertake these reviews simply to meet their regulatory obligations may miss out on the opportunities for continuous improvement.

REGULATIONS

The United States Food and Drug Administration (FDA) requirement to conduct an *annual product review* (APR) is found in 21 CFR 211.180(e). As the name suggests, FDA GMP regulations require that pharmaceutical companies, on an annual basis (or, minimally, one time per year), complete a thorough review of data associated with each pharmaceutical product.

The European requirement to conduct a *product quality review* (PQR) is found in Chapter 1 of Volume 4, *European Union Guidelines to GMP* (as well as Chapter 1 of the *PIC/S* [Pharmaceutical Inspection Convention and the Pharmaceutical Inspection Co-operation Scheme] PE-009-11 PIC/S GMP Guide—Part I, *Guide for Medicinal Products*). Similarly to the FDA requirement, pharmaceutical companies must, on an annual basis, complete a thorough review of specified data elements. Unlike the FDA GMP requirements, however, this annual assessment must take into account data from previous review periods (previous years). The data elements that must be reviewed differ from the FDA requirements.

ANNUAL PRODUCT REVIEWS

General Requirements

FDA GMP regulations specify that pharmaceutical companies maintain records associated with the production, control, or distribution of each batch of drug product and retain those records for at least one year after the expiration date of the batch (or, in the case of certain *over-the-counter* [OTC] drug products, three years after distribution of the batch). Additional records related to raw materials, packaging containers, closures, and labeling must be retained according to a similar timeline. The data associated with these records are used for evaluating, at least annually, the quality standards of each drug product.

Under FDA requirements, pharmaceutical companies are required to establish a written procedure for conducting annual evaluations and for ensuring that their procedure is followed as written. Additionally, while not specifically identified in the regulations, firms should document the results of each APR in a written report and submit the reports to senior management for review. The reports typically include summary conclusions on the quality of the product and any corrective/preventive actions initiated and/or completed during the review period. The APR has a strong link to a firm's *corrective and preventive action* (CAPA) program, and any identified CAPA items should be tracked appropriately and completed in a timely fashion.

Data Elements

Required. An evaluation of specific data elements, as specified in the FDA GMP regulations, must be included in the APR:

- Representative number of batches, whether approved or rejected

- Product complaints

- Recalls

- Returned or salvaged drug products

- Investigations

Expected. In addition to the required data elements, the FDA has identified, through the issuance of form FDA 483s and other guidance documents, other data elements that they typically expect to see as part of the APR:

- Deviations or nonconformances

- In-process and finished product testing results and a discussion of any adverse trending

- Product stability results and a discussion of any adverse trending

- Changes to processes that occurred during the review period

In the spirit of continuous improvement, additional data elements may need to be included in the review process. Firms should assess all of the data that are gathered throughout their operations and determine what makes the most sense for their particular products and processes.

PRODUCT QUALITY REVIEWS

General Requirements

European Union (EU) regulations call for regular, periodic, or rolling quality reviews of all licensed medicinal products, including those that are designated as "export only." The reviews, similarly to FDA requirements, should be conducted and documented annually.

Despite the similarities, there are a number of aspects of the EU regulations that differ from FDA regulations. The primary differences between the EU and FDA requirements related to the quality reviews include:

- EU regulations explicitly require an assessment of the results of the review to determine whether corrective or preventive actions are needed, or whether revalidation is required. FDA likely expects firms to perform this type of analysis, but it is not explicit within the regulations.

- EU regulations require the assessment of current data against data from previous reviews in an attempt to identify adverse trends. FDA does not require firms to look at data from previous review periods. Depending on the number of batches manufactured, however, this type of "prior period" data may be necessary to adequately analyze the data for trends.

- According to EU regulations, quality reviews may be grouped by product type (for example, solid dosage forms, liquid dosage forms, sterile products) where scientifically justified. FDA regulations do not allow products to be grouped; APR must be conducted on individual products.

- EU regulations do not specify a requirement for a written procedure that outlines the PQR process. FDA requirements do explicitly specify that firms adopt a written procedure for the APR process. It is likely best to adopt a written operating procedure that outlines the process for completing these annual product assessments to ensure compliance with expectations of the regulatory agencies involved.

- EU regulations include a number of data elements not required by FDA regulations. It is important to be aware of the differences to ensure compliance with appropriate regulations.

Data Elements Mandated by EU Regulations

Required. An evaluation of the following data elements, as specified in the EU GMP regulations, must be included in the PQR:

- Starting materials, including packaging materials used in the product, with emphasis on those from new sources

- Critical in-process controls and finished product results

- All batches that failed to meet established specification(s) and their respective investigation(s)

- Significant deviations or nonconformances, their respective investigation(s), and the effectiveness of resultant corrective or preventive actions taken

- Changes to processes or analytical methods

- Marketing authorization variations submitted, granted, or refused, including those for export only

- Results of stability programs, and any adverse trends

- Quality-related returns, complaints, and recalls and their respective investigation(s)

- Adequacy of any other previous product, process, or equipment corrective actions

- Post-marketing commitments for new marketing authorizations or variations to marketing authorizations

- Qualification status of relevant equipment and utilities

- Contractual arrangements

Expected. In addition to the required data elements, salvaged products should be included as part of the PQR process.

ADDITIONAL CONSIDERATIONS

It is important to understand that the use of contractors (for example, contract manufacturers, contract laboratories) does not negate the requirement for the marketing application holder to gather the required data. The application holder is responsible for either ensuring that the contractor completes the APR on their behalf or obtaining the required data from the contractor and completing the annual review on their own. It is critical that the responsibilities for completing the annual reviews be specified in any contracts and/or quality agreements between the contracting parties.

Chapter 18

Supplier and Contractor Quality Management

Suppliers (also referred to as *vendors*) provide goods or services to another organization. Pharmaceutical products are created to improve the health of patients; the pharmaceutical manufacturer is responsible for ensuring that all of its suppliers contribute to product quality.

In Figure 18.1, the pharmaceutical manufacturer has five suppliers: the raw material manufacturer provides chemicals or biologics that become part of the batches of drugs; the filter manufacturer provides filters that are used in the manufacturing process; the vial manufacturer makes the containers for the product; the sterilization contractor sterilizes the vials before they are received at the pharmaceutical manufacturer; and the contract laboratory performs some of the release tests that determine whether the product meets its predetermined specifications. The pharmaceutical manufacturer is a supplier to the distributor, and the distributor is a supplier to the pharmacies that supply drug products to the patients who need them.

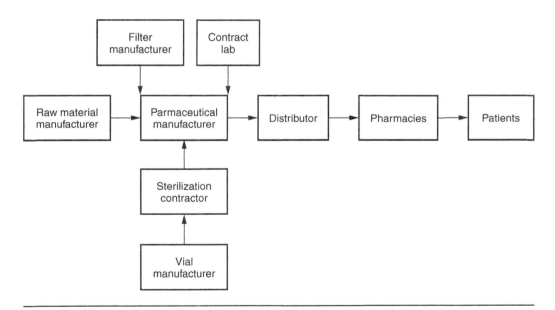

Figure 18.1 Example of suppliers to a pharmaceutical company.

Source: Figure courtesy of the ASQ Food, Drug, and Cosmetic Division. Used with permission.

Pharmaceutical *good manufacturing practices* (GMP) vary in the level of detail used to describe the ways that pharmaceutical manufacturers should ensure that their suppliers contribute to the quality of the products they create, but they also have some similarities. In Chapter 7 of the European Union (EU) GMP, *Contract Manufacture and Analysis*, the responsibilities of the contract giver and contract acceptor are defined for subcontracted manufacturing and testing. ICH Q7 addresses controls for contract manufacturers in Section 16, communication of supplier information to customers in Section 17.6, and complaint handling in section 17.7. Q7 indicates in Section 7.11 that manufacturers should evaluate the suppliers of critical materials, where "critical" is a parameter that "must be controlled within predetermined criteria to ensure that the active pharmaceutical ingredients (API) meet its specification." FDA GMP require that the *quality unit* (QU) be "responsible for approving or rejecting drug products manufactured, processed, packed, or held under contract by another company" [21 CFR 211.22(a)].

ISO/IEC 17025:2005, *General requirements for the competence of testing and calibration laboratories*, provides requirements for the competence of these suppliers to perform tests and/or calibrations. If testing and calibration laboratories comply with ISO/IEC 17025, their *quality management system* (QMS) will also meet the requirements of ISO 9001, *Quality management systems—Requirements*. The unique aspects of this ISO standard regarding supplier competence include:

- Providing appropriate supervision when using staff to perform tasks while training

- Qualifying personnel based on their education, training, and experience, including demonstration of skills required for the position

- Ensuring that personnel have knowledge of the technology used for manufacturing the items tested and the defects or degradations that may occur during service

In general, pharmaceutical manufacturers develop requirements for their finished product and for the materials they use to manufacture the product. They select suppliers who meet those requirements after evaluating them by conducting on-site audits or surveys. For contract manufacturing and testing, manufacturers develop a written contract to document the agreements between the manufacturer and subcontractor. They monitor the quality of the products and services received, and ensure that the quality requirements are fulfilled over multiple receipts of the products and services. Manufacturers may certify a raw material supplier that has consistently met requirements and whose own quality systems have proven to be in control, and thus be able to reduce the testing of the incoming raw materials. They ensure that the supply chain is reliable as close to the original source of the material as possible.

REQUIREMENTS FOR MATERIALS AND SERVICES

Suppliers of raw materials, components, and contract services need to meet requirements for the product or service they provide to the pharmaceutical organization. When a pharmaceutical product is being developed, specifications are written to define the quality characteristics that must be met for raw materials and components that are used in the manufacture of the product. Contracted services such as manufacturing, testing, and sterilization have defined requirements to ensure that their activities support product quality.

When written specifications or requirements are available for a purchased material or contracted service, the supplier must meet these requirements. The specifications are developed to ensure that the final product will have the safety, identity, strength, quality, and purity as designed. Two different aspects of contracts are purchasing requirements and quality requirements.

Purchasing requirements, often defined in a purchase order or purchase agreement, that need to be considered include:

- Minimum order quantities

- Lead times for filling orders after they are placed

- Batch sizes

- Price and payment terms

- Liability and insurance

- Confidentiality requirements

- Warranty

Quality requirements include:

- Quality attributes as defined in written specifications

- Permission to periodically audit the supplier

- Preapproval of subcontracting to other suppliers

- Preapproval of changes to the product or service

- Shipment methods (if they could impact quality, such as refrigeration, overnight delivery)

- Packaging materials (for example, tamper-proof, temperature maintenance and monitoring, humidity control through desiccant packs, prevention of contamination)

- Length of time to retain documentation related to manufacturing or provision of services

- Communication and investigation of nonconformances that may impact the product or services provided

- Identification of material (labeling)

- Documentation of testing results

Quality agreements may also be known as *technical agreements* or *supplier quality agreements*, or another term may be used. Some pharmaceutical companies may require quality agreements for all of their suppliers; others may use them only for contracted services, for raw materials that are critical to product quality (for example, excipients), for single-sourced materials, for custom materials, or for materials for which they would like to reduce testing upon receipt.

According to ISO/IEC 17025, when laboratories review contracts when preparing to test or calibrate for a potential customer, the review should include:

- Clearly defined and understood requirements (including the methods to be used)

- Determination of whether the laboratory has the capability and resources needed (including personnel skills and expertise)

- Selection of the appropriate test and/or calibration method

Once the supplier has been identified and the quality agreement has been approved by the supplier and manufacturer, the manufacturer starts receiving the supplier's products or services. The supplier should be evaluated by audit or survey and by trending information about receipt of product or services provided. In addition, changes to the supplied product or service should be monitored to ensure that the changes do not impact product quality. To improve the likelihood that a supplier will provide products or services that meet requirements, the supplier can be qualified or certified.

In the FDA guidance *Quality Systems Approach to Pharmaceutical CGMP Regulations*, issued in September 2006, FDA recommends periodic auditing of suppliers based on a risk assessment. Suppliers who provide *active pharmaceutical ingredients* (APIs), which are an important component of product quality, would be audited more frequently than a manufacturer of sodium chloride. The API manufacturer's quality systems should be thoroughly examined to ensure that they can reliably provide an API that meets the pharmaceutical manufacturer's specifications.

If the pharmaceutical manufacturer accepts the test results on the *certificate of analysis* (COA) from the API manufacturer and does not perform full analytical tests itself, the pharmaceutical manufacturer should evaluate the API release testing processes during the audit of the API manufacturer. In addition, if the pharmaceutical manufacturer accepts the supplier's COA for test results, the pharmaceutical manufacturer should, at a minimum, perform an identity test for each receipt of material.

Additional assurance that a critical supplier, such as a contract manufacturer for an API, will be able to meet requirements can be achieved by the pharmaceutical manufacturer placing a person-in-the-plant at the contract manufacturer to observe manufacturing and/or to review batch records and test results on site. A person-in-the-plant will be able to work in a timely manner with the contract manufacturer on any issues that may arise during manufacturing or testing.

ON-SITE AUDIT

Suppliers must be evaluated periodically, and the primary way of performing the evaluation is an on-site audit. Some suppliers who have many customers charge a fee to permit an audit to be conducted at their facility, or they offer one day when multiple customers can perform audits at the same time to minimize the time the supplier spends hosting audits. Suppliers such as contract laboratories may be audited once a week because they have so many customers, which requires a large amount of resources to support the audits and respond to audit observations.

An audit of a supplier should be performed by a qualified auditor. The auditor performs the audit against specific requirements, such as specifications for the product, the quality agreement, and any applicable regulatory requirements for the type of supplier being audited. Suppliers of pharmaceutical manufacturers may not be subject to pharmaceutical GMP regulations themselves. Some suppliers may be ISO 9001 certified, which provides some assurance of understanding of quality; others may have few controls in place to assure quality. The auditor should work with the supplier to ensure that the supplier has sufficient quality management systems in place so that their product or services will meet requirements.

After an audit is performed of a supplier, the pharmaceutical manufacturer provides the supplier with an audit report. The audit report summarizes the results of the audit, including any nonconformances (observations) from the requirements against which the supplier was audited. Typically, a response to the audit observations is requested within a month from the report issuance. The supplier is requested to respond with corrective action plans for the observations. When the audit response is received, the pharmaceutical manufacturer reviews the response to determine whether the corrective action plans adequately address the observations. If the supplier refuses to respond or to take action on critical observations, the pharmaceutical manufacturer has to determine a path forward. The supplier may need to be replaced with one who will cooperate with efforts to ensure that the items or services supplied to the pharmaceutical manufacturer meet the specifications.

QUALITY SYSTEM SURVEY

An alternative method to an on-site audit for evaluation of a supplier is a written *quality system survey*. Surveys may be used to evaluate suppliers whose products are a low risk to pharmaceutical product quality, or to monitor suppliers' quality systems in years when on-site audits are not performed. The survey contains questions about the quality systems that the supplier has implemented to ensure that their products or services meet requirements. Surveys can be customized based on the type of supplier: calibration suppliers, raw material manufacturers, or packaging materials manufacturers. The manufacturer sends the survey to the supplier and requests completion in a timely fashion. The manufacturer reviews the response to ensure that quality systems are implemented. If the supplier is not FDA regulated or ISO certified, the manufacturer will need to carefully evaluate the survey response to ensure that the minimum quality system elements are implemented.

In some cases, the survey is sent to the supplier as part of the initial approval of the supplier with the purchase agreement and quality agreement, before the supplier is approved for use. Many suppliers who are frequently requested to complete surveys for their customers have prepared documents that describe their quality systems to minimize their time spent completing surveys. These documents are sent to the pharmaceutical manufacturer in place of a survey response. The pharmaceutical manufacturer can accept the quality system document in place of a response to the quality systems survey if it addresses the required information in the survey.

CHANGE CONTROL

In addition to evaluating suppliers periodically, the pharmaceutical manufacturer needs to ensure that any changes made by the supplier are evaluated before implementation, if possible, to prevent potential impact to the drug product. The quality agreement between the supplier and manufacturer should include a section that makes it clear to the supplier that any changes that could potentially impact the supplied item or service should be preapproved by the pharmaceutical manufacturer.

For example, if a rubber stopper supplier changes the formulation of the silicone coating applied to the stoppers to prevent them from sticking together, the pharmaceutical manufacturer should be provided with some samples to test with the drug product to ensure that the silicone coating does not interact with the drug. The pharmaceutical manufacturer should be provided with adequate time to test the stoppers before the change is implemented at the stopper supplier's facility. If a contract laboratory changes to a new instrument using a state-of-the-art technology to perform a test, the contract laboratory should work with the pharmaceutical manufacturer to ensure that the test result is the same as before the instrument was upgraded.

If a change is made by the supplier, but the pharmaceutical manufacturer is not given advance notice, an unanticipated product impact may result in deviations, investigations, and retroactive analysis of product implications. If product was released before the impact was known, the change may lead to a product recall and possible adverse impact to patient health. The supplier should clearly understand that changes need to be preapproved by the pharmaceutical manufacturer.

TRENDING

FDA guidance *Quality Systems Approach to Pharmaceutical CGMP Regulations* recommends that data for acceptance and rejection of materials be trended to evaluate supplier performance. If 0.1% of a supplier's batches received by the pharmaceutical manufacturer were rejected over the past year, and the frequency of rejection is increasing, it is time to address the issue with the supplier. If occasional noncritical issues arise between audits of the supplier, they can be addressed at the time of the next audit. When an auditor is preparing for a periodic audit of a supplier, the auditor should obtain the trended acceptance and rejection data to determine whether any issues should be addressed during the audit. If a quality issue such as contamination is observed in incoming material, a for-cause audit should be scheduled at the supplier as soon as possible. In addition, the supplier should work with the pharmaceutical manufacturer to communicate how the investigation is progressing toward the root cause of the contamination, and what corrective actions will be implemented to ensure that future receipts of the material are not contaminated.

SUPPLIER CERTIFICATION

Pharmaceutical manufacturers have several options for categorizing a supplier after the supplier meets the requirements for approval. The pharmaceutical manufacturer can maintain a list of approved suppliers and those that have been evaluated as not meeting requirements for approval. The pharmaceutical manufacturer can also choose to take extra steps to certify a high-performing supplier in order to document that the supplier understands the pharmaceutical manufacturer's requirements and has the quality systems in place to ensure that they will meet or exceed the pharmaceutical manufacturer's requirements.

Certification usually entails building a partnership between the supplier and pharmaceutical manufacturer. In addition to normal approval steps, according to the *Supplier Management Handbook* (Bosse 2004), certification requires the supplier to document the process control details to show how critical parameters are controlled to deliver the desired result. Statistical process control, process capability, and process reliability analysis can contribute to control of critical parameters. The review for certification should include cost, quality, delivery, technical support, and management attitude over an extended period of time. After the certification is approved by both the supplier and the pharmaceutical manufacturer, the supplier is recognized to celebrate the new status of the supplier. Finally, the supplier's performance is monitored to ensure that the certification can be maintained.

SUPPLY CHAIN

One aspect of supplier quality management that has received more attention in recent years is the identification of the supply chain and the pharmaceutical manufacturer's responsibility for ensuring the quality of materials used in drug products. The heparin contamination that originated with pig intestine processing in China demonstrated the complexity in tracing the supply chain and ensuring quality at each hand-off.

The pharmaceutical manufacturer should do its best to determine the original source of the materials used in its drug products, and should evaluate the quality systems of the manufacturers in the supply chain as far back as they can. The pharmaceutical manufacturer is responsible for ensuring the safety, identity, strength, quality, and purity of its products as designed, and evaluation of its suppliers plays a critical role in fulfilling this responsibility.

Part III

Laboratory Systems

Chapter 19

Compendia (US, Europe, and Japan)

This chapter covers a subset of a much larger but out-of-scope topic: namely, knowing, understanding, navigating, and applying information found within the three major pharmaceutical compendia to the selection and implementation of qualitative or quantitative release tests for drug substances (*active pharmaceutical ingredients* [APIs]), drug products, or excipients). While regulatory and consensus standard references cited and annotated herein are important, proper, real-time lookup and learning from the current or effective-in-future General Chapters (plus specific monographs) of the three major compendia are required for full understanding and knowledge. Detailed interpretation of General Chapter content is confined to only those mandatory and informational General Chapters considered to be a minimum for *good manufacturing practices* (GMP) literacy.

A compendium is simply a collection or compilation of distinct pieces of writing or chapters. Vis-à-vis drug substances, drug products, and excipients (collectively referred to as official articles contained within the Unites States Pharmacopeia [USP]), the term "compendium" refers to the USP, the European Pharmacopeia (PhEur), or the Japanese Pharmacopeia (JP). The USP, PhEur, and JP comprise General Notices, General Chapters, and official article-specific chapters called *monographs* that contain the official article's definition, packaging, storage, and other requirements and specifications. The USP General Chapters provide frequently cited procedures common to multiple official articles. For drug substances and drug products, the USP General Chapters <1> through <999> are mandatory, whereas General Chapters <1000> through <1999> are intended to be informational only by the USP. In reality, the United States Food and Drug Administration (FDA) considers the latter General Chapters to represent good science, which translates into FDA often enforcing informational General Chapters as extensions of *current good manufacturing practices* (cGMP).

Bulk pharmaceutical water serves as a pharmaceutical component (a manufacturing material that is later completely evaporated or sublimated) or a material that decontaminates, cleans, and/or sanitizes product-contact equipment. It is produced and distributed by a system that undergoes initial qualification and that must be monitored. Thus, bulk pharmaceutical water is a utility, a process material, an excipient, or all three items.

Total organic carbon (TOC) and water conductivity make up the common tests prescribed by the USP, PhEur, and JP. *Water for injection* (WFI) additionally requires the *bacterial endotoxin test* (BET) with a specification of not more than 0.25 endotoxin units/mL (international units/mL in Europe). The Japanese aseptic processing guidance (Appendix A2, "Pharmaceutical Waters") states, "Whenever water quality is monitored and controlled by conductivity and TOC testing, it is not usually necessary to monitor individual metals or inorganic ions." Therefore BET, TOC, and water conductivity may be considered sufficient process control and monitoring tests for maintaining a pharmaceutical water storage and delivery system in control.

For *quality control* (QC) monitoring tests of pharmaceutical water, neither USP nor JP require heavy metals or other specific ion testing of the pharmaceutical waters because the Environmental Protection Agency (EPA)'s National Primary Drinking Water Regulations have sufficiently tight specifications to preclude their retesting in the more purified water. Unfortunately, the PhEur is not in harmony with USP or JP by the requirement of several tests (Table 19.1).

Though not a compendial specification, the PhEur suggests a *total aerobic microbial count* (TAMC) action limit of 10 CFU/100 mL in its WFI monograph, which agrees with the 1993 FDA *Guide to Inspections of High Purity Water Systems.* The PhEur and the 1993 FDA guide give a TAMC action limit of 100 CFU/mL for purified water. The USP, in its informational General Chapter <1231> "Water for Pharmaceutical Purposes," explains that microbial specifications would be inappropriate for a continuously produced material such as bulk pharmaceutical water and for such a validated process. The microbial incubation time lag inherently defeats the real-time production and usage of bulk pharmaceutical water.

The PhEur TAMC action limit statement, in both the purified water and WFI monographs, specifies the use of agar medium S, which is R2A media. Neither the USP nor JP specifies an agar for TAMC of bulk pharmaceutical water, permitting different process validation results to dictate the appropriate medium.

Two guides exist for the frequency and location of bulk pharmaceutical water sampling for monitoring or testing off-line. The 1993 FDA guide also created the generally accepted sampling frequency and sampling locations within a bulk pharmaceutical water distribution system, namely, daily sampling (except during shutdown) from a minimum of one point of use, with all points of use tested weekly. USP General Chapter <1231> states that "sampling frequencies should be based on system validation data and should cover critical areas including unit operation sites. . . . samples should be collected from use points using the same

Table 19.1   Tests and specifications for the principal pharmaceutical waters as per European Pharmacopeia.

Pharmaceutical water → QC release test ↓	Purified water	Water for injection in bulk
Nitrates	0.2 ppm	0.2 ppm
Heavy metals	0.1 ppm	0.1 ppm

ppm = parts per million, QC = Quality control

delivery devices, such as hoses, and procedures, such as preliminary hose or out-let flushing, as are employed by production from those use points."

Pure steam is manufactured such that, when condensed, it satisfies WFI spec-ifications. Guidelines for monitoring pure steam are less well defined to non-existent compared with those for bulk pharmaceutical waters. Providing it is manufactured within a system that already passes TOC and water conductivity, it is presumed not to deviate significantly from its source pharmaceutical water. In addition, pure steam is inherently self-sterilizing such that TAMC is highly unlikely to provide trends on the steam but only on incorrectly sampled conden-sate. BET results on pure steam use points or sampling points provides enough assurance against grossly contaminated (by Gram-negative bacteria) draw-off valves.

Water conductivity monitoring/testing may be performed off-line or in-line. In-line conductivity monitoring inherently prevents the progression to stage 2 or stage 3 of the USP or PhEur water conductivity test; however, the distribution sys-tem must be designed such that an *out-of-specification* (OOS) result (based on con-ductivity versus water temperature) automatically results in either diversion to drain or recirculation into the water generation system. If using the off-line phar-macopeial water conductivity test, stages 2 or 3 must be performed if the previous stage fails. No OOS investigation (per FDA out-of-specification guidance) or stop-page of the conductivity or any multistage compendial test may occur between stages. USP General Chapter <645> requires an electronic calibration of the con-ductivity meter by replacing the conductivity sensor with a nationally traceable resistance device, for example, Wheatstone Bridge.

The TOC compendial test for bulk pharmaceutical water is harmonized among the USP, PhEur, and JP. The apparatus for measuring TOC, like water con-ductivity, is either in-line or off-line. The periodic suitability testing of the appara-tus is specified as employing both a standard solution of compendial sucrose and a system suitability standard solution of 1,4-Benzoquinone. The diluent/solvent is reagent water having a TOC of not more than 0.10 mg/L.

A monitoring test required for, and applicable only to, WFI and pure steam is the BET. The test, being highly dependent on the particular *Limulus amebocyte lysate* (LAL) and corresponding test equipment and instruments, is not a candidate for compendial test suitability verification, but must undergo complete method validation for parenteral products. For WFI and pure steam, pharmacopeial test verification of suitability may suffice. The LAL reagent used in the BET has been classified as a biologic, and is licensed by the Center for Biologics Evaluation and Research (CBER). FDA requires that a finished parenteral pharmaceutical manu-facturer operating in the US or shipping to the US use an LAL reagent licensed by CBER in all validation, in-process, and end-product LAL tests.

Portions of the BET General Chapter have been harmonized among the three compendia. USP, PhEur, and JP permit and describe six methods (Figure 19.1). All three compendia contain similar wording that "in the event of doubt or dis-pute, the final decision is made based upon method A [Gel-clot method: limit test] unless otherwise indicated in the monograph [for a specific finished parenteral pharmaceutical]."

- Gel-clot method
- Semiquantitative test
- Turbidmetric endpoint method
- Turbidmetric kinetic method
- Chromogenic endpoint method
- Chromogenic kinetic method

Figure 19.1   Six methods for testing for bacterial endotoxins.

Chapter 20

Laboratory Investigations of Aberrant Results

The International Conference on Harmonization (ICH) defines specifications as a "list of tests, references to analytical procedures, and appropriate acceptance criteria that are numerical limits, ranges, or other criteria for the test described." Specifications establish the set of criteria to which a material should conform to be considered acceptable for its intended use. "Conformance to specification" means that the material (for example, raw material, finished drug product), when tested according to the listed analytical procedures, will meet the listed acceptance criteria. The term *"out-of-specification* (OOS) results" includes all test results that fall outside the specifications or acceptance criteria established in drug applications, *drug master files* (DMF), official compendia, or by the manufacturer. The term also applies to all in-process laboratory tests that are outside of established specifications.

An OOS result requires a concerted effort to determine whether it is due to a product failure or a laboratory error. In either case, an investigation is required to determine the source of the OOS result, the disposition of the product, and the impact on associated products and processes.

REGULATORY GUIDANCE

ICH Q7 Guidance for Industry, *Good Manufacturing Practice Guidance for Active Pharmaceutical Ingredients,* states that OOS results must be immediately reported to laboratory supervisors and/or managers and must be fully investigated. The guidance further states that any OOS result obtained should be investigated and documented according to a procedure. This procedure should include analysis of the data, assessment of whether a significant problem exists, allocation of the tasks for corrective actions, and conclusions. Any resampling and/or retesting after OOS results should be performed according to a documented procedure.

The United States Food and Drug Administration (FDA) OOS guidance further elaborates how to conduct an OOS investigation: To be meaningful, the investigation should be thorough, timely, unbiased, well documented, and scientifically sound. The first phase of such an investigation should include an initial assessment of the accuracy of the laboratory's data. Whenever possible, this should be done before test preparations (including the composite or the homogenous source of the aliquot tested) are discarded. If this initial assessment indicates that no meaningful errors were made in the analytical method used to arrive at the data, a full-scale OOS investigation should be conducted. For contract laboratories, the laboratory should convey its data, findings, and supporting documentation to the manufacturing firm's *quality control unit* (QCU), who should then initiate the full-scale OOS investigation.

A microbiological OOS, referred to as a *microbial data deviation* (MDD) is often associated with the aforementioned guidance documents, as well as with United States Pharmacopeia (USP) <1117>, but these references either exclude microbiological tests and biological assays or intimate the difficulties associated with resolving a microbiological OOS. A better guideline to use when conducting an MDD investigation is the FDA aseptic processing guidance, *Sterile Drug Products Produced by Aseptic Processing—Current Good Manufacturing Practice*. Although this guideline addresses positive sterility results, it can be judiciously applied to investigate an MDD for a non-sterile raw material, product, and assay.

CONDUCTING AN OOS INVESTIGATION

The FDA guidance for conducting an OOS investigation applies to chemistry-based laboratory testing of drugs regulated by the Center for Drug Evaluation and Research (CDER). It is directed toward traditional drug testing and release methods. These laboratory tests are performed on *active pharmaceutical ingredients* (APIs), excipients, and other components, in-process materials, and finished drug products to the extent that *current good manufacturing practices* (cGMP) regulations (21 CFR 210 and 211) and the Federal Food, Drug, and Cosmetic Act (FDCA) [Section 501(a)(2)(B)] apply. The principles in this guidance also apply to in-house testing of drug product components that are purchased by a firm. This guidance can be used by contract firms performing production and/or laboratory testing activities on behalf of the marketing authorization holder. This guidance does not apply to biological assays (for example, in vivo, immunoassays) or microbiological testing.

Specifically, the FDA OOS guidance discusses how to investigate OOS test results, including the responsibilities of laboratory personnel, the laboratory phase of the investigation, additional testing that may be necessary, when to expand the investigation outside the laboratory, and the final evaluation of test results. It is important to remember, however, that FDA guidance documents, including the OOS guidance, do not establish legally enforceable responsibilities. Instead, guidance documents describe the Agency's current thinking on a topic, and should be viewed only as recommendations unless specific regulatory or statutory requirements are cited. The use of the word "should" in Agency guidance documents means that something is only suggested or recommended, but establishes the current thinking of the agency.

Analytical OOS Investigations

FDA regulations require that an investigation be conducted whenever an OOS test result is obtained (21 CFR 211.192). The purpose of the investigation is to determine the cause of the OOS result. The source of the OOS result should be identified either as an aberration of the measurement process or an aberration of the manufacturing process. Even if a batch is rejected based on an OOS result, an investigation is necessary to determine whether the result is associated with other batches of the same drug product or other products. Batch rejection does not negate the need to perform the investigation. The regulations require that a written record of the investigation be made, including the conclusions and follow-up.

Responsibility of the Analyst. In accordance with the cGMP regulations in 21 CFR 211.160(b)(4), the analyst should ensure that only those instruments meeting established performance specifications are used, and that all instruments are properly calibrated. Systems not meeting suitability requirements should not be used. If reference standard responses indicate that the system is not functioning properly, all data collected during the suspect time period should be properly identified and should not be used. The cause of the malfunction should be identified and, if possible, corrected before a decision is made whether to use any data before the suspect period.

Analysts should check the data for compliance with test specifications before discarding test preparations or standard preparations. When unexpected results are obtained and no obvious explanation exists, test preparations should be retained, if stable, and the analyst should inform the supervisor. An assessment of the accuracy of the results should be started immediately.

If errors are obvious, such as the spilling of a sample solution or the incomplete transfer of a sample composite, the analyst should immediately document what happened. Analysts should not knowingly continue an analysis they expect to invalidate at a later time for an assignable cause (that is, analyses should not be completed for the sole purpose of seeing what results can be obtained when obvious errors are known).

Responsibility of the Laboratory Supervisor. The supervisor's assessment should entail:

- Discussing the test method with the analyst; confirming analyst knowledge of, and performance of, the correct procedure.

- Examining the raw data obtained in the analysis, including chromatograms and spectra, and identifying anomalous or suspect information.

- Verifying that the calculations used to convert raw data values into a final test result are scientifically sound, appropriate, and correct; determining whether unauthorized or nonvalidated changes have been made to automated calculation methods.

- Confirming the performance of the instruments.

- Determining that appropriate reference standards, solvents, reagents, and other solutions were used and that they met quality control specifications.

- Evaluating the performance of the test method to ensure that it is performing according to the standard expected, based on method validation data and historical data.

- Fully documenting and preserving records of this laboratory assessment. The assignment of a cause for OOS results will be greatly facilitated if the retained sample preparations are examined promptly. Hypotheses regarding what might have happened (for example, dilution error, instrument malfunction) should be tested. Examination of the retained solutions should be performed as part of the laboratory investigation.

Laboratory management should ascertain not only the reliability of the individual values obtained, but also the significance these OOS results represent to the laboratory quality assurance program. Laboratory management should be especially alert to developing trends, and upper management should appropriately monitor these trends and ensure that any problem areas are addressed.

Laboratory error should be relatively rare. Frequent errors suggest a problem that might be due to inadequate training of analysts, poorly maintained or improperly calibrated equipment, or careless work. Whenever laboratory error is identified, the firm should determine the source of that error and take corrective action to prevent recurrence. To ensure full compliance with the cGMP regulations, the manufacturer also should maintain adequate documentation of the corrective action. When clear evidence of laboratory error exists, laboratory testing results should be invalidated. When evidence of laboratory error remains unclear, a full-scale OOS investigation should be conducted by the manufacturing firm to determine what caused the unexpected results. It should not be assumed that OOS test results are attributable to analytical error without performing and documenting an investigation. Both the initial laboratory assessment and the following OOS investigation should be documented fully.

Full-Scale OOS Investigation

When the initial assessment does not determine that laboratory error caused the OOS result, and testing results appear to be accurate, a full-scale OOS investigation using a predefined procedure should be conducted. This investigation may consist of a production process review and/or additional laboratory work. The objective of such an investigation should be to identify the root cause of the OOS result and take appropriate corrective and preventive action. A full-scale investigation should include a review of production and sampling procedures, and will often include additional laboratory testing. Such investigations should be given the highest priority. Among the elements of this phase is evaluation of the impact of OOS result(s) on already distributed batches.

Production Review

The investigation should be conducted by the *quality control unit* (QCU) and should involve Manufacturing, Process Development, Maintenance, and Engineering. In cases where manufacturing occurs off-site (for example, performed by a contract manufacturer), all sites potentially involved should be included in the investigation. Other potential problems should be identified and investigated.

The records and documentation of the manufacturing process should be fully reviewed to determine the possible cause of the OOS result(s). A full-scale OOS investigation should consist of a timely, thorough, and well-documented review. A written record of the review should include, at a minimum:

- A clear statement of the reason for the investigation

- A summary of the aspects of the manufacturing process that may have caused the problem

- Results of a documentation review, with the assignment of actual or probable cause

- Results of a review made to determine whether the problem has occurred previously

- Description of corrective actions taken

If this part of the OOS investigation confirms the OOS result and is successful in identifying its root cause, the OOS investigation may be terminated and the product rejected. A failure investigation that extends to other batches or products that may have been associated with the specific failure must also be completed (21 CFR 211.192). If any material was reprocessed after additional testing, the investigation should include comments and the signatures of appropriate production and QC personnel.

OOS results may indicate a flaw in product or process design. In such cases, it is essential that redesign of the product or process be undertaken to ensure reproducible product quality.

Retesting. The sample used for the retesting should be taken from the same homogeneous material that was originally collected, tested, and yielded the OOS results. For a liquid, it may be from the original unit of liquid product or composite of the liquid product; for a solid, it may be an additional weighing from the same sample composite prepared for the original test.

Retesting is indicated when instrument malfunctions or sample handling problems (for example, a dilution error) are suspected. Decisions to retest should be based on the objectives of the testing and sound scientific judgment. Predefined retesting plans should include retests performed by an analyst other than the one who performed the original test. A second analyst performing a retest should be at least as experienced and qualified in the method as the original analyst.

The practice of testing into compliance is unscientific and objectionable under cGMP. The maximum number of retests to be performed on a sample should be specified in advance in a written *standard operating procedure* (SOP). The number should be based on scientifically sound principles and should not be adjusted depending on the results obtained. The firm's predetermined retesting procedures should contain a point at which the additional testing ends and the batch is evaluated. If the results are unsatisfactory at this point, the batch should be considered suspect and rejected or held pending further investigation [21 CFR 211.165(f)]. Any deviation from this SOP should be rare and done in accordance with 21 CFR 211.160(a), which states that any deviations from written specifications, sampling plans, test procedures, or other laboratory control mechanisms shall be recorded and justified. In such cases, before starting additional retesting, a protocol should be prepared (subject to approval by the QCU) that describes the additional testing to be performed and specifies the scientific and/or technical handling of the data.

In the case of a clearly identified laboratory error, the retest results would substitute for the original test result. All original data should be retained, however, and an explanation recorded. This record should be initialed and dated by the involved persons and include a discussion of the error, and supervisory comments. If no laboratory or calculation errors are identified in the first test, there is no scientific basis for invalidating initial OOS results in favor of passing retest results. All test results, both passing and suspect, should be reported and considered in batch release decisions.

Resampling. *Resampling* involves analyzing a specimen from any additional units collected as part of the original sampling procedure or from a new sample collected from the batch, should that be necessary. The original sample from a batch should be sufficiently large to accommodate additional testing in the event an OOS result is obtained. It may be appropriate to collect a new sample from the batch. Control mechanisms for examination of additional specimens should be in accordance with predetermined procedures and sampling strategies [21 CFR 211.165(c)].

When all data have been evaluated, an investigation might conclude that the original sample was prepared improperly and was therefore not representative of the batch quality [21 CFR 211.160(b)(3)]. Improper sample preparation might be indicated, for example, by widely varied results obtained from several aliquots of an original composite (after determining there was no error in the performance of the analysis).

Resampling should be performed using the same qualified, validated methods that were used for the initial sample. If, however, the investigation determines that the initial sampling method was inherently inadequate, a new accurate sampling method must be developed, documented, and reviewed and approved by the QCU [21 CFR 211.160 and 211.165(c)].

Reporting Testing Results

Averaging—Appropriate Uses. If the sample can be assumed to be homogeneous (that is, an individual sample preparation designed to be homogeneous), using averages can provide a more accurate result. In the case of microbiological assays, the USP prefers the use of averages because of the innate variability of the biological test system.

If a test consists of a specific number of replicates to arrive at a result (for example, a *high-performance liquid chromatography* [HPLC] assay result is determined by averaging the peak responses from a number of consecutive, replicate injections from the same preparation), then the assay result would be calculated using the peak response average. This determination is considered one test and one result, distinctly different from the analysis of different portions from a lot—intended to determine variability within the lot—and from multiple full analyses of the same homogenous sample.

The use of replicates to arrive at a single reportable result, and the specific number of replicates used, should be specified in the written, approved test method. Acceptance limits for variability between the replicates should also be specified in the method. Unexpected variation in replicate determinations should trigger remedial action as required by 21 CFR 211.160(b)(4). If acceptance limits for replicate variability are not met, the test results should not be used.

If a series of complete tests (full run-throughs of the test procedure), such as assays, are part of the test method, it may be appropriate to specify in the test method that the average of these multiple assays is considered one test and represents one reportable result. In this case, limits on acceptable variability between the individual assay results should be based on the known variability of the method and should be specified in the test methodology. A set of assay results not meeting these limits should not be used. These appropriate uses of averaging test data should be used during an OOS investigation only if they were used during the original testing that produced the OOS result.

Averaging—Inappropriate Uses. All individual test results should normally be reported as separate values. Where averaging of separate tests is appropriately specified by the test method, a single averaged result can be reported as the final test result. In some cases, a statistical treatment of the variability of results is reported (for example, in a test for dosage form content uniformity), and the standard deviation (or relative standard deviation) is reported with the individual unit dose test results.

Averaging can conceal variations in different portions of a batch, or within a sample, for example, when performing powder blend/mixture uniformity or dosage form content uniformity determinations. In these cases, testing is intended to measure variability within the product, and individual results provide the information for such an evaluation.

For additional testing performed during an OOS investigation, averaging the result(s) of the original test that prompted the investigation and additional retest or resample results obtained during the OOS investigation may hide variability among the individual results. These data can be misleading when some of the results are OOS and others are within specifications. The laboratory must provide all individual results for evaluation and consideration by the QCU, which is responsible for approving or rejecting, for example, drug products or in-process materials (21 CFR 211.22).

Outlier Tests. The cGMP regulations require that statistically valid QC criteria include appropriate acceptance and/or rejection levels [21 CFR 211.165(d)]. A value that is markedly different from the others in a series obtained using a validated method may qualify as a statistical outlier. An outlier may result from a deviation from prescribed test methods, or it may be the result of variability in the sample. It should never be assumed that the reason for an outlier is error in the testing procedure rather than inherent variability in the sample being tested.

Outlier testing is a statistical procedure for identifying from an array those data that are extreme, and the possible use of outlier tests should be determined in advance. It should be written into an SOP for data interpretation and be well documented. The SOP should include the specific outlier test to be applied, with relevant parameters specified in advance, and should specify the minimum number of results required to obtain a statistically significant assessment from the specified outlier test.

For biologic assays having a high variability, an outlier test may be an appropriate statistical analysis to identify those results that are statistically extreme observations. The USP describes outlier tests in the General Chapter on "Design and Analysis of Biological Assays." In these cases, the outlier observation is omitted from calculations. The USP states that "arbitrary rejection or retention of an apparently aberrant response can be a serious source of bias . . . the rejection of observations solely on the basis of their relative magnitudes is a procedure to be used sparingly."

An outlier test is only a statistical analysis of the data obtained from testing and retesting validated chemical tests with relatively small variance, and when the sample being tested can be considered homogeneous. It will not identify the cause of an extreme observation and should not be used to invalidate the suspect result. Outlier tests have no applicability in cases where the variability in the product is what is being assessed, such as for content uniformity, dissolution, or release rate determinations. In these applications, a value perceived to be an outlier may in fact be an accurate result of a nonuniform product.

When using these practices during the additional testing performed in an OOS investigation, the laboratory will obtain multiple results. It is critical for the laboratory to provide all test results for evaluation and consideration by the QCU in its final disposition decision. In addition, when investigation by a contract laboratory does not determine an assignable cause, all test results should be reported to the customer on the *certificate of analysis* (COA).

Concluding the Investigation

To conclude the investigation, the results should be evaluated, the batch quality should be determined, and a release decision should be made by the QCU. The SOP should be followed in arriving at this point. Once a batch has been rejected, there is no limit to further testing to determine the cause of the failure so that a corrective action can be taken.

Interpretation of Investigation Results

The QCU is responsible for interpreting the results of the investigation. An initial OOS result does not necessarily mean the subject batch fails and must be rejected. The OOS result should be investigated, and the findings of the investigation, including retest results, should be interpreted to evaluate the batch and reach a decision regarding release or rejection (21 CFR 211.165).

When an investigation has revealed a cause, and the suspect result is invalidated, the result should not be used to evaluate the quality of the batch or lot. Invalidation of a discrete test result may be done only upon the observation and documentation of a test event that can reasonably be determined to have caused the OOS result.

When an investigation indicates that an OOS result is caused by a factor affecting the batch quality (that is, an OOS result is confirmed), the result should be used in evaluating the quality of the batch or lot. A confirmed OOS result indicates that the batch does not meet established standards or specifications, and should result in the batch's rejection, in accordance with 21 CFR 211.165(f), and proper disposition.

For inconclusive investigations that do not reveal a cause for the OOS test result, the investigation changes from an OOS investigation into a batch failure investigation, which must be extended to other batches or products that may have been associated with the specific failure (21 CFR 211.192). For inconclusive investigations that do not confirm the OOS result, the QCU might still ultimately decide to release the batch. Any decision to release a batch despite an initial OOS result that has not been invalidated should come only after a full investigation has shown that the OOS result does not reflect the quality of the batch. In making such a decision, the QCU should always err on the side of caution.

An assay result that is low, but within specifications, should raise a concern. One cause of the result could be that the batch was not formulated properly. Batches must be formulated with the intent to provide not less than 100% of the labeled or established amount of active ingredient [21 CFR 211.101(a)]. This situation includes where the analytical result meets specifications, but caution should be used in the release or reject decision.

All records pertaining to the OOS test result should be retained. Records must be kept of complete data derived from all tests performed to ensure compliance with established specifications and standards (21 CFR 211.194).

MICROBIOLOGY OOS INVESTIGATIONS

No definitive guideline exists on how to conduct a microbiological OOS investigation. The FDA OOS guidance essentially excludes microbiological and biologic assays; the ICH Q7A OOS guidance states that OOS investigations are not normally needed for in-process tests that are performed for the purpose of monitoring and/or adjusting the process; and USP <1117> intimates the difficulties associated with resolving a microbiological OOS. In fact, the term "microbiological OOS" is better served by the term "MDD."

One guideline, the FDA aseptic processing guidance, addresses an MDD, albeit it is focused on sterile products. As sterility is the most critical attribute of a product, however, application of these stringent investigational principles can be applied to other products or raw materials to ensure that the decision to retest or fail a product has been made with the greatest scientific scrutiny and the lowest risk. When applied judiciously, the guidance is an effective tool that can be used to perform an MDD investigation.

The aseptic processing guidance identifies seven areas that should be scrutinized when conducting an MDD (Figure 20.1). Four additional areas of investigation not included in the guideline complete the cycle for investigating an MDD, and include API source, excipient source, satellite facilities (if used), and laboratory (in-house or contract).

The principles of conducting an analytical OOS investigation heretofore described should be invoked throughout an MDD investigation, including proper documentation, collection of data, and interpretation of data by the QCU and final disposition by the QCU and company management. In both instances, the investigation must be conducted using sound scientific principles, and the conclusion must be based on empirical data that are elucidated during the process. The underlining assumption of an MDD is that it evaluates the microbiological disposition of a product or material, and the product must be placed on hold until it is proven that the MDD is a result of laboratory or operator error that does not affect product integrity.

- Identification (speciation) of the organism
- Records of laboratory tests and deviations
- Monitoring of production area environment
- Monitoring of personnel (laboratory and production)
- Product presterilization bioburden
- Production record review
- Manufacturing history (including media fills)

Figure 20.1   The aseptic processing guidance identifies seven areas that should be scrutinized.

Standard Operating Procedures and Protocol

The firm should have an SOP that describes how an MDD investigation will be conducted, and should include a section for preparing a protocol subject to approval by the QCU that describes the additional testing to be performed and specifies the scientific and/or technical handling of the data. The protocol should be based on scientifically sound principles and should clearly state when retesting is appropriate. It should indicate that any unsatisfactory results incriminate the batch, which must be rejected or held pending further investigation [21 CFR 211.165(f)]. Any deviation from this SOP should be rare and done in accordance with 21 CFR 211.160(a), which states that any deviations from written specifications, sampling plans, test procedures, or other laboratory control mechanisms shall be recorded and justified. In such cases, before starting additional retesting, a protocol should be prepared (subject to approval by the QCU) that describes the additional testing to be performed and specifies the scientific and/or technical handling of the data.

Identification (Speciation) of the Organism

Microorganism isolates should be identified to the species level. Microbiological monitoring data should be reviewed to determine if the organism is found in laboratory and production environments, personnel, or product bioburden. Advanced identification methods (for example, nucleic acid based) are valuable for investigational purposes. When comparing results from environmental monitoring and product/production positives, both identifications should be performed using the same methodology. Identifying the same organism from environmental and product/production is helpful in determining the source of the contamination but by itself does not prove it. Additional data must support the findings.

Based on the species, an initial determination of the source can be made. For example, isolation of *Staphylococcus hominis* would indicate the source to be human skin while *Bacillus sphaericus* would implicate an environmental source. Interpretation of data by a qualified microbiologist is an essential element of the MDD investigational process.

Record of Laboratory Tests and Deviations

Review of laboratory deviations and investigations can help to eliminate or to implicate the laboratory as the source of contamination. If the organism is seldom found in the laboratory environment, product contamination is more likely than laboratory error. If the organism is found mainly in the laboratory and seldom in the production environments, product contamination may still be more likely than laboratory error. Laboratory test and deviation data review from at least one year before the MDD is suggested to develop a comprehensive understanding of the dynamics associated with the laboratory testing procedures and environment.

Proper handling of deviations is an essential aspect of laboratory control. When a deviation occurs, it should be documented, investigated, and remedied. If any deviation is considered to have compromised the integrity of the microbial testing, the test should be invalidated immediately without incubation.

An MDD result can be viewed as indicative of production or laboratory problems, and the entire manufacturing process should be comprehensively investigated as such problems often can extend beyond a single batch. To more accurately monitor potential contamination sources, maintaining separate trends by appropriate categories such as product, container type, filling line, sampling, and testing personnel is recommended. Where the degree of test sample manipulation is similar to that during production and an MDD is found, the production process may be implicated more than the laboratory.

Microbial monitoring of the testing area of the laboratory and personnel can reveal trends that are informative. Upward trends in the microbial load in the testing area of the laboratory should be promptly investigated as to cause, and corrected. In some instances, such trends can appear to be more indicative of laboratory error as a possible source of an MDD.

Where a laboratory has a good track record with respect to errors, this history can lower suspicion of the laboratory as a source of contamination as chances are greater that the contamination arose from production; however, the converse is not true. Specifically, where a laboratory has a poor track record, firms should not assume that the contamination is automatically more attributable to the laboratory and consequently overlook a genuine production problem. Accordingly, it is essential that all MDDs be thoroughly investigated.

Monitoring of Production Area Environment

Trend analysis of microorganisms in the critical and immediately adjacent areas is especially helpful in determining the source of contamination in an MDD investigation. Consideration of environmental microbial data should not be limited to results of monitoring the production environment for the lot, day, or shift associated with the suspect lot. Results showing little or no recovery of microorganisms can be misleading, especially when preceded or followed by a finding of an adverse trend or atypically high microbial counts. It is therefore important to look at both short- and long-term environmental trend analyses. A review of at least the past year of environmental monitoring data from the production area is useful in determining trends and overall performance of the area. It can help identify areas that are more susceptible to microbial contamination, facilitating *corrective and preventive action* (CAPA).

Monitoring Personnel (Laboratory and Production)

The review of data and associated trends from daily monitoring of personnel can provide important information indicating a route of contamination. The adequacy of personnel practices and training also merit significant review and consideration. Trending these data can help pinpoint specific technicians and operators who may be the source of the contamination, and appropriate remedial actions can be taken, including decertifying them to perform their jobs, if necessary. In certain instances, the technician or operator may be removed and asked to undergo comprehensive training and evaluation to ensure he or she meets standards established in corresponding SOPs.

Product Bioburden

A review of product bioburden is required to determine if adverse bioburden trends have occurred in the past. One-year data analysis will help ascertain if the bioburden levels contributed to the MDD. Excipients and APIs that show increased levels of microbial activity may be implicated as the source of the MDD, and remedial actions should be taken, including bioburden-reduction procedures or a change in the supplier. High-quality starting materials are necessary to produce high-quality finished products.

Production Record Review

Complete batch and production control records should be reviewed to detect any signs of failures or anomalies that could have a bearing on product integrity. The investigation should include:

- Events that could have impacted a critical zone.

- Batch and trending data that indicate whether utility and/or support systems are functioning properly. For example, records of air quality monitoring for filling lines could show a time at which there was improper air balance or an unusually high particle count.

- Review of information on construction or maintenance activities that could have had an adverse impact.

- Review of production records from at least the past year to determine if trends were apparent.

Manufacturing History (Including Media Fills Where Applicable)

The manufacturing history of a product or similar products should be reviewed as part of the investigation. Past deviations, problems, or changes (for example, process, components, equipment) are among the factors that can provide an indication of the origin of the problem. Depending on the product(s) produced, sterility, bioburden, personnel, and environmental data from at least the past year should be reviewed to determine if trends were apparent.

API Source

As part of the total quality system, microbiological testing should be performed on every batch of API received into the firm's plant(s) to confirm the microbiological acceptability of the material and to generate data for trending purposes. If a monograph exists for the API and includes microbial testing, those tests should be performed. For APIs with no microbial monographs, the firm should determine what microbiological tests are critical in assuring the microbial integrity of the material and perform the appropriate tests, including bioburden, microbial limits, endotoxin, and sterility testing. As part of the MDD investigation, a microbiological review of at least the past 15 batches should be conducted to ascertain both the species of organisms that are inherent in the material and any trends that may exist.

Confirmation of the indigenous microbes in the API with those found in the affected product implicate the API as a probable root cause of the organism, and appropriate preventive measures in the manufacture of the API should be conducted:

- Suspend delivery of new API lots to the firm

- Place all existing in-house lots of the material on *quality assurance* (QA) hold

- Place all in-process finished product lots containing the API on QA hold

- Require a written investigation from the manufacturer, including CAPA

- Reinspect the API facility

- Increase incoming testing and inspection of the material

- Consider elimination of the manufacturer as a provider of the API

- Conduct a formal investigation, including risk analysis, of the MDD to determine the disposition of the product and any affected batches of products from any of the firm's production plants using the API

Excipients

It is highly recommended to perform incoming microbiological testing on excipients to ensure their integrity. Although it may not be feasible to test every lot or batch of excipient, they should all be tested on a regular basis as governed by the firm's supplier certification SOP. The same process and criteria for investigating an API MDD should be applied to the excipient manufacturer, including a risk analysis. Microbial testing for certain products known not to harbor micro-organisms (for example, concentrated acids and bases) may be waived. As part of the MDD investigation, a microbiological review of at least the past 15 batches should be conducted to ascertain both the species of organisms that are inherent in the material and any trends that may exist. Purified water or water for injection should be treated as an excipient, and a review of the microbial water quality from the past year should be included in the investigation.

Satellite Facilities

Some firms use multiple production facilities to formulate products, (for example, they may weigh the API and/or excipients in one facility and transport them to another facility, either off site or at the same site). Each facility must be treated in the same manner as the main production facility, and the areas to be investigated should be the same as described earlier:

- Speciation of the organism from the API/excipient/environment

- Production area environment

- Personnel (laboratory and production)

- Production record review

- Manufacturing history (including media fills)

Trend analysis is critical in ascertaining whether the organism has been associ-ated with a satellite site, and the satellite should be under continuous microbiolog-ical surveillance to ensure it supports the microbial integrity of the process.

Contract Laboratories

Many firms use contract laboratories to test APIs, excipients, and bulk and fin-ished products, and ask the laboratories to conduct an investigation of an MDD. Whenever possible, the firm should request that they be allowed to conduct the investigation of the laboratory; this request is not to indict the laboratory, but only serves the best interest of the firm. Generally, a contract laboratory has many clients, and serving one client over the others is not in their best interest. This philosophy is applicable not only to microbiological testing but also to analytical testing and to contract manufacturers. Allowing a firm access to the inner work-ings of the laboratory may be the best method to uncover the source of an MDD, or OOS in the case of analytical deviations.

If the laboratory does not allow outside personnel to conduct an investiga-tion, the firm should require the laboratory to provide written documentation of these items:

- *Receiving area.* The physical condition of the receiving area may be indicative of the manner in which the laboratory operates. Good laboratories have well-defined areas that are organized, and materials are quickly logged in and sent to the appropriate departments. Sample log-in, whether manually recorded or electronically recorded, is a critical component of the area, and an SOP should cover sample receipt and tracking.

- *Sample staging area.* Similarly to the receiving area, the sample staging area should be well organized and clean, and this should be documented.

- *Autoclave cycles.* Autoclave cycles should be reviewed for the past year to determine if any excursions occurred.

- *Cleaning agents and processes.* Cleaning agents and frequencies should be reviewed for the past year, and trends should be documented.

- *Environmental isolates.* One-year environmental monitoring data should be reviewed and the organisms found compared to those found in the product. Additionally, the isolated organisms should be reviewed in relation to the cleaning agents being used. If *Bacillus* are frequently found and no sporocidal agent is used, there is a possibility that *Bacillus* spores may be a potential problem.

- *Personnel.* Personnel may contribute to an MDD, and the records from the past year of technicians conducting the testing should be thoroughly reviewed. Organisms associated with the technicians should be compared with those found in the MDD. If retraining is required, the training records should be reviewed.

- *Incubators.* A review of the cleaning and environmental monitoring of and organisms found in the incubators should be conducted. Incubators are a major source of environmental excursions and may contribute to an MDD.

- *Filters* (including *high-efficiency particulate air* [HEPA] filters, if used). Cleaning, maintenance, and environmental monitoring of filters from the past year should be reviewed and the organisms found compared with those found in the MDD.

- *Purchased media.* The manufacturer of the purchased media should be asked to provide a one-year review of the batches used to test the product in question. Media producers occasionally issue a recall of contaminated media, which can be a source of the MDD.

- *Equipment.* A one-year review of the microbiological history of biohazard hoods, work top spaces, pipettes, hockey sticks, and other areas and tools should be conducted to determine if they contributed to the MDD.

- *Sterility testing.* A one-year review of the anteroom, sterility suite, HEPA filters, and failure rate should be conducted, and any organisms should be compared with those in the MDD.

- *General supplies.* Many supplies are shipped in cardboard boxes that are a major source of contamination. Sampling of the cardboard may reveal the source of the MDD.

- *Media preparation and growth promotion.* A one-year review of media preparation and growth promotion should be conducted and correlated with the autoclave cycles used and test organisms used for the media preparation and growth promotion, respectively. Although not a common source of contamination, these areas should be well controlled as an overall investigational assessment.

- *Training.* Properly trained technicians are the most important component of well-functioning laboratories. Their records should be examined to ensure they received appropriate training for the tests they are performing. Aseptic training may be the most critical area to examine.

- *Observation of testing.* If possible, the firm should be allowed to observe the technician(s) who originally performed the testing perform a mock testing from start to finish, including receipt, preparation, handling, dispensing, diluting, and incubating samples. Minor inconsistencies may be revealed, which could be the source of the MDD.

CASE STUDY

A contract testing laboratory encountered an MDD in a sterility test. After conducting an MDD investigation, the firm was allowed to observe the laboratory's technicians perform a mock test. As part of the test, 20 ampules were pooled into sterile containers before filtration. The sterile containers were urine sample containers that were sterilized by gamma radiation; they were shipped to the laboratory in a large cardboard box containing a polyethylene bag filled with 1000 containers. The containers were not individually wrapped as it was cost-efficient to purchase them in bulk. The laboratory had recently made the change from individually wrapped containers to the bulk package containers. The laboratory was asked to sample the inside, outside, and flaps of the cardboard box, and the polyethylene bag. Two samples were found to harbor the offending microorganism, which allowed the original test to be invalidated and retesting to be performed. Had the firm not been within the core observing the testing, the source of the contamination might not have been found, and the product would have been rejected. The laboratory discontinued purchasing in bulk and returned to purchasing individually wrapped sample containers. Witnessing the operation enabled appropriate CAPA to be conducted: the corrective action was to sample the cardboard and invalidate the original testing and retest according to USP <71>; the preventive action was to purchase individually wrapped sample containers.

OBJECTIONABLE MICROORGANISMS

Many companies believe that if their nonsterile product meets the USP requirements, it will be safe from FDA dispute. This belief is correct, and the manufacturer is responsible for all contents of its drug product. Should question arise over the appropriateness of a particular organism, the manufacturer is expected to have a justification for the presence of that organism, preferably as part of the batch release document. 21 CFR 211.113 requires that medicines should be "free of objectionable microorganisms."

USP <1111> provides little specific guidance other than "The significance of microorganisms in nonsterile pharmaceutical products should be evaluated in terms of the use of the product, the nature of the product, and the potential hazard to the user." The USP recommends that certain categories be routinely tested for total counts and specified indicator microbial contaminants, including natural plant, animal, and some mineral products for *Salmonella*, oral liquids for *E. coli*, topicals for *P. aeruginosa* and *S. aureus*, and articles intended for rectal, urethral, or vaginal administration for yeasts and molds.

Other than these listed microorganisms, no others are mentioned as objectionable in the USP. FDA has a publication of objectionable microorganisms that is used for the food industry but can also be applied to pharmaceutical sciences: the *Bad Bug Book*. This publication details numerous microorganisms that may present a health hazard, and whose presence may invoke a rejection or recall of a product or excipient; however, the difficulty facing the industry is determining how objectionable a microorganism actually is. For products that are not labeled as "sterile," circumstances exist where an objectionable microorganism could be acceptable for product release based on a risk assessment analysis.

Similarly to an MDD, little guidance exists to conduct a risk assessment for objectionable microorganisms. FDA suggests that once all organisms grown in the total count studies (total aerobic as well as total yeast and mold) are identified, a qualified microbiologist would conduct a risk analysis on the presence of those organisms in the medication. This risk analysis should incorporate a minimum of five separate analyses (Figure 20.2).

Absolute Number of Organisms Seen

Most products have microbial specifications for total bacterial counts. When the counts exceed these limits, even if the organisms identified are nonpathogenic or objectionable, an MDD should be conducted, most likely resulting in the rejection of the batch and possibly other batches. Although high numbers of nonpathogenic organisms may not pose a health hazard, they may affect product integrity. An unusually high number of organisms seen in the product may indicate a problem during the manufacturing process, or an issue with an excipient or API. The high

- Absolute numbers of organisms seen
- Microorganism's characteristics
- Product characteristics
- Route of administration
- Potential impact on patients

Figure 20.2   Risk analysis should incorporate a minimum of five separate analyses.

bacterial counts may indicate that the microorganisms are thriving in the product. For a preserved product, this indication could suggest that the product's preservative system is not functioning, is missing, or incorrectly formulated.

The Characteristics of the Microorganism

The characteristics of the microorganism can be determined by textbook, library, or Internet searches, and should include synonyms of the organism. The *Bad Bug Book* is an excellent reference for determining whether the organism is a known pathogen or an objectionable. The potential for the organism to cause spoilage of the product is another important factor. If the substances used by the microorganism for growth are found in the product, the risk is great that it will degrade the product, supporting the rejection of the batch and associated batches.

A microorganism is *objectionable* if it has the potential to degrade the product's stability. Evaluate the microorganism's tolerance to unusual conditions, such as low or high pH, high salt concentration, high sugar concentration (osmotic conditions), low water activity, and growth temperatures. Organisms with a proclivity for harboring plasmid-mediated antibiotic resistance may be considered objectionable, particularly if the product is to be used in vulnerable patients with compromised immune systems.

Product Characteristics

The characteristics of the product affect the ability of the microorganism to grow within it. Some of these include anhydrous versus water based (that is, enough free water to support microbial growth) and container design and closure (that is, the container should be designed to minimize contamination and subsequent spoilage and should also retard access to the environment and prevent contamination from the environment). Special consideration should be given to an anhydrous medication's exposure to water, providing the potential for microbial proliferation. And a review of the production records, environmental monitoring trends, and product complaints is also warranted, and comprises part of an MDD investigation.

Route of Administration

Some microorganisms that could be tolerated in a topical medicine could cause severe distress to a patient if taken orally or inhaled. Similarly, a medication orally administered can tolerate some microorganisms that would be devastating in a medication meant to be applied topically to abraded skin or to rashes. Inhalants, although not required to be sterile, are a particularly sensitive area, and great care should be taken in classifying any contaminate as "nonobjectionable."

Patient Population

The targeted patient plays a critical role in assessing the risk of a potential objectionable microorganism. Microorganisms isolated from products intended for pediatric or immune-compromised patients present a greater risk to these patients than microorganisms in those products intended for use in relatively healthy patients. *Burkholderia cepacia* in cough medicine poses a greater risk than if it was found in a topical cream. Although the manufacturer can not control patient abuse or off-label use of the product, the reasonable use of it should be considered as part of the risk analysis. Certain patient populations may be exposed to increased risk if they use the medication harboring the particular microorganism.

Chapter 21

Instrument Control and Record Keeping

All laboratory instrumentation must be maintained to ensure proper functioning. Instrumentation is numbered so it can be easily identified during testing. If an instrument is used in a *good manufacturing practices* (GMP) environment, it will have the appropriate qualification and calibration performed. In a research and development environment, instrumentation does not require routine calibration, although a minimum standard for verification should be established to ensure data accuracy.

As an instrument is acquired in a GMP environment, it should be assigned a unique identification number. Some companies will use an abbreviation of the instrument with a set of numbers for the unique identification (for example, balances will be numbered as Bal 22, Bal 23, Bal 24). The associated documentation links this unique identification to the instrument type, model, and serial number. Documentation includes when an instrument was put into service and when it was retired.

Instrumentation can be classified into one of three categories (minor, intermediate, or major). Appropriate categorization of instruments depends on the intended use of the end user. Minor instruments, such as stirring plates, water baths, and sonicators, that do not perform any measurements do not require any calibration or qualification. Intermediate instruments such as thermometers and timers have little or no configurability, and typically perform a single task. Qualification for intermediate instruments is typically limited to *installation qualification* (IQ) and *operational qualification* (OQ), with the OQ consisting of calibration. Major instruments are those that are multifunctional and configured with multiple components, such as *high-performance liquid chromatography* (HPLC), *gas chromatography* (GC), *infrared* (IR), and *ultraviolet* (UV)-Vis spectrophotometers. These instruments require full qualification (IQ, OQ, and *performance qualification* [PQ]).

Based on the instrument category, IQ, OQ, and PQ may be required when a new instrument is introduced into the laboratory, a critical part is replaced, or instrumentation is moved from one location to another. A protocol defines the purpose or objective, test procedures to be followed, parameters to be evaluated, and the criteria to demonstrate acceptability. This may be done through the change control process.

The IQ is conducted to ensure that the instrument and software, if applicable, were installed in the proper environment and manner as intended by the manufacturer. The OQ is conducted to ensure that the instrument and software, if applicable, operate as designed and generate accurate data. The PQ is conducted to ensure that the instrument and software, if applicable, meet the end user specific requirements and function as intended in the production environment. A report summarizes the test results for the qualifications and any deviations. Upon completion of the qualification, the instrument can be put into service.

For instruments in the GMP environment, routine maintenance and calibrations are required. The maintenance and calibration schedules for laboratory instrumentation can be established based on severity of environment, severity of use, frequency of use, durability of the instrument, accuracy of measurement required, precision of measurement required, and history of maintenance and calibration. Each type of instrumentation should have a procedure that specifies its operation, maintenance, and calibration. The procedure must specify what activity should be conducted, what the acceptance criterion is, and the frequency. An instrument logbook may be used to track the usage, repair, and calibration of the instrument. All maintenance and calibration information, which includes reagents or standards used, must be documented. When an instrument requires repair or calibration, it should be flagged as out of service in some manner, such as with an "Out of Service" sticker. If an instrument fails the calibration, an impact assessment must be performed. During the impact assessment, all data generated since the last successful calibration must be evaluated. Upon completion of the repair or calibration, the out-of-service indicator is removed and the instrument is placed back into service. If the instrument was being calibrated, a new calibration sticker, which designates the next calibration due date, is applied.

Chapter 22

Specifications

Specifications are an important element of the overall quality strategy to ensure that the materials used to produce the final drug product, and the drug product itself, are acceptable for their intended use. It is important to understand what constitutes a specification, how specifications are developed, the different types of specifications, and what is required to change a specification once they are approved (either by a regulatory agency in the case of submitted drug products, or as part of the initial validation effort for non-submitted drug products).

The International Conference on Harmonization (ICH) defines *specifications* as "a list of tests, references to analytical procedures, and appropriate acceptance criteria, which are numerical limits, ranges, or other criteria for the tests described." Specifications are established (proposed and justified) by the manufacturer and serve as the basis for quality evaluation. "Conformance to specifications" means that the materials and/or drug product, when tested according to the listed analytical procedures, will meet the established acceptance criteria. It is important to note, however, that specifications are established to confirm the quality of these items and are not intended to provide complete characterization. As a result, the specifications should focus on those characteristics that are most critical to ensuring the safety and efficacy of the particular material or drug product.

DEVELOPMENT OF SPECIFICATIONS

Specifications for raw materials, intermediates, packaging components, and the finished product are first established during the drug development process. Like the drug product itself, specifications evolve over time as more information about the product and manufacturing process is generated. After drug product approval and/or launch, the experience and data generated during commercial manufacture of the drug product may result in changes to the established specifications.

At the early stages of drug product development, pharmaceutical companies have limited knowledge of the product. Different raw materials are being assessed, different manufacturers of the materials may be involved, and the manufacturing process has not been established. This limited knowledge of the product and manufacturing process is further compounded by limited experience in the clinic with the investigational drug product. As a result, the specifications that are established for the drug product during the early stages of development should be focused on product safety.

As drug product development progresses, and more information is gathered about the product, its components, and the processes used to manufacture the product, additional quality characteristics are identified and incorporated into the specifications. The final specifications that are ultimately developed are the quality standards (that is, tests, analytical procedures, and acceptance criteria) that are used to assess the quality and performance of the drug substance, excipients, container closure systems, intermediates, and drug product to ensure safety and efficacy. Final specifications are approved as part of the regulatory approval process, or must be approved before validation of the drug product manufacturing process for non-submission drug products. Once they are approved, they are subject to change control processes to ensure that proposed changes to the specifications are adequately justified and that no negative impact on product quality, safety, and efficacy will occur.

CRITERIA FOR ESTABLISHING SPECIFICATIONS

It is important to consider three categories of requirements when establishing specifications for a particular material, component, or product:

- *Compendial requirements.* Quality attributes, test methodology, and acceptance criteria that have been established by national or international compendia. Pharmacopoeial requirements establish the base or the minimum quality standards for evaluating a material. Additional quality attributes and tests may be necessary to ensure that the material is fit for its intended use.

- *Regulatory requirements.* Quality attributes and acceptance criteria that are well defined by regulatory agencies (for example, specifically identified in regulatory guidance).

- *Product-specific requirements.* Quality attributes and acceptance criteria that are unique and critical to the material or product itself.

RAW MATERIAL SPECIFICATIONS

Drug Substances

According to ICH guidelines, tests and acceptance criteria for drug substances typically fall into one of two categories: universal tests (tests applicable to all substances) and product-specific tests (tests unique to the substance itself or the specific form of the drug substance). Table 22.1 identifies the typical universal and product-specific tests for a chemical drug substance. A similar outline of tests for biologic drug substances can be found in ICH Q6B. Additional tests may be critical, and the manufacturer of the drug substance should have fully characterized the material and is in the best position to identify the tests that are needed to establish the quality of the material.

Inactive Ingredients (Excipients)

Excipients are defined as ingredients added to the drug formulation for purposes other than the therapeutic or medicinally active effect. They are largely

Table 22.1   Typical universal and product-specific tests for chemical drug substances.

Universal tests	Description	Qualitative statement about the state (for example, solid, liquid) and color of the drug substance
	Identification	Test(s) to discriminate between compounds of closely related structure that are likely to be present; specific for the new drug substance; if the new drug substance is a salt, identification testing should be specific for the individual ions
	Assay	A specific, stability-indicating test to determine the content of the new drug substance
	Impurities	Test(s) for organic and inorganic impurities and residual solvents
Specific tests	Physiochemical properties	Properties, such as pH of an aqueous solution, melting point/range, and refractive index; test(s) determined by the physical nature of the drug substance
	Particle size	Test to determine the particle size distribution
	Polymorphic forms	Test(s) to determine the crystalline form(s) of the new drug substance
	Water content	Test (for example, loss on drying, Karl Fischer titration) for residual moisture in the drug substance; may be important for hygroscopic substances or substances known to degrade due to moisture
	Inorganic impurities	Inclusion of tests (for example, residue on ignition) is based on the knowledge of the manufacturing process and the types of impurities likely to be present
	Microbial limits	The type of microbial test(s) and acceptance criteria are based on the nature of the drug substance, method of manufacture, and the intended use of the finished dosage form manufactured with the drug substance
Additional considerations	Chiral drug substances	New drug substances which are optically active may need specific identification testing

inert substances that are added to the formulation to aid in delivery of the active ingredient(s).

Well-established and well-characterized excipients are typically covered by a national or international compendium, and most pharmaceutical companies will adopt the compendial specifications and test methodology. When establishing specifications for compendial items, however, it is important to note that there may be specific attributes of the inactive ingredient that are important for the company's product and/or manufacturing process but that are not identified as part of the compendial specifications. A good understanding of the manufacturing process, as well as knowledge of the inactive ingredient's function in the finished dosage form, is necessary to ensure that the compendial specification captures all of the tests necessary to ensure that the inactive ingredient will perform as expected in the final drug formulation.

INTERMEDIATES

Specifications for intermediates are necessary to ensure that the material is acceptable for continued processing. Full characterization of the intermediate may not be necessary, however, and the specifications (appropriate tests and acceptance criteria) identified should be those that provide additional assurance that the final product will conform to established specifications.

PACKAGING COMPONENTS

Packaging components are initially qualified during drug development. It is through the development process that it is shown that the selected packaging components adequately protect the product, that they do not interact with the product, and that they are constructed of materials that will not leach harmful or undesirable substances into the product during routine storage.

Once the packaging components are qualified (that is, shown to be suitable for their intended use), specifications must be established for routine quality control. Primary packaging components—those that are intended to have direct product contact—are most critical, and specifications need to be established to ensure batch-to-batch consistency of these components.

According to the United States Food and Drug Administration (FDA) guidance *Container Closure Systems for Packaging Human Drugs and Biologics, quality control* (QC) specifications for packaging components typically include physical characteristics (dimensional criteria, physical parameters, performance characteristics) and chemical composition (colorants, material of construction). For most drug products, a pharmaceutical company may accept a packaging component lot based on acceptable results documented on a *certificate of analysis* (COA) or *certificate of compliance* (COC) from the packaging component vendor, and the performance of an appropriate identification test. This type of reduced testing is acceptable provided that the vendor's test data are periodically validated/revalidated (21 CFR 211.84). Additional specifications may be appropriate for components used in the packaging of injectable or inhalation products.

FINISHED DRUG PRODUCT

Similarly to the requirements for drug substances, tests and acceptance criteria for drug products typically fall into one of two categories: universal tests (tests applicable to all drug products) and product-specific tests (tests unique to the drug product itself and/or the dosage form). Table 22.2 describes the analytical tests that are typical to chemical drug products.

Other dosage forms (for example, oral liquids, parenteral products) will have tests specific to the type of product. Other tests may be critical, in which case the manufacturer of the drug product should have fully characterized the product during drug development and thus will be in the best position to identify the tests that are needed to ensure the quality of the finished drug product.

Finished Product Specifications

Acceptance Limits. The acceptance limits for specifications of the different quality characteristics are established by taking into account all significant elements related to the quality of the drug (medicinal) product (constancy of its characteristics), its activity (level of active constituent), and, if necessary, its safety (risk of microbial contamination, breakdown products).

Table 22.2   Typical analytic tests for chemical drug products (for tablets and capsules).

Universal tests		Description	Qualitative statement about the state (for example, solid, liquid) and color of the drug substance
		Identification	Test(s) to discriminate between compounds of closely related structure that are likely to be present; specific for the new drug substance; if the new drug substance is a salt, identification testing should be specific for the individual ions
		Assay	A specific, stability-indicating test to determine the content of the new drug substance
		Impurities	Test(s) for organic and inorganic impurities and residual solvents
Specific tests	Tablets/capsules	Dissolution	Test to measure the release of drug substance from the drug product
		Disintegration	Testing is most appropriate when a relationship to dissolution has been established or when disintegration is shown to be more discriminating than dissolution
		Hardness/friability	If the characteristics of hardness and friability have a critical impact on drug product quality, acceptance criteria should be included in the specification
		Uniformity of dosage units	This term includes both the mass of the dosage form and the content of the active substance in the dosage form
		Water content	Test for water content should be included and justified with data on the effects of hydration or water absorption on the drug product
		Microbial limits	Tests for the total count of aerobic microorganisms, the total count of yeasts and molds, and the absence of specific objectionable bacteria should be conducted except when its components are tested before manufacture and the manufacturing process is known, through validation studies, not to carry a significant risk of microbial contamination or proliferation

Continued

Table 22.2   *Continued.*

	Oral Liquids	Tests may be required for: • Uniformity of dosage units • pH • Microbial limits • Antimicrobial preservative content • Antioxidant preservative content • Extractables • Alcohol content • Dissolution • Particle size distribution • Redispersibility • Rheological properties • Reconstitution time • Water content
Additional considerations	Parenternal Drug Products	Tests may be required for: • Uniformity of dosage units • pH • Sterility • Endotoxins/pyrogens • Particulate matter • Water content • Antimicrobial preservative content • Antioxidant preservative content • Extractables • Functionality testing of delivery systems • Osmolarity • Particle size distribution • Redispersibility • Reconstitution time

Acceptance Limits of Pharmacotechnical Parameters. For most pharmacotechnical specifications, the European Pharmacopoeia, or failing this, the national pharmacopoeias of the member states, describes general test procedures with, in some cases, standards or maximal limits. In the context of these specifications, it is necessary to establish minimal and/or maximal limits, specific and adapted to the medicinal product that is the object of the marketing authorization, to guarantee the reproducibility of the finished product at manufacture.

Maximum Acceptable Deviation in Content of Active Substances. Directive 75/318/EEC states that the maximum acceptable deviation in the active substance content of the finished products shall not exceed 5% at the time of manufacture. On the basis of the stability tests, the manufacturer must propose and justify maximum acceptable tolerance limits in the active substance content of the finished product up to the end of the proposed shelf life:

• Release limits of 5% are acceptable without further justification.

- Release limits wider than 5% would need to be justified in the development pharmaceutics documentation with experimental results, which are normally based on a confidence level of 95%. The wider limits also include both the variation of the production and of the test procedure for the assay.

- Use of inadequate manufacturing procedures or inadequate test procedures (low precision) will not be accepted as a justification for wider release limits.

- To satisfy the 5% requirements, it is left to the responsibility of the manufacturer to apply an adjustment of the amount of active substance in the production of the finished product. In such a case, the overage must be clearly stated. The release limit will remain within 5% of the stated content.

- References to pharmacopoeias can not normally be accepted as a justification for wider limits as monographs do not describe a defined composition of the medicinal product, and do not pertain to release, but to recontrol by official laboratories over the whole shelf life of the product.

- Exceptionally, for certain products with a well-known degradation process and that pose no safety problems (for example, vitamins), an overage at release can be tolerated. This overage, the aim of which is to guarantee a sufficient level at the end of shelf life, must not cause an excessive level at release, and release limits must be adapted accordingly.

- At recontrol by official laboratories, the release limits of the manufacturer will be taken into consideration despite the fact that the limits used at recontrol may not be identical to the release limits of the manufacturer (due to interlaboratory variability). Where recontrol tests are carried out by another laboratory, the test procedures must be validated in their hands.

- Overfilling to guarantee the delivery of the theoretical unit dose must be justified. The acceptance limits for determination of unit content are adapted in consequence.

Acceptance Limits for Excipients

Excipients that affect the bioavailability of an active substance must be the object of a quantitative determination in each batch, unless bioavailability is guaranteed by other appropriate tests, established on a case-by-case basis as a function of development studies. In the case of preservatives, content limits of 90% to 110% at release should be acceptable without further justification, except in special cases. On expiry, the lower limit of antimicrobial preservatives may be reduced subject to the results of satisfactory preservative efficacy testing. For chemical preservatives (antioxidants), the lower limit may be considerably lower than 90% during the shelf life because of the preferential degradation of these agents.

ADDITIONAL CONSIDERATIONS

For all incoming materials (those purchased from third-party suppliers), the specifications should clearly identify the approved suppliers for the raw material in question. Documentation specific to the approved manufacturing sites is important as many suppliers have multiple manufacturing sites, and all of them may not be approved to supply the material. Care should be taken if the material is provided by a broker or agent for the manufacturer to ensure that the materials received are coming from the approved supplier and the approved manufacturing sites.

In addition to documenting the approved supplier(s), the specifications should include a description of the approved shipping containers (these are typically the containers that the supplier has used to establish the raw material shelf life) and any special environmental conditions for maintaining the quality of the material during storage. Specifications should include the name and internal (company-specific) code for the material(s); the name should include any reference to a pharmacopoeial monograph (for example, United States Pharmacopeia [USP]).

Finally, information should be provided that is related to the sampling plan to be used to sample the raw materials and any special instructions necessary to protect the individual sampling the material, as well as any precautions to protect the material itself. Directions for sampling may be included in the specification (or reference provided to procedures that describe the sampling process).

SPECIFICATION REVISION

Post-approval changes (or post-launch changes in the case of non-submission products) in the laboratory are not uncommon. As the manufacturer gains experience with the drug product and the analytical methodology, changes may be necessary to ensure that the methods are robust and are capable of producing consistent and reliable analytical results. Changes made in the manufacturing process, or in the pharmaceutical product itself, may have an impact on the analytical methodology; revisions to the methodology may be necessary to accommodate these changes.

Compendial changes are not uncommon. Pharmaceutical manufacturers should have mechanisms in place to track proposed compendial changes and to evaluate the impact of the changes on applicable drug products. Pharmaceutical manufacturers need to have a robust change control process in place to capture and incorporate necessary changes.

Changes to a packaging component (for example, changes to the materials of construction or the manufacturing process used to produce the component) must be assessed and, if appropriate, reported to the applicable regulatory agency. The filing requirements vary depending on the type and impact of the change. The finished dosage form manufacturer is responsible for conducting the appropriate studies to demonstrate that the change in question does not have an adverse impact on the drug product. Specifications are updated to incorporate the change(s) once the change has been shown to be acceptable and the change has been approved by the regulatory agency, if required.

Chapter 23

Laboratory Record-Keeping and Data Requirements

The laboratory is responsible for testing incoming material and finished products. The laboratory uses their approved specifications and test methods, which have been validated or verified for suitability, to perform the required testing. When testing is conducted, all the pertinent information must be documented in real time (as the test is conducted). The analyst must use permanent ink, blue or black, when making data entries. The analyst is responsible for accurately recording the pertinent information on a controlled document, which can be a standard laboratory notebook or controlled analytical data forms or a validated software package. Analytical data forms can be blank, so the analyst is required to document everything, or prepopulated with pertinent information, so the analyst only has to fill in identification numbers, reagent batch numbers, calibration dates, and so on.

The analyst records the date the testing is being started. The product name, batch number, and sample identification number are entered on the controlled document, and the method number and revision number recorded. As a sample is weighed, the weighing information is documented. If a printer is attached to the balance, the analyst ensures that the sample identification, balance number, and calibration date are recorded on the weigh tape. If the weigh tape is thermo paper, the analyst must make a copy of the tape, which will ensure that the information captured on the tape is not lost as the thermo paper fades over time. Both the original weigh tape and the copy, if applicable, are securely adhered to the controlled document. One can securely attach raw data to the controlled document by initialing and dating across the edge of the raw data in a manner such that the initials/ date are partly on the attachment and partly on the controlled document, then all four sides must be taped down (Figure 23.1). Clear tape that is not easily removed must be used, and the attachment must not cover any information on the page.

Preparation of solutions to be used in the analysis can be documented on the controlled document or in a logbook designated for such preparations. Most laboratories have a solution preparation book where all solution preparations are documented. All pertinent information, such as chemical name, manufacturer, grade/purity, lot number/identification number, and expiration date, pertaining to reagents used and the method used to prepare the solution are documented. A unique identification number is assigned to the solution along with the appropriate expiry date. The solution is labeled with the unique numbers, solution description, and expiration date for future use. As the analyst follows the test method, all standard, if applicable, and sample preparations must be documented. If the analyst is making further dilutions, the dilution scheme must be documented. If the

```
ADF09192803
TM-450-02

Bal 25    Cal Due: 5-11-09
05/11/2009           12:42
ID                   09-1928

1                    1.7288 g
2                    1.7653 g
```

Figure 23.1   Raw data attachment example.

analyst uses timers, thermometers, sonicators, or water baths, all associated identification numbers and calibration/service due dates are recorded.

Once the sample preparation is complete, the analyst prepares the instrument used in the analysis. The analyst verifies that the instrument is within calibration; if not calibrated, the analyst ensures that the calibration is completed before use. The analyst captures the instrument identification number and calibration due date on the controlled document. The analyst conducts the analysis. If the instrument requires a sample sequence, the analyst will complete the necessary data entry before starting the analysis. Most computerized systems have a set method of analysis in the system; the analyst will verify that the correct method is used for the analysis. In most data acquisition systems, only system administrators with a certain level of authority are allowed to set up methods and revise them. The analyst conducting routine testing only has access to create run sequences. The analyst either documents or prints out the parameters used in the analysis. All printouts generated must be labeled with notebook and page/controlled document number, sample identification, number of pages, and the analyst name/date.

Once the run is complete, the analyst can evaluate the data. In some instances, the data acquisition system used has validated templates in which the data require no further calculations. If there is no associated template, the analyst may need to manually calculate the results or use a nonvalidated template in Excel. A sample calculation should be included to demonstrate how the analyst calculated the result. Once the analyst has completed the calculations, all paperwork can be completed, including reporting the final results on an analytical result form or in a data management system.

The analyst must review his or her work to ensure there are no obvious errors and must initial/date it to signify the work is complete. If errors were made, the error must be crossed out with a single line and initial/date/explanation included, then the correct information can be added (Figure 23.2). If one digit of a number or one letter of a word is incorrect, the analyst must cross out the entire number or word and make the correction. Any deviations from the method must be documented either as a planned or unplanned deviation and approved by management.

The analyst can begin to clean up the work area, but keeps all glassware in the bench area until it can be verified by a second analyst. All solutions are maintained until the analysis is complete and known to be correct.

~~stoed~~
stored
ABC 5-11-09 spelling

Figure 23.2   Correct documentation of an error example.

Once the analysis is complete and documented, a second individual must review and understand the data and calculations. The reviewer ensures that all documentation is complete and accounted for. The data reviewer must ensure that the correct method and revision were used to perform the analysis. The data reviewer checks that all solutions used were prepared correctly and that all materials used were within expiry dating. The reviewer verifies that all instrumentation used was identified and within calibration. The data reviewer ensures that all the documentation is clear, and that comments are appropriate and easily understood. All laboratory investigations and deviations are reviewed, which will ensure that laboratory management has approved them. Any calculations made that are not part of a validated template must be verified. The data reviewer initials and dates the controlled document and any attachments to signify review. If any information needs to be corrected or added, the data reviewer does not sign until the analyst has made the correction/addition. When adding information after the analyst had added the final sign-off, he or she must designate the additional information with a late entry/initials/date to flag the additional information.

If a company has a validated electronic system, data are captured electronically. Such validated electronic systems include instrumentation data acquisition systems or electronic notebooks. These systems have routine backups and built-in security. System administrators are designated to maintain and qualify the system, and change controls are used to document any changes to the validated system. Each user must have a unique user name and a password to access the system. For a review, some validated electronic systems will flag the errors, such as *out of specification* (OOS) or *out of calibration* (OOC). Calculations do not need to be verified each time since the system was validated. All analyst and administration activities are documented in an audit trail that the reviewer can view. The audit trail review will indicate any suspicious activity that may require additional investigation.

Upon completion of the final data review, laboratory management conducts a final review to approve the data. Management ensures that all results meet the approved acceptance criteria and that all documentation is complete. Upon completion of the management assessment, laboratory management approves the data.

Once the raw data have been reviewed, they will be archived. If raw data are on paper, all raw data will be filed in a document control system. If the raw data have been collected electronically, the electronic information will be saved to a server that has routine backup and scheduled maintenance. Each company establishes its own document retention policy. Typically, raw data are maintained for seven years.

Once the data are approved, a *certificate of analysis* (COA) is generated. If data are stored in a validated electronic system, a COA may be generated automatically.

The COA contains pertinent batch information, such as batch number and expiration date, and the test, acceptance criteria, and results. In some cases, a *good manufacturing practices* (GMP) compliance statement may be included. The COA may contain an electronic signature or a wet signature that indicates all results have been reviewed or approved. If a COA is manually generated, all information must be reviewed and approved to ensure accuracy. The COA is not considered raw data and does not need to be retained. In most cases, the COA is produced upon request from a customer, and the original is sent to them.

Chapter 24

Laboratory Handling Controls

All samples and reagents coming into the laboratory must be checked and logged in before use. Laboratory procedures should be in place so materials are consistently received.

INCOMING MATERIAL RECEIPT, INSPECTION, AND SAMPLING

Receiving personnel in the warehouse are responsible to verify that the material received matches the associated paperwork and is what was ordered. This check is typically done by reviewing what was received against what was ordered on the purchase order. Once material is received into the system, warehouse personnel move the appropriate number of containers (based on the predefined sampling plan) to the inspection area. The containers moved into the inspection area are selected randomly by the warehouse personnel.

The quality inspectors compare the name of the material and vendor/ manufacturer's lot number on the container label against the information on the paperwork, which provides documentation that the material was received from an approved vendor. The quality personnel verify the shipping container to ensure it is appropriate, which is required to ensure that the packaging configuration is appropriate for use in production, as well as confirmation that the material is stable in the specific container. If there are specific storage requirements, the quality inspector will ensure that all documentation is in order to ensure that the material had been stored appropriately during transit.

The quality inspector prepares a sample container with the appropriate identifying information, such as material name, batch number, and vendor batch number, if applicable. The person performing the sampling and the date sampled are recorded on the sample container. Proper labeling is a *good manufacturing practices* (GMP) requirement and helps avoid costly mistakes and rework. Typically, laboratory samples are given a unique sample identification number.

The quality inspector ensures that the container is clean and places the container in an appropriate sampling area. Depending on what is being sampled, the sampling area may be a room or tent with appropriate *high-efficiency particulate air* (HEPA) ventilation up to a class I clean room. Once the quality inspector has donned the appropriate personal protective gear, the sampling can occur. The tools used in sampling must be clean to prevent contamination. Disposable sampling tools are often used; the benefit of this approach is that it nearly eliminates the potential of contaminating the sample with an improperly cleaned sampling tool.

153

The quality inspector opens the appropriate number of containers and begins to sample from each drum. Depending on the testing requirements for the material, individual samples may be pulled from each container, or a smaller amount may be pulled from each container and combined to make a composite sample. A reserve sample is often pulled in conjunction with the laboratory sample. Upon completion of sampling, the sample is delivered to the laboratory for testing. The sample is logged into the laboratory system and is scheduled for testing.

SAMPLES FOR PRODUCTS MANUFACTURED IN-HOUSE

During the manufacturing process for a material, operations personnel remove a representative composite sample from the manufacturing line as designated in their batch record or associated paperwork. Depending on the nature of the material being manufactured, the sample may come from an in-process manufacturing step, completed semifinished good, or final packaged product.

The batch record, or associated paperwork, should detail how and when to pull the sample. The sample container is typically identified in these procedures. The operator should use the appropriate sampling method as defined in the written instructions. The sample container should be labeled with at least the product name, batch number, and sampled-by date. Depending on the nature of the sample, other pertinent identifying information may be included on the label. If the manufacturing of the batch occurs over several shifts, staff performing the sampling should initial and date their activities on the sample label. At the completion of the sampling, the sample is sent to the laboratory. The sample is logged into the laboratory system and is scheduled for testing.

Stability Samples

Depending on regulatory commitments as well as the nature of the product being manufactured, stability testing will vary. Once a packaging batch is identified for a stability study, operations personnel pull an adequate amount of packaged product throughout the packaging run to meet the study requirements. At the completion of the sampling, the samples are transported to the laboratory and placed under appropriate environmental stability testing conditions. At the appropriate intervals, a sample is pulled and scheduled for testing.

Reagents or Solutions

Proper control and identification of reagents and solutions in the laboratory ensures that the materials used in the analysis of products are appropriate. A *material safety data sheet* (MSDS) should accompany each receipt of a reagent. The MSDS contains much of the information needed to ensure proper handling and use of the material, what to do in the event of a spill, and so on. Before the material is handled, the MSDS should be reviewed to ensure that appropriate precautions are taken. The containers must be inspected to ensure their integrity. If a seal is broken, the solution has been frozen, the container is leaking, or the labeling is inconsistent with what was ordered, the material should not be used. A label containing information (Figure 24.1) should be secured on each of the reagent or solution bottles.

Often, reagents inventory is managed though a *laboratory information management system* (LIMS). If this is the case, the information listed on the label may be derived from the database by a bar code instead of being listed on the label.

The expiration date of the reagent should be readily apparent on the container. For commercially procured reagents, the manufacturer-assigned expiration date is often used. If no expiration date is available, and the material is stable, a company may have a procedure in place that would allow it to assign a predefined expiration period based on the date of receipt. Shorter expiration dates may be required if stability is an issue for the material. For example, solutions that are prone to microbial growth, such as *high-performance liquid chromatograph* (HPLC) water, an opened date and use-by date may be added to the container upon opening. Table 24.1 contains some typical expiry dating periods for common solutions.

Some reagents and solutions may be used past their expiration date if the material can be recertified or re-qualified. For example, it is common to re-standardize or recertify volumetric solution upon use or at monthly intervals.

Received by/Date: _____

Expiration date: _____

Open by/Date: _____

Use-by date: _____

Figure 24.1 Typical label for purchased reagents.

Table 24.1 Solution expiry dates.

Solution	Expiry
Water	1 week after opening
Buffers/dissolution media	pH 6–8: 1 week
	Others: 2 weeks
Buffers/dissolution media (purchased)	5 years unless otherwise stated by manufacturer
Laboratory solvents < 10% organic	1 month
Laboratory solvents ≥ 10% organic	3 months
Storage solvents (50% organic)	6 months
Test solutions	1 year (unless otherwise specified by USP)
Test solutions (purchased)	5 years (unless otherwise specified by manufacturer)
Volumetric solutions	1 year (unless otherwise specified by USP)
Volumetric solutions (purchased)	Manufacturer certified date

The current compendia (European Pharmacopeia [PhEur], Japanese Pharmacopeia [JP], and United States Pharmacopeia [USP]) typically define the process for re-standardizing the most commonly used volumetric solutions.

The preparation of all solutions prepared in the laboratory must be documented. The prepared solution should be identified with, at a minimum, the name/composition of the solution, concentration, storage, re-standardization date, expiration date, reference, and analyst/date.

STANDARDS

Laboratories use primary and secondary standards to determine material results and equipment calibration. A primary standard is purchased from an official source, such as USP, British Pharmacopeia (BP), or National Institute of Standards and Technology (NIST). If no official source of a standard exists, material can be thoroughly characterized to ensure its identity, strength, quality, purity, and potency. Secondary or in-house standards are raw materials that have been assayed against a primary standard.

When standards are received into a laboratory, traceability must be established. Most laboratories will assign a unique standard number and complete corresponding paperwork indicating the standard's name, lot number, purity, expiration date, and drying requirements. USP has a bimonthly publication that reports expiration dates. Analysts must verify they are not using expired standards. Based on the USP publication, most companies will establish a bimonthly review of their standards to ensure no expired ones are in the laboratory.

SAMPLE STORAGE

The storage of samples is extremely important to ensure the integrity of the material. Once sample containers are received into the laboratory, the containers should be stored in a centralized location until testing is started. Samples should have some form of unique identification to differentiate them from the other samples in the laboratory. Once testing has been started, procedures will dictate how samples are prepared and stored. For example, if a sample is light sensitive, amber glassware is used in the sample preparations. During method validation, solution stability is determined. Upon completion of testing, most laboratories require solutions to be retained, even if the solution has expired, until data review is complete. If there is a need for an investigation, the expired solutions may be used for information.

21 CFR 211.170 requires a reserve sample that is representative of the batch to be retained. The reserve sample consists of at least twice the quantity necessary to conduct all required testing. Reserve samples are typically pulled during inspection sampling and/or final packaging. The reserve samples are maintained at warehouse conditions and evaluated once a year for signs of deterioration. The finished product reserve samples are maintained for one year past their expiration date. The raw material reserve samples must be maintained one year past the expiration of the last finished product they were used in. Most pharmaceutical companies have finished products with a maximum of 36-month expiration

dating; thus, they can assign a five-year expiration date to the raw material reserve sample, which ensures they will meet the CFR requirement.

REAGENTS OR SOLUTIONS

Chemicals, reagents, and solutions must be stored in the laboratory in a manner that considers safety, chemical integrity, and efficient management. Materials must be stored in tightly sealed and chemically resistant containers. Strong bases should not be stored in glass containers because the hydroxide will slowly react with the silica. Exposure of materials to heat or direct sunlight should be avoided. If a material is easily oxidized, it may be stored with a layer of nitrogen. Some companies store those chemicals in desiccators and flush with nitrogen. Materials requiring refrigeration or freezing should be stored as such. Chemically incompatible materials will be segregated according to their MSDS requirements. Acids and bases are not stored together.

STANDARDS

Standards are stored according to the label instructions. Typically, standards are maintained in desiccators until use. If drying is required before use, the analyst should take only the amount needed and dry in an appropriate container. Once dry, the analyst can store the dried standard in a desiccator until it is needed. Unless otherwise specified, standards are typically weighed and diluted within 24 hours of removal from the oven. After weighing, the remaining dried material is discarded. The appropriate storage of the standard solution should be outlined in the company's method. During method validation, standard solution stability should be determined.

Chapter 25

Stability Programs

L aboratory testing, which is required by 21 CFR 211.160 and 211.165, is necessary to confirm that components, containers and closures, in-process materials, and drug products conform to appropriate standards of identity, strength, quality, and purity. Release testing provides evidence that the materials conform to appropriate standards at the time of release. Stability testing provides evidence on how the quality of a drug substance or drug product varies over time. Environmental factors and product-related factors may impact the stability of the drug substance/drug product over time. The impact of environmental factors, such as temperature, humidity, and light, must be evaluated. The impact of product-related factors, such as the chemical and physical properties of the drug substance/drug product, the manufacturing process, and the container-closure system, must also be evaluated.

Stability programs can be divided into three main types: product development stability, commercial support stability, and change management stability. While there are overlaps in the execution of the stability studies, the objectives of each of the stability types are different.

TYPES OF STABILITY STUDIES

Product Development Stability

The type of product that is being considered defines the activities of the development stability program. For generic drug products, the stability requirements for submission of the Abbreviated New Drug Application (ANDA) include the comparison of the final drug product stability data to those of the innovator product. Stability data on the innovator product are of further value, as they provide insight into formulation and packaging requirements.

For new drug products, no innovator studies can be performed; however, clinical studies frequently are conducted using another therapeutic compound as a comparator, as well as a placebo product. Since these clinical studies are often blinded, the identity of the target formulation, the comparator formulation, and the placebo must be hidden by over-encapsulation or other means of obscuring the identity. Stability testing of these formulations is required to evaluate impact to drug release of the obscuration process and to ensure patient safety throughout the duration of the clinical study.

Other stability studies common to both types of products include photostability testing, excipient compatibility testing, stress testing, and packaging evaluation studies. Further, through well-planned *design of experiments* (DOE) studies, appropriate ranges and tolerances in component ratios and processing parameters can be established. Stability is an integral part of these DOE studies as the various changes may not result in observable differences in the release results.

Photostability studies are performed as two distinctive studies; one as a form of forced degradation, and the other to demonstrate appropriate protective qualities of container closure systems (also known as *confirmatory photostability studies*). For the forced degradation photostability study, the test article is exposed to high levels of visible light and *ultraviolet* (UV) radiation with the intent of degrading the test article. The results from this testing help to identify potential degradation pathways and provide guidance in formulating and packaging the product. Confirmatory photostability studies are performed as indicated by International Conference on Harmonization (ICH) guidance Q1B *Photostability Stability Testing of New Drug Substances and Products*. Studies are performed in the least protective packaging available (such as open petri dish), progressing to more protective packaging (primary commercial packaging) as required. The data generated from these studies will be used to demonstrate that the packaging provides adequate protection from light.

Excipient compatibility studies are performed to determine if any intended components contribute to instability of the product. Forced degradation studies are performed as a tool in developing stability-indicating analytical methods, while the packaging evaluation studies help to identify appropriate packaging configurations and material.

Stress testing is performed to help identify likely degradation products and validate stability-indicating methods. Most companies target to degrade a material 5% to 15%, but no more than 20%. Successful degradation is demonstrated when the analysis clearly indicates the presence of degradation peaks and a lowered assay. Companies may use acid stress, base stress, thermal degradation, or oxidative degradation to degrade their material. An appropriate stability-indicating method will have appropriate resolution between the analyte and degradation peaks and will demonstrate mass balance.

A company can acid-stress the analyte and placebo of the drug substance and/or drug product by adding HCl such that the pH $\leq$ 3. Samples are maintained in that environment up to a week. The sample is neutralized before analysis. If no degradation occurs, a higher concentration of acid (maximum of 6N) and/or an elevated temperature (60 °C to 80 °C) can be used. The base stressing is done by stressing the analyte and placebo of the drug substance and/or drug product by adding NaOH such that the pH $\geq$ 9. Samples are maintained in that environment up to a week. The sample is neutralized before analysis. If no degradation occurs, a higher concentration of base (maximum of 6N) and/or an elevated temperature (60 °C to 80 °C) can be used.

The thermal degradation is done by stressing the analyte and placebo of the drug substance and/or drug product by heating in an oven or water bath to temperatures of 70 °C to 105 °C, but at least 10 °C below the melting point. Samples are maintained in that environment up to a week. Lower temperatures can be selected if the sample melts or excessive degradation occurs. If no degradation occurs, a combination of thermal exposure and humidity (for example, 50 °C/80% *relative humidity* [RH]) can be used. The oxidative degradation is done by stressing the analyte and placebo of the drug substance and/or drug product by adding up to 3% H_2O_2. Samples are maintained in that environment up to a week.

Packaging evaluation studies are performed near the end of the development process when a likely formulation and process have been identified. For these studies, a firm would place the same batch of material in various container-closure systems and submit them to the same storage conditions. Results can be compared side by side to determine if one package provides more protection than another. The results obtained from all these studies will be used to help select a final formulation, establish appropriate specifications, and determine product shelf life.

The final stability study from the development program is the *submission study*. This study is conducted following the guidance provided in ICH Q1A (R2) *Stability Testing of New Drug Substances and Products* (referred to as "Q1A guidance"). The batches used in the submission study represent the final formulation, manufacturing processes, and commercial packaging. Sample material is stored at controlled conditions (Table 25.1) for specific time periods and tested. The data generated from these studies are evaluated and submitted to regulatory bodies as part of the drug approval process.

Commercial Support Stability

As part of the submission process, a company will include a commitment to continue stability evaluation over the commercial life of the product. The stability commitment may vary depending on the properties of the product, but generally specifies that one representative batch per year be held at the long-term storage condition (Table 25.1) and tested at the same time points and by the same methodology as used to generate the submission data.

The results generated for a commitment batch have far-reaching implications. Thus, a batch that fails to meet specification during shelf life would cause all batches of the same packaging configuration to be evaluated. In such a scenario, a firm could be required to reduce expiry or recall product from the market.

Table 25.1   Definitions of ICH conditions.

Condition set points	Acceptance criteria	Suggested use
25 °C/60% RH	± 2 °C/±5% RH	• General case long-term stability
		• Refrigerated product accelerated stability
30 °C/65% RH	±2 °C/±5% RH	• General case long-term stability
		• General case intermediate stability
40 °C/75% RH	±2 °C/±5% RH	• General case accelerated stability
5 °C/Humidity not controlled	±3 °C	• Refrigerated product long-term stability
–20 °C/Humidity not relevant	±5 °C	• Frozen product long-term stability

Change Management Stability

The components, processing, packaging, and labeling of a drug product are specified in the approved application. A change to any of these requires evaluation to ensure that the change has no deleterious effect on the product. Stability testing is frequently a part of this evaluation. For example, a firm may wish to change the supplier of the *active pharmaceutical ingredient* (API) in their drug product. This change would require stability testing. Just as in the original application, the results will be evaluated and submitted to regulatory authorities for approval. The magnitude of change and the tolerances established during registration will influence the type of stability program required to support the change.

EXECUTION OF STABILITY STUDIES

As with any good scientific evaluation, stability studies begin with outlining the steps to be taken and the rules for interpreting the results (that is, this plan is the stability protocol). Minimally, a protocol should specify the sample storage conditions/testing time points/packaging configuration and provide reference to the test methods/acceptance criteria against which the test article is being evaluated. Studies performed to support a regulatory submission generally include the criteria for evaluating the data.

Conditions

The ICH Q1A (R2) guidance outlines the generally accepted conditions at which studies are to be performed (Table 25.1). Exceptions to these conditions, with a written justification, can be made depending on the nature of the product and the intended use of the data.

Time Points

The Q1A guidance provides recommended time points for testing. These are typically one, two, three, and six months for accelerated studies; and three, six, nine, 12, 18, 24, and 36 months for long-term studies. The intermediate storage condition is set up to provide additional information should a study fail to meet acceptance criteria during the accelerated study. Like the storage conditions, these may be adjusted as needed to fulfill the purpose of the study.

Packaging Configurations

Each unique presentation of a product must be represented in the commercial support stability program. For example, a drug product that has one strength and is in four package configurations would have four unique presentations of the product. Thus, the four presentations need be represented on stability.

A stability program can be established by *bracketing*. Bracketing is based on the extremes, which are put on stability, and the intermediates are assumed to be represented. For example, bracketing can be applied to different container sizes that are made from the same resin, filled with the same product. If a drug product is packaged in the same bottle with three different tablet counts (30-count, 90-count, and 100-count) and in a unit-dose blister, only three presentations (30-count, 100-count, and unit-dose blister) will be on stability. The fourth configuration (90-count), which is bracketed by the 30-count and 100-count, is assumed to be represented. Matrixing can be used. With matrixing, a selected subset of the total number of possible samples with all factor combinations is tested at a specified time point.

Once data are generated from the study, they will need to be evaluated. The first step in this process is to compare them against the acceptance criteria. The second step is to look at the trending. Trending is typically performed on sets of data that include the same formulation and packaging configuration. An approach for analyzing stability data, which is expected to change over time, is to determine the time at which the 95% one-sided confidence limit for the mean curve intersects the acceptance criterion (Figure 25.1).

Based on the stability data extrapolation, companies can infer information about future data and establish dating. This information can aid in establishing acceptance criteria/expiry dating for the new product based on a high degree of confidence. After approval of a new material, the ongoing stability study data will permit the detection of a stability issue, such as change in impurity levels. In general, certain quantitative attributes, such as assay and degradation products, can be assumed to be zero-order kinetics during long-term storage, thus the trending and regression statistics can be applied to these stability-indicating tests. Although the kinetics of other quantitative attributes, such as pH and dissolution, are not known, the same statistical analysis model can be applied.

Results that do not meet the acceptance criteria or demonstrate adverse trending must be investigated both from a laboratory perspective (was the testing

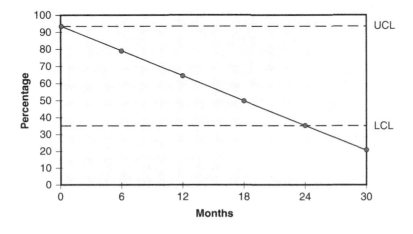

Figure 25.1   Shelf life estimation for assay.

performed correctly?) and from a product perspective (were formulation, man-ufacturing, packaging, and delivery performed correctly?). Typically, an *out-of-specification* (OOS) procedure will be followed to conduct the investigation. For approved products, and if the stability study is representative of product in com-merce, a confirmed OOS result will require notification to the United States Food and Drug Administration (FDA) within three days of the confirmation. Depend-ing on the failure and product evaluation, a company may potentially reduce the expiry dating or recall the product.

Chapter 26

Reserve Samples and Retains

21 CFR 211.170 requires an appropriately identified reserve sample that is representative of each lot in each shipment of each active ingredient. The reserve sample consists of at least twice the quantity necessary for all tests required to determine whether the active ingredient meets its established specifications, except for sterility and pyrogen testing. The retention time is as follows:

- For an active ingredient in a drug product the reserve sample shall be retained for 1 year after the expiration date of the last lot of the drug product containing the active ingredient.

- For an active ingredient in a radioactive drug product, except for nonradioactive reagent kits, the reserve sample shall be retained for:

  o Three months after the expiration date of the last lot of the drug product containing the active ingredient if the expiration dating period of the drug product is 30 days or less;

  o Or Six months after the expiration date of the last lot of the drug product containing the active ingredient if the expiration dating period of the drug product is more than 30 days.

- For an active ingredient in an OTC drug product that is exempt from bearing an expiration date the reserve sample shall be retained for 3 years after distribution of the last lot of the drug product containing the active ingredient.

It is important that samples are appropriately identified, representative of each lot or batch of drug product, and shall be retained and stored under conditions consistent with product labeling in the same immediate container-closure system in which the drug product is marketed or in one that has essentially the same characteristics.

The FDA's Division of Scientific Investigations (DSI) and FDA field investigators conduct inspections of clinical and analytical sites that perform bioavailability (BA) and bioequivalence (BE) testing for drug manufacturers seeking approval of a drug product.

Retention samples should be kept at the testing facility where the study was conducted. The study sponsor should provide the testing facility with a supply of the test article and the reference standard sufficient to complete the study and retain the appropriate number of dosage units as reserve samples. The study sponsor should not separate out the samples to be reserved prior to sending the batches to the testing facility. The testing facility will randomly select the reserve samples from the supply sent by the sponsor. This is to ensure that reserve samples are in fact representative of the same batches provided by the study sponsor for the testing. The testing facility should retain enough quantify to permit FDA to perform five times all of the release tests required in the application.

Samples shall consist of a sufficient quantity to permit FDA to perform five times all of the release tests required in the application or supplemental application. Each reserve sample shall be adequately identified so that the reserve sample can be positively identified as having come from the same sample as used in the specific bioavailability study. Each reserve sample shall be stored under conditions consistent with product labeling and in an area segregated from the area where testing is conducted and with access limited to authorized personnel. Each reserve sample shall be retained for a period of at least 5 years following the date on which the application or supplemental application is approved, or, if such application or supplemental application is not approved, at least 5 years following the date of completion of the bioavailability study in which the sample from which the reserve sample was obtained was used.

Part IV

Infrastructure: Facilities, Utilities, Equipment

Chapter 27

Facilities

INTRODUCTION

Good manufacturing practices (GMP) were invoked to maintain the quality of pharmaceutical and biopharmaceutical products manufactured for human consumption. The predicate regulatory documents, 21 CFR 210 and 211, outline the minimum GMP for methods to be used in, and the facilities or controls to be used for, the manufacture, processing, packing, or holding of a drug to assure that such drug meets the requirements of the Act as to safety, and has the identity and strength and meets the quality and purity characteristics that it purports or is represented to possess. Failure to comply with the regulations renders a drug adulterated, and the drug, as well as the person(s) and company responsible for the failure to comply, are subject to regulatory action. In GMP, buildings and facilities are the second major topic addressed, indicating their importance in the overall manufacturing of quality products.

DESIGN AND CONSTRUCTION FEATURES (21 CFR 211.42)

Building design is the first imperative to ensure that products are manufactured safely. Buildings should facilitate cleaning, maintenance, and proper operations, and therefore need to be large enough and constructed in a manner to accommodate these processes. They should have adequate space for the orderly placement of equipment and materials to prevent cross-contamination between different components, drug product containers, closures, labeling, in-process materials, or drug products. They should also be designed to prevent contamination through the unidirectional flow of components, drug product containers, closures, labeling, in-process materials, and drug products from minimally controlled areas to those in which control is greater. As these materials move through the production area, each area is subject to higher scrutiny and control. For example, the loading dock where raw materials and components are received will have fewer environmental controls than the area where bulk product is filled into containers.

Specifically defined areas of adequate size are required for each operation and are designed to prevent contamination or mix-ups. Specific areas are typically demarcated for:

- Receipt, identification, storage, and holding of components, drug product containers, closures, and labeling pending the appropriate sampling, testing, or examination by the quality control unit before release for manufacturing or packaging

- Holding rejected components, drug product containers, closures, and labeling before disposition

- Storage of released components, drug product containers, closures, and labeling

- Storage of in-process materials

- Manufacturing and processing operations

- Packaging and labeling operations

- Quarantine storage before release of drug products

- Storage of drug products after release

- Control and laboratory operations

- Aseptic processing, including floors, walls, and ceilings with smooth, hard surfaces that are easily cleanable; temperature and humidity controls; air supply filtered through high-efficiency particulate air filters under positive pressure, regardless of whether flow is laminar or not laminar; system for monitoring environmental conditions; system for cleaning and disinfecting the room and equipment to produce aseptic conditions; and system for maintaining any equipment used to control the aseptic conditions

LIGHTING (21 CFR 211.44)

The GMP are very specific and succinct regarding lighting. The facilities must have sufficient lighting to ensure that all work can be easily viewed by personnel to allow them to conduct their activities properly. Most companies provide fluorescent lighting, which produces bright, nonglaring light, facilitating visual assessment of each operation.

One area of lighting that overlaps with design and construction is cleaning and maintenance of the lighting fixtures. Since lights are placed above the working area, any particles and/or microorganisms that accumulate on them are potential contaminates that could lead to an adulterated product. Therefore, companies should design lighting systems that facilitate cleaning and maintenance to prevent unwanted contamination, such as lights that are enclosed in metal housings with removable bottom panels. Additionally, cleaning schedules should be generated and implemented. Operators and supervisors should conduct daily visual inspections of the lighting fixtures to ensure that insects or other visible contaminants have not infiltrated the lighting fixtures. An insect finding its way into a fixture before the scheduled cleaning or maintenance is indicative that the frequency of cleaning is too long and should be modified.

VENTILATION, AIR FILTRATION, AIR HEATING AND COOLING (21 CFR 211.46)

The GMP requirements stipulate that adequate ventilation shall be provided, and equipment for adequate control over air pressure, microorganisms, dust, humidity, and temperature shall be provided when appropriate for the manufacture, processing, packing, or holding of a drug product. The GMP also require air filtration systems, including prefilters and particulate matter air filters, to be used when appropriate on air supplies to production areas. If air is recirculated to production areas, measures are to be taken to control recirculation of dust from production. In areas where air contamination occurs during production, exhaust systems or other systems adequate to control contaminants are required. Air-handling systems for the manufacture, processing, and packing of penicillin are to be completely separate from those for other drug products for human use.

Ventilation, air filtration, and air heating and cooling are areas that may contribute to contamination, both particulate and microbiological, and these systems should be closely monitored and controlled. Similarly to lighting, a company should generate a schedule for cleaning and maintaining air vents, ducts, and cooling systems, but human observation on a daily basis should also be practiced. For example, visual observation of blackened areas on vents is evidence that the frequency of cleaning and maintenance needs to be increased to avoid unwanted contaminants from entering the area.

PLUMBING (21 CFR 211.48)

The GMP requirements for water state that potable water shall be supplied under continuous positive pressure in a plumbing system free of defects that could contribute contamination to any drug product. Potable water must meet the standards prescribed in the Environmental Protection Agency's (EPA) National Primary Drinking Water Regulations set forth in 40 CFR 141. Water not meeting such standards is not permitted in the potable water system. Drains must be of adequate size and, where connected directly to a sewer, must be provided with an air break or other mechanical device to prevent back-siphonage.

Supply of water to the facility may significantly contribute to the overall quality of the manufacturing operation. Although a facility can not control the type of water it receives from a municipality, it should monitor the water on a scheduled basis and take appropriate actions to ensure that the water meets the current EPA regulations. The EPA specifies specific levels of organic, inorganic, and microbial agents that are allowed in municipal water supplies, and typically the municipality reports these levels annually. Pharmaceutical manufacturing facilities should exert increased diligence regarding the requirements, and may adopt a practice of testing the water more frequently than annually to ensure that the incoming supply does not overwhelm its water purification system that removes these agents. This process is critical in assessing the life-span of the filters, carbon beds, resins, and ozone or other components used to reduce the amount of agents in the water supply.

Most facilities have installed plumbing that diverts sewage, including liquids used in manufacturing, directly to a closed drain equipped with air breaks downstream from the point of entry. It is good practice to ensure that all drains are capped, even those used for discharging washing solutions after a room is cleaned. In this instance, the drains should remain capped until the room is cleaned and subsequently recapped when cleaning is concluded.

SEWAGE AND REFUSE (21 CFR 211.50)

The GMP for sewage and refuse state that sewage, trash, and other refuse in and from the building and immediate premises must be disposed of in a safe and sanitary manner. Firms should have written procedures to ensure that sewage and refuse are properly removed and disposed of. Medical waste should be removed by qualified vendors who provide complete documentation of removal and ultimate disposal, be it by incineration or other means. Liquid medical waste should be removed by the same vendors, or the firm should have written procedures documenting its inactivation before disposing of it into the municipal waste or the sewage system. They must also be in compliance with all EPA regulations before disposal. Nonmedical and nontoxic waste should be removed by general waste haulers, and the firm should have written procedures to document the details of the process.

WASHING AND TOILET FACILITIES (21 CFR 211.52)

The GMP for washing and toilet facilities require that adequate washing facilities be provided, including hot and cold water, soap or detergent, air driers or single-service towels, and clean toilet facilities easily accessible to working areas. The firm is responsible not only for providing washing and toilet facilities but also for cleaning and sanitizing them on a regular basis, as described in written procedures. The firm's training program should include a section devoted to teaching proper washing techniques for all employees after they visit a washroom.

SANITATION (21 CFR 211.56)

The GMP for sanitization are:

- Any building used in the manufacture, processing, packing, or holding of a drug product shall be maintained in a clean and sanitary condition. Any such building shall be free of infestation by rodents, birds, insects, and other vermin (other than laboratory animals). Trash and organic waste matter shall be held and disposed of in a timely and sanitary manner.

- Written procedures are needed to assign responsibility for sanitation and describing in sufficient detail the cleaning schedules, methods, equipment, and materials to be used in cleaning the buildings and facilities; such written procedures shall be followed.

- There shall be written procedures for use of suitable rodenticides, insecticides, fungicides, fumigating agents, and cleaning and sanitizing agents. Such written procedures shall be designed to prevent the contamination of equipment, components, drug product containers, closures, packaging, labeling materials, or drug products, and shall be followed. Rodenticides, insecticides, and fungicides shall not be used unless registered, and used in accordance with the Federal Insecticide, Fungicide, and Rodenticide Act.

- Sanitation procedures shall apply to work performed by contractors or temporary employees as well as work performed by full-time employees during the ordinary course of operations.

These regulations provide enough specificity such that a firm can follow them verbatim. Whatever written programs the firm establishes to assure adequate sanitization should be supplemented with proper training of all affected employees.

MAINTENANCE (21 CFR 211.58)

The GMP for maintenance state that any building used in the manufacture, processing, packing, or holding of a drug product must be maintained in a good state of repair. Firms must have written procedures that describe the frequency and type of maintenance they will conduct in the facility. Typically, the more critical areas, such as the aseptic core, will be more frequently maintained, and the type of maintenance will be more highly scrutinized. In many cases, the batch records will include a section for line clearance and maintenance before the run and after the run. It may include a section for cleaning and for specific areas that require maintenance. For example, many more areas in an aseptic filling suite will be scrutinized as compared to a bulk processing area. Again, training is an essential component of maintaining a facility, and individuals should be continuously trained to ensure they are vigilant in keeping the facility as impeccable as possible.

Chapter 28

Cleanrooms

Cleanrooms are an essential function in the processing of pharmaceuticals, biologics, and medical devices that are safe and effective. Cleanrooms provide an environment that minimizes sources of potential contaminates such as dust, microbes, particles, and vapors. Cleanrooms are classified by the maximum number of particles allowed per cubic meter. The controlled dispersion of particulates or contaminates by airflow is essentially how a cleanroom maintains a clean environment. ISO 14644-1:1999 defines a cleanroom as a "room in which the concentration of airborne particles is controlled, and which is constructed and used in a manner to minimize the introduction, generation, and retention of particles inside the room, and in which other relevant parameters, e.g. temperature, humidity, and pressure, are controlled as necessary."

Two types of cleanrooms exist: unidirectional and non-unidirectional. Each type of cleanroom has its unique advantages and disadvantages. *Unidirectional* cleanrooms are necessary when an ISO class 6 or better cleanroom is required. *Non-unidirectional* cleanrooms are generally less expensive to construct and rely on a high volume of air to disperse contaminates. Air filtration is essential to maintain acceptable particulate/contaminate counts. Two types of filters can be used: *high-efficiency particulate air* (HEPA), which are at least 99.97% efficient, and *ultra-low penetration air* (ULPA), which are at least 99.999% efficient. HEPA filters are used for ISO class 6 to 8 cleanrooms and ULPA filters are used for ISO class 1 to 5 cleanrooms. Cleanrooms are classified by the maximum number of particles allowed per cubic meter (Table 28.1 through Table 28.4). Cleanrooms rely on the dispersion of particulates/contaminates by airflow (Table 28.5).

When it is necessary to control the environment, specifications for parameters such as temperature, humidity, *colony-forming units* (CFUs), and particulates per cubic foot should be established. No United States Food and Drug Administration (FDA) guidances for these parameters presently exist for environmentally controlled areas such as cleanrooms.

A review of 21 CFR 210, 211, and 820 yields no direct requirements for the use or classifications of controlled environments or cleanrooms. These parts of 21 CFR do have references requiring the need for environmental and contamination controls where a lack of control could reasonably be expected to have an adverse effect on product quality. However, FDA has issued a guidance for industry, *Sterile Drug Products Produced by Aseptic Processing—Current Good Manufacturing Practice*. This guidance document recommends the use of an ISO class 5 cleanroom (European Union [EU] Grade A) in areas deemed to be critical. A critical area is defined

Table 28.1   Cleanroom classification (ISO 14644-1:1999).

ISO class	Maximum permitted number of particles/m³					
	≥0.1 µm	≥0.2 µm	≥0.3 µm	≥0.5 µm	≥1.0 µm	≥5.0 µm
1	10	2				
2	100	24	10	4		
3	1,000	237	102	35	8	
4	10,000	2,370	1,020	352	83	
5	100,000	23,700	10,200	3520	832	29
6	1,000,000	237,000	102,000	35,200	8,320	293
7				352,000	83,200	2,930
8				3,520,000	832,000	29,300
9*				35,200,000	8,320,000	293,000

*Equivalent to normal outside air

Table 28.2   Recommended limits for microbial contamination (ISO 14644-1:1999).

ISO class	Microbiological active air action levels (CFU/m³)	Microbiological setting plates action levels (diam 90 mm; CFU/4 hr)
5	1	1
6	7	3
7	10	5
8	100	50

CFU = colony-forming units, diam = diameter, hr = hour

Table 28.3   Maximum permitted number of particles/m³ (*European Union Guidelines to Good Manufacturing Practice*).

Grade	Maximum permitted number of particles/m³			
	At rest		In operation	
	≥0.5 mm	≥5 mm	≥0.5 mm	≥5 mm
A	3,500	0	3,500	0
B	3,500	0	350,000	2,000
C	350,000	2,000	3,500,000	20,000
D	3,500,000	20,000		

Table 28.4   Recommended limits for microbial contamination (*European Union Guide to Good Manufacturing Practices*).

Grade	Recommended limits for microbial contamination			
	Air sample CFU/m³	Settle plates (diam 90 mm), CFU/4 hr	Contact plates (diam 55 mm), CFU/plate	Glove print 5 fingers CFU/glove
A	< 1	< 1	< 1	< 1
B	10	5	5	5
C	100	50	25	—
D	200	100	50	—

CFU = colony forming unit, diam = diameter, hr = hour

Table 28.5   Rule of thumb for recommended air changes per hour based on class of cleanroom (Whyte 2010).

ISO class	Air changes per hour
1	
2	
3	Use unidirectional airflow
4	
5	
6	> 100
7	10–100
8*	2–10

* FDA Guidance for Industry *Sterile Drug Products Produced by Aseptic Processing—Current Good Manufacturing Practice* recommends a minimum of 20 air changes per hour as acceptable.

as "one in which the sterilized drug product, containers, and closures are exposed to environmental conditions that must be designed to maintain product sterility." FDA recommends that areas directly supporting aseptic processing activities be at a minimum ISO class 7 while in operation. Consistent with Volume 4 EU *Guidelines to Good Manufacturing Practice Medicinal Products for Human and Veterinary Use, Annex 1 Manufacture of Sterile Medicinal Products*, it is recommended that microbiological contamination (bioburden) counts remain at < 1 at all times.

SPECIFIC ISO SECTIONS RELATED TO CLEANROOMS

ISO 14644-2:2000

Specifications for testing and monitoring to prove continued compliance with ISO 14644-1 provide guidance and direction for testing requirements to ensure the proper operation and compliance for cleanrooms. According to ISO 14644-1:1999, cleanrooms may be classified in one of three states:

- *As-built.* Condition where the installation is complete, with all services connected and functioning, but with no production equipment, materials, or personnel present

- *At-rest.* Condition where the installation is complete, with equipment installed and operating in a manner agreed on by the customer and supplier, but with no personnel present

- *Operational.* Condition where the installation is functioning in the specified manner, with the specified number of personnel present and working in the manner agreed on

The minimum number of sampling points is derived from the following equation:

$$NL = \sqrt{A}$$

Where:

NL = The minimum number of sampling locations (rounded up to a whole number)

A = The area of the cleanroom or clean zone in square meters

Table 28.6, derived from ISO 14644-2:2000, lists the required and optional testing necessary to ensure proper cleanroom operation and continued compliance.

ISO 14644-1:1999

This part of ISO 14644 (*Cleanrooms and associated controlled environments—Part 1: Classification of air cleanliness*) covers the classification of air cleanliness in cleanrooms and associated controlled environments exclusively in terms of concentration of airborne particles. Only particle populations having cumulative distributions based on threshold (lower limit) sizes ranging from 0.1 µm to 5 µm are considered for classification purposes. This part does not provide for classification of particle populations that are outside of the specified particle size range, 0.1 µm to 5 µm. Concentrations of ultrafine particles (particles < 0.1 µm) and macroparticles (particles > 5 µm) may be used to quantify these populations in terms of ultrafine descriptors and macroparticle descriptors, respectively. This part of ISO 14644 can not be used to characterize the physical, chemical, radiological, or viable nature of airborne particles.

Table 28.6 Required and optional testing necessary to ensure proper cleanroom operation and compliance (ISO 14644-2:2000).

Test parameter	Class	Maximum time interval (months)
Required tests		
Particle count test	≤ ISO 5	6
	> ISO 5	12
Airflow volume or airflow velocity	All	12
Air pressure difference	All	12
Optional tests		
Installed filter leakage	All	24
Airflow visualization	All	24
Recovery	All	24
Containment leakage	All	24

ISO 14644-2:2000

This part of ISO 14644 (*Cleanrooms and associated controlled environments—Part 2: Specifications for testing and monitoring to prove continued compliance with ISO 14644-1*) specifies requirements for periodic testing of a cleanroom or clean zone to prove its continued compliance with ISO 14644-1 for the designated classification of airborne particulate cleanliness. These requirements invoke the test described in ISO 14644-1 for classification of a cleanroom or clean zone. Additional tests are also specified to be carried out in accordance with the requirements of this part of ISO 14644. Optional tests, to be applied at the user's discretion, are also identified. This part of ISO 14644 specifies requirements for monitoring of a cleanroom or clean zone (hereafter referred to as an *installation*) to provide evidence of its continued compliance with ISO 14644-1 for the designated classification of airborne particulate cleanliness.

ISO 14644-3:2005

ISO 14644-3:2005 (*Cleanrooms and associated controlled environments—Part 3: Test methods*) specifies test methods for designated classification of airborne particulate cleanliness and for characterizing the performance of cleanrooms and clean zones. Performance tests are specified for two types of cleanrooms and clean zones: those with unidirectional flow and those with non-unidirectional flow, in three possible occupancy states: as-built, at-rest, and operational. ISO 14644-3:2005 is not applicable to the measurement of products or of processes in cleanrooms or separative devices.

ISO 14644-4:2001

This part of ISO 14644 (*Cleanrooms and associated controlled environments—Part 4: Design, construction and start-up*) specifies requirements for the design and construction of cleanroom installations but does not prescribe specific technological or contractual means to meet these requirements. It is intended for use by purchasers, suppliers, and designers of cleanroom installations and provides a checklist of important parameters of performance. Construction guidance is provided, including requirements for start-up and qualification. Basic elements of design and construction needed to ensure continued satisfactory operation are identified through the consideration of relevant aspects of operation and maintenance.

Application of this part of ISO 14644 is restricted in that user requirements are represented by the purchaser or specifier; specific processes to be accommodated in the cleanroom installation are not specified; fire and safety regulations are not considered specifically, so the appropriate national and local requirements should be respected; and process media and utility services are only considered with respect to their routing between and in the different zones of cleanliness. Regarding initial operation and maintenance, only cleanroom construction–specific requirements are considered.

ISO 14644-5:2004

ISO 14644-5:2004 (*Cleanrooms and associated controlled environments—Part 5: Operations*) specifies basic requirements for cleanroom operations. Aspects of safety that have no direct bearing on contamination control are not considered in this part of ISO 14644, so national and local safety regulations must be observed. This document considers all classes of cleanrooms used to produce all types of products. Therefore, it is broad in application and does not address specific requirements for individual industries. Methods and programs for routine monitoring within cleanrooms are not covered in detail in this part of ISO 14644, but reference should be made to ISO 14644-2 and ISO 14644-3 for monitoring particles, and ISO 14698-1 and ISO 14698-2 for monitoring microorganisms.

ISO 14644-6:2007

ISO 14644-6:2007 (*Cleanrooms and associated controlled environments—Part 6: Vocabulary*) establishes a vocabulary of terms and definitions related to cleanrooms and associated controlled environments.

ISO 14644-7:2004

ISO 14644-7:2004 (*Cleanrooms and associated controlled environments—Part 7: Separative devices [clean air hoods, gloveboxes, isolators and mini-environments]*) specifies the minimum requirements for the design, construction, installation, test, and approval of separative devices, in those respects where they differ from cleanrooms as described in ISO 14644-4 and 14644-5. The application of ISO 14644-7:2004 takes into account several limitations: user requirements are as agreed by customer and supplier, application-specific requirements are not addressed, specific processes to be accommodated in the separative-device installation are not specified, fire, safety, and other regulatory matters are not considered specifically, and where appropriate, national and local regulations apply.

ISO 14644-8:2013

ISO 14644-8:2013 (*Cleanrooms and associated controlled environments—Part 8: Classification of air cleanliness by chemical concentration [ACC]*) establishes the classification of *air chemical cleanliness* (ACC) in cleanrooms and associated controlled environments in terms of airborne concentrations of specific chemical substances (individual, group, or category) and provides a protocol to include test methods, analysis, and time-weighted factors within the specification for classification. ISO 14644-8:2013 currently considers only concentrations of air chemical contaminants between 100 and 10 to 12 g/m^3 under cleanroom operational conditions. ISO 14644-8:2013 is not relevant for application in those industries, processes, or productions where the presence of airborne chemical substances is not considered a risk to the product or process. It is not the intention of ISO 14644-8:2013 to describe the nature of air chemical contaminants. ISO 14644-8:2013 does not give a classification of surface chemical contamination.

ISO 14644-9:2012

ISO 14644-9:2012 (*Cleanrooms and associated controlled environments—Part 9: Classification of surface cleanliness by particle concentration*) establishes the classification of cleanliness levels on solid surfaces by particle concentration in cleanrooms and associated controlled environment applications. Recommendations on testing and measuring methods, as well as information about surface characteristics, are also given. ISO 14644-9:2012 applies to all solid surfaces in cleanrooms and associated controlled environments such as walls, ceilings, floors, working environments, tools, equipment, and products. The *surface particle cleanliness* (SPC) classification is limited to particles between 0.05 μm and 500 μm. Several issues are not considered, including requirements for the cleanliness and suitability of surfaces for specific processes, procedures for the cleaning of surfaces, material characteristics, references to interactive bonding forces or generation processes that are usually time dependent and process dependent, selection and use of statistical methods for classification and testing, and other characteristics of particles, such as electrostatic charge, ionic charges, and microbiological state.

ISO 14698-1:2003

ISO 14698-1:2003 (*Cleanrooms and associated controlled environments—Biocontamination control—Part 1: General principles and methods*) establishes the principles and basic methodology of a biocontamination control (formal system) for assessing and controlling biocontamination when cleanroom technology is applied for that purpose. It specifies the methods required for monitoring risk zones in a consistent way and for applying control measures appropriate to the degree of risk involved. In zones where risk is low, it can be used for information.

ISO 14698-2:2003

ISO 14698-2:2003 (*Cleanrooms and associated controlled environments—Biocontamination control—Part 2: Evaluation and interpretation of biocontamination data*) gives guidance on methods for the evaluation of microbiological data and the estimation of results obtained from sampling for viable particles in risk zones for biocontamination control. It should be used, where appropriate, in conjunction with ISO 14698-1.

Chapter 29

Utilities

Utilities play an important part in the production of safe and effective biologics, pharmaceuticals, and medical devices. To consistently provide products that are safe and effective, utilities must be properly designed, installed, monitored, and maintained. Utilities include, but are not limited to, electrical power; compressed air; *heating, ventilation, and air conditioning* (HVAC) systems; steam; gases, including medicinal; water, including potable and *water for injection* (WFI); vacuum; and drains. Each of these items provides its own set of unique challenges to properly support production operations and prevent contamination and cross-contamination.

The selection and design of utilities should be made on the premise of properly supporting production operations and preventing contamination and cross-contamination. Considerations should be made for the types of materials used, washing, sterilizing, and depyrogenation. Use of medical-grade materials will help minimize contamination and reduce potential biocompatibility issues.

The Pharmaceutical Inspection Convention's Pharmaceutical Inspection Co-Operation Scheme (PIC/S) P1 009-3 details a seven-step process for pharmaceutical water systems that includes key design parameters, qualification, inspection, *quality control* (QC) testing, monitoring, maintenance and calibration, and documentation.

Design considerations for water used in the production of pharmaceuticals, including WFI, should use *good engineering practices* (GEP) using a risk-based approach that is planned and structured throughout the entire life cycle of the system. The system should consider the required water quality and its intended use, the initial water source, and storage considerations. Water shall be supplied under continuous positive pressure in a system that prevents the possibility of contamination. Additional design considerations should include weld quality, passivation, vent filters, suitability of construction materials, slope of pipe works, recirculation velocities and temperatures, check valves to prevent backflow, sanitary joints, capacity relative to demand, vales, draining and flushing, and sampling ports and locations.

Particularly important is the passivation stainless steel piping. The passivation process uses nitric or citric acid to coat the surface, thereby improving the corrosion-resistance properties by dissolving iron that has been embedded in the surface during the manufacturing process, creating a thin, transparent oxide film. When materials are not passivated, the iron can corrode and react with other materials, causing stains, discoloration, and product contamination.

Design considerations for compressed air and gas systems in the production of pharmaceuticals should use GEP with a risk-based approach that is planned

- Out-of-specification (OOS) events
- Frequent out-of-calibration events
- Out-of-tolerance (OOT) events
- Additional load to the system
- Decreased load on the system
- Frequent breakdowns
- New technology

Figure 29.1   Conditions that may require the revalidation of utilities.

and structured throughout the entire life cycle of the system. The system should consider the required gas quality and its intended use, the initial source, and storage considerations.

Once utility systems have been designed and installed, qualification/ validation should be done to ensure the system is capable. At this time, the company should determine and set operational, cleaning, sanitization, and sterilization parameters for the systems. Appropriate consideration should be given to maintenance and calibration activities.

Quality-testing methods, along with acceptable thresholds, should be developed and documented in appropriate procedures and work instructions. These procedures should document who will conduct the sampling, when samples will be taken, the minimum required sample volume, handling and storage of the samples, chemical, biological, and particulate levels, and how to handle *out of specification* (OOS) results. Frequent monitoring (for example, temperature, pressure, velocity), maintenance, and calibration activities should be conducted according to established procedures to ensure that the system(s) are functioning as intended.

Once utility systems have been installed, qualified, and validated, any change made to the system should be preapproved and formally documented to ensure that the system properly functions as designed. The change control process should begin with a formal *facility change request* (FCR). The FCR should document the scope of the proposed change, potential effect of product, materials, or processes, whether the change will require a full or partial qualification/revalidation, and maintenance and calibration activities. The approval should include signatures from appropriate departments, including operations, maintenance, and quality, before making the changes. Figure 29.1 provides a list of scenarios that may indicate revalidation activities.

Chapter 30

Equipment

The basic good manufacturing practices (GMP) requirement is to ensure that production equipment is designed, located, and maintained to serve its intended purpose. This requirement helps ensure that active pharmaceutical ingredients (APIs) and drugs of consistent quality are fabricated. Equipment GMP are designed to prevent the contamination of drugs by other drugs, by dust, and by foreign materials such as rust, lubricant, and particles coming from the equipment. Contamination problems can occur from poor maintenance, the misuse of equipment, exceeding the capacity of the equipment, and the use of worn-out equipment.

Major equipment should be identified with a distinctive number, name, or code that is recorded in batch records. This identification requirement is intended to help document which pieces of equipment were used to make which batches of drug product.

A label indicating the status of maintenance is not required by regulations; however, records demonstrating maintenance should be available. A firm should be able to provide records documenting when a specific piece of equipment was last calibrated/maintained, the results or action, and when its next maintenance is scheduled. The absence of such documentation or failure to provide these records is considered a GMP deviation.

DESIGN

Equipment should be of appropriate design and adequate size, and the design and construction of equipment should permit cleaning, sanitizing, and inspection of the equipment. Equipment should be designed for closed or contained processes wherever appropriate. Where open equipment is used, or equipment is opened, appropriate precautions should be taken to minimize the risk of contamination. Equipment should be equipped with fittings that can be dismantled and cleaned, allowing validated *clean-in-place* (CIP) equipment to be dismantled for periodic verification. Equipment should be sterilizable/sanitizable, where appropriate, and have filter assemblies designed for easy dismantling. Equipment documentation should include design validation, installation, operation, and performance qualification documentation.

Equipment should be suitably located for its intended use. Major equipment (for example, reactors, storage containers) and permanently installed processing lines used during the production of an intermediate or API should be appropriately identified. Fixed pipework should be clearly labeled to indicate the contents and, where applicable, the direction of flow. Equipment should be part of an appropriate, defined maintenance program. Equipment should only be used within its qualified operating range, and dedicated production equipment should be provided where appropriate. Where applicable, chain drives and transmission gears should be enclosed or properly covered. Tanks, hoppers, and other similar fabricating equipment should be equipped with covers.

MATERIALS OF CONSTRUCTION

GMP requirements stipulate that equipment parts that come in contact with raw materials, intermediates, APIs, in-process drugs, or drugs should be designed and constructed so that they are accessible for cleaning or are removable. Equipment parts should be designed and constructed so that surfaces that contact raw materials, intermediates, or APIs do not alter the quality of the intermediates and APIs beyond the official or established specifications. The parts of the production equipment that come into contact with the product must not be reactive, additive, or absorptive to such an extent that it will affect the quality of the product and present any hazard. Surfaces that come in contact with raw materials, in-process drugs, or drugs should be smooth and made of material that is nontoxic, corrosion resistant, nonreactive to the drug being fabricated or packaged, and capable of withstanding repeated cleaning or sanitizing. Equipment made of material that is prone to shed particles or to harbor microorganisms should not contact or contaminate raw materials, in-process drugs, or drugs.

LUBRICANTS

The design of equipment should be such that the possibility of a lubricant or other maintenance material contaminating the drug is minimized. Any substances associated with the operation of equipment, such as lubricants, heating fluids, or coolants, should not contact intermediates or APIs so as to alter their quality beyond the official or established specifications. Any deviations should be evaluated to ensure that the fitness for purpose of the material is not affected detrimentally. Wherever possible, food-grade lubricants and oils should be used.

Equipment Layout

Equipment should be arranged in an orderly manner that permits cleaning of adjacent areas and does not interfere with other processing operations. Equipment should be:

- Located to suit its intended purpose

- Located so that production operations undertaken in a common area are compatible, and so that cross-contamination between such operations is prevented

- Located to optimize the flow of material and to minimize the circulation of personnel (unidirectional flow)

- Installed to prevent any risk of error or of contamination, and to ensure that equipment is not operated where contaminants may fall into the material

- Easily cleaned, sanitized, and inspected

- Located at a sufficient distance from other equipment and walls to permit cleaning of the equipment and adjacent area

- Sealed at the base of immovable equipment along points of contact with the floor

EQUIPMENT CLEANING VALIDATION

Regulations require that APIs and drug products be fabricated and packaged in areas that are free from environmental contamination and free from contamination by another drug. Washing and cleaning equipment should be chosen and used in a manner so as not to be a source of contamination.

The objective of the cleaning validation is to verify the effectiveness of the cleaning procedure for removal of product residues, degradation products, preservatives, excipients, and/or cleaning agents, as well as the control of potential microbial contaminants. In addition, the company needs to ensure that there is no risk associated with cross-contamination of active ingredients.

Equipment should be cleaned at appropriate intervals to prevent buildup and carry-over of contaminants (for example, degradants or objectionable levels of microorganisms). A written cleaning (sanitization) process validation program provides some assurance that levels of cleanliness in the plant are maintained and that the provisions of Sections 8 and 11 of the Food and Drug regulations are satisfied. The cleaning validation program should demonstrate that cleaning procedures are robust and effective, establish the maximum time that may elapse between the completion of processing and equipment cleaning (dirty hold time), establish the maximum time that equipment may be held clean before use (clean hold time), and document and justify the amount of carry-over from batch to batch.

Cleaning validation is used for equipment used in continuous or campaign production of successive batches of the same intermediate or API, and non-dedicated equipment cleaned between production of different materials to prevent cross-contamination.

GMP of Cleaning Validation and Analytical Methods

GMP state that a cleaning program must be implemented and be effective in preventing unsanitary conditions. Cleaning procedures for manufacturing equipment are validated based on the cleaning validation guidelines. Residues from the cleaning process itself (for example, detergents, solvents) are removed from equipment during cleaning.

It is necessary to provide evidence demonstrating that routine cleaning and storage does not allow microbial proliferation, and that analytical methods used to detect residues or contaminants are validated. The analytical methods used to detect residuals or contaminants should be specific for the substance or the class of substances to be assayed (for example, product residue, detergent residue, and/or endotoxin) and be validated before the cleaning validation study is done.

In the case of biologic drugs, the use of product-specific assay(s) such as immunoassay(s) to monitor the presence of biological carry-over may not be adequate; a negative test may be the result of denaturation of protein epitope(s). Product-specific assay(s) can be used in addition to *total organic carbon* (TOC) for the detection of protein residue.

The analytical method and the percentage recovery of contaminants should be challenged in combination with the sampling method(s) used to show that contaminants can be recovered from the equipment surface, and to show the level of recovery and the consistency of recovery. This step is necessary before any conclusions can be made based on the sample results. A negative test may be the result of poor sampling technique. Acceptance criteria for residues and the choice of cleaning procedures and cleaning agents should be defined and justified, and equipment should be visually examined to verify cleaning.

Cleaning Validation and Sampling, Rinsing, Rinse Samples, and Detergents

Two types of sampling that are generally considered to be acceptable are *direct surface sampling* (swab method) and *indirect sampling* (use of rinse solutions). A combination of the two methods is the most desirable, particularly in circumstances where accessibility of equipment parts can mitigate against direct surface sampling:

- *Direct surface sampling*. Areas hardest to clean and that are reasonably accessible can be evaluated by the direct surface sampling method. This method allows establishment of a level of contamination or residue per given surface area. This method ensures that dried out or insoluble residues can be sampled.

- *Rinse samples*. Rinse samples allow sampling of a large surface area and of inaccessible systems or ones that can not be routinely disassembled. Limitations include insoluble contaminants or contaminants remaining on the equipment surface.

Indirect testing, such as conductivity and TOC testing, may be of some value for routine monitoring once a cleaning process has been validated. This process could be applicable to reactors or centrifuges and piping between such large equipment that can be sampled only using rinse solution samples.

When detergents are used in the cleaning process, their composition should be known to the user, and their removal should be demonstrated. The manufacturer should ensure that they are notified by the detergent supplier of any changes in the formulation of the detergent. Acceptable limits should be defined for detergent residues after cleaning. The possibility of detergent breakdown should be considered when validating cleaning procedures. Indirect testing such as conductivity and TOC testing may be of some value for assessing the effectiveness of removing the cleaning agent.

Water for injection (WFI) should be used as the last rinse for product-contact equipment to be used in the fabrication of sterile products. Purified water is considered acceptable as the last rinse for product-contact equipment used in the fabrication of non-sterile products or sterile products for ophthalmic use. Tap water should not be used in the last rinse of any cleaning procedure for product-contact equipment because of the presence of varying levels of organic and inorganic residues, as well as chlorine.

Establishment of Cleaning Validation Limits

No established standard acceptance limits exist for cleaning validation. Companies must establish limits that reflect the capability of the cleaning processes and analytical test methods used. Considerations for cleaning include evaluation of the therapeutic dose carryover, toxicity of the potential contaminant, concentration of the contaminant in rinse and swab samples, removal of cleaning agents, limit of detection of the analytical test method, and identification of critical areas (hardest to clean).

The approach for setting acceptance limits can be product-specific cleaning validation for all products; grouping into product families and choosing a worst-case product; grouping by properties (for example, solubility, potency, toxicity or formulation ingredients known to be difficult to clean); setting limits on not allowing more than a certain fraction of carryover; and different safety factors for different dosage forms.

Carryover of product residues should meet defined criteria, for example, the most stringent of criteria:

- No more than (NMT) 0.1% of the normal therapeutic dose of any product is to appear in the maximum daily dose of the following product.

- NMT 10 ppm of any product is to appear in another product.

- No quantity of residue may be visible on the equipment after cleaning procedures are performed. Spiking studies should determine the concentration at which most active ingredients are visible.

- For certain highly sensitizing or highly potent ingredients (such as penicillins, cephalosporins, or potent steroids and cytotoxics), the limits should be below the limit of detection by the best available analytical methods. In practice, it may mean that dedicated plants are used for these products.

If levels of contamination or residuals are not detected, it does not mean that no residual contaminant is present after cleaning. It only means that the levels of contaminant greater than the sensitivity or detection limit of the analytical method are not present in the sample.

Documentation

Required documentation for cleaning validation includes detailed cleaning procedure(s) documented in *standard operating procedures* (SOPs), and a cleaning validation protocol defining how the cleaning process will be validated. The protocol should include the objective of the validation process; responsibilities for performing and approving the validation study; description of the equipment to be used; the interval between the end of production and the beginning of the cleaning procedure; the number of lots of the same product that could be manufactured during a campaign before a full cleaning is done; detailed cleaning procedures to be used for each product, each manufacturing system, or each piece of equipment; the number of cleaning cycles to be performed consecutively; and any routine monitoring requirement. Other information in the cleaning protocol includes sampling procedures, including the rationale for why a certain sampling method is used; clearly defined sampling locations; data on recovery studies, where appropriate; validated analytical methods, including the limit of detection and the limit of quantitation of those methods; the acceptance criteria, including the rationale for setting the specific limits; other products, processes, and equipment for which the planned validation is valid according to a bracketing concept; change control and revalidation; and approval by management

Manual cleaning procedures are inherently variable. Operators should be trained, monitored, qualified, and periodically assessed on the effectiveness of performing cleaning operations. Manual cleaning methods should be reassessed at more frequent intervals than CIP systems. Cleaning processes should be reassessed at defined intervals, and revalidated as necessary. As a general rule, if cleaning validation has not been performed, equipment should be dedicated to prevent cross-contamination.

Equipment Cleaning

Equipment and utensils should be cleaned, stored, and, where appropriate, sanitized or sterilized to prevent contamination or carryover of a material that would alter the quality of the intermediate or API beyond the official or other established specifications.

Cleaning GMP require that procedures contain sufficient details to enable operators to clean each type of equipment in a reproducible and effective manner. Cleaning procedures must strictly follow carefully established and validated methods. These procedures should include:

- Personnel responsible for carrying out cleaning procedures

- Requirement to identify equipment with contents and cleanliness status

- Intervals for cleaning/sanitizing, including the maximum time that may elapse between the completion of processing and equipment cleaning (dirty hold time), when appropriate

- Instructions for the removal or obliteration of previous batch identification

- When appropriate, instructions for disassembling and reassembling equipment to ensure proper cleaning

- Complete description of agents, materials, and equipment/apparatus to use for cleaning and disinfection, including dilution of cleaning agents used to clean equipment

- Disposal procedures for waste material and debris

- Instructions for storing equipment in clean and dry conditions

- Instructions for the protection of clean equipment from contamination before use

- Inspection of equipment for cleanliness immediately before use

Maintenance

Elements of a maintenance program should include a way to identify equipment with a distinctive name, number, or code. The equipment must be maintained in a good state of repair when in use, and where a potential for the contamination of the drug being fabricated or packaged exists, surfaces must be free from cracks, peeling paint, and other defects. Gaskets must be verified as functional, and the use of temporary devices such as tape is avoided. Equipment parts that come in contact with drugs must be maintained in such a manner that drugs are fabricated or packaged within specifications. Finally, records of maintenance documenting the performance of these activities must be kept.

Schedules and procedures (including assignment of responsibility) should be established for the preventive maintenance of equipment. Defective equipment should, if possible, be removed from production and quality control areas, or at least be clearly labeled as defective. For equipment not requiring maintenance, the firm must be able to support its decision to not include the equipment in the maintenance program.

Equipment Change Control

A change control system should be in place to ensure that impact to cleaning processes or function is assessed, documented, and approved. Methods for verifying that a change control system is defined and implemented should include a way to verify that a documented procedure is in place. The procedure should require that changes are properly documented, evaluated, and approved by the quality function. The implementation/effective date of the change should be identified. Significant changes are assessed to determine if revalidation is necessary. A review of nonroutine maintenance, calibration, or nonconformance records can be used to determine whether changes to equipment have been made using appropriate change controls. Examples of changes that require evaluation and may require revalidation include:

- Changes to the cleaning procedure

- Changes in raw material sources

- Changes to product formulation

- Changes to the production process

- Introduction of new products, new cleaning agents or detergents, or changes to cleaning agents or detergents

- Modifications to equipment

Chapter 31

Qualification and Validation

INTRODUCTION

In the pharmaceutical environment, qualification and validation are required for any *good manufacturing practices* (GMP) facility, utility, equipment, or process. The intent of qualification and validation activities is to provide documented evidence that the facility, utilities (for example, water, gases, air), and processes are designed and operate in accordance with GMP requirements. An infinite amount of detail can be provided in each phase of the validation life cycle. Regulations are vague when determining specific requirements for what constitutes a qualification or validation document. Industry standards have provided content and activities of the qualification and validation documentation.

To ensure that the facility, utilities, and equipment have been designed, built, and installed properly, and operate as intended, proper qualification and validation activities must occur. The foundation of a successful qualification and validation program begins with design. During the design phase, the specifications, requirements, and critical aspects are developed and documented. *Specifications* are prescribing attributes that are required to provide a quality of work for something to be built, installed, or manufactured. *Requirements* are detailed necessities for the item being built, installed, or manufactured. Requirements can be defined as *user* requirements or as *functional* requirements. *Critical aspects* are specification and design requirements that focus on those attributes that are critical to product quality and patient safety, and these aspects may be outlined within the specification and requirements documents. Another document that is required to outline and plan the requirements for the life cycle process is a *validation master plan* (VMP).

The VMP document or a suitable equivalent defines the overall structure, philosophy and approach of the phases of the validation life cycle. The VMP should define the structure and required documentation for design, qualification, and validation activities, to include prerequisites, and stage-gate requirements to move on to the next phase in the validation life cycle. The VMP should detail key criteria within each stage and phase, and other qualification and validation requirements and considerations, including lists of products, processes, and systems to be validated, documentation format, required *standard operating procedures* (SOPs), and planning and scheduling.

The facility, utilities, and equipment should be designed to predetermined requirements and specifications. The critical aspects are used to create and document the design requirements and specifications. The design is documented through *design qualification* (DQ).

DESIGN QUALIFICATION

DQ should establish and provide evidence that the equipment is designed in accordance with the requirements of GMP. DQ is a formal document that requires *quality assurance* (QA) oversight. This document uses critical aspects from approved requirements (user and functional requirements) and other approved specifications as the source documents. Typical items that may be found in the scope of a DQ document include verification that:

- The design will achieve the user requirements
- The design is GMP and will conform to applicable national standards and guidelines
- The utility services are appropriate and are qualified or will be qualified
- All the required support documentation is specified
- The system will be able to be calibrated
- The system will be able to be maintained
- Personnel training requirements will be met

At the completion of the design phase, the project moves to the next phase—the commissioning and installation phase.

COMMISSIONING AND QUALIFICATION

Once the facility, utility, or equipment has been designed, built, and/or installed, a commissioning program should encompass the additional testing to establish a qualified state, which can be performed through *factory acceptance testing* (FAT), testing that is performed at the vendor's factory before shipping the equipment. This task is important, as equipment that does not meet the requirements of design should not be shipped to the manufacturing facility until it does meet the necessary specifications and requirements. Once the equipment or system is at the manufacturing site and its final destination, as part of a commissioning, a *site acceptance testing* (SAT) exercise may be conducted. These activities as part of commissioning are prerequisites to site qualification exercises.

The commissioning program should encompass as much testing as possible to include, but not be limited to, testing the vendor or manufacturer's functional and operational requirements, the design requirements and other aspects that are critical to quality, business continuity, and safety. This testing ensures that the systems and equipment are challenged to test the full functionality and operational ability in a noncommercial environment to avoid any potential impact to GMP equipment, areas, and/or product. Qualification activities may be introduced in the commissioning program as long as the program is well documented and QA oversight exists. The commissioning program requires *good documentation practices* (GDP) and *good engineering practices* (GEP) to ensure that the testing activities that are conducted are properly documented and can be used for qualification activities.

Many regulatory guidance documents, such as European Union (EU) Annex 15, United States Food and Drug Administration (FDA) process validation guidance (*Process Validation: General Principles and Practices*), and Pharmaceutical Inspection Convention and the Pharmaceutical Inspection Co-operation Scheme (PIC/S) P006-3, require and discuss the elements of *installation qualification* (IQ) and *operational qualification* (OQ). Some additional publications in the last few years include installation and operational qualifications. ASTM E2500-7 *Standard Guide for Specification, Design, and Verification of Pharmaceutical and Biopharmaceutical Manufacturing Systems and Equipment* introduced concepts of streamlining the traditional IQ and OQ program to eliminate some of the formal documentation requirements and QA oversight that are typically required for formal validation programs. The ASTM E2500 standard proposes the concept of verification, where traditional qualification activities are conducted as verification exercises. The QA oversight is acceptable during the development and approval of requirements, specifications, and critical aspects. The commissioning and verification test requirements and acceptance criteria are defined in a verification plan. QA is not involved at the implementation level of protocol writing and test plan execution as long as the approved verification plan has not been deviated from. Although new standards and publications exist with the intent of providing guidance on performing and documenting commissioning, qualification, and/or verification activities, the relevant intent of installation and operational qualification is that the facility, utility, and equipment/systems are designed properly, installed properly, and operate as intended by design and as per GMP requirements.

It is a requirement of the regulatory guidance documents and GMP that the documentation provided by each pharmaceutical company proves a state of control in that the "drug meets the requirements of the Act as to safety, and has the identity and strength and meets the quality and purity characteristics that it purports or is represented to possess." The commissioning and qualification program must have adequate QA governance.

INSTALLATION QUALIFICATION

Elements of the traditional IQ may be incorporated into the commissioning program. The regulatory guidance documents such as EU Annex 15 and FDA process validation guidance require IQ and OQ. Although the installation verification may have occurred during the commissioning stage, the regulatory expectation is that an IQ protocol and report documents that the facility, utilities, and/or equipment were installed properly. The intent of commissioning and/or the IQ is to verify that the facility, utilities, and/or equipment are installed properly. The IQ program includes, but is not limited to:

- Verification of components and parts

- Identification and verification of serial numbers and model numbers

- Identification and documentation of software versions and correct level of installation

- Verification of calibration

- Verification that installation is as specified per appropriate drawings and specifications (including sloping, dimensions, and so on)

- Verification that support utilities conform with national standards and other guidance documents

OPERATIONAL QUALIFICATION

OQ is the documented evidence that the system operates as designed and for its intended use. Commissioning activities can include operational testing, which should include the full range of parameters for which the equipment was designed. The OQ testing may be reduced if the full testing was conducted in commissioning, and may include only challenging the ranges or parameters of the intended use of the system. The OQ program includes, but is not limited to:

- Verification of integrated loop testing

- Testing of alarms

- Testing of interlocks and permissive conditions

- Testing of data storage integrity

- Verification of the functionality of the equipment

- Testing of security levels to prevent unauthorized access or changes

- Testing to verify and document power loss recovery

- Verification of procedures (operation, preventive maintenance, and calibration)

- Challenge of the system by stressing the equipment or system to the edge of failure to determine proven acceptable ranges

Once the equipment is qualified, the equipment can be released for *performance qualification* (PQ) and commercial manufacturing. The facility, utility, and equipment will be under a formal change control system and GMP environment. The OQ must be successfully completed before beginning PQ.

PERFORMANCE QUALIFICATION

PQ ensures that the equipment or integrated systems function under normal operating conditions to confirm that the equipment/system functions as intended. During the PQ phase, systems, processes, and utilities are challenged at nominal operating characteristics. This process includes studies that ensure the system properly functions under various conditions, such as evaluating seasonal changes for the water system, evaluating a circuit or piping/equipment configuration for steam in-place validation, or evaluating load patterns for sterilization in autoclaves. The PQ program includes at least three consecutive successful runs or qualifications within the study. The definition of a run or qualification can be designated and predetermined by a description and definition of the run or qualification in the protocol or VMP.

The PQ program is a confirmatory exercise of verification of predefined critical aspects and critical quality attributes. Elements traditionally in a PQ include, but are not limited to:

- Definition of performance criteria and test procedures

- Identification of critical control parameters, critical quality attributes, and key process parameters (for example, predefined specifications and acceptance criteria)

- Determination of the sample size and test intervals (including the rationale to support these requirements)

- Definition of corrective actions if the system does not meet the established criteria

Upon completion and successful verification of PQ, validation of the commercial manufacturing process may begin. The PQ may not be entirely completed but may be released for commercial manufacturing or process validation activities. Stage II PQ for utilities may not be completed (due to required seasonal testing); however, stage I of utility PQ must be completed. The system has demonstrated the required performance characteristics at the end of stage I.

PROCESS VALIDATION

The traditional term *process validation* under the FDA process validation guidance document covers all elements of the validation life cycle (Figure 31.1). The FDA

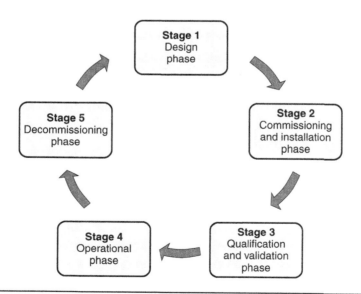

Figure 31.1   Validation life cycle.

Source: Figure courtesy of the ASQ Food, Drug, and Cosmetic Division. Used with permission.

document refers to that activity as a *process performance qualification* (PPQ). For the purposes of this chapter, the term "process validation" will be retained as its traditional activity where the verification of the manufacturing process is completed.

Cleaning validation may be conducted during the PQ phase or the traditional process validation phase in parallel with the manufacturing of the validation batches. The details of the philosophy and approach for process and validation activities must be detailed in the site's VMP. Validated laboratory test methods are required for the execution of process and cleaning validation studies.

After successful completion of the process validation batch campaign, the next stage in the validation life cycle approach is *operational phase* or continuous monitoring/sustaining of operations, also termed *continued process verification*. During routine manufacturing, continuous monitoring of the critical quality attributes provides a continuous loop of information. The continuous monitoring aspect of the validation life cycle creates a feedback mechanism that is used to improve the process. Any proposed changes to improve the process must be formally documented in the change control system. Information gained during the continuous monitoring program is feedback into various systems, including updating and improving calibration and preventive maintenance systems.

VALIDATION LIFE CYCLE

Validation is a prospective and confirmatory exercise. The difference between *qualification* and *validation* is that equipment is individually qualified, and the system or process is validated. The intent of validation activities, including PQ and process validations, is to confirm the knowledge gained during design, development, installation, and challenge exercises, and as a confirmatory exercise of a process that is already known and in control. A few types of validation are discussed in some regulatory guidance documents, which include prospective, retrospective, and concurrent. The chapter has discussed and outlined *prospective validation*. Prospective validation is the most preferable and defendable nature of validation. This type of validation aligns with the validation life cycle approach and provides the most confidence in the documentation generated that the drug is produced as required by GMP.

Retrospective validation is a look-back approach to validation and an attempt to justify legacy systems based on a retrospective gathering of documentation. Retrospective validation is not normally considered acceptable. There is an expectation of understanding and documenting processes, including the site's legacy processes and equipment. Retrospective validation is difficult to document as the data gathered must be statistically based and analyzed.

Concurrent validation occurs when manufactured batches are released one lot at a time before the completion of the three or designated number of batches for the process validation campaign, and should only be used when drugs are medically necessary and an approved plan that outlines the nature of concurrent release is approved by required regulatory agencies.

Qualification and validation are regulatory guided programs for GMP pharmaceutical companies. Although these programs are mandated by various regulatory bodies, the intent of a robust qualification and validation program is to ensure that facilities, utilities, equipment, systems, and processes are designed with the end in mind. Requirements are tested and verified to predetermined specifications, and there is verification that the facilities, utilities, or equipment are installed and operate properly. These programs provide documented evidence that what was purchased meets expectations and produces a drug product that meets the requirements of 21 CFR 210.1.

Chapter 32

Maintenance and Metrology Systems

All instruments that control manufacturing facilities, utilities, and equipment must be maintained to ensure they are functioning as intended. Instrumentation should be uniquely numbered so it can be easily identified during calibration, maintenance, commissioning, and validation. Each instrument should have appropriate unique identification labeling permanently affixed; if the item is too small, the container that holds the device can be appropriately labeled. Associated documentation will link this unique identification to the instrument type, model, and serial number. Documentation includes when an instrument was put into service, its intended range of use, and when it was retired.

Based on the instrument category, *installation qualification* (IQ), *operational qualification* (OQ), and *performance qualification* (PQ) may be required when a new instrument, facility, utility, or equipment is introduced or replaced, or if instrumentation is moved from one location to another. A protocol should be written to define the purpose/objective, test procedures to be followed, parameters to be evaluated, and the criteria to demonstrate acceptability.

The IQ is conducted to ensure that the instrument and software, if applicable, were installed in the proper environment and manner as intended by the manufacturer. The OQ is conducted to ensure that the instrument and software, if applicable, operate as designed and generate accurate data. The PQ is conducted to ensure that the instrument and software, if applicable, meet the end user specific requirements and function as intended in the production environment. A report is generated to summarize the test results for the qualifications and any deviations. Upon completion of the qualification, the instrument can be put into service.

Facilities, utilities, or equipment used in the *good manufacturing practices* (GMP) environment will require routine maintenance and calibrations. The maintenance and calibration schedules can be established based on severity of environment, severity of use, frequency of use, durability of instrument, accuracy of measurement required, precision of measurement required, and history of maintenance and calibration. Each type of instrumentation should have a procedure that specifies its operation, maintenance, and calibration. The procedure must specify what activity should be conducted, what the acceptance criterion is, and the frequency. A logbook or software program may be used to track the usage, repair, and calibration. All maintenance and calibration information, which includes standards used, must be documented. When an instrument requires repair or calibration, it should be flagged as *out of service* (OOS) in some manner, such as with an "Out of Service" sticker. If an instrument fails the calibration, an impact assessment must be performed. During the impact assessment, all data generated since the last successful calibration must be evaluated. Upon completion of the repair or calibration, the OOS indicator is removed and the instrument is placed back into service. If the instrument was being calibrated, a new calibration sticker, which designates the next calibration due date, is applied.

Chapter 33

Cleaning, Sanitization, and Pest Control

WASHING FACILITIES AND CLEANING PROCEDURES

"Washing and cleaning equipment should be chosen and used in order not to be a source of contamination." This statement is a fundamental starting point for any discussion of *good manufacturing practices* (GMP) equipment and parts cleaning. In a pharmaceutical manufacturing environment, rooms and areas are classified based on the risk to the product. Four grades (A, B, C, and D) or classifications (ISO 100 to 100,000) of areas allow various levels of particulates or microbial challenges. These areas extend from cleanest (grade A) to less stringent requirements (grade D).

Sponges and mops used in grades A or B must be of material and design to minimize shedding of particles. Large and small GMP equipment and parts amenable to *clean out of place* (COP) must have facilities or a set of suites equipped with the necessary utilities (for example, water meeting World Health Organization [WHO] drinking water standards, purified water, and possibly water for injection [WFI]). Take-offs and/or hoses from the purified water and WFI loops must have mechanisms (for example, backflow preventers/check valves) or procedures that prevent back-siphonage of cleaning solutions or detergents. Flow of equipment and/or cleaning facility layout must preclude dirty equipment and parts from contaminating or mixing with clean equipment and parts. Annex 1 of the European Union (EU) GMP guidelines section on premises prohibits sinks and drains in grade A or B areas. Therefore, equipment and parts cleaning may not occur in these aseptic core suites. If equipment and parts cleaning suites exist within grade C or D areas, any floor drains should be fitted with traps or water seals to prevent backflow. Sink drains, glassware or equipment washer drains, and autoclave drains must have air breaks between the machine or sink and the drains.

GMP equipment and parts cleaning must be proceduralized to ensure consistency over time and from operator to operator. Pharmaceutical product and *active pharmaceutical ingredients* (APIs) can be contaminated by other pharmaceutical products or APIs, by cleaning agents, by microorganisms, or by other material (for example, airborne particles, dust, lubricants, raw materials, intermediates, auxiliaries). The cleaning process must be qualified and/or validated to demonstrate repeatability and robustness of the cleaning procedure and process. Whenever possible, the cleaning process should be automated to ensure repeatability. In cases where automation is not feasible, very strict requirements must be placed on manual cleaning methods to ensure consistency. These restrictions include identifying and controlling critical control parameters such as cleaning agent concentration, soak and/or scrub time, rinse time, temperature and volume of water, scrubbing parameters, and rinsing parameters.

Dependent on the nature of the product, process soil, and/or active ingredient, cleaning procedures may require cleaning agents and/or sanitizers. Typically, cleaning procedures and cleaning validation studies to confirm the cleaning procedure include only product-contact surface areas. Full understanding of the manufacturing process and equipment train must be attained to determine whether there are other areas in the process or equipment that are not direct product-contact surfaces that may be a source of contamination.

The intent of the cleaning validation program is to provide documented evidence of a robust and repeatable cleaning process that removes contaminates to predetermined acceptable levels. A robust cleaning validation program is established through the development and approval of a *cleaning validation master plan* (CVMP). The CVMP establishes the philosophy and approach for the site's cleaning program. This document should include the requirements for development, confirmation, and sustainability of the cleaning program.

The CVMP establishes the acceptable residual limits that determine level of acceptability for the cleaning process. These limits should be achievable, verifiable, and based on the most toxic residue and/or the residue that has the highest risk to the product and/or process. These limits can be reflected in equations (for example, 10 ppm, *no observable effect level* [NOEL], therapeutic dose) that calculate maximum allowable carryover of residual. These limits are used during validation of the analytical methods to ensure that they are within the linear range of the method. Cleaning validation methods require full validation under International Conference on Harmonization (ICH) Q2 guidance, including limit of detection, limit of quantitation, specificity, and spike swab and coupon recovery studies. When setting acceptance limits for cleaning agents and sanitizers, the expectation is that no residual exists; ensure that the limits are appropriate. For sanitizers, residue is not acceptable on the surfaces of the equipment, and limits ensure that the cleaning procedure and analytical method can detect that the sanitizer has been removed from the product-contact surfaces.

Four elements are typical to every cleaning validation study to determine the effectiveness of a cleaning procedure and/or cycle. Each of these elements must have predetermined, defined, and approved acceptance criteria. Visual inspection is the first element and protocol test function. Once the equipment is inspected visually for any residual, the microbiological samples are collected to ensure that the surface equipment area is not contaminated by the cleaning validation sampling process. Product and process soil samples follow microbial sampling, and lastly, cleaning agent and sanitizer sampling. These sampling schemes can be adjusted based on the understanding of the cleaning process and potential product impact.

The cleaning procedure is considered robust and repeatable upon completion of three successful runs (the number of runs may be more or less dependent on the knowledge of the process), which indicate that all data met predetermined acceptance criteria, the data were reviewed, and the data were summarized in a final report and approved by the *quality unit* (QU).

To ensure that the cleaning process is sustainable, the CVMP must include requirements that the life cycle is maintained, including requirements on periodic monitoring to assess changes in acceptance criteria, changes in equipment, changes in product or process soil, and changes in the cleaning process. The CVMP outlines requirements for revalidation activities based on changes in the process, equipment, product mix, and acceptance criteria.

SANITIZATION PROCEDURES

The United States Environmental Protection Agency (EPA) licenses chemicals for which its manufacturers claim efficacy in disinfecting inanimate objects. The EPA evaluates disinfectant efficacy chiefly by either of two methods originated by the Association of Official Analytical Chemists (AOAC):

- *Use/dilution method.* An organism is dried to a rod made of glass, stainless steel, polished porcelain, or other nonreactive material. The rod is submerged for 10 minutes or other claim time in a container with the disinfectant being tested (without touching the side of the container). The rod is raised and allowed to drain. A *replication organism detection and counting* (RODAC) plate with agar and the appropriate nutrient is placed on the rod to remove organisms for testing and incubated a set time. Zero growth permits disinfectant to pass the test.

- *Spray method/ hard surface carrier test.* An organism is dried to a measured surface area of a specific material. The disinfectant product is sprayed according to manufacturer's directions, and the surface is left until sufficient contact time according to directions. The surface is scraped and applied to a RODAC plate of appropriate media, then incubated a set time. Zero growth permits disinfectant to pass the test.

Regarding the EU requirement for monitoring of disinfectant prepared at *ready-to-use* (RTU) dilution and in its final applicator bottle, unless the site has created and validated a production-like aseptic sterilizing filtration process and validated the sterility through expiration date along with validating the container closure of the application container, the full expectation by European Medicines Agency (EMA) is for monitoring of the solution over its shelf life. Alternatively, the supplier of prefilled, presterilized (aseptic filtered or terminally sterilized) vials must have had its validation data audited by the drug manufacturer, including container closure validation. This requirement holds true for liquid, gel-like, and moist pad antiseptics used in the sterile core. The latter, due to their exposure (sheets are pulled like tissues from a container), can not avoid the requirement for drug manufacturing site monitoring. The alternative, onerous requirement for monitoring entails sampling the disinfectant solution or wipe on a media containing a validated neutralizer against the bactericidal active ingredients.

LITERATURE EFFICACY OF VARIOUS SANITIZERS

Chlorhexidine has a wide spectrum of antibacterial activity against both Gram-positive and Gram-negative vegetative bacteria. A *quaternary ammonium compound* (QAC) has high antimicrobial activity (vegetative cells) if its carbon chain length is C8 to C18 (if aliphatic). These compounds, being positively charged, are also surfactants (that is, have detergent/cleaning properties to get inside crevices). Unfortunately, QAC are not mycobactericidal (for example, active against tuberculosis-causing organism) or effective against the Gram-negative bacteria *E. coli*, *P. aeruginosa*, and *S. typhimurium*. They are more active at alkaline or neutral pH than at acid pH levels.

Phenolics are effective against both Gram-positive and Gram-negative vegetative bacteria, but only slowly effective against bacterial spores. The virucidal activity of phenolics can not be generalized (that is, enveloped viruses are more susceptible than other organisms).

Glutaraldehyde (usually 2% v/v supplied alkaline but made acidic before use) possesses sporicidal activity (that is, vegetative cells), mycobacterial, and fungal spore efficacy. It is active against various types of viruses. Formaldehyde, which is a carcinogen, is widely bactericidal, sporicidal, and virucidal; it is effective against protozoa. Iodophors are surface-active agents and surfactants that can solubilize iodine to form compounds containing microbicidal activity over a wide pH range (for example, povidone-iodine solution of 10% w/v). These are sporicidal.

The most common chlorine-releasing compounds are hypochlorites and N-chloro compounds. All of these compounds are irritants and corrosive but have high antimicrobial activity, including sporicidal activity and some mycobacterial activity. These compounds are active against lipid and nonlipid viruses. Sodium hypochlorite (NaOCl) is more active at acid than at alkaline pH. Diluted RTU solutions have short shelf life and must be qualified.

Chlorine dioxide (ClO_2) is an alternative to NaOCl and retains biocidal activity over a wide pH range. Oxine is a sodium chlorite solution that, when acidified, generates chloride dioxide, giving a mixture of chlorite and chlorine dioxide; it is more efficacious against pathogenic bacteria than chloride dioxide alone, and it is virucidal.

Peroxygens include hydrogen peroxide (H_2O_2) and peracetic acid (CH_3CO_3H). H_2O_2 is used at varying strengths (35%, 50%, and 90%) and is bactericidal and a sporicide. H_2O_2 can be used as a sanitizing agent and an antiseptic. Peracetic acid is available commercially as a 15% aqueous solution (35% is potentially explosive). Peracetic acid has a broad spectrum of activity, including bacteria and their spores, molds, yeasts, algae, and viruses.

Ethylene oxide (C_2H_4O) uses its alkylating properties on proteins (used at proper concentration, temperature, and relative humidity) to act as a potent sterilant and sporicide. Ozone (O_3) is another agent that is bactericidal, virucidal, and sporicidal. Sodium hydroxide (NaOH) or lye is active against all microorganisms, including protozoa and prions.

PEST CONTROL

Any building used in the manufacturing, processing, packaging, or storage of pharmaceutical products must be free of infestation. The pest control program requires appropriate QU oversight. Procedures must describe the use of suitable rodenticides, insecticides, fungicides, or fumigating agents. Rodenticides, insecticides, fungicides, or fumigating agents should be of the appropriate grade, approved by local regulations, and approved by the drug manufacturing site QU.

Pest control records must be generated and retained, and a system must exist for the continual capture of crawling and flying pests by an entomologist or pest control expert for identification and analysis. When the latter is contracted by a manufacturing site, a quality/technical agreement must describe all the activities and responsibilities of the contract giver and the contractor. A system should be in place for the reporting/recording of pest sightings by any personnel besides the contractor.

Chapter 34

Automated or
Computerized Systems

A utomated or computerized systems are powerful business tools selected to meet business needs for such tasks as research and development, production, and maintenance. These tools can also generate and store evidence for meeting regulatory requirements. As in most industries, automated systems have fostered operational simplicity, efficiency, reliability, repeatability, and accuracy in all business areas from procurement to human resources. Automated systems can increase safety in the monitoring and control of risky processes and regulate processes through real-time feedback.

Regulatory agencies recognize that these systems, under certain conditions, are reliable tools that can provide benefits for all stakeholders. 21 CFR 211.68 and ICH Q7 (Section 5.4) both specifically address the conditions under which automation is considered acceptable. *Good automated manufacturing practices* (GAMP) 5 includes information about automation.

Automated or computerized systems, regardless of whether they are embedded in equipment or products (such as medical devices) or exist as support systems, are company assets that should be subject to all of the scrutiny and control that would be expected with any asset. The pharmaceutical professional will not necessarily be expected to know the inner workings of a computerized system, but he/she should know the characteristics of system evolution, maintenance, and regulatory compliant use.

SYSTEM LIFE CYCLE

All systems evolve through a predictable life cycle (Figure 34.1). Understanding where a system is in its life cycle is important in knowing how it got there and where it is going. The life cycle is a road map with typical characteristics. A number of phases and expectations exist that the pharmaceutical professional should expect when dealing with automated or computerized systems:

- *Identifying the need*. Will an automated or computerized system provide the best solution to the business problem?

- *Proposing solutions*. Solutions can be technical (that is, the computer system is expected to do it all, perhaps without any human intervention), procedural (that is, people will do it all by following a procedure), or, as is most common, a blend of the technical and procedural approaches where procedural steps are supported by the computer system with some human oversight.

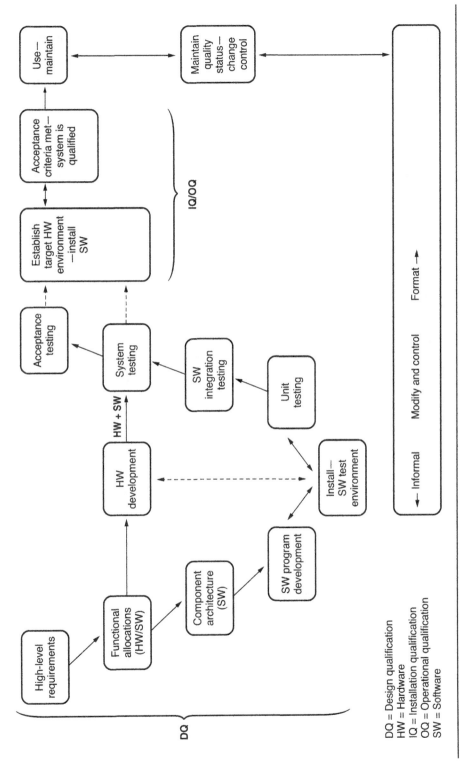

DQ = Design qualification
HW = Hardware
IQ = Installation qualification
OQ = Operational qualification
SW = Software

Figure 34.1   Automated and computerized systems are recognized to have a typical life cycle. This life cycle is often represented in a V-diagram format. The far right side of the model eventually leads to system retirement and decommissioning.

Source: Figure courtesy of the ASQ Food, Drug, and Cosmetic Division. Used. with permission.

- *Deciding how to develop the system with its business use as a major goal.* Should the effort be to build (that is, develop a specific program using in-house or vendor resources), buy (that is, use a program, usually a commercial product that will meet the need), or modify (that is, buy an existing product and customize it to meet the need)?

- *Installing the system.* Have we correctly anticipated the infrastructure and supporting systems needed? How will we replace the old system? How disruptive will it be to ongoing activities?

- *Testing and acceptance.* How much should we test and at what level of detail? Do the test results unequivocally and thoroughly demonstrate that the system can reliably meet the business needs?

- *Training.* Now that the system has been shown to be functionally appropriate, do the people who need to use it know how to use it? Will it be as useful as expected?

- *Change control.* All systems change, and the changes must be controlled. Systems constantly undergo three types of changes: corrective, perfective, and adaptive. Is there a clearly defined and thorough (that is, proceduralized and documented) methodology for guiding a system from its current state (the as-is) to its desired state (the to-be)?

- *Backup and disaster recovery.* Although hardware and software failures are becoming less frequent, they do happen. All systems bring this inherent risk. Are backup and recovery systems in place so that potential data loss is minimized? Data loss should generally be considered unacceptable, but loss of *good manufacturing practices* (GMP) data should be considered a failure to meet regulatory requirements.

- *Decommissioning.* The system will eventually become outdated, hardware and supporting systems will change, or a better way of meeting the changing business need will be found. The system may become obsolete, but the data might, for regulatory, legal, or historical reasons, need to be protected and retained. Consideration must be given to addressing the need to replace the system and maintaining (to some working degree) the old system. Not all information and processes can be easily transferred to a new system. Not all new systems can handle existing data formats and processes.

- *Records.* Keeping documented evidence is a regulatory must, and good business practice, but it is not practical to keep everything. Legal considerations, as well as direction from regulatory agencies, should guide what records are kept and for how long.

VALIDATION AND QUALIFICATION

Two important terms associated with but not exclusive to automated systems need to be understood: validation and qualification. In essence, these activities both meet the need for proving that a system is reliable and does what it claims to do, before and during its use, in its intended environment. *Validation* comprises identifying all aspects of testing that need to be completed before a product or process can be deployed for business use. It is common to write a *validation master plan* (VMP) to document the intent, scope, resources, schedules, activities, documentation, test types, and acceptance criteria required to achieve a validated state. Validation plans may address training and methods of change control to be used to maintain a validated state. Software and components will change, but the essential business goals regarding safety, quality, and regulatory compliance must always be met. The VMP provides guidance in achieving and maintaining qualified facilities and validated processes.

Qualification contributes to determining when a system is reliable and stable enough to support validated processes. Typical qualification phases include:

- *Design qualification* (DQ) is conducted to assure that the system is designed to do what is intended. This phase consists of documenting such topics as user requirements (functional and operational specifications) and includes identifying *critical components*, which are those features that directly impact product and process characteristics such as safety and quality. Critical components can include power supplies, equipment safety features, temperatures, pressures, weights, and alarm features. These features are implemented design features that must remain in control for the process to act predictably. In systems of great complexity where not every possible logic avenue can be practically checked, or every combination of events predicted, designing the system such that critical components or parameters are easily tested and monitored is crucial. If everything can not be tested, at least test what is critical to the safety and quality of the process or product. The design should facilitate this goal.

- *Installation qualification* (IQ) comprises activities for ensuring that the system is installed safely and that it will function in the environment in which it is intended. IQ, relative to automated systems, includes establishing a complete inventory of components (that is, model numbers, serial numbers, locations, part numbers, revision numbers), making sure that the components are correctly installed (that is, reliable power, correct wiring, proper grounding, working interfaces), making sure that installations are in compliance with vendor recommendations, and doing nominal checks to make sure that information is flowing through the system as expected in the design specifications.

- *Operational qualification* (OQ) proves that the design, its implementation, and supporting components will operate reliably together in a way that will meet the business need. OQ tests the system as it is intended to be used.

- *Component qualification* (CQ) (manufacturing to the correct design criteria) and *performance qualification* (PQ) (consistent performance over time) are other qualification types that are sometimes needed on a specific project. DQ, IQ, and OQ are commonly used for software-intensive systems. IQ, OQ, and PQ are commonly used for equipment. The series DQ, IQ, OQ, PQ might be used for a system that includes both software and equipment. Qualification expectations and acceptance should be documented in a plan.

Addressing these needs will lead a system to be validated (it does or can do what it claims to do) or qualified (it does what, in a business sense, it is needed or expected to do). If a system has been validated and it needs to change, documented evidence must be produced that confirms that the system still performs as effectively as it did when it was originally validated, in spite of the modification.

REGULATORY REFERENCES

Pertinent regulatory references include 21 CFR 211.68, "Automated System Requirements," and ICH Q7, GMP for API. Numerous references can be found concerning written records. 21 CFR 11 does set rules for providing written records in electronic form. In the past, record keeping relied on human observation and interpretation to supply information about which decisions would be made. The constantly improving capabilities, efficiency, and reliability of automated and computerized systems has allowed many industries, including the pharmaceutical industry, to confidently move from paper records (that were subject to human error) to electronic records (that provide greater technical accuracy).

The current regulations are clear and specific concerning what written records the United States Food and Drug Administration (FDA) needs from pharmaceutical manufacturers. In an effort to take advantage of technological improvements, provide improved consistency, and reduce paperwork, industry leaders asked FDA to set standards by which electronic records and signatures would be acceptable in meeting government regulations for written records. Federal regulations, designated 21 CFR 11, were formulated in response to this request and became law in March 1997. The discussion of electronic records is covered in the section addressing closed and open systems. Electronic signatures are acceptable in meeting regulatory needs if the signatures have the specific characteristics cited in 21 CFR 11.

OPEN AND CLOSED SYSTEMS

A few definitions exist for what constitutes open and closed computerized systems, but both systems are centered on who has access to the system and who controls the content. *Open* and *closed* refer to who has jurisdiction over the code (as in open source or closed source systems). Commercial products (commercial off-the-shelf [COTS] software) are usually written with proprietary restrictions and are closed systems; the user can not alter the basic code (or should not, as it will invalidate the warranty and infringe on copyrights). If, however, a computer system is developed in-house (or perhaps through a vendor), the pharmaceutical company will want access to the code so that modifications can be made. When purchasing a custom-developed product from a vendor (also known as a *bespoke system*), it is important to make sure that the agreement ensures that the purchaser will be the recipient of the code. Open systems can become closed systems if the correct restrictions are imposed.

In the pharmaceutical world, open and closed systems are distinctly defined when it comes to using electronic records and electronic signatures to meet regulatory needs. 21 CFR 11, "Electronic Records; Electronic Signatures," provides definitions for closed and open systems. Closed systems are usually local, proprietary workplace type systems that handle unique business needs. These can be systems (that is, automated systems) that operate specific equipment or are timekeeping systems, data gathering systems, or monitoring systems. This information is important to the business and is protected from the outside world. The Internet is an open system; few restrictions are placed on access, and very little checking is done to ensure the integrity (or veracity) of the electronic records. Open systems are public-access systems. Thus, in general, closed and open systems are at opposite ends of the spectrum. Closed systems usually require the user to be granted specific access to the system (usually after some type of background check) and often require a unique log-in and password. Closed systems are strictly controlled. Open systems are for public use. If, in the pharmaceutical industry, a company would like to keep and submit electronic records to meet regulatory needs, a closed system is suggested.

CHANGE MANAGEMENT

All systems change, and pharmaceutical professionals should be familiar with the characteristics of proper change management. Regulatory agencies refer to systems as being either *in control* or *out of control*. Keeping a system in control can be tedious and painstaking, but allowing a system to drift out of control can be fatal to a business. Systems that are prone to unauthorized and uncontrolled modification are a huge risk from both safety and regulatory views. Simply put, once a system is proven to produce an acceptable product, any change to the system is presumed to change the product. Based on that concept, any modification to a system is assumed to produce a modified (that is, adulterated) product. It is crucial that any change to an automated or computerized system be accurately proposed, and reviewed for its potential impact on the product. Various methods can keep a system, and by extension the product, in control. The way that a system is kept in control is through *change management*. Change management has two elements: change control and configuration management.

Change control is the methodology that defines and reviews changes. Change control evolves during a system's life cycle as the system evolves from the conceptual to productive phases. Basically, change control should not be too restrictive during the development phase, and should be rigorous during the deployment phase. The closer a system gets to the product, the more change control account-ability must be demanded. It is acceptable for a developer to try things in the labo-ratory and to debug an evolving system to make it function, but it is not acceptable to adopt that philosophy in a system that is producing drugs for marketing. A change control methodology should, at a minimum, document:

- *Who.* Who needs the change? If the change is needed because of a malfunction, who witnessed or found the malfunction? Stakeholders, technical reviewers, approvers, task assignees, customers/patients, *quality assurance* (QA), and so on, are involved with this category.

- *What.* Describe the issues, problems, and enhancements, and what tasks need to be completed to resolve them. What items need to be modified to maintain control? What has been done?

- *When.* When did this impact the process/product, and when does it need to be fixed? If this issue has been ongoing, when did it begin, and how much product was produced during this time? In this situation, follow-up investigations are needed to determine how much product may have been affected.

- *Where.* What physical locations need to change? Is it a local problem, or does this have regional or global impact? If it is a functional change, where else is this function used?

- *How.* How does this impact the system/process/product? To what degree (that is, how severely), and how are the issues resolved?

- *Why.* Why does this affect the process or product? Why did it occur (that is, cause analysis)?

Configuration management is a discipline that can be thought of as software accounting. *Configuration management* collects and provides information about software characteristics over time and provides for protection of entities in terms of backups, vaulting, and archiving. Critical configuration management informa-tion includes:

- *Identification.* Configuration item identifiers (for example, part numbers, revisions) must be unique, and their characteristics clearly must be defined. The methods used to maintain the unique identification are referred to as *version control.* The goal is to ensure that a version comprises a unique set of characteristics. If modifications are made to version 3, it is no longer version 3; it needs another unique identifier (based on the chosen version control scheme).

- *Control.* Controlled configuration items must be beyond compromise either physically or electronically, and this goal can be accomplished by physical vaulting (for example, safes, limited access rooms) or by establishing electronic storage areas with limited access. Typically, electronic storage is divided into working and controlled areas. A controlled check-out/check-in scheme is recommended. Configuration items must be retrievable. Off-site storage for physical items is fine and recommended in potentially dangerous situations, but, if needed to restore functionality, the items must be quickly retrievable.

- *Authorization.* Use must be authorized and clearly scoped. Configuration management programs must have rules to ensure authorized deployment of items, which is usually done by requiring signatures of stakeholders such as managers and QA. The deployments should be strictly defined so that it is known where everything is and when its use began and ended.

- *Accountability.* When and where do we use it, and how long do we need to keep it? Configuration management should be able to answer questions such as "What versions were we running on this piece of equipment three years ago?" In addition, configuration management should maintain an inventory in compliance with company record retention requirements. When items are no longer needed, they should be properly discarded.

TESTING CHANGES

When considering testing needed relative to modifications made to a computerized system, it is helpful to categorize the type of software and what the appropriate level of testing should be. Testing at some level must be conducted to ensure that the system does what it is intended to do (that is, that it is in control). This process is referred to as maintaining the *validated state*. A system that has been formally tested and accepted for use should maintain that original level of reliable functionality even as it undergoes change. In this regard it is useful to be familiar with the GAMP classifications for software types and their associated validation expectations (Table 34.1).

The characteristics mentioned in regulatory requirements as being important to ensuring that automated systems are in control include access control, data protection, change control, data backup and protection, and audit trail.

Two major aspects of access control are physical and logical access. *Physical access* is meant to limit personnel from restricted areas (that is, doors, locks, signs). Physical restrictions comprise legitimacy checks and should include training considerations (that is, should people who do not know how to properly use the equipment be allowed access). *Logical access* refers to the restrictions placed on computerized systems usually in the form of identifiers, passwords, biometric restrictors, tokens, and so on. Identification restrictions apply, such as having employees have a unique personnel identifier, and password rules such as not sharing passwords and changing passwords on a regular basis. Biometric methods such as fingerprint and retinal scanners might be used. Logical controls are used to limit access to system functionality and to data, and to restrict system modification.

Table 34.1   GAMP classifications for software types, and associated validation expectations.

GAMP class	Category	Validation action
1	Operating systems	Record version
2	Instruments and controllers	Record configuration and calibration
3	Configurable packages	Audit supplier, validate any bespoke code. Apply full life cycle requirements.
4	Systems where the codes, or part of the code, are configurable	Audit supplier and code, validate that any bespoke configurations apply full life cycle requirements
5	Systems using custom or bespoke code that develop predicate rules information	Audit supplier, validate all code, and apply full life cycle requirements

In general, data protection refers a system's ability to do a number things (that is, gather, process, and transfer data accurately, maintain data integrity across interfaces, protect data such that it is beyond compromise or unauthorized modification, and retrieve data accurately). Data that can be modified should be subject to audit trails, and the audit trails must travel with the data (the data and their metadata must be linked). Importantly, data that are of regulatory interest and are kept electronically must be able to survive technological changes. It might not be useful to have batch records stored on floppy disks as not all systems are capable of handling that type of physical input. Data protection includes being able to recover data quickly regardless of its media or format. In a simple form, data protection can refer to adhering to proper environmental conditions when storing media.

Backups are created as duplicate files (direct copies of files) kept in case of system failures or other disasters. Using backups to recover files and data is referred to as *restoration. Archiving* is a technique of moving data that are no longer actively used to a separate data storage device (or media) for long-term retention. Off-site storage of archived data is common. Data archives comprise older data that might be important and necessary for future reference. Archives may contain data that would be kept for regulatory compliance or needed to support business continuity. Again, these data must be retrievable, regardless of their format.

A system has four major components—hardware, software, documentation, and personnel—and four aspects of system maintenance. Change control (for software and documentation) and training (for personnel) are important aspects of maintenance in general, but hardware has some special considerations. Of these four categories, hardware is the most prone to physical erosion. Hardware must be maintained and calibrated to make certain that it functions as expected. *Calibration* is the act of periodically checking, setting, or otherwise adjusting a device to a specified operational level. Suffice to say that instruments, devices, and other hardware components used in automated systems must be calibrated.

Maintenance can be thought of as three types—*reactive* (fix it when it breaks or degrades), *preventive* (change the part, usually on a periodic basis, before it breaks or degrades), or *predictive* (monitor the part and change it when it begins to show out-of-trend behavior).

An audit trail in terms of automated or computerized systems is an electronic accounting of who has accessed a system, when it was accessed, and what changes have been made. The audit trail often exists as a separate file but must be capable of being linked to the file that it describes. The integrity of the audit trail must be maintained as strictly as an actual system file. Keeping an accurate audit trail is an important feature of Part 11 compliance.

Periodic system monitoring may refer to many aspects of the system or the system life cycle. It can broadly refer to access monitoring (that is, who is using the system), resource monitoring (that is, how effectively is electronic traffic handled during use), assessing the state of the system (that is, are instruments properly calibrated), or checking the integrity of the system (that is, have changes had negative impact on the process or the products produced by the process). Relative to change control, periodic reviews are recommended when a system has undergone a number of changes over time. Each change may have maintained the integrity of the system, but unintended interactions between the changes may affect the overall operation of the system. In this case, a revalidation, rerunning the protocols (or portions thereof), would be used to confirm that the system remains in the validated state. Periodic reviews of unchanged operating procedures are common.

Chapter 35

Societal Security—Business Continuity Management Systems

AN OVERVIEW OF ISO 22301:2012

ISO 22301 specifies requirements to plan, establish, implement, operate, monitor, review, maintain, and continually improve a documented management system to prepare for, respond to, and recover from disruptive events when they arise. Natural disasters, environmental accidents, technology mishaps, and man-made crises have demonstrated that severe incidents can and will happen, impacting the public and private sectors alike. The challenge goes beyond providing an emergency response plan or using disaster management strategies that were previously used.

ISO 22301:2012 *Societal security—Business continuity management systems—Requirements* is the world's first international *business continuity management standard* (BCMS). It was developed by ISO Technical Committee 223. ISO published this standard on June 15, 2012. It cancels and replaces the old BS 25999 business continuity standard, which is obsolete and has been officially withdrawn.

The purpose of ISO 22301:2012 is to show individuals how to set up and manage a BCMS. These requirements can be found in seven sections within the standard (Table 35.1). The requirements specified in ISO 22301:2012 are generic and intended to be applicable to all organizations (or parts thereof), regardless of type,

Table 35.1 ISO 22301:2012 requirements for setting up and managing a business continuity management system.

Clause	Topic
4	Context of the organization
5	Leadership
6	Planning
7	Support
8	Operation
9	Performance evaluation
10	Improvement

size, and nature of the organization. The extent of application of these requirements depends on the organization's operating environment and complexity.

THE PDCA APPROACH

Similarly to ISO 9001 and ISO 13485, ISO 22301 uses what is called the plan–do–check–act (PDCA) cycle, which uses this model to organize the standard:

- *Plan*. Parts 4, 5, 6, and 7 expect you to plan the establishment of your organization's BCMS

- *Do*. Part 8 expects you to establish your BCMS

- *Check*. Part 9 expects you to evaluate your BCMS

- *Act*. Part 10 expects you to improve your BCMS

BRIEF OVERVIEW OF KEY CLAUSES OF ISO 22301:2012 BUSINESS CONTINUITY STANDARD

Following the new structure of ISO Guide 83, ISO 22301 is organized into seven main clauses (Table 35.1), and the key activities for each clause are summarized.

Clause 4: Context of the Organization

Understand your organization, its purpose, and objectives context while understanding the needs and expectations of interested parties in light of legal and regulatory requirements. Organizations should consider how disruptive incidents could impact the organization.

Clause 5: Leadership

Provide leadership and support for your organization and ensure that managers demonstrate their commitment and support and encourage employee involvement. Allocate responsibility and authority for carrying out business continuity roles to the appropriate people within your organization.

Clause 6: Planning

Identify and determine the risks and opportunities that could influence the effectiveness of your organization or disrupt its operation. Define actions and prepare plans to address the risks and opportunities that could influence the effectiveness of your organization or disrupt its operation.

Clause 7: Support

Identify and provide the resources that your organization needs, including procedures and communication tools. Determine the competence requirements of the people under your organization's control who have an impact on its performance, and ensure that people are aware of their responsibilities.

Clause 8: Operation

Plan and develop your BCMS processes by studying potential disruptions and analyzing business risks, and set your priorities. Establish a formal process that your organization can use to evaluate and set business continuity and recovery priorities, objectives, and targets; document, implement, and maintain your priority-setting process.

Clause 9: Performance Evaluation

Determine how you will monitor and measure the performance and effectiveness of your organization. Make sure that your audit program is capable of determining whether your system conforms to requirements.

Clause 10: Improvement

Identify, react to, and evaluate nonconformities when they occur. Implement corrective actions to address causes, and review the effectiveness of your corrective actions. Continuously improve the performance, suitability, adequacy, and effectiveness of your system.

Part V

Materials Management and Supply Chain

Chapter 36

Receipt of Materials

Upon the receipt of any material, all documents associated with the shipment or delivery must be reviewed to ensure accuracy and completeness. Starting materials, both *active pharmaceutical ingredients* (APIs) and excipients should be purchased only from approved suppliers, according to the European Union (EU) *good manufacturing practices* (GMP) Section 5.26 and the World Health Organization (WHO) GMP Section 14.8.

INCOMING INSPECTION

The EU and WHO GMP have similar requirements. Each container should be inspected for at least integrity of package and seal and for correspondence between the order, the delivery note, and the supplier's labels. If a company receives material made of different supplier lot numbers, each batch must be considered separately for sampling testing and release, according to EU GMP Sections 5.27 and 5.28 and WHO GMP Sections 14.9 and 14.10. Containers should be cleaned where necessary and labeled with the prescribed label. Any damage to containers or other problem that could adversely affect the quality of the material should be recorded and reported to the *quality unit* (QU) as per WHO GMP Section 14.11. Both GMP (EU GMP Section 5.30 and WHO GMP Sections 14.14 and 17.15) further prescribe that appropriate measures should be taken to assure the identity of the contents of each container of starting material either by identity testing of each container or validation of the supplier.

The United States 21 CFR 211.80a–d includes requirements for procedures to receive materials, to store them appropriately, and to identify them. The United States Food and Drug Administration (FDA) 21 CFR 211.82a states that "Upon receipt and before acceptance, each container or grouping of containers of components, drug product containers, and closures shall be examined visually for appropriate labeling as to contents, container damage or broken seals, and contamination."

Written procedures and records are required for the receipt of each delivery of starting material and primary and printed packaging materials. The record of the receipts should include the name of the material on the delivery note and the containers, the in-house name and/or code of material if different, date of receipt, the supplier's name, and, if possible, the manufacturer's name, the manufacturer's batch or reference number, the total quantity and number of containers received, the batch number assigned after receipt, and any relevant comment (for example, state of the containers).

Written procedures for the internal labeling, quarantine, and storage of starting materials, packaging materials, and other materials, as appropriate, are needed, according to EU GMP Chapter 4, Section 4.19–4.21, WHO GMP 15.32–15.34, and 21 CFR 211.80(a–d), 82(a,b).

IDENTIFICATION AND LABELING OF STARTING MATERIALS

The information that should be recorded on the label for each delivery is prescribed in the EU GMP Section 5.29, WHO GMP Section 14.13, and 21 CFR 211.80d and includes the designated name of the product and internal code reference, the supplier's batch number and control (lot number) provided on the receipt, the status of the contents, and an expiry date or date beyond which retesting is necessary. When fully validated computer systems are used, not all of the above information needs to be legible on the label. Material must be restricted until appropriate testing is performed and disposition obtained from the site's QU.

API GMP FOR RECEIPT OF MATERIALS

In addition to the requirements for starting materials used for drug products, receipt of starting materials used in API manufacturing should comply with specific requirements. Before incoming materials are mixed with existing stocks (for example, solvents or stocks in silos), they should be identified as correct, tested (if appropriate), and released. Procedures should be available to prevent wrongly discharging incoming materials into the existing stock. If bulk deliveries are made in non-dedicated tankers, assurance of no cross-contamination from the tanker is advisable. Means of providing this assurance could include a certificate of cleaning, testing for trace impurities, and/or audit of the supplier. One or more of these processes should be used. Some starting materials may not be tested for compliance because of the hazards involved (for example, phosphorus pentachloride and dimethyl sulfate), and this nontesting is acceptable when a batch *certificate of analysis* (COA) is available from the vendor and when there is a reason based on safety or other valid considerations.

Chapter 37

Sampling Processes

GENERAL SAMPLING REQUIREMENTS

It is desirable to have written procedures for sampling that include the names of person(s) authorized to take samples, the methods and equipment to be used, the amounts to be taken, and any precautions to be observed to avoid contamination of the material or any deterioration in its quality. Documented sampling procedures and sampling plans approved by the quality unit for all materials should be in place.

The European Union (EU) and World Health Organization (WHO) both have *good manufacturing practices* (GMP) that further prescribe that the sampling procedures should contain the instructions for any required subdivision of the sample, the type of sample container to be used, whether it is for aseptic sampling or normal sampling, labeling, storage conditions, and instructions for cleaning and storage of sampling equipment. Samples should be representative of the material being sampled and should be taken in a manner that does not compromise the integrity of the sampled material or the sample.

Each container of starting materials should be sampled for identification testing unless supplier validation has been done to permit reduced testing. Such reduced testing is not permissible for parenteral product actives or for materials coming from a broker. Acceptable means of validating the supplier processes are listed in EU Annex 8 and WHO Section 17.15. This validation should take account of:

- Nature and status of the manufacturer and of the supplier and their understanding of the GMP requirements of the pharmaceutical industry

- *Quality assurance* (QA) system of the manufacturer of the starting material

- Manufacturing conditions under which the starting material is produced and controlled

- Nature of the starting material and the medicinal products in which it will be used

WHO GMP Section 17.16 lists minimum information to be included on the supplier's *certificate of analysis* (COA) as identification, name, and address of the issuing supplier, signature of the competent official and statement of his/her qualifications, name of the material tested, batch number of the material tested, specifications and methods used, test results obtained, and the date of testing.

SAMPLING FACILITIES, UTENSILS, AND EQUIPMENT

The sampling facilities should meet the general requirements described in EU GMP Chapter 3 and WHO GMP Chapter 7 for cleanliness and dust control, and should not result in cross-contamination or sample confusion. The WHO guidance (*WHO Guidelines for Sampling of Pharmaceutical Products and Related Materials*) provides details on facilities and equipment to be used in sampling.

Sampling facilities should be designed to prevent contamination of the opened container, prevent cross-contamination by other materials, product, and the environment, and protect the individual who samples during the sampling procedure. Where possible, sampling should be performed in an area or booth designed for the purpose. The area in which the sample was taken should be recorded. Some materials should be sampled in special or dedicated environments (for example, aerosol valves, hormones, and penicillins).

SAMPLE CONTAINERS AND LABELING

Sample containers should not be reactive, additive, or absorptive so as to alter the safety, identity, strength, quality, or purity of the material being sampled, and should provide adequate protection from external factors in storage and use that can cause deterioration. Finally, sample containers should be clean and, where required, sterilized and pyrogen free.

Samples should be labeled to maintain traceability and identity. WHO Section 17.12 and EU GMP Section 6.13 specify label content for samples, with WHO being more prescriptive. Section 17.12 lists the following requirements for sample label content:

- Name of the sampled material
- Batch or lot number
- Number of the container from which the sample was taken
- Number of the sample
- Signature of the person who has taken the sample
- Date of sampling

TRAINING OF PERSONNEL

Each GMP requires personnel to adequately train for the jobs they perform, including 21 CFR 211.25, EU GMP Chapter 2, and WHO GMP Section 10. EU GMP Annex 8 further specifies that personnel should receive initial and ongoing training in the disciplines relevant to correct sampling. The training should include sampling plans, written sampling procedures, techniques and equipment for sampling, information about the risks of cross-contamination, the precautions to be taken with regard to unstable and/or sterile substances, the importance of considering the visual appearance of materials, containers, and labels, and the importance of recording any unexpected or unusual circumstances.

SAMPLING OF STARTING MATERIALS FOR API MANUFACTURING

At least one test to verify the identity of each batch of material should be conducted, with certain exceptions: processing hazardous or highly toxic raw materials, other special materials, or materials transferred to another unit within the company's control do not need to be tested if the manufacturer's COA is obtained, showing that these raw materials conform to established specifications. Visual examination of containers and labels and recording of batch numbers should help in establishing the identity of these materials. The lack of on-site testing for these materials should be justified and documented.

Samples should be representative of the batch of material from which they are taken. Sampling methods should specify the number of containers to be sampled, which part of the container to sample, and the amount of material to be taken from each container. The number of containers to sample and the sample size should be based on a sampling plan that takes into consideration the criticality of the material, material variability, past quality history of the supplier, and the quantity needed for analysis. Sampling should be conducted at defined locations and following procedures designed to prevent contamination of the material sampled and contamination of other materials. Containers from which samples are withdrawn should be opened carefully and subsequently reclosed. They should be marked to indicate that a sample has been taken.

SAMPLING OF PACKAGING MATERIALS

EU GMP Annex 8 states that the sampling plan for packaging materials should take account of the quantity received, the quality required, the nature of the material (for example, primary packaging materials and/or printed packaging materials), the production methods, and what is known of the QA system of the packaging materials manufacturer based on audits. The number of samples taken should be determined statistically and specified in a sampling plan.

WHO guidance cautions against mixing of printed packaging materials. Only one material should be sampled at a time, and the WHO guidance explicitly states that samples of packaging materials should never be returned to the consignment. It considers sources of nonhomogeneity in packaging material batches and recommends that sampling take these potential sources of nonhomogeneity into account. The sources of nonhomogeneity include materials manufactured on different days or machines, materials manufactured on one machine but at different stations (for example, molding stations), packaging manufactured with different source materials, and change in quality during the process (for example, container wall thickness and text legibility).

Chapter 38

Material Storage, Identification, and Rotation

MATERIAL STORAGE

Storage locations should meet the general principles outlined for pharmaceutical manufacturing facilities in each of the *good manufacturing practices* (GMP), that is, United States 21 CFR Subpart C, European Union (EU) GMP Chapter 3, and World Health Organization (WHO) GMP Section 12. Additional requirements for storage areas are included in 21 CFR 211 Subpart H, WHO GMP Annex 9, WHO Technical Report Series 908 and Annex 5, and WHO Technical Report Series 937.

Storage areas should be of sufficient capacity to permit the orderly storage of materials and to facilitate cleaning and inspection, and materials should be stored off the floor. Storage areas should be designed to maintain any required label storage conditions, such as controlled temperature and humidity. Records should be maintained of temperature monitoring, and the monitoring equipment should be checked periodically and calibrated. WHO specifies that temperature mapping should show temperature uniformity. Areas should be clean and free from pests. Receiving and dispatch bays should protect materials from the weather and should enable cleaning of the materials before storage.

If quarantine status is maintained by storage in separate areas, these areas should be clearly marked, with access restricted to authorized personnel. Any system replacing physical quarantine should provide equivalent security, particularly for rejected, expired, recalled, or returned materials or products. The status of all materials should be identified.

Highly active materials, narcotics, and hazardous materials should be stored in dedicated areas and subject to additional safety and security measures. Materials should be handled and stored to prevent mix-ups and cross-contamination. They should be stored under conditions that assure their quality is maintained, and stock should be appropriately rotated.

Printed packaging materials should be stored in secure conditions with limited access. Cut labels and other loose printed materials should be stored and transported in separate closed containers to avoid mix-ups. Packaging materials should be issued for use by designated personnel in accordance with defined procedures.

Rejected materials and products should be identified and controlled to prevent their use before a final disposition by the *quality unit* (QU). Broken or damaged items should be segregated and withdrawn from usable stock.

MATERIAL IDENTIFICATION

Each container should be identified, and the status of the material should be controlled either by physical labeling and segregation or by electronic systems that provide equivalent security.

STOCK ROTATION AND CONTROL

WHO GMP contain more detailed guidance on stock rotation and control than either EU or United States Food and Drug Administration (FDA). Periodic stock reconciliation should be performed by comparing actual and recorded stocks, and any significant discrepancies should be investigated. Partly used containers should be securely closed and resealed to prevent contamination. Materials from opened containers should be used before those in unopened containers. Damaged containers should not be used unless the quality of the material has been shown to be unaffected. The QU should be notified of damage, and any actions taken should be documented.

CONTROL OF OBSOLETE AND OUTDATED MATERIALS AND PRODUCTS

Stocks should be checked periodically for obsolete and outdated materials. Procedures should be in place to prevent the issuance and use of outdated materials. Approved procedures should be in place for control of returned goods. All returns should be placed in quarantine pending disposition by the QU. Products returned from the market and that have left the control of the manufacturer should be destroyed; they may be considered for resale, relabeling, or recovery in a subsequent batch only after they have been critically assessed by the QU in accordance with a written procedure.

Chapter 39

Shipping and Distribution

A finished pharmaceutical's labeling and/or pharmacopeia monograph provide specific directions for the temperature and humidity conditions of storage and shipment to the consumer, which is ultimately based on stability data. The United States Pharmacopeia (USP) General Notices section on *preservation*, *packaging*, *storage*, and *labeling* provides working definitions for the temperature ranges/storage devices designated as freezer, cold, cool, controlled cold temperature, room temperature, controlled room temperature, warm, excessive heat, and protection from freezing.

Warehousing/storage temperatures should be controlled and monitored using calibrated monitoring devices and records of temperature, and alarms, where applicable, should be maintained. Refrigerators and freezers used to store drugs should:

- Be well maintained

- Be equipped with alarms

- Be free from frost buildup

- When combined, be a two-door unit with separate freezer compartment and door

- Allow for adequate air distribution and orderly storage within the chamber; storage practices and loading configurations should not lead to the obstruction of air distribution

- Have sensors for continuous monitoring, and alarms located at the points representing the temperature extremes

If an alarm is associated with the refrigerator or freezer, the functionality of the alarm should be checked periodically at the upper and lower set points. Warehouses must undergo temperature profiling using a suitable number of temperature-recording instruments placed strategically (for example, based on sun-facing walls, ceiling height). Temperature profiles should occur at least over three consecutive 24-hour periods and during days of extreme outdoor winter cold and summer heat. Products should not be stored in areas shown by temperature mapping to present a risk.

The calculation of a *mean kinetic temperature* (MKT) is necessary for compliance with 21 CFR 203.32 "Drug Sample Storage and Handling Requirements" (part of 21 CFR 203 "Prescription Drug Marketing"). MKT is a single derived temperature that, if maintained over a defined period, would afford the same thermal challenge to a pharmaceutical product as would have been experienced over a range of both higher and lower temperatures for an equivalent defined period. In other words, MKT is a calculated, fixed temperature that simulates the effects of temperature variations over a period of time. It expresses the cumulative thermal stress experienced by a product at varying temperatures during storage and distribution. The calculation of MKT is given in USP <1150> and usually requires 52 weeks of continual temperature monitoring or weekly high-temperature and weekly low-temperature recordings.

The formula for MKT is:

$$MKT = (-DH/R)/\text{Ln}\{(\text{SUM}(\exp(-DH/R \times Tn)))/n\}$$

Where

DH = Activation energy

R = The universal gas constant (0.0083144 kJ/molK)

T = The temperature in degrees K

n = The total number of (equal) time periods over which data are collected

Ln = The natural log

exp = The natural log base

Various temperature measurement technologies exist that are distinguished by their fragility and their measurement precision. USP <1118> describes several temperature measuring devices: alcohol or mercury thermometer, *infrared* (IR) device, *resistance temperature detector* (RTD), thermistor, thermocouple, data loggers, and time-temperature integrators (typically single use). Temperature and humidity monitoring devices should be calibrated at predetermined intervals. Single-use monitoring devices should be qualified.

Selection of a shipping container and/or box should be based on:

- Storage and transportation requirements of the drugs

- Space required for the amount of drugs to be transported

- Anticipated external temperature extremes

- Estimated maximum length of time required for transportation of the drugs, including any in-transit storage

Measures should be in place to prevent unauthorized persons from entering and/or tampering with vehicles and/or equipment and to prevent the theft or misappropriation thereof. Monitoring data recorded during vehicular transport should be reviewed upon receipt of the pharmaceutical products to assess maintenance of any special storage conditions. Any deviations from storage conditions that are considered to be acceptable (that is, small, brief excursions) should be determined in consultation with the marketing authorization holder and/or manufacturer.

At a port of entry into a country, consignments of pharmaceutical products should be stored under suitable conditions for as short a time as possible. All reasonable steps should be taken by importers to ensure that products are not mishandled or exposed to adverse storage conditions at wharves or airports. Where necessary, persons with pharmaceutical training should be involved with the customs procedures, or should be readily contactable.

Any counterfeit or suspected drugs found in the pharmaceutical supply chain should be segregated immediately from other pharmaceutical product. The marketing authorization holder and relevant competent authorities should be informed immediately.

21 CFR 211.132 requires *over-the-counter* (OTC) retail drug products sold in the United States (except a dermatological, dentifrice, insulin, or lozenge product) to have a tamper-evident (primary and/or secondary) package. Such a package has one or more indicators or barriers to entry that, if breached or missing, can reasonably be expected to provide visible evidence to consumers that tampering has occurred. Each retail package of a drug product having a tamper-evident feature(s) must bear a statement that identifies all tamper-evident feature(s) and any capsule sealing technologies, is prominently placed on the package, and is so placed that it will be unaffected if the tamper-evident feature of the package is breached or missing.

Chapter 40

Traceability and Sourcing

TRACEABILITY

Traceability refers to the ability to determine (trace) what materials have been brought into the facility, which materials, equipment, and personnel were used to manufacture a specific batch of finished product, and where the finished goods were distributed for commercial sale. To achieve complete traceability, companies must have systems in place to record the receipt and use of materials, by unique identifier (either a batch or control number), that go into the manufacture of the drug product, and systems for identifying where the finished product batches were distributed. Good documentation is key to meeting the traceability requirements and ensuring, in the case of a recall, that all impacted product is identified and can be removed from the field, if necessary. The United States Food and Drug Administration (FDA) *good manufacturing practices* (GMP) regulations illustrate the concept of traceability throughout a finished dosage form facility.

Raw Materials and Components

Before a raw material or component arrives at the receiving dock of the pharmaceutical company, it is imperative that the company has done its homework on the material and the vendor that supplies the material. Establishing the quality and integrity of the raw materials and components that are used in manufacturing and packaging the drug product begins with an understanding of how these materials are manufactured and packaged by the vendor. It is important to qualify vendors to ensure the receipt of quality raw materials and components. It is also important, through the qualification process, to verify that the vendor has mechanisms in place to trace the manufacture of its products, and that the product label is a unique identifier that can be traced forward into the manufacture of the finished dosage form.

Proper receipt of raw materials and components is crucial from a traceability perspective. When materials and/or components arrive on the dock, a verification of the vendor's bill of lading should be conducted. Upon receipt, GMP regulations require that the finished dosage form manufacturer assign a unique code (batch or control number) to each lot of incoming materials, for each shipment received. The vendor's unique identifier (batch or lot number) should be recorded to allow traceability back to the vendor in the event of a problem. The regulations direct the pharmaceutical company to verify the vendor's packaging, labeling, and tamper-evident seal (if applicable) to ensure that the material received is legitimate and not counterfeit. Finally, it is important to understand that multiple shipments of the same batch of material require unique batch or control numbers to be assigned to each receipt. It is not acceptable to assign the same batch or control number to multiple receipts of the same vendor-supplied material or component batch.

Product Manufacturing and Packaging

GMP regulations require that each manufactured batch is assigned a unique identifier, typically a batch or lot number, that is specific to the product being manufactured. As raw materials are weighed and dispensed for use in manufacturing, the batch or control number of the raw materials must be recorded. As these materials are charged into the manufacturing equipment, their identity (by batch or control number) and quantity must be recorded on the manufacturing batch documentation. It is important to note that the addition of raw materials to the batch is typically viewed as a critical step and, as a result, requires two individuals to verify that the correct materials were added and to record the correct batch information on the associated documentation.

As manufacturing progresses, appropriate documentation of the manufacturing process (for example, the equipment used, personnel involved) is needed. The use of processing aids (for example, lubricants) should be documented. If individual batches are blended together to produce a single, larger batch for further processing, there should be traceability to the individual batches that were used to manufacture the larger batch. Batches should only be combined in this manner according to preestablished procedures and validated processes. Batches that failed to meet required specifications should not be combined with batches that have met specifications in hopes of producing a larger batch that meets the predetermined specifications for the product.

Water is a raw material that is commonly used in a number of pharmaceutical dosage forms and manufacturing processes. Documentation of water usage, and traceability to the water used, is always a bit of a problem as most companies use a continuous flow loop for their process water. A specific batch number or unique identifier can not be easily applied to the water that is used in the manufacturing process. As a result, traceability with respect to water is typically time-based, and any issues that arise with the quality of the water have the potential of impacting all of the batches that used the water since the date of the last acceptable testing results.

Finally, similarly to the requirements during manufacturing, each batch or control number of the packaging and labeling components must be recorded on the batch documentation to meet traceability requirements.

Finished Dosage Form

GMP regulations require the identification of each packaged lot of product with a batch or lot number that permits the determination of the history of the manufacturing and packaging operations, as well as the control and testing of the batch.

Distribution Practices

GMP regulations require the maintenance of distribution records containing at a minimum:

- Name and strength of product

- Name and address of the consignee

- Batch or lot number of the finished drug product shipped

- Quantity shipped

- Date shipped

These distribution records enable the tracking of each finished drug product, and should include shipments to commercial customers, transfers to internal departments (for example, samples for *quality control* [QC] testing), as well as samples to physicians or other healthcare providers. A system should be in place to account for 100% of the packaged finished dosage form and allow for complete notification of customers in the event of a product recall.

BIOLOGICAL AGENTS

Transmission spongiform encephalopathies (TSE) came to the forefront in the mid-1980s with the identification of the bovine form (*bovine spongiform encephalopathy* [BSE]) in British cattle. This discovery of mad cow disease, and the risk of transmission to humans, highlighted the need for greater controls over the sourcing of animal-derived materials for use in the pharmaceutical industry.

The ideal situation when sourcing raw materials for the manufacture of drug products would be to avoid the use of bovine-derived materials, or materials from other animal species in which TSE naturally occurs. Therefore, when a pharmaceutical company has a choice between materials of animal or nonanimal origin, the materials of nonanimal origin are clearly preferred. Unfortunately, sourcing materials of nonanimal origin is not always possible and, as a result, it is critical for a pharmaceutical company to take steps to minimize the risk of transmitting animal TSE through their drug products.

The European Medicines Agency (EMA) identifies mechanisms to minimize the risk of transmitting TSE:

- Sourcing materials produced from animals residing in geographic areas of low risk for the disease

- Cleaning and control procedures that minimize the risk of cross-contamination between production batches

- Removal or inactivation of TSE agents during production processing

Of these activities, the well-controlled sourcing of animal-derived materials is the most critical as this prevents the introduction of TSE into the drug manufacturing

- Understand the source of all of the materials that are used in the manufacture of the drug product and identify those that are animal derived.

- For animal-derived products, understand the country of origin of the starting materials and ensure that the country is rated as low risk.

- Understand the controls that the supplier of the animal-derived material has in place to minimize the introduction of these agents into their facility.

- Obtain a BSE/TSE statement from each supplier of animal-derived materials that demonstrates their commitment to ensure that their materials are free from these types of agents.

- Closely monitor the suppliers of animal-derived materials as the risk of TSE can not be entirely eliminated.

Figure 40.1   Steps to ensure that materials used in manufacture of finished dosage forms do not contain harmful biologic agents.

facility. To ensure that the materials used in the manufacture of the finished dosage form do not contain these types of biological agents, defined steps are recommended (Figure 40.1).

GMP regulations place responsibility for ensuring the quality of the materials used to manufacture drug products squarely on the shoulders of the pharmaceutical company. The globalization of the pharmaceutical supply chain, and the increasing use of materials manufactured in emerging countries (from a pharmaceutical perspective) such as India and China, has made this responsibility increasingly difficult to achieve.

Over the last few years, much debate and discussion has occurred regarding the establishment of a drug pedigree to ensure the integrity and authenticity of each and every drug product that enters the pharmaceutical supply chain. Much of this discussion has arisen as a result of the increase in counterfeit pharmaceutical products entering the supply chain and putting consumers and patients at significant risk. It is imperative that every organization involved in the pharmaceutical supply chain does their part to minimize or eliminate the introduction of counterfeit materials or products.

PHARMACEUTICAL SUPPLY CHAIN

A typical supply chain for a pharmaceutical company is shown in Figure 40.2. Inputs (for example, raw materials, packaging components) into the finished dosage form manufacturing process typically are purchased from outside suppliers. Once the finished dosage form is manufactured, packaged, tested, and released, it is shipped to a wholesaler who may store it for a period of time. The wholesaler may sell the product to a chain drug store (which requires the product to pass through the chain drug store warehouse before reaching the pharmacy) or directly to a pharmacy customer. The finished product typically passes through a number of hands before it reaches the end customer or patient.

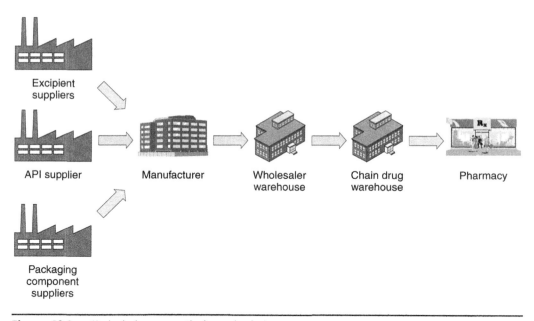

Figure 40.2   Typical pharmaceutical supply chain.

Source: Figure courtesy of the ASQ Food, Drug, and Cosmetic Division. Used with permission.

Chapter 41

Salvaged/Returned Goods and Destruction

ood manufacturing practices (GMP) regulations were designed to ensure that pharmaceutical products that are manufactured and released for distribution are safe, pure, and effective, and that they have a level of quality commensurate with their use in humans or animals. This level of quality needs to be maintained throughout the distribution network to ensure that products are not negatively impacted during transit and subsequent storage. When pharmaceutical products are returned to the company, or salvaged after a natural disaster, it is imperative that appropriate measures are taken to verify the quality of the product before reconditioning or releasing the product back into the supply chain. It is critical that returned or salvaged product that is ultimately rejected is disposed of appropriately.

RETURNED DRUG PRODUCTS

Drug products that are returned to the pharmaceutical company, for whatever reason, need to be identified during the receiving process and segregated from other saleable product until an appropriate disposition is made. Documentation of the receipt of returned goods, including the product name, strength, lot number, reason for the return, and quantity returned, must be recorded. If the reason for the drug product return implicates other batches, an investigation should be conducted to determine the extent of the issue.

After receipt, returned goods need to be evaluated to determine an appropriate disposition (for example, return to stock, reprocessing, or rejection). This evaluation should take into account the length of time outside the control of the pharmaceutical company, the likely conditions under which the product was distributed or held before return, and the condition of the drug product, its container, carton, or labeling. In the case of an error in shipment, or if the drug products have been in the distribution channel for a brief time, this evaluation may be limited to a physical examination of the returned product. In this case, if the physical examination demonstrates that the product was not damaged during the short period of time that it was outside the control of the company, it can be returned to stock as saleable product.

In situations where the product has been in the distribution channels for some time, or there is a question about how the product was stored, additional testing may be necessary to ensure that the product meets appropriate standards of safety, identity, strength, quality, and purity. In general, products that have been outside the control of the pharmaceutical manufacturer for some time should not be returned to saleable stock unless:

- Products are in their original unopened containers and are in good condition

- Products appear to have been stored and handled appropriately

- Remaining shelf life is suitable for continued distribution

- Products have been tested to ensure that they meet the appropriate quality standards

European regulations require that returned goods be examined and assessed by a person authorized to do so. The company needs to weigh the benefit of returning the product to stock against the cost of additional verification testing to ensure that the product has not been negatively impacted. In addition, the pharmaceutical company should look closely at the labeling of the returned drug product before returning it to stock to ensure that the product labeling includes the latest safety information. Reprocessing of returned drug product is allowed provided that the subsequent drug product meets the appropriate standards, specifications, and characteristics of the original drug product. Reprocessing is a viable option where an update to the labeling is warranted to ensure that the latest safety information is available for patient use.

In all cases, the holding, evaluation, inspection, and testing, if necessary, to disposition a returned product should be documented. Release of returned product back into the supply chain should be done only after review of all of the relevant information by the *quality unit* (QU) or *qualified person* (QP). The activities surrounding returned goods, and the functional areas involved in the process, need to be outlined in a formal procedure, and records of the returns process need to be maintained.

Finally, returned drug products may serve as an indication of quality problems related to the product itself or how the product was handled during the distribution process. As a result, it is imperative that the root cause for the return be identified and documented so that the returns data can be reviewed as part of the annual product review process.

SALVAGED DRUG PRODUCTS

When it is clear that pharmaceutical products have been subjected to improper storage conditions (for example, extremes in temperature or humidity) or exposed to atypical conditions (for example, smoke or chemical fumes) due to natural disasters, fires, accidents, or equipment failures, they should not be salvaged and returned to the marketplace. Whenever it is unclear, or there is some level of doubt regarding whether the drug products have been subjected to these types of conditions, salvaging operations may be conducted, but only when it is evident from analytical testing that the drug products meet all applicable standards of identity, strength, quality, and purity, and it is evident from an inspection of the facility where the salvaged drug products were held that the drug products were not subjected to improper conditions as a result of the natural disaster or accident.

In the case of salvaged drug products, a preponderance of evidence that demonstrates the acceptability of these types of products is required. Without a substantial body of evidence, salvaged drug products should be rejected and disposed of appropriately. The outcome of the evaluation of salvaged drugs should be documented.

Reverse logistics is the term used to describe the process of returning products back through the distribution network for reimbursement, product assessment, and appropriate disposal. Recognizing that the effective management of the reverse logistics process is essential for the company and the environment, some pharmaceutical firms have turned to third-party reverse logistics companies to handle all aspects of the returned goods process. In general, the product that flows through these processors will ultimately be rejected, and therefore no evaluation of the product is deemed necessary.

Like any third-party service provider that conducts a GMP operation on behalf of the pharmaceutical company, these providers must be assessed to ensure that they are capable of doing the work, providing adequate data back to the pharmaceutical company for quality evaluation, and that they are disposing of product in compliance with the appropriate laws and regulations.

DISPOSAL OF DRUG PRODUCTS

Public awareness and concern are growing over the disposal of pharmaceutical products and the potential for adverse impact on the environment. An article ("Pharmaceuticals, Hormones, and Other Organic Wastewater Contaminants in U.S. Streams, 1999–2000: A National Reconnaissance," published in 2002 by the US Geological Survey) outlined the presence of pharmaceuticals and other organic wastewater contaminants in streams across the country. This report highlighted the need for improving the handling and disposal of pharmaceutical waste. Proper disposal of potentially dangerous pharmaceutical products is now of critical importance not just in the United States but around the world.

All drug products that are rejected by the pharmaceutical company need to be disposed of in accordance with applicable laws and in a manner that protects consumers as well as the environment. Many drug products are considered hazardous waste and must be disposed of by companies that are licensed to handle these types of materials. In the United States, the Environmental Protection Agency (EPA) is responsible for defining hazardous chemicals and the procedures to be followed to properly dispose of these materials. Drug formulations are considered hazardous waste if they fall into one of two primary categories: listed hazardous waste or characteristic hazardous waste. It is critical to understand the EPA (or other relevant environmental regulatory agency) requirements as they pertain to a company's specific products, that the products are assessed to determine the appropriate category for disposal and, ultimately, that they are disposed of in accordance with the laws and regulations that govern the operations in the area. The complexity of the laws has increased the use of third-party vendors by pharmaceutical companies, but it is important to understand that these vendors need to be adequately assessed and qualified by the pharmaceutical company to ensure that they are abiding by the laws for handling and disposal of returned drug products.

Controlled substance drug products are another special category that requires very tight control on the inventory and destruction of these products. The destruction of controlled substance products requires specific documentation (Form 41) for the Drug Enforcement Agency (DEA) in addition to the documentation that is required to be maintained for GMP purposes. The disposal of controlled substances often requires witnessing the actual disposal to ensure that the product does not inadvertently reenter the supply chain.

The processing of pharmaceutical product returns and salvaged drug products can be a daunting task and requires knowledge of laws and regulations outside the GMP regulations. Proper disposition and disposal of pharmaceutical products ensures that consumers receive drugs that have the required quality, and that they, and the environment, are not inadvertently harmed by inadequate disposal of rejected or expired drug products.

Part VI

Sterile and Non-sterile Manufacturing Systems

Chapter 42

Master Batch and Completed Batch Records

Clearly written, detailed batch records are critical to ensuring product quality. The *master batch record* (MBR) accurately describes the production processes required to make the product the same way every time, to meet the defined product specifications. MBRs are written and approved by the department that manufactures the product and are approved by the *quality unit* (QU). MBRs should be written to precisely describe the required information for trained operators to execute consistently.

ISSUANCE

The MBR contains a section for documenting issuance of *production batch records* (PBRs) generated from the MBR. This section provides signature spaces for the person who generated the PBR and for a second person who verifies the PBR. Their signatures indicate that the PBR is of the correct current version and that it is an accurate, legible copy of the MBR.

YIELD

Include the expected (theoretical) yield at key processing steps in the MBR. Actual yields are tracked in the PBR to ensure that product is not unexpectedly lost in processing. Production yields should be predictable, within acceptable tolerances, if the manufacturing process is in control. Calculation of percentage of theoretical yield is performed by one person and verified by a second person. If the percentage of theoretical yield is not within the defined range, an investigation is conducted to determine the reason for the unexpected result.

CRITICAL STEP VERIFICATION

Significant processing steps that are critical to product quality should be verified by a second person to ensure that they are performed in accordance with the batch record, creating product that meets predetermined specifications. For example, addition of materials to a batch of product is performed by one person and verified by a second person.

PROCESSING INSTRUCTIONS

The instructions in the MBR for making the product should include identifying information describing the product, a list of all of the materials that are used to make the product, including quantity, and the location and equipment used to make the product. The identifying information can include the name of the product, the processing step (for example, fermentation of product X), the concentration or strength of the product, and an identification number.

The MBR includes processing steps in the order in which they must occur. Identify any critical processing parameters that could impact product quality and the allowable ranges around these parameters that must be maintained, such as pressure, temperature, elapsed time, and speed in revolutions per minute. Example: Set centrifuge to run for 15 ± 1 minutes at 7500 ± 200 rpm.

The MBR includes in-process samples that are taken to check product quality against defined acceptance criteria. Conductivity or pH is frequently checked during processing to determine if the levels are appropriate before performing the next step. Example: pH acceptance criteria is 6.8 ± 0.2.

The processing instructions include packaging and labeling requirements. The primary packaging (product container) and secondary packaging (cartons, shipping boxes, and shrink-wrap) are included in the list of materials required for the batch. Labeling text is documented to ensure that the product is accurately identified. Requirements for the label material are included that describe the type of label that will adhere securely to the product while remaining legible throughout storage and distribution of the product to the customer.

Storage conditions of the intermediate or finished product, with any storage time limits, are included in the batch record to ensure that the product is stored in conditions (temperature, humidity, protection from light) that maintain the quality of the product.

HOLD TIMES

Any time limits for processing steps, hold times between steps, and maximum length of time to perform the total process that could impact product quality are included in the batch record. Sampling and testing requirements to measure product attributes to determine whether the product meets specifications are included in the MBR. When a PBR is issued from the MBR, a unique identification number is assigned to the PBR, often called a *batch number*. The issuer signs and dates the PBR to indicate it is an accurate, legible reproduction of the approved MBR, and a second person reviews the PBR to confirm its accuracy.

COMPLETED BATCH RECORDS

As the PBR is used to make a batch of product, several items need to be documented at the time the significant processing steps are performed:

- Date (and time, if important) of execution, with the date and initials of the persons who performed and checked the step

- Equipment used

- Weight, lot number, and actual quantity of materials used

- Actual measured values of the critical processing parameters

- Samples collected and results for in-process and release tests

- Actual yield where theoretical yields are identified

- Description of packaging, labeling, and labels, as well as a sample of the label

- Documentation of any deviation and its related investigation if the deviation has potential impact to product

REVIEW AND DISPOSITION OF PBR

The responsibility for review and disposition of the product by examination of the PBR should be defined in a written procedure. Production personnel are responsible for reviewing PBRs, ensuring they are completed and signed, and that any related deviations are documented and investigated.

QU personnel are responsible for reviewing and approving the completed batch records and releasing or rejecting product. Part of the QU's review is to ensure that any deviations and related investigations that could impact product, and any *out-of-specification* (OOS) test results, are satisfactorily addressed. The QU ensures that the product complies with established specifications before any product is released from the organization's control.

Chapter 43

Production Operations

GENERAL

Production operations must comply with *good manufacturing practices* (GMP) to manufacture quality product that meets regulatory requirements. GMP for manufacturing operations include requirements for the prevention of cross-contamination during production, process validation, and environmental conditions, based on the types of manufacturing performed. These GMP should be written and approved, with procedures and documentation for production operations. The GMP for production operations include:

- Access to production premises should be restricted to designated personnel.

- Before any processing operation is started, steps are taken and documented to ensure that the work area and equipment are clean and free from any raw materials, products, product residues, labels, or documents not required for the current operation.

- At all times during processing, all materials, bulk containers, major items of equipment, and the rooms used are labeled or otherwise identified with an indication of the product or material being processed, its strength, and the batch number or status. The processing status of major units of equipment should be indicated either on the individual units of equipment or by appropriate documentation, computer control systems, or alternative means.

- Contemporaneous and complete batch production documentation is necessary.

- Process steps must be verified by a second person. Process steps can be performed using a validated computer system.

- Other critical activities should be witnessed or subjected to an equivalent control.

- Any deviation from instructions or procedures is avoided. Any deviation should be documented and explained. Any critical deviation should be investigated. Qualified personnel write a report that describes the deviation, the investigation, the rationale for disposition, and any follow-up activities required. The report is approved by *quality control* (QC).

241

- Rejected materials and products are clearly marked as such and are either stored separately in restricted areas or controlled by a system that ensures that they are either returned to their vendors or, where appropriate, reprocessed or destroyed. Actions taken are recorded.

Provided that changeover procedures are validated and implemented, nonmedicinal products may be fabricated or packaged/labeled in areas or with equipment that is also used for the production of pharmaceutical products.

PROCESS VALIDATION

Process validation includes the validation and security of computerized or automated data handling systems. Validation studies are conducted in accordance with predefined protocols. A written report summarizing recorded results and conclusions is prepared, evaluated, approved, and maintained.

APPLICATION FACTORS

Human Drugs

Production requirements for human drugs are regulated by 21 CFR 211, while production requirements for biologics are regulated by 21 CFR 600, 601, and 610. Animal drugs are regulated by 9 CFR. Sterile drugs are susceptible to particulate, pyrogenic, and microbiological contamination. Due to the health hazard associated with the use of contaminated sterile products, special precautions are required in the production of these products. The skill, training, and competency of all personnel involved are critical. *Quality assurance* (QA) is important, and the production must follow carefully established and validated methods of preparation and sterilization.

To maintain product sterility, it is essential that the environment in which aseptic operations (for example, equipment setup, filling) are conducted be maintained in a controlled manner and at an appropriate quality. Activities conducted in critical areas include manipulations (for example, aseptic connections, sterile ingredient additions) of sterile materials before and during filling and closing operations.

High-efficiency particulate air (HEPA)–filtered air should be supplied in critical areas at a velocity sufficient to sweep particles away from the filling/closing area and to maintain unidirectional airflow during operations. The velocity parameters established for each processing line should be justified and appropriate to maintain unidirectional airflow and air quality under dynamic conditions within the critical area.

Supporting clean areas can have various classifications and functions. Many support areas function as zones in which non-sterile components, formulated products, in-process materials, equipment, and container/closures are prepared, held, or transferred. These environments are soundly designed when they minimize the level of particle contaminants in the final product and control the microbiological content (bioburden) of articles and components that subsequently are sterilized.

The nature of the activities conducted in a supporting clean area determines its classification. The United States Food and Drug Administration (FDA) recommends that the area immediately adjacent to the aseptic processing line meet, at a minimum, class 10,000 (ISO 7) standards under dynamic conditions. Manufacturers can classify this area as class 1000 (ISO 6) or maintain the entire aseptic filling room at class 100 (ISO 5). An area classified at a class 100,000 (ISO 8) air cleanliness level is appropriate for less-critical activities (for example, equipment cleaning). European Union (EU) GMP recommend that the supporting areas cascade, so that supporting area from grade A is grade B, which cascades down to grade C, and again down to grade D.

Non-sterile Manufacturing and Manufacturing of Liquids, Creams, and Ointments

Production prevention of microbiological contamination of drug products purporting to be sterile, including the validation of any sterilization process, is the prevention of objectionable microorganisms in non-sterile drug products. FDA guidance is found in sections of 21 CFR regarding topical drug products, and similar information can be found in Eudralex Volume 4, Parts I and II and Annexes.

SANITIZATION AND PROTECTION

Gowning Requirements

Every person entering the manufacturing areas should wear protective garments appropriate to the operations to be carried out. Where a potential for the contamination of a raw material, in-process material, or drug exists, individuals wear clean clothing and protective covering. Personal hygiene procedures, including the use of protective clothing, apply to all persons entering production areas. The hygiene program clearly defines clothing requirements and hygiene procedures for personnel and visitors.

Clothing used in clean and aseptic areas should be laundered or cleaned in such a way that it does not gather additional particulate contaminants that can later be shed. Separate laundry facilities for such clothing are desirable. If fibers are damaged by inappropriate cleaning or sterilization, the risk of shedding particles is increased. Washing and sterilization operations follow *standard operating procedures* (SOPs), and repair of clothing is done using appropriate materials (for example, non-shedding thread). Cleanroom gowning requirements as specified by EU GMP, International Conference on Harmonization (ICH), and Health Canada are listed in Table 43.1.

Sanitization and Hygiene

Clean areas should be cleaned thoroughly according to documented procedures. Detailed hygiene programs should be established. They should include procedures relating to the health, hygiene practices, and clothing of personnel. Hygiene procedures should be understood and followed in a very strict way by every person whose duties take him/her into the production and control areas. The hygiene

Table 43.1   Cleanroom gowning requirements as specified by EU GMP, ICH, and Health Canada.

Grade A (Class 100, ISO 5)	Grade C	Grade D
Headgear totally encloses the person's hair, as well as any beard or mustache; the headgear is tucked into the neck of the suit; a face mask is worn to prevent the shedding of droplets.	The person's hair, as well as any beard or mustache, is covered.	The person's hair, as well as any beard or mustache, is covered.
Trouser bottoms are tucked inside the footwear, and garment sleeves are tucked into the gloves.	A one- or two-piece trouser suit, gathered at the wrists and with a high neck, and appropriate shoes or overshoes are worn.	Protective clothing and appropriate shoes or overshoes are worn.
The protective clothing sheds virtually no fibers or particulate matter and retains particles shed by the body.	The protective clothing sheds virtually no fibers or particulate matter.	
Sterilized, non-powdered rubber or plastic gloves and sterilized or disinfected footwear are worn.		
Outdoor clothing should not be brought into changing rooms.	Outdoor clothing should not be brought into changing rooms.	

program should be promoted by management and discussed during training sessions. Every person entering the manufacturing areas should wear protective garments appropriate to the operations to be carried out. Where a potential for the contamination of a raw material, in-process material, or drug exists, individuals wear clean clothing and protective covering. Unsanitary practices such as eating, drinking, chewing gum, or smoking, or the storage of food, drink, smoking materials, or personal medication in the production and storage areas should be prohibited. Requirements concerning personal hygiene, with an emphasis on hand hygiene, are outlined and are followed by employees. Personnel should be instructed to use the hand-washing facilities. Direct skin contact between the operator's hands and raw materials, primary packaging materials, intermediate or bulk drug, or exposed product, as well as with any part of the equipment that comes into contact with the products, should be avoided. Houseplants are not permitted in fabrication, packaging/labeling, and storage areas or in any other areas where they might adversely influence product quality. Requirements concerning cosmetics and jewelry worn by employees are outlined and are observed by employees. Soiled protective garments, if reusable, are stored in separate containers until properly laundered and, if necessary, disinfected or sterilized. Steps should be taken to ensure as far as is practicable that no person affected by an infectious disease or having open lesions on the exposed surface of the body is engaged in the manufacture of medicinal products. Personal hygiene procedures, including the use of protective clothing, apply to all persons entering production areas. The hygiene program clearly defines clothing requirements and hygiene procedures for personnel and visitors. It must be the manufacturer's responsibility to provide instructions ensuring that health conditions that can be of relevance to the quality of products are brought to the manufacturer's attention. In general, any unhygienic practice within the manufacturing areas or in any other area where the product might be adversely affected should be forbidden.

In addition, some jurisdictions require medical examinations, particularly at time of recruitment. After the first medical examination, examinations should be carried out when necessary for the work and personal health.

Chapter 44

In-Process Controls

21 CFR 211.110 AND EUDRALEX VOLUME 4

21 CFR 211.110 "Sampling and Testing of In-process Materials and Drug Products"; Eudralex Volume 4, Part I, Documentation 4, Production 5; and Eudralex Volume 4, Part II, (ICH Q7) 8.3 "Production and In Process Controls" are regulations that require written procedures describing in-process controls, sampling, tests, or examination of in-process materials. These procedures should be subject to review and approval of the *quality unit* (QU). In-process controls should be established to monitor the production output and to validate the performance of the manufacturing processes that may be responsible for causing variability in the characteristics of in-process materials and the product. In-process monitoring and tests are performed during the manufacture of each batch according to specifications and methods devised during the development phase. Where appropriate, types of in-process controls may include:

- Tablet or capsule weight variation

- Disintegration time

- Adequacy of mixing to assure uniformity and homogeneity

- Dissolution time and rate

- Clarity, completeness, or pH of solutions

Risk management can help identify areas of process weakness, areas of higher risk, and factors that can influence critical quality. Less-stringent in-process controls may be acceptable in early processing, with tighter controls in later processing steps.

Good manufacturing practices (GMP) regulations and quality systems models call for the monitoring of critical processes that may be responsible for causing variability during production. For example, the process steps must be verified by a second person (21 CFR 211.188); process steps can also be performed using a validated computer system. Batch production records must be prepared contemporaneously with each phase of production [21 CFR 211.100(b)]. Although time limits for production can be established, when they are important to the quality of the finished product (21 CFR 211.111), the manufacturer should have the ability to establish production controls using in-process parameters that are based on desired process end points measured using real-time testing or monitoring apparatus (for example, blend until mixed versus blend for 10 minutes). Procedures must be in place to prevent objectionable microorganisms in finished products not required to be sterile and to prevent microbial contamination of finished products purported to be sterile. Sterilization processes must be validated for sterile drugs [21 CFR 211.113(b)].

A quality systems approach calls for the manufacturer to develop procedures that monitor, measure, and analyze the operations (including analytical methods and/or statistical techniques). Procedures should be revisited as needed to refine operational design based on new knowledge. Selected data should be used to evaluate the quality of a process or product and identify opportunities for improvement. Data trends should be continually identified and evaluated to identify potential variances before they become problems, bolster data already collected for the annual review, and facilitate improvement throughout the product life cycle.

Eudralex Volume 4, Part II, (ICH Q7) 8.3 further specifies:

- Critical in-process controls should be documented and approved by the QU.

- Critical process monitoring should be documented and approved by the QU.

- Sampling plans and procedures should be based on scientifically sound practices.

- Sampling should be conducted in such a manner as to prevent contamination of the product.

- Procedures for ensuring the integrity of samples should be established.

- *Out-of-specification* (OOS) investigations are not normally needed for in-process tests that are performed for the purpose of monitoring and/or adjusting the process.

21 CFR 211.110(b)

In-process specifications should be consistent with final product specifications. They should "be derived from previous acceptable process average and process variability estimates where possible and determined by the application of suitable statistical procedures where appropriate." Testing of in-process samples ensures that in-process and drug product material conforms to specifications.

21 CFR 211.110(c) In-Process Material Testing

In-process materials shall be tested for identity, strength, quality, and purity as appropriate, and approved or rejected by the quality control unit, during the production process (for example, at commencement or completion of significant phases or after storage for long periods).

21 CFR 211.110(d) Rejected In-Process Materials

Rejected in-process materials must be identified and controlled under a quarantine system designed to prevent their use in manufacturing or processing operations for which they are unsuitable.

FDA Guidance—Powder Blends and Finished Dosage Units

Guidance was drafted to assist manufacturers in meeting requirements of 21 CFR 211.110 to demonstrate the adequacy of mixing and ensure uniformity of in-process dosage units. This guidance describes the procedures, sampling, and testing that should be performed during development of the product, including performing an assessment of and validating powder mix uniformity, correlating powder mix uniformity with stratified in-process dosage unit data, and correlating stratified in-process samples with final product.

Section VI, "Verification of Manufacturing Criteria," describes methods for establishing in-process acceptance criteria. The resulting data are used to establish stratified sample locations. At least 10 locations during capsule filling or tablet compression should be identified to represent a batch.

Time Limits

Both 21 CFR 211.111, "Time Limitations on Production," and European Union (EU) GMP Part II, (ICH Q7) 8.2 "Time Limits" establish time limits to assure the quality of the product, where appropriate. Time limits should be met to ensure the quality of intermediates and product. Deviation from time limits may be acceptable if it does not compromise the quality of the product. Acceptability of deviation must be justified and documented; however, time limits may be inappropriate when processing to a target value, such as pH, or drying to specified values. Manufacturers should have the ability to establish production controls using in-process parameters based on desired end points measured using real-time testing or monitoring equipment.

Microbiological Contamination

Both 21 CFR 211.113, "Control of Microbiological Contamination," and EU GMP Part II, (ICH Q7) 8.51 and 8.52 state that a company needs written procedures designed to prevent objectionable microorganisms. Operations should be conducted in a manner that prevents contamination by other materials. Handling of *active pharmaceutical ingredients* (APIs) after purification should include precautions to avoid contamination.

Contamination Control

Eudralex Volume 4, Part I, Production 5.18, and EU GMP Part II, (ICH Q7) 8.5 address contamination control. Residual material carryover into successive batches of the same intermediate or API may be acceptable if there is adequate control. Carryover should not result in carryover of degrades or microbial contamination that can adversely affect the API impurity profile.

21 CFR 211.115 REPROCESSING

Written procedures are needed for reprocessing batches that do not conform to standards or specifications. The procedures should include steps to ensure that the reprocessed material conforms to specifications. These procedures need to include review and approval by the QU.

COMBINATION PRODUCTS

The United States Food and Drug Administration (FDA) does not have GMP regulations for combination products. Each constituent part (drug, device, biologic) is subject to specific GMP regulation if it is marketed separately. For combination products sold as one unit (for example, drug-filled syringes), both sets of regulations are applicable to the whole product after joining. The FDA recommends speaking with the Agency during product development to discuss how best to achieve compliance to regulations for combination products.

BIOTECHNOLOGY PRODUCTS

Bioreactor fermentation parameters should be specified and monitored. Review of parameter profiles should verify that run parameters are consistent or have an established pattern from batch to batch. Parameters may include growth rate, pH, waste by-product level, viscosity, addition of chemicals, density, mixing, aeration, foaming, and culture purity. Written procedures are needed to assure proper aseptic techniques during cell inoculation and absence of adventitious agents, including criteria for rejecting contaminated runs. The procedures should describe what investigations and corrective actions will be performed in the event that growth parameters exceed established limits.

Once the fermentation process is completed, the desired product is harvested, and if necessary, refolded to restore configurational integrity, and purified. For recovery of intracellular proteins, cells must be disrupted (lysed) after fermentation. After disruption, cellular debris can be removed by centrifugation or filtration. Centrifugation can be open or closed. The adequacy of the environment must be evaluated for open centrifugation. Ultrafiltration is commonly used to remove the desired product from the cell debris. The porosity of the membrane filter is calibrated to a specific molecular weight, allowing molecules below that weight to pass through while retaining molecules above that weight. For recovery of extracellular protein, the primary separation of product from producing organisms is accomplished by centrifugation or membrane filtration. Initial separation methods can be used after centrifugation to concentrate the products.

Further purification steps primarily involve chromatographic methods to remove impurities and bring the product closer to final specifications. Chromatographic separation techniques are multistage separation methods in which the components of a sample are distributed between two phases, one of which is stationary, while the other is mobile. The stationary phase may be a solid or a liquid supported on a solid or a gel. The stationary phase may be packed in a column, spread as a layer, or distributed as a film. The mobile phase may be gaseous or liquid or supercritical fluid. The separation may be based on adsorption, mass distribution (partition), or ion exchange, or may be based on differences in the physicochemical properties of the molecules, such as size, mass, or volume.

The purification process is primarily achieved by one or more column chromatography techniques, such as affinity chromatography, *ion-exchange chromatography* (IEC), gel filtration, *hydrophobic interaction chromatography* (HIC), and reverse-phase *high-performance (pressure) liquid chromatography* (HPLC).

Various types of filtration methods, such as diafiltration, ultrafiltration, and microfiltration, may be used in the purification of vaccine products. Some of the filters used may be single-use and some may be multiuse. The filters are usually placed within a filter-housing apparatus. The criteria used for the evaluation of the column purification should be applied to the filter housings and the multiuse filters.

Viral Clearance

For products derived from cells or source material of human or animal origin, viral inactivation/removal should be performed in accordance with the process in the approved license application. In some manufacturing operations, there will be a specific viral inactivation/removal step; in other operations, viral inactivation/removal will be accomplished by a step or steps in the manufacturing process that are not specifically considered to be viral inactivation/removal steps. In some instances, more than one viral clearance step is used for a given product. Pre- and post-viral inactivation/removal steps (with the exception of products such as albumin, which are virally inactivated in final containers) should be completely separated. Separate areas with a dedicated *air-handling unit* (AHU) or single-pass air should be used for those steps that occur after viral clearance procedures.

Heat treatment is one method of clearing infectious agents from biologics. Heat treatment is sometimes referred to as *pasteurization,* and heating equipment such as large water baths may be referred to as *pasteurizers.* Technically, however, pasteurization is heating at 63 °C for 30 minutes, which is not sufficient to render plasma derivatives virally inactive.

The parameters specified in the batch record should be achieved such that the validated process for viral inactivation/removal is accomplished. Changes made to the process that do not require submission of a supplement to the Center for Biologics Evaluation and Research (CBER) should be validated.

Inactivation

If the active ingredient is a killed or inactivated version of a live bacteria or virus, the methods for inactivation will have been established and reviewed during product approval. Either heat or chemical treatment may be used for inactivation. The manufacturer should have validated the process and followed the validated procedures during production. All inactivation parameters should be monitored and the appropriate testing performed with acceptable results.

Manufacturing and Aseptic Processing

Aseptic processing in-process controls include environmental monitoring methods, such as surface monitoring, which can be performed with touch plates, swabs, and contact plates, active and passive air monitoring, container weight variation, fill weight, leak testing, established microbial specifications for in-process testing for the lots made, and aseptic connections and transfers. Procedures should be in place for interruption of the fill, should it occur, and for limiting access to controlled and classified areas. Filters should be evaluated before use to assure they meet specifications, and integrity testing should be performed on filters post-fill; results should be in keeping with the manufacturer's and validated specifications. Written procedures for gowning should be in place and followed.

Some bulk products are held after sterile filtration and before filling. The holding period and storage conditions should have been validated. For lengthy filling operations, time limits should be set and validated to assure that the duration of the fill does not affect the potency of the product and its susceptibility to microbial contamination.

Lyophilization

Lyophilization, or freeze-drying, is a process in which water is removed from a product after it is frozen and placed under a vacuum, allowing the ice to change directly from solid to vapor without passing through a liquid phase. The process consists of three separate, unique, and interdependent processes: freezing, primary drying (sublimation), and secondary drying (desorption). The lyophilization process generally includes dissolving the drug and excipients in a suitable solvent, usually *water for injection* (WFI), sterilizing the bulk solution by passing it through a 0.22-micron bacteria-retentive filter, filling into individual sterile containers and partially stoppering the containers under aseptic conditions, and transporting the partially stoppered containers to the lyophilizer and loading them into the chamber under aseptic conditions. The solution is frozen by placing the partially stoppered containers on cooled shelves in a freeze-drying chamber or prefreezing in another chamber. A vacuum is applied to the chamber, and the shelves are heated to evaporate the water from the frozen state. The final step is complete stoppering of the vials, usually by hydraulic or screw-rod stoppering mechanisms installed in the lyophilizers.

It is desirable after freezing and during primary drying to hold the drying temperature (in the product) at least 4 °C to 5 °C below the eutectic point of the product. The lyophilizer should have the necessary instrumentation to control and record the key process parameters, including shelf, product, and condenser temperature, and chamber and condenser pressure. Other process controls that should be specified in manufacturing procedures are time, temperature, and pressure limits. The monitoring of product temperature is particularly important for those cycles for which there are atypical operating procedures, such as power failures or equipment breakdown.

Chapter 45

Dispensing and Weighing Controls

Dispensing and weighing controls should be such that the identity, purity, and quality of the raw materials are maintained throughout the process. In addition, the controls should be such that there is complete traceability of the materials. The requirements for weighing controls are covered in 21 CFR 211.101.

WEIGHING EQUIPMENT

Clearly written procedures for use and maintenance of weighing equipment should be available for training the operators. The procedures dictate the scales to be used for each range of weights. Weighing and measuring devices should be of suitable accuracy for the intended use, and they are be calibrated to ensure accurate results within appropriate ranges. Weighing scale calibration is performed every three to six months as per the procedures. In addition, a daily weight check in the range the scale is used within is performed with a National Institute of Standards and Technology (NIST)–calibrated weight set, and the information is logged in. The weight set should be calibrated annually. These procedures ensure that the scales are accurate when they are used for weighing of materials for commercial batches of pharmaceutical products.

DISPENSING UTENSILS

Utensils used for dispensing materials should be nonreactive to the material. If the utensils are reusable, they should be clean, sanitized, and dry before each use. The cleaning process needs to be validated to ensure that no cross-contamination occurs. Clean utensils should be stored properly in clean, labeled areas/bins and separated in the weigh room from used utensils that need cleaning.

If weighed material needs to be transferred to a secondary container, the secondary container should be clean, sanitized, dry, and nonreactive. The secondary container must be labeled immediately with the component name or item code, control or lot number of component, weight or measure transferred to the container, and batch number of product for which this component was weighed.

STAGING AREAS

A clearly marked staging area for materials that need to be weighed is necessary. This area should be large and free-flowing enough to maintain adequate separation between materials and for operators to easily take one item at a time to the weigh room. Components for each batch of product need to be segregated from each other. Material being returned to inventory after removal of required component should be staged in a separate area. These areas should be clean and with a good flow to prevent mixing of chemicals. The material names, item code, and lot number should be clearly visible at all times in order for operators to easily pick the items they need.

WEIGH ROOM

The weigh room should be separated from the rest of the production area to allow for easy material handling and dispensing without the material flying and settling on or otherwise contaminating other processes in the production area. Proper environmental controls (ISO 14644) need to be maintained as per the requirements of the raw materials that are to be weighed and the stringency of the product being manufactured. Even in the least stringent pharmaceutical product manufacture, at a minimum, the area should be ISO 14644 class 8. Only one chemical is taken into and handled in the weigh room at a time. Materials needed for each batch of product are weighed, reconciled, and removed from the weigh room before starting on a second batch. Material weighed for each product batch is separated from other batches. The pallets used to store the weighed material are labeled with the batch number, product name, pallet number, and total number of pallets. The pallets are staged in a labeled designated area for further batching.

WEIGHING PROCESS

Weighing, measuring, or subdividing operations for components must be adequately supervised. Each container of component dispensed must be examined by a second person to assure that the component was released by the *quality control* (QC) group, the weight or measure is correct as per the production batch record, and the containers are properly identified as per 21 CFR 211.101.

Electronic processes can be used to increase controls over the weighing process, but these processes need to be validated. The most common electronic process is attaching a printer to the weigh scales to print the tare, gross, and net weights dispensed. The printers can be programmed with readers that can read bar codes of the items being weighed. These printers can be made to communicate to the material resource planning software to reconcile the material weighed from inventory. These processes do decrease the sources of errors if the programs are all validated completely to ensure that they are free of ambiguity.

AUDIT

Periodic audit of production batch records should be conducted to ensure that the dispensing process retains all traceability of materials used in any batch of product. Ensure that when multiple lots of one component are used in a production batch, there is information about the quantities of each lot used in the batch record.

Chapter 46

Requirements for Critical Unit Processes

HAZARD ANALYSIS

Critical process parameters (CPPs) can be identified through the use of *hazard analysis and critical control points* (HACCP) analysis. HACCP is a process control system designed to identify and to prevent microbial, chemical, and physical hazards in production. It includes steps designed to prevent problems before they occur and to correct deviations as soon as they are detected. Such preventive control systems with documentation and verification are widely recognized by scientific authorities and international organizations as the most effective approach available for producing products safely. HACCP consists of seven principles: hazard analysis, critical control point identification, establishment of critical limits, monitoring procedures, corrective actions, record keeping, and verification procedures.

Hazard Analysis

Facilities determine the safety hazards and identify the preventive measures the facility can apply to control these hazards.

Critical Control Point Identification

A *critical control point* (CCP) is a point, step, or procedure in a process at which control can be applied and, as a result, a safety hazard can be prevented, eliminated, or reduced to an acceptable level. A safety hazard is any biologic, chemical, or physical property that may cause a pharmaceutical product to be unsafe for use.

Establishment of Critical Limits

It is important to establish critical limits for each critical control point. A *critical limit* is the maximum or minimum value to which a physical, biological, or chemical hazard must be controlled at a critical control point to prevent, eliminate, or reduce it to an acceptable level.

Monitoring Procedures

Monitoring activities are necessary to ensure that the process is under control at each critical control point.

Corrective Actions

Corrective actions are to be taken when monitoring indicates a deviation from an established critical limit. The final rule requires a plant's HACCP plan to identify the corrective actions to be taken if a critical limit is not met. Corrective actions are intended to ensure that no product injurious to health or otherwise adulterated as a result of the deviation enters commerce.

Record Keeping

HACCP regulation requires that all plants maintain certain documents, including its hazard analysis and written HACCP plan, and records documenting the monitoring of critical control points, critical limits, verification activities, and the handling of processing deviations.

Verification Procedures

Procedures for verifying that the HACCP system is working as intended are required. *Validation* ensures that the plans do what they were designed to do, that is, they are successful in ensuring the production of safe product. *Verification* ensures that the HACCP plan is adequate, that is, working as intended. Verification procedures may include such activities as review of HACCP plans, CCP records, and critical limits, and microbial sampling and analysis.

GOOD MANUFACTURING PRACTICES

The production of safe products requires that the HACCP system be built upon a solid foundation of prerequisite programs. This process traditionally has been accomplished through the application of *good manufacturing practices* (GMP). These conditions and practices are now considered to be prerequisite to the development and implementation of effective HACCP plans. Prerequisite programs provide the basic environmental and operating conditions that are necessary for the production of safe products. Common prerequisite programs may include, but are not limited to:

- *Facilities.* The establishment should be located, constructed, and maintained according to sanitary design principles. Linear product flow and traffic control minimize cross-contamination.

- *Supplier control.* Each facility should ensure that its suppliers have in place effective GMP and safety programs. These may be the subject of continuing supplier guarantee and supplier HACCP system verification.

- *Specifications.* Written specifications for all components, products, and packaging materials are needed.

- *Production equipment.* All equipment should be constructed and installed according to sanitary design principles. Preventive maintenance and calibration schedules should be established and documented.

- *Cleaning and sanitation.* All procedures for cleaning and sanitation of the equipment and the facility should be written and followed. A master sanitation schedule should be in place.

- *Personal hygiene.* All employees and other persons who enter the manufacturing plant should follow the requirements for personal hygiene.

- *Training.* All employees should receive documented training in personal hygiene, GMP, cleaning and sanitation procedures, personal safety, and their role in the HACCP program.

- *Chemical control.* Documented procedures must be in place to ensure the segregation and proper use of chemicals in the plant. These include cleaning chemicals, fumigants, and pesticides or baits used in or around the plant.

- *Receiving, storage, and shipping.* All raw materials and products should be stored under sanitary conditions and the proper environmental conditions, such as temperature and humidity, to assure their safety.

- *Traceability and recall.* All raw materials and products should be lot-coded and a recall system in place so that rapid and complete traces and recalls can be done when a product retrieval is necessary.

- *Pest control.* Effective pest control programs should be in place.

Other examples of prerequisite programs might include *quality assurance* (QA) procedures, *standard operating procedures* (SOPs) for sanitation, processes, and product formulations, glass control, procedures for receiving, storage, and shipping, labeling, and ingredient handling practices. Figures 46.1 and 46.2 can be used to determine whether a process parameter is a CCP.

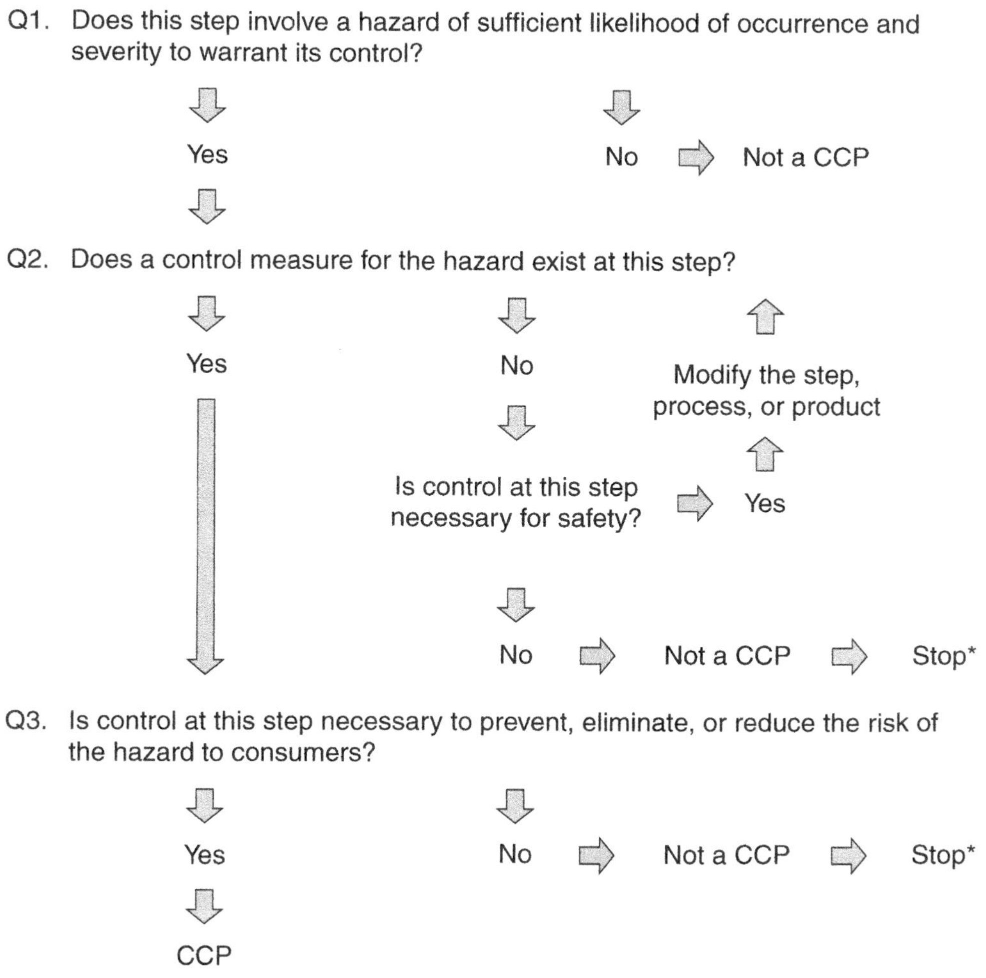

Q1. Does this step involve a hazard of sufficient likelihood of occurrence and severity to warrant its control?

Yes   No ⇨ Not a CCP

Q2. Does a control measure for the hazard exist at this step?

Yes   No   Modify the step, process, or product

Is control at this step necessary for safety? ⇨ Yes

No ⇨ Not a CCP ⇨ Stop*

Q3. Is control at this step necessary to prevent, eliminate, or reduce the risk of the hazard to consumers?

Yes   No ⇨ Not a CCP ⇨ Stop*

CCP

Figure 46.1 Critical control point decision tree example number 1.

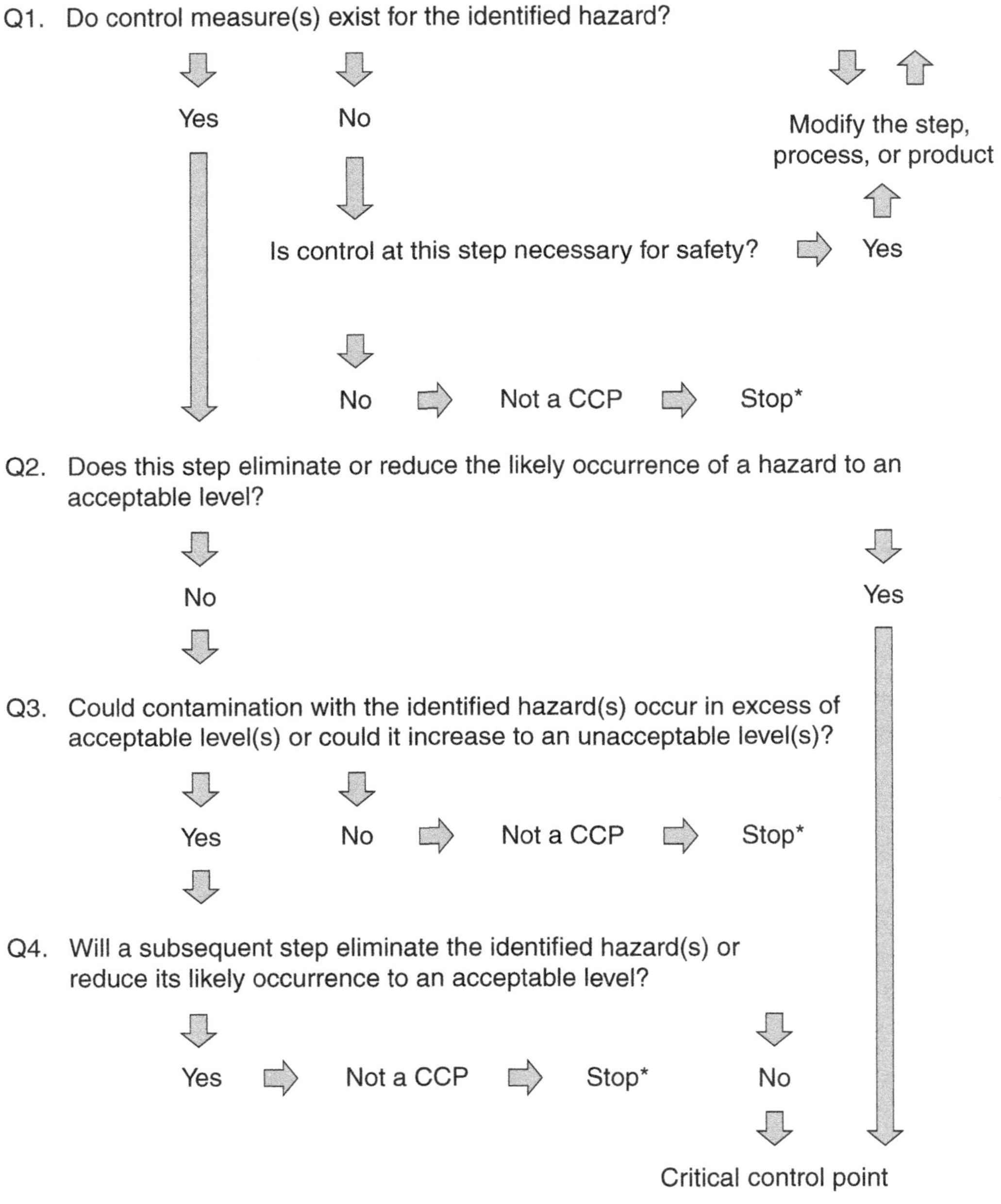

Q1. Do control measure(s) exist for the identified hazard?

Yes No   Modify the step,
process, or product

Is control at this step necessary for safety? ⇨ Yes

No ⇨ Not a CCP ⇨ Stop*

Q2. Does this step eliminate or reduce the likely occurrence of a hazard to an acceptable level?

No   Yes

Q3. Could contamination with the identified hazard(s) occur in excess of acceptable level(s) or could it increase to an unacceptable level(s)?

Yes No ⇨ Not a CCP ⇨ Stop*

Q4. Will a subsequent step eliminate the identified hazard(s) or reduce its likely occurrence to an acceptable level?

Yes ⇨ Not a CCP ⇨ Stop* No

Critical control point

Figure 46.2 Critical control point decision tree example number 2.

Chapter 47

Contamination and Cross-Contamination

INTRODUCTION

It is important to take away the sense of urgency the United States Food and Drug Administration (FDA) exudes when addressing issues of pharmaceutical contamination and cross-contamination. In fact, the Agency makes reference to the word "contamination" 23 times in 21 CFR 211 (Figure 47.1). That being said, it becomes an immensely important and often daunting task for the manufacturers of pharmaceuticals to implement and employ the appropriate controls to ensure that product contamination and the potential for product cross-contamination never occur during routine processing.

Warning Letter Citations

Failure of pharmaceutical companies to adequately protect production lines from contamination and cross-contamination is a frequently cited Form 483

- 21 CFR, Part 211
  - Subpart B—Organization and Personnel; Sec. 211.28 Personnel responsibilities
  - Subpart C—Buildings and Facilities; Sec. 211.42 Design and construction features
- Sec. 211.46 Ventilation, air filtration, air heating and cooling
- Sec. 211.48 Plumbing
- Sec. 211.56 Sanitation
  - Subpart D—Equipment; Sec. 211.67 Equipment cleaning and maintenance
  - Subpart E—Control of Components and Drug Product Containers and Closures
- Sec. 211.80 General requirements
- Sec. 211.82 Receipt and storage of untested components, drug product containers, and closures
- Sec. 211.84 Testing and approval or rejection of components, drug product containers, and closures
- Sec. 211.94 Drug product containers and closures
  - Subpart F—Production and Process Controls; Sec. 211.113 Control of microbiological contamination
  - Subpart G—Packaging and Labeling Control; Sec. 211.130 Packaging and labeling operations

Figure 47.1 "Contamination" cited in 21 CFR 211.

observation noted during establishment inspections. The focus on product contamination has increased significantly since the New England Compounding Center Recall, driven by product contamination resulting in multiple deaths from fungal meningitis.

Causes of Contamination and Cross-Contamination

Unfortunately, no single cause or event results in the contamination or cross-contamination of pharmaceuticals; otherwise, industry professionals would not need to traverse FDA's enforcement page and read about the ongoing issues impacting the pharmaceutical industry. The causes are as diverse as the industry itself, with many high-profile incidents linked directly to poor *good manufacturing practices* (GMP) for finished pharmaceuticals. FDA placed much considertion, including the querying of industry, before scripting 21 CFR 211. The prevention of contamination and cross-contamination rests squarely on the shoulders of manufacturers and the practices they employ, or fail to employ.

One of the primary causes of contamination and cross-contamination is linked to a lack of properly documented and validated cleaning processes used by pharmaceutical manufacturers. Additionally, the improper labeling of drug ingredients and the lack of effective line clearance processes rate high on the list of causes for contamination and cross-contamination of products.

TOOLS FOR PREVENTING CONTAMINATION AND CROSS-CONTAMINATION

Equipment Cleaning

First and foremost, pharmaceutical manufacturers must establish written procedures that delineate the cleaning requirements for every piece of manufacturing equipment. The procedures must contain sufficient granularity to ensure that each piece of equipment can be adequately cleaned. In some cases, it may be necessary to remove equipment from the manufacturing environment to do a proper cleaning. Regardless, the cleaning process must be properly validated as validation is a salient requirement of 21 CFR 211 and a regulatory requirement for most regulatory bodies outside the United States.

When scripting the procedures for cleaning, multiple parameters require consideration for inclusion into each written procedure. For example, five components of the cleaning process that require consideration are:

- Equipment-related parameters

- Type of residual material (residues) that require cleaning and removal

- Identification of the types of cleaning agents to be used

- Specific type(s) of cleaning processes to be used

- Process variables associated with the actual cleaning of the equipment

Equipment-Related Parameters

From an equipment standpoint, each piece of equipment should have its own equipment file that captures all preventive maintenance activities, including cleaning and, if necessary, calibration. Included in the equipment file should be the *installation qualification* (IQ) for each piece of equipment. Equipment-related parameters that need to be considered include identification of equipment sections that may be a problem for cleaning, identification of the physical/mechanical properties of the equipment (for example, 17-4 stainless steel), and disassembly instructions as appropriate (that is, identification as to whether the equipment can be cleaned in place or requires removal from the production environment).

Residue Removal

Removal of unwanted residue is the underlying reason for the proper cleaning of equipment. Four elements that need to be considered in support of the removal of residue are proper identification of all residues requiring removal as part of the cleaning process, residue reactivity and toxicity, establishment of cleaning limits, and residue solubility.

Cleaning Agents

The selection of cleaning agents and the establishment of parameters for safe and effective use is immensely important. Some of the requirements to be considered when selecting cleaning agents include the chemical composition of the cleaning agent, instructions for properly mixing and using the cleaning agent, establishment of proper handling of cleaning agents, identification of special environmental considerations, and health and safety considerations. A *material safety data sheet* (MSDS) should be available for all cleaning agents selected and employed.

Cleaning Processes

The cleaning process and all parameters relating to the cleaning process must be clearly defined within a written procedure. Elements requiring consideration for inclusion in the procedure include:

- Defining whether the cleaning process is manual or portions of it can be automated

- Identifying whether the equipment can be adequately cleaned in place

- Availability of a user manual to assist with the cleaning process

- Training requirements for personnel performing the cleaning

- Time required to properly clean a piece of equipment

- Frequency of the cleaning process (daily, weekly, and so on)

- Testing or other requirements necessary before placing cleaned equipment back into service

Process Variables

All cleaning processes, regardless of the equipment being cleaned, have variables associated with the process. Process variables requiring consideration for equipment cleaning are the temperature required for the cleaning agent, the duration of each cleaning cycle, including the number of cleaning cycles required, the time frame allocated for each cleaning, operator variability, and the outsourcing of cleaning and maintenance to a third party versus performing the work in-house with the pharmaceutical establishment's personnel.

Proper Identification and Labeling

Upon receipt, all drug ingredients must be properly identified and labeled. It is imperative that product traceability for drug ingredients be maintained to the individual lot/batch level. Additionally, it is incumbent upon pharmaceutical companies to properly store drug ingredients until such time as the ingredients are used. Special consideration should be made for special environmental requirements needed for product storage, as appropriate, for example, storage temperature.

Line Clearance

Pharmaceutical establishments are expected to have appropriate line clearance procedures in place to prevent potential contamination and cross-contamination. The line clearance procedure should clearly define lot/batch controls, documentation practices, product separation, product quarantine (if required), and the overall handling of materials during the manufacturing process.

SUMMARY

FDA is extremely vigilant when it comes to ensuring that pharmaceutical establishments have adequate infrastructure in place, including written procedures, to prevent contamination and cross-contamination. Some of the most effective tools manufacturers can use are validated cleaning procedures that define, in great detail, the cleaning requirements for all pieces of equipment. Additionally, the proper identification and labeling of all drug ingredients and an effective line clearance process are needed as the first line of defense in the prevention of contamination and cross-contamination of pharmaceuticals.

Chapter 48

Reprocessed and Reworked Materials

REPROCESSING

The reprocessing of any lot or batch of drug is given approval by *quality control* (QC). Approval of a reprocessed lot or batch of a drug by QC is based on documented scientific data, which may include validation. The reprocessing of products that fail to meet their specifications, or rejected product, is generally a rare occurrence. Materials to be reprocessed should be appropriately controlled/ quarantined to prevent unauthorized use.

Good manufacturing practices (GMP) state that reprocessing is permitted only when the following conditions are met:

- Reprocessing shall not be performed without the review and approval of the *quality unit* (QU).

- The quality of the finished product is not affected.

- The reprocessed lot meets specifications.

- The reprocessing is done in accordance with a defined procedure approved by QC.

- All risks have been evaluated, including the consideration of potential formation of by-products and/or overreacted materials.

- Complete records of the reprocessing are kept.

- A new batch number is assigned.

- Validation demonstrates that the quality of the finished product is not affected.

Reprocessing activities including introducing an intermediate or *active pharmaceutical ingredient* (API)—including one that does not conform to standards or specifications—back into the process and reprocessing by repeating a crystallization step or other appropriate chemical or physical manipulation steps (for example, distillation, filtration, chromatography, milling) that are part of the established manufacturing process are generally considered acceptable. Introducing unreacted material back into a process and repeating a chemical reaction is considered to be reprocessing unless it is part of the established process.

If reprocessing of a specific step is used for most batches, this information should be included as part of the standard manufacturing process. Continuation of a process step after an in-process control test has shown that the step is incomplete is considered to be part of the normal process. This action is not considered to be reprocessing.

REWORKING

Reworking is the process of performing additional manufacturing process steps on in-process or final material that does not meet standards or specifications, which is typically performed when there is an unexpected occurrence, and this new additional processing step is not preapproved as part of the marketing authorization. The reworked lot may be subject to additional regulatory approvals before release for distribution. Materials to be reworked should be appropriately controlled or quarantined to prevent unauthorized use. The GMP for reworking are:

- Written procedures shall be established and followed, prescribing a system for reprocessing batches that do not conform to standards or specifications and the steps to be taken to ensure that the reprocessed batches will conform with all established standards, specifications, and characteristics.

- The reworking of any lot or batch of drug is given approval by the quality control department.

Approval of a reworked lot or batch of a drug by the quality control department is based on documented scientific data, which may include validation. The reworking of products that fail to meet their specifications is undertaken only in exceptional cases. Reworking is permitted only when:

- An investigation into the reason for nonconformance of batches to established standards or specifications is performed prior to reworking batches.

- All risks have been evaluated, and a new batch number is assigned.

- The lot is reworked in accordance with a defined procedure approved by QC.

- The quality of the finished product is not affected.

- The reworked lot meets specifications. Batches that have been reworked should be subjected to appropriate evaluation, testing, stability testing, if warranted, and documentation to show that the reworked product is of equivalent quality to that produced by the original process.

- Complete records of the reworking are kept.

- The reworked lot is included in the ongoing stability program.

Before acceptance and use, reprocessed material must meet appropriate standards, specifications, and any other relevant criteria. Concurrent validation is often the appropriate validation approach for rework procedures, and this allows a protocol to define the rework procedure, how it will be carried out, and the expected results. If there is only one batch to be reworked, then a report can be written and the batch released once it is found to be acceptable.

Part VII
Filling, Packaging, Labeling

Chapter 49

Filling Operations and Controls

Filling operations and controls should be such that the identity, strength, purity, and quality of the product are maintained throughout the process. The requirements for filling and packaging controls are covered in 21 CFR 211, Subpart G. Written procedures that govern the filling processes of each product fill, and the execution of these procedures, must be documented as process controls, and any deviations must be documented and reviewed. These procedures help prevent contamination and ensure that filled product is of the strength, identity, purity, and quality it is purported to have.

MATERIALS CONTROL

Filling operations begin after the bulk manufacturing process has been completed. At this point the blend/bulk has been tested to be uniform, passed all bulk specifications, and been released for filling. Filling processes should be such that the identity, strength, and purity of the bulk are not altered. Clear written filling procedures (filling assembly procedures) specific to each type of product are required. *Filling assembly procedures* (FAPs) should be maintained through a change control process to ensure the correct versions are being used in operations. Each FAP is to be verified against the master FAP before a filling operation. The FAP should contain the product name, strength of dosage, dosage form, dosage unit, net contents, and all details and specifications regarding its filling process. The FAP or *bill of materials* (BOM) will contain the appropriate components, their part numbers, the process of assembly, and specifications of assembling to complete the filling process. The *quality unit* (QU) group will ensure that all components and bulk product needed for filling have been appropriately tested and released for filling operations.

FILLING ASSEMBLY PROCEDURES

FAPs are formally authorized packaging instructions that should exist for each product, pack size, and type. These should normally include, or make reference to, the name of the product; a description of its pharmaceutical form, strength and, where applicable, method of application; the pack size expressed in terms of the number, weight, or volume of the product in the final container; and a complete list of all the packaging materials required for a standard batch size, including quantities, sizes, and types, with the code or reference number relating to the specifications for each packaging material. Where appropriate, an example or reproduction of the relevant printed packaging materials and specimens, indicating where the batch number and expiry date of the product have been marked, should be included, as well as any special precautions to be observed, including a careful examination of the packaging area and equipment to ascertain the line clearance before and after packaging operations; a description of the packaging operation, including any significant subsidiary operations, and equipment to be used; and details of in-process controls with instructions for sampling and acceptance limits.

FILLING EQUIPMENT CONTROLS

Filling equipment should be qualified through valid *installation qualification* (IQ), *operational qualification* (OQ), and *performance qualification* (PQ) protocols to ensure it is installed as per its design specifications, and can operate and perform as required to yield desired results within preset specifications. The equipment should be maintained regularly and is to be included in the preventive maintenance program. Any replacement of parts should be like for like and should be managed within a change control process. Each piece of equipment should be assigned a unique identifier, and this number should be noted in filling records of operations that use the equipment.

Filling operations of a pilot or test batch of product should be used to determine the appropriate filling equipment needed for the process to yield filled product for preset specifications. This process should be incorporated in the FAP and is to be validated to ensure uniformity in every fill. Further, at predetermined intervals filled goods from every fill should be taken and tested for fill criteria to ensure that filling operations are under control throughout the run. These data are recorded in a filling record that is verified by a second person or QA as part of filled goods release.

CONTAMINATION CONTROLS

Contamination in filling of a product can occur from other filling processes, from the environment, or from personnel. Filling operations should be such that there is physical or spatial separation between different product filling operations to prevent contamination. Filling areas should be inspected immediately before use to ensure that all materials not required for the next fill have been removed, and this inspection should be documented.

Filling of dry powders requires special precautions to prevent generation and spreading of dust. Proper air control measures are needed for such filling operations, with a regulated supply and extraction of air of suitable quality. Contamination of one product by another product must be avoided. The significance of the contamination risk varies with the type of contaminant and type of product being contaminated. Facilities manufacturing highly sensitive materials such as hormones, biologic preparations, living organisms, cytotoxic substances, or highly active materials should use dedicated equipment in self-contained areas. Products in which contamination is likely to be most significant are products administered by injection, products applied to open wounds, and those given in large doses

> - Self-contained areas and dedicated equipment
> - Campaign production followed by appropriate cleaning with validated cleaning procedure
> - Appropriate air locks, pressure differentials
> - Pretreatment of air in the facility
> - Appropriate clothing and gowning procedures
> - Validated cleaning and decontamination procedures
> - Testing for residue

Figure 49.1 Several measures that can help avoid cross-contamination.

or for a prolonged time. Several measures can help avoid cross-contamination (Figure 49.1). Measures to prevent cross-contamination and their effectiveness should be checked periodically according to *standard operating procedures* (SOPs). Production areas where susceptible products are processed should undergo periodic environmental monitoring (for example, for microbiological monitoring and particulate matter where appropriate [ISO 14644]).

STAGED MATERIALS

Staging materials properly is a key process that prevents contamination or substitutions in a filling process and is accomplished through good line-clearance procedures with appropriate checklists and documentation of activities for each fill. The staging area for filling should be clearly marked for each filling process or line. All components needed for that fill should be brought to the corresponding staging area for the fill, and only components needed for that fill should be there. QA should check and ensure that all components are tested and released before staging for fill. Filled goods should have a location of their own and should not be commingled with components staging. Different products should not be packaged in close proximity unless there is clear physical segregation. The name and batch/lot number of each product being staged for fill, and the fill line, should be clearly displayed in the area. Filled goods should also be labeled immediately with the product name, batch number, and its release status. All staged materials should be reconciled at the end of the fill process, including any labels printed during the fill process.

STATUS LABELING

Products should be labeled immediately after fill, preferably in-line with the fill process to avoid any mistakes. Appropriate procedures for labeling in-line and off-line should be in place in case of any delays. All products at all stages should have a status label. The product should at a minimum have the batch number, product name, and release status. If a particular filled product is removed from the line for any reason, then the status label for that product should contain the reason, for example, QA sample, retain, nonconforming sample, and so on. Any filled goods without a status label are considered contaminated product. Therefore, care must be taken to have status assigned to products at all stages. Once the filling process is completed, all filled goods are removed from the line and located in a designated area with the status of "Hold."

For each batch/lot of drug product, appropriate laboratory tests should be used to determine conformity to the finished product specifications. The filled goods taken from the filling process periodically as per filling procedures for *quality control* (QC) testing are tested for the criteria specified. Once these tests have been satisfactorily completed, the filled goods of that lot can be released. The products of that lot can be moved to released inventory. Products failing to meet the established specifications must be quarantined and a nonconformance process initiated. Products not meeting the specifications must be rejected and appropriately disposed of.

Chapter 50

Environmental Monitoring

Environmental monitoring is considered by regulators (United States Food and Drug Administration [FDA]) necessary to ensure that the material/products produced are in accordance with 21 CFR 211.113, "Control of Microbiological Contamination." This section of the Code of Federal Regulations (CFR) specifically states the "appropriate written procedures . . . shall be established and followed."

A robust environmental monitoring program provides valuable information regarding the point-in-time conditions of the manufacturing environment as well as the ancillary clean areas. It allows for manufacturers to be able to potentially identify areas of contamination and be able to implement *corrective and preventive action* (CAPA) accordingly, such as additional cleaning regimens, different cleaning solutions, evaluation of personnel, and optimized material flow. It is important to note that a low level of contamination may not always be detected, and a trending program may alert manufacturers to future issues.

The specific cleanroom environment that a material/product would be manufactured in would dictate the frequency of monitoring and the specific techniques associated with the environmental monitoring program.

NONVIABLE PARTICLE MONITORING

As part of any controlled environment, nonviable particle monitoring is important both for the identification and control of *nonviable* (nonliving particles, such as dust) and *viable* (living microorganisms) contamination. This monitoring is most critical in an ISO Class 5 (Class 100) environment, typically used for aseptic processing of injectable preparations. Meeting the specifications of the established cleanroom standards is a necessity to perform manufacturing according to the certification specific (and predefined) to the cleanroom.

Typically, the size of most concern is 0.5 microns. This size is representative of the approximate size of a single microorganism. It has been shown that microorganisms can attach themselves to particles and therefore become a biologic contaminant.

Testing may be performed in two different conditions, either dynamic or static. *Dynamic* conditions are those in which activities in the cleanrooms are occurring during normal operations. Testing in these types of conditions is more desirable when in production to ensure that the cleanrooms are meeting specifications during potentially worst-case operations. *Static* conditions are those in which no operations are occurring and minimal or no personnel are in the cleanroom (with the exception of the analyst), and do not give a representative picture of cleanliness in the room with personnel flow, components, and active machine operations.

With today's technology, multiple ways exist to perform nonviable monitoring. One method is by a portable particle counting instrument, whereby an analyst performs a system verification of the instrument and, with the instrument's internal vacuum, draws a programmed volume of sample air through the system for analysis (typically through use of a laser). Particle counter sensors may be installed in critical locations in cleanrooms, which are connected to a centralized unit and computer system. They enable alarms to be sent to multiple e-mail addresses or cell phones. These units are typically continuously run and can provide real-time results as well as significant amounts of data for trending purposes.

CONTACT PLATES

Contact, surface, or RODAC (replicate organism detection and counting) testing is necessary in an environmental monitoring program. RODAC is a brand name commonly used in the pharmaceutical industry and is a registered trademark of Becton Dickinson, a manufacturer of these agar plates, although several other organizations sell such plates. Contact plates use a slightly convex surface of microbiological media to make direct contact with a flat surface. Predetermined work sites are tested by gently pressing the media surface onto the site and immediately recapping the plate. After testing, the site is wiped down with isopropyl alcohol and a lint-free wipe to ensure that no media residue is left behind. If media residue is left behind, it may become an inadvertent viable area for the growth of microorganisms. Critical areas should be tested at the end of processing to avoid contamination of a sterile processing area.

The contact plates are approximately 65 mm × 15 mm and provide a testing surface area of 25 cm². For routine monitoring, *trypticase soy agar* (TSA) with lecithin and polysorbate 80 is the media of choice. The trypticase soy agar is the nutrient media for the microorganisms (specifically bacteria) to grow in. Lecithin and polysorbate 80 are added to deactivate disinfectant residue. TSA contact plates are incubated at 30 °C to 35 °C for 48 to 72 hours.

Another formulation of media, *Sabouraud dextrose agar* (SDA), is used for monitoring of mold and yeast. The main difference between the TSA and SDA agar is that the lower pH of SDA provides for a more favorable environment of growth for fungi. SDA plates are incubated at 20 °C to 25 °C for five to seven days.

Contact plates may be used for personnel monitoring. Four fingers are closed together and the contact plate is lightly applied to the fingertips, and the thumb is lightly pressed on the surface as well. After testing, either the gloves are changed out (in the gowning area for an aseptic area) or disinfected with isopropyl alcohol and wiped with a lint-free wipe to prevent media transfer to work surfaces from gloves. In situations where media fills are occurring, sleeve monitoring may be performed as well. Contact plates should not be used on irregular or textured surfaces, only smooth surfaces. For irregular surfaces, a swab method may be used.

SWAB MONITORING

In areas that are not able to be accessed and tested with contact plates (for example, machine parts, tubing, or rough or uneven areas), swab monitoring may be performed. A lint-free swab is moistened with a buffer and placed in a sterile, capped tube. When ready for use, which would be at the end of a sterile processing operation, the swab is carefully removed from the tube, using impeccable aseptic technique, and wiped across the surface, rotating the swab to ensure the entire swab is used. The swab is re-submerged in the buffer solution and vortexed (or similar mixing) to ensure that any microbiological contamination is transferred from the swab to the solution. The solution is aseptically poured onto agar plates (TSA or SDA) and incubated. Another swab method may be used: a slightly moistened swab housed in a sterile, capped tube is wiped across the surface and, using the same rotation motion, swabbed directly on the agar plate and incubated.

Regardless of swab method used, a large potential margin for error exists due to the sheer number of steps that may lead to unintentional personnel contamination. The swab monitoring method must undergo method validation to ensure that proper recovery is achieved.

SETTLE PLATES

Settle plates are used as part of an environmental monitoring passive air-sampling program. This type of air testing is considered to be qualitative in that no predetermined quantity of air is being sampled, but rather the quality of the air (types of organisms present) is being tested by plates being placed in critical locations and the agar exposed for a specific amount of time, usually an hour.

Settle plates are composed of TSA or SDA. The plates are exposed and recapped, then incubated. One drawback of settle plates is that they desiccate with extensive exposure time and/or high airflows. In the pharmaceutical industry, this phenomenon displays a "potato chip" appearance when incubated and therefore would inhibit the potential growth of microorganisms. A maximum exposure time should be validated.

ACTIVE VIABLE AIR MONITORING

A more representative method of monitoring air quality is *active air monitoring*. Varieties of samplers include impaction, centrifugal, and membrane. These devices allow testing of the number of organisms per volume of air sampled. This method of air testing is considered to be quantitative, that is, the number of organisms can be calculated by the volume of air sampled. Active air samplers draw in a predetermined volume of surrounding air and aim the air stream at the culture medium (agar plate or agar strip) for incubation. These active air samplers are placed in critical areas of an operation, although they should not disrupt the unidirectional airflow.

Chapter 51

In-Process and Finished Goods Inspections

The pharmaceutical industry has recognized the need for better and faster systems for inspection of in-process and finished goods. A wide range of inspection solutions exist, including visual inspection systems, vacuum decay technology, seal quality inspection, blister package inspection, and container leak testing. The implementation of one or more of these inspection methodologies allows drug manufacturers to eliminate catastrophic primary packaging failures and reduce the probability of product recalls while maintaining patient confidence.

In the case of sterile products, inspection methods such as vacuum decay testing, seal force, and dye penetration testing offer an alternative to the required sterility testing to ensure that the primary container maintains the integrity and quality of the drug product throughout its lifespan. According to the United States Food and Drug Administration (FDA) guidance "Container and Closure System Integrity Testing in Lieu of Sterility Testing as a Component of the Stability Protocol for Sterile Products," some of the advantages of using these inspection methods are:

- A breach in container/closure system integrity can be detected before contamination enters the product.

- Results are timely. Sterility testing typically requires at least seven days of incubation to obtain results.

- The potential for false positive results can be reduced.

INSPECTION METHODOLOGIES

Most of the companies that provide this type of inspection technology offer non-destructive and noninvasive inspection methods that have the advantage of producing less waste. Some of the current technologies in the marketplace include seal quality inspection, nondestructive leak testing, and blister package inspection.

Seal Quality Inspection (Airborne Ultrasound)

This method is commonly used to inspect the seal quality of medical pouches and other types of flexible packages by transmitting an ultrasonic signal along the seal. The signal creates a high-resolution image of the seal structure and quality. By using this method, container defects such as abrasion, blisters, contamination, incomplete and/or misaligned seal, delamination, wrinkles, flex cracks, crooked seal, and cut seal can be identified.

Nondestructive Leak Testing (Vacuum Decay)

This technology uses the principle of changes in vacuum to determine if leaks are present in the container, thus giving an indication of the quality and integrity of the primary package container. This inspection methodology is used to inspect filling components such as presterilized stoppers and presterilized caps, and drug product packaged in vials, syringes, and ampules. One of the advantages of this method is that the test is nondestructive and noninvasive; therefore, no sample preparation is required.

Blister Package Inspection and Container Leak Testing

Blister package inspection (vacuum decay with indirect imaging) is a nondestructive and noninvasive method used for inspection of drugs packaged in blister packages. Leak detection is accomplished by detecting the change in pressure inside the test chamber resulting from gas or vapor egress from a blister package challenged with vacuum. If leaks are present, the inspection diagnostics are capable of identifying the defective blister cavities. The container leak testing (pressure decay) method uses changes in pressure to detect the presence of leaks in the container.

Freeze-Dried Product Leak Testing

Freeze-dried (lyophilized) products were previously inspected for vacuum using a spark test, but new methods are being implemented. The leak testing is performed by analyzing the headspace pressure inside the vial using laser absorption spectroscopy (optical measurement of any gas that is present). This method is nondestructive and gives an indication of the actual vacuum level in the vial. Typically, the equipment used for this type of testing has an automatic self-test system that challenges the machine by using calibrated check vials, thus ensuring the reliability of the equipment.

Vision Inspection Systems

These types of systems help the drug manufacturer analyze the quality of the product, identify product or container defects, and ensure that the data printed on the primary and secondary containers are accurate (for example, drug facts, labels). Most visual inspection system companies agree that the key factors in a visual inspection technology are lighting and optics. Lighting in relation to the geometry of the container being inspected should be considered when choosing a visual inspection system, and optics can help when trying to increase contrast between the region of interest (container or drug being inspected) and the background. For example, drug companies use visual inspection systems to inspect blister packages to make sure that they contain the correct color tablets.

Qualification and Calibration

Drug manufacturers must ensure that the inspection technology used is qualified and that any inspection processes used in their operations are validated. The inspection technology selected must be appropriate for the product that will be inspected, and the qualification needs to prove that the equipment is reliable when identifying the characterized product/container defects.

This type of equipment should be routinely calibrated, inspected, and checked according to a written program designed to ensure proper performance. Written procedures for cleaning, operating, and maintaining the automated equipment should be in place. All such programs and procedures must be approved and followed.

Chapter 52

Parenteral Product Inspection

Filled containers of parenteral products must be inspected individually for extraneous contamination and other defects that may adversely affect the integrity of the product. Units found defective in this manner must be rejected. Such inspection is one of many activities that a parenteral manufacturer uses in its effort to assure that its drug product meets the quality and purity characteristics that it purports or is represented to possess. Parenteral product inspection can be accomplished through manual visual inspection or by fully automated methods of inspection.

The inspection process must be designed and qualified to ensure that every lot of all parenteral preparations is essentially free from visible particulates. Every container whose contents show evidence of visible particulates must be rejected. Likewise, evidence of any other serious (critical or major) product/container defect provides grounds for rejecting that final container. Defect rates should be calculated at the end of each inspection process. Maximum allowable reject rates must be established.

Trends in types and size of particulates should be monitored and evaluated (for example, as part of an overall quality system). Intrinsic particulates (from the manufacturing process) are to be treated separately from extrinsic particulates (from environmental sources external to the manufacturing process itself). Three classifications of common defects have been defined (Table 52.1). Container or closure defects include cracked containers, broken finish (vial), damaged stopper or seal that compromises integrity (vial), or wrong or missing component (for example, a vial stopper or seal) or container. Examples of product defects include foreign material or particulate matter, precipitates and agglomerates, underfills and overfills, and melted cake (or a collapsed cake in some cases) for lyophilized products.

Table 52.1 Three classifications of common defects.

Critical	Affects the safety, identity, strength, quality, or purity of the product and could cause injury to patient
Major	Potential to affect the quality of the product, or can lead to serious container impairments of a lesser degree (a functional risk, whereby the product is impossible or difficult to use)
Minor	Affects the cosmetic appearance only (no potential to affect the quality of the product)

Each person engaged in parenteral product inspection operations must have the education, training, and experience, or any combination thereof, to perform his or her assigned function, whether that function involves a manual, semiautomated, or automated visual inspection process or operation. Likewise, written production and process control procedures must be followed in the execution of the parenteral product inspection, and those inspection activities are documented at the time of their performance. These personnel, procedural, and documentation requirements apply to reinspection activities as well.

Parenteral product inspection activities must be performed in accordance with established specifications, standards, sampling plans, and test procedures that are scientifically sound and appropriate to assure that the drug product conforms to appropriate standards of identity, strength, quality, and purity. The inspection process can occur as a separate process or in-line with an associated process such as filling, labeling, or packaging. Drug product containers undergoing inspection are fully assembled (container/closure assembly) and as such can be inspected in an unclassified area. Adequate facilities, equipment, and materials must be available and used to execute the inspection process, regardless of the methodology and technology being used. Special considerations must be given to drug product solutions that are prone to forming product-related particulates (for example, protein formulations). The consideration should include specific product-related training and inspection techniques, and/or characterization data for product storage time and conditions.

Reinspections may be permitted, but the number of reinspections should be limited, specified, and justified, and any special characteristics of the product should be taken into consideration, if applicable (for example, temperature and light exposure and sensitivity). The need for any reinspection event should be evaluated and authorized by the appropriate quality function. Additional, and oftentimes specialized, training and/or qualification for a reinspection activity is customary and expected.

Quality control (QC) acceptance criteria must be applied to the parenteral product inspection process, and the results must be considered when assessing a drug product batch's condition for approval and release. Each appropriate specification and appropriate statistical quality control criterion must be met. The statistical QC criteria must include appropriate acceptance levels and/or appropriate rejection levels. Statistically sound sampling plans for *acceptable quality level* (AQL) inspection must be used. ISO 2859.1 or ANSI/ASQ Z1.4 level II sampling commonly is used for the quality assurance acceptance sampling, after the inspection event, and serves as a *quality assurance* (QA) audit of the entire process (the manufacturing process, as well as the 100 percent inspection process). AQLs for particulate and other serious defect attributes are generally within the range of 0.065% to 1.0%. Reinspections are also subject to additional AQL sampling and inspection.

MANUAL VISUAL INSPECTION

The basic manual visual inspection process typically involves the individual viewing of 100 percent of the filled containers of a parenteral drug product lot. Viewing distance, particle motion in the liquid, and container volume are important factors to be considered in the design of any manual visual inspection program. The viewing must be performed against a nonglare black-and-white background under a specified nonglare light intensity. The viewing is performed by a person who has been trained and qualified to inspect for specified defects.

The purpose of the inspection is to detect container or drug product solution defects according to the established training and qualification procedures, under a controlled setting and specified inspection parameters. Containers considered defective are segregated from containers considered acceptable. Further handling of the segregated containers must be delineated in the firm's procedures.

Lighting may be fluorescent, incandescent, spot, and/or polarized, and must be nonglaring. The light intensity at the container viewing area must be specified and of a strength that facilitates defect detection. Common acceptable illumination intensities are between 2000 and 3750 lux. Higher intensities can be used for colored glass and plastic containers, and for certain types of products (for example, colored solutions). Higher intensities should be justified and characterized by the firm. Light intensity must be monitored to ensure it is within the parameters specified in the inspection procedures. Procedures should be in place to ensure sufficient relamping frequency.

The rate of the manual visual inspection process must be specified. This rate is oftentimes referred to as the "pace." A common pace, per container, is five seconds of viewing against the black background and five seconds of viewing against the white background. Otherwise, the pace or rate must be defined and characterized. Rate consistency is customarily accomplished with the aid of a pacing mechanism (for example, an LED or other type of light prompting). Pacing is the methodology used for achieving a uniform and effective rate of inspection within the defined and acceptable quality standards and levels.

Another form of manual visual inspection of parenteral products typically involves a *presentation machine*. These machines typically use many of the same features of the standard manual inspection process (that is, lighting, inspection zone, container movement to create particle movement), yet handle and present the vial to the operator in a controlled and repeatable manner. Although this process is referred to as *semiautomated* visual inspection of parenteral product, it has many of the same requirements for operator training and qualification. The machine manipulates the container during viewing, yet the operator performs the inspection.

Training

Each person engaged in manual visual inspections must have the education, training, and experience, or any combination thereof, to perform the visual inspection with reproducibility. Inspectors must be trained in relevant inspection-related procedures, theory discussion, and defect recognition (using examples). Training and testing conditions should be in alignment with those of the actual inspection process and environment. Should trainees inspect product during probationary periods, all units inspected by the trainees should be reinspected by qualified inspectors to assure the quality of the inspection and the development of the trainee.

Qualification

The *qualification* process consists of passing an eye examination, successful completion of the training and qualification activities, and a number of successful consecutive passes of the qualification kits as established by the firm's procedures. The qualification process tests the trainee's ability to identify and segregate defective units from acceptable units by using a test panel (qualification kit) composed of known defective and acceptable containers representative of the process and product, if applicable. Inspectors should be re-qualified at least annually, and the re-qualification process should include at least one successful test on the qualification kit. Quality personnel assigned to perform the verification of inspected lots (AQL inspection) should have, as a minimum, the same training and qualification as would be expected for personnel performing 100 percent manual visual inspection.

As an alternate method to the 100 percent visual inspection, fully automatic inspection machines exist for particle, cosmetic defect, and leak detection (container/closure defect) inspection. When using an automated method, it must provide at least the same level of inspection security as the manual visual inspection method. Any automated method used must provide detection rates at confidence levels that are equal to or greater than those achieved by manual inspection. Automated inspection machines should be challenged using defects obtained from the production operation.

As with any other process, equipment, or system used in the manufacture of finished pharmaceuticals, automated inspection machines and processes must be validated and documented under the company's overall validation policy. Typical performance qualification for automated inspection equipment would involve the inspection of three consecutive lots to assure reproducibility of results. Likewise, the equipment must be routinely calibrated, inspected, and checked according to a written program designed to assure proper performance. Written procedures for cleaning, operating, and maintaining the automated equipment are required. All such programs and procedures must be approved and followed.

Defect libraries, or sample sets (also referred to as *qualification/test panels* or *kits*), should be representative of those particles and defects found in the operation. Particle sizes and the types of defects present in the sets should represent the range of sizes and defects that have been, or could be, found in the production environment. When automated inspection equipment is used, it can be calibrated using the standard sets. Defect libraries must be reviewed at some appropriate frequency and modified, augmented, or revised to assure that the kits are maintained in a state that supports the inspection program's needs.

Personnel assigned to perform 100 percent manual visual inspection must pass eye examinations as part of their initial qualification and on some routine basis thereafter. Vision may be corrected, as long as acceptable results are achieved. The examinations should include visual acuity and a color and contrast assessment as well. Routine annual eye examinations for these parameters are common.

Inspector concentration, ergonomic comfort, and level of fatigue are important considerations for successful visual inspection results. Inspectors should be provided appropriate relief from the inspection rigor, which can be accomplished through rest breaks and/or job rotation.

Chapter 53

Packaging Operations and Controls

One of the most important functions that the product packaging provides is the protection of its contents. The identity, strength, and purity of the drug product can become compromised if the packaging component that is in direct contact with the dosage form contaminates the product and/or fails to protect it from environmental conditions such as temperature, humidity, and moisture.

In addition to the evaluation and qualification of the primary packaging components (those that come in direct contact with the product), drug manufacturers need to evaluate the suitability of the secondary packaging components, as a failure in packaging performance may translate to potential quality problems. For example, secondary packaging components such as cartons that are intended for additional light-exposure protection need to be controlled to ensure that the cartons are not removed while the product is in storage.

The regulations for manufacturing of container closure systems detail the qualification and controls around the primary packaging components, as well as the variables to consider when selecting a primary packaging component (for example, vial, syringe, ampule, stopper) for the dosage form. This chapter, however, only addresses the aspects of operations and controls related to the secondary packaging components (for example, cartons, pallets) and how the secondary packaging plays a role in the protection of the product.

CONTENT PROTECTION

According to the United States Food and Drug Administration (FDA) guidance for industry, "Container Closure Systems for Packaging Human Drugs and Biologics," the secondary packaging components are used for several purposes:

- To provide protection from excessive transmission of moisture or solvents into or out of the packaging system

- To provide light protection for the packaging system

- To provide additional microbiological protection by protecting the packaging system from microbial intrusion

- To provide protection from excessive transmission of reactive gases (atmospheric oxygen, inert headspace filler gas, or other organic vapors) into or out of the packaging system

The secondary packaging offers a means for product identification and presentation. For example, cartons and packaging inserts commonly are used to display information related to drug facts, dosage, and expiration dates, and as such, the information presented on them is governed by *good manufacturing practices* (GMP). On this subject, the Federal Food, Drug, and Cosmetic Act (FD&C) states that a drug or device shall be deemed to be misbranded if packaging and labeling are inappropriate, unrecognizable, misleading, or allow inks or adhesives in contact with the product. A particular type of packaging that grants additional security to the final drug product is the tamper-evident package, which can be designed as the primary packaging, secondary packaging, or a combination of both packaging systems. Currently, the Agency requires this type of package for most *over-the-counter* (OTC) drug products. The definition as stated in 21 CFR 211.132 is "A tamper-evident package is one having one or more indicators or barriers to entry which, if breached or missing, can reasonably be expected to provide visible evidence to consumers that tampering has occurred. To reduce the likelihood of successful tampering and to increase the likelihood that consumers will discover if a product has been tampered with, the package is required to be distinctive by design or by the use of one or more indicators or barriers to entry that employ an identifying characteristic (e.g., a pattern, name, registered trademark, logo, or picture)."

In summary, drug manufacturers are facing numerous challenges when it comes to ensuring the compliance and security of the final package while maintaining brand recognition and shelf presence (especially for OTC drugs). As a result, manufacturers need to balance cost efficiency, regulations, and the new trends around child-resistant and senior-friendly packaging.

PACKAGING OPERATION CONTROLS

To ensure adequate control of the packaging and labeling operation, drug manufacturers must exercise at minimum several GMP:

- Packaging line identification, indicating the type of product and lot number being packaged.

- Inspection of production facilities before the packaging/labeling operation to ensure that packaging and labeling materials from other lots are not present. An additional inspection of the facilities should be conducted at the end of the packaging operation.

- Examination of packaging and labeling materials before use to determine their suitability for the packaging operation.

- Proper maintenance and calibration of the packaging and labeling equipment.

- Label control, including packaging insert controls.

- Clear and detailed standard operating procedures and batch production records that allow for documentation of the key steps of the packaging operation (lot number, line-clearance procedures, label reconciliation, number of units packed, and results of the work-in-progress [WIP] inspection and packaged product inspection).

• Segregation of packaged product that needs to undergo inspection by the quality unit.

• Prevention of cross-contamination or errors by physical separation of different packaging/labeling operations.

• Controls over contract manufacturers that perform the secondary packaging and labeling operations.

• Control of labels. Most manufacturers are changing from cut labels to roll labels; however, where cut labels are used, drug manufacturers need to control the packaging operation by dedicating packaging lines using automated or semiautomated equipment for inspection of packaged product, and ensuring 100 percent visual inspection of the finished product for hand-applied labeling. Generally, the visual inspection is verified by a second individual who did not perform the initial 100 percent inspection.

Additionally, the personnel involved in the packaging and labeling operation must have the required training and experience to perform their assigned duties. Personnel qualifications must be current in order to support the different inspection activities performed throughout the packaging and labeling operations. Equipment changeovers and setup are critical when the production lines are used for packaging and labeling of different products. FDA has issued Form 483 observations for drug manufacturers failing to maintain control of the packaging line as a result of deficiencies in personnel training. An FDA 483 observation regarding this subject cited the manufacturer for failure to adequately train employees engaged in the manufacture, processing, or holding of a drug product in GMP or in the particular operations performed by the employees [21 CFR 211.25(a)]. For example, employees engaged in the production of 260 mg/26 mL liquid oral product, lot #XYZ, which was mislabeled as 20 mg/2 mL, did not follow the company's written procedures pertaining to product changeover on the Auto Labe labeling system or those requiring documentation of filler settings.

THE PACKAGING LINE

Figure 53.1 depicts the steps in a typical final packaging process. Common operations in the packaging of pharmaceuticals include:

• Inspection of packaging and labeling materials to determine suitability for use.

• Inspection and verification of the packaging line (equipment) to ensure that the equipment is ready for use.

• Other preparation activities, which include verification of batch records being present in order to document the packaging/labeling operations.

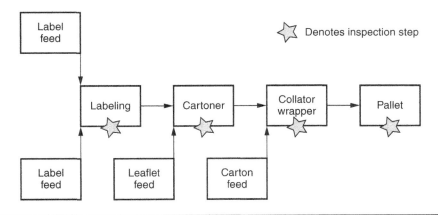

Figure 53.1   Typical final packaging process. Inspection of the product as it goes from the labeling operation to the palletizing operation occurs at every step to assure that containers and packages have the correct label. At the end of the process, the quality unit performs a visual examination of a representative sample of the packaged product.

Source: Figure used with permission of Dixie A. Dean, Roy Evans, and Ian Hall, eds. 2000. *Pharmaceutical Packaging Technology.* London and New York: Taylor & Francis.

- Label application to primary packaging (labeling equipment).

- Packaging inserts application (cartoner).

- Product in its primary packaging is placed in cartons (cartoner), that is, single dose per cartoner or multiple doses per cartoner.

- Product is collated and arranged on pallets for storage or distribution.

Chapter 54

Labeling Operations and Controls

L abels are an integral part of the drug product packaging process and the marketing of the final drug product. They provide essential information regarding the contents of the drug product, such as strength, dosage, medical claims, and drug warnings. According to the United States Food and Drug Administration (FDA), drug products that are mislabeled can pose a threat to public health, cause product recalls, and seriously damage the image of the drug manufacturer.

As a result, labels are designed, produced, and controlled to meet *good manufacturing practices* (GMP) that ensure the identity and quality of the product. Additionally, it is the ultimate responsibility of the drug manufacturer to ensure that the label integrity is never compromised (print quality, label adhesion, and so on) during the life span of the drug product, from distribution to its intended use. The requirements for label control and packaging components are becoming increasingly stringent. To address these requirements, drug manufacturers, as well as label manufacturers, are moving toward electronic verification of the printed labels, and improved inventory control systems that allow tracking using bar codes printed on each label.

In February 2004, FDA released a rule requiring bar codes on human drugs and biologic products. By implementing bar code tracking, FDA hopes to reduce the number of medication errors, thus ensuring that health professionals provide patients with the right drug and proper dosage. The rule also applies to establishments that handle blood components that will be used for transfusions. According to FDA, this new rule will help prevent nearly 500,000 adverse events and transfusion errors and concurrently will help save US$93 billion in healthcare costs over 20 years.

FDA's final rule requires the use of a linear bar code to code the *National Drug Code* (NDC) on most prescription drug products and certain *over-the-counter* (OTC) drug products.

LABEL RECEIPT

In general, the labels destined for the packaging operation of the drug product are printed by a vendor that has been certified by the drug manufacturer. To ensure that the correct labels are received, each shipment of labels that arrives at the manufacturing site is subjected to several steps:

- The receiving department at the drug manufacture receives the labels. Records must be maintained for each shipment of labels received from the vendor (printer).

- A quarantine area or controlled area is designated to store the received labels while incoming inspection is done by the *quality unit* (QU).

- The labels are sampled for inspection against defined reject criteria (*acceptable quality level* [AQL] inspection method).

- The QU releases or rejects the labels. If the label is released, an identification or lot number typically is assigned.

- The labels are maintained in a secured and controlled area while awaiting release for packaging use. Access to this controlled area should be granted only to a few individuals. Additionally, labels destined for different products or different strengths of the same product need to be stored separately to avoid potential errors.

LABELING ISSUANCE TO MANUFACTURING

GMP guidelines are in place to ensure that not only the type of label but also its quantity are controlled strictly when being issued for packaging of the drug product. The manufacturers of the drug must have *standard operating procedures* (SOPs) that detail the steps to follow when labels are issued to manufacturing.

Label specimen verification is required to ensure that the current version of the label is being documented on the drug product batch record. Label verification is required to guarantee that all labels to be used match the identity of the label template (specimen) specified in the drug product batch record. The label verification step implies a 100 percent inspection of all labels that will be installed in the labeling equipment. Each label is counted and verified either by manual methods or by electronic verification. Several methods of electronic verification currently are used by drug manufacturers, and they typically use an electronic visual inspection of each label by means of a camera that compares a photograph of each label with the approved label specimen.

SOPs specify how many labels will be issued against the planned number of containers to be labeled. Furthermore, the completed batch records must show comparisons between the number of labels that were issued to manufacturing, the number of labels used, and the number of labels not used during the operation. An investigation is initiated and completed if any discrepancies are found during the label reconciliation process.

Unused labels can be returned to the controlled storage area if they have not been printed with the drug product batch number; however, most companies have procedures requiring that unused labels be destroyed in an effort to prevent label errors.

LABEL QUALITY AND LABEL OPERATIONS

Label control is extremely important for all drug products, as labeling mix-ups and printing errors continue to be a major source of product recalls. Drug manufacturers need to ensure that the information printed on the labels does not degrade over time. Thus, it becomes fundamental that the inks used for label manufacturing are light resistant, do not smear, and do not leave traces of odor. Additionally,

> - Labeling equipment identification, and confirmation of calibration status
>
> - Names of personnel involved in labeling operations
>
> - Line clearance verification before and after label operations
>
> - Label segregation to avoid mix-ups
>
> - Label reconciliation numbers
>
> - In-process examination of label quality (that is, label adherence, location on container)

Figure 54.1   Labeling operations.

the printing must conform to the approved label specimen (for example, uniformity, art specification).

Another factor that is controlled by drug manufacturers is the labeling operation. Just as batch records are required to document label issuance operations, they are also required for recording key aspects of the actual labeling operation (Figure 54.1).

EXPIRATION DATING

The guidelines for GMP require that the drug expiration date is noted on the label. Moreover, if the drug product is to be reconstituted at the time of use, the label must include the expiration dates for the reconstituted and unreconstituted drug product.

EXAMPLES OF FDA WARNING LETTERS

Failure to ensure that strict control is exercised over labeling issued for use in drug product labeling operations as required by 21 CFR § 211.125(a). Your firm does not exercise adequate controls over the labeling issuance and labeling operation of the drug products being handled at your facility. Your firm's personnel were not aware of the labeling requirements set forth by the abovementioned regulation.

Failure to ensure that written procedures are designed and followed to assure that correct labels, labeling, and packaging materials are used for drug products as required by 21 CFR § 211.130. Your firm had not established or implemented procedures to assure that correct labels were applied to your . . . products.

Failure to control labeling operations to prevent labeling mix-ups and to document the labeling used in the DHR as required by 21 CFR § 820.120(d). For example, implant . . . was manufactured and released on 10/28/08 with labeling that indicated that the device was non-sterile. However, this implant was returned to . . . for sterilization and the sterilization record found in the *device history record* (DHR) for this implant shows that the implant was sterilized on 11/5–6/07. The sterilization record was signed off on 11/8/07, and the product was shipped on 11/18/07. The only label included with this DHR indicates that the product was labeled as nonsterile.

Other Examples of FDA Warning Letters

Your product labeling specifies a 10-day use limit under the "Warnings" heading in the "Drug Facts" panel (that is, "Stop use and ask a doctor if . . . pain gets worse or lasts more than 10 days") but this warning appears only within the Drug Facts panel of the retail package. Its placement within the perimeter of the Drug Facts panel suggests that it applies exclusively to the analgesic use discussed in that panel. It is contradicted by the statement elsewhere on the labeling "For calcium, adults and children 12 years and over, take up to 4 caplets per day . . . ," without any limitation on duration indicated.

Your product labeling warns against use by children and teens, to prevent Reye's syndrome (that is, "Warning—Reye's syndrome: Children and teenagers should not use this medicine for chicken pox or flu symptoms before a doctor is consulted about Reye's syndrome, a rare but serious illness reported to be associated with aspirin."), but this warning appears only within the "Drug Facts" panel of the retail package. Its placement within the perimeter of the Drug Facts panel suggests that it applies exclusively to the analgesic use discussed in that panel. It is contradicted by the statement elsewhere on the labeling "For calcium, adults and children 12 years and over, take up to 4 caplets per day . . . ," without any warning that there are circumstances where it is not appropriate for children and teenagers to take the product.

Chapter 55

Filling and Packaging Records

An essential aspect of a robust documentation program is the existence of records that provide a detailed history of the manufacturing stages, testing, and any relevant event that was part of the execution of a batch of drug product. As a result, it is expected that the regulations for *good manufacturing practices* (GMP) of finished pharmaceuticals (21 CFR 211, Eudralex Volume 3, Chapter 4, among others) require companies to establish not only written procedures for the production of the finished drug products, but also batch production and process control records to assure product identity, strength, quality, and purity. The written procedures, as well as the batch records, provide clear instructions on how to execute a batch of drug product per approved procedures, and at the same time they guarantee uniformity from batch to batch.

REGULATIONS AND GUIDANCE DOCUMENTS

Filling and Packaging Records

Separate batch production record(s) are prepared for each batch of drug product to cover the different manufacturing steps from filling to packaging. The batch production records should be designed in such a way that they provide clear instructions on how to manufacture the batch and ensure consistency in execution from batch to batch even when differently qualified individuals execute the manufacturing operation. The filling batch production record should include:

- Initials or signature of the staff performing the operation.

- Dates.

- Component information including, but not limited to, material description, material number, quantity used, and expiration dating.

- Checks on the work area, such as line clearance procedures before the filling operation begins (area free of items not intended for use in the operation).

- Yield calculations at the end of each manufacturing step; these calculations are performed by a qualified individual and independently verified by another organizational unit staff member.

- Documentation on any major equipment used during the production of the batch and documentation of equipment suitability verification (for example, checks on calibration due dates, cleaning status).

- Manufacturing time constraints. When appropriate, time limits should be established for the completion of the filling step to guarantee the quality of the drug product; when deviation to the production time limit occurs, the event should be documented with a justification on the batch record.

- Fill weight calculation/verification

- Interventions and line stoppages on the filling batch record listing the time of the event and the duration of the intervention or line stoppage

- Any sampling performed

The packaging batch production record should include:

- Initials or signature of the staff performing the operation

- Product description (name, type, strength, pack size)

- Product specifications

- Inventory record of each component used during the packaging operation (cartons and labels, among others)

- Review of the label information against the established label specifications, including a copy of each label signed and dated by the staff responsible for label approval

- Line clearance operation of the packaging area before and after use

- Special precautions to be observed during the packaging process

- Any sampling performed

Production, Process Control, and Laboratory Record Review

The filling, packaging, and labeling records must be reviewed by the corresponding organizational unit and the *quality unit* (QU) to ensure that the finished drug product was manufactured according to the established and approved procedures. The review of the production and process control records must include an assessment of any event failures or deviations that could potentially affect the sterility of the product. Where deviations to the written procedures exist, the appropriate organizational units must document the changes and their corresponding justification. The production record review should include, but it is not limited to:

- Events that could have impacted the environment in the *critical zone* (an area designed to maintain sterility of sterile materials). Sterilized product, containers, closures, and equipment may be exposed in the critical zone.

- Review of maintenance activities that could have impacted the execution of the batch.

- Batch and trending data for utility and support systems (*heating, ventilation, and air conditioning* [HVAC], particle monitoring system, and so on).

- Documentation concerning adherence to critical process parameters such as fill time limits and sterilization expiration dates.

The laboratory records are reviewed to ensure compliance with specifications and standards. The information contained in these records comprises descriptions of the samples received for testing, batch number, quantity, the date the samples were taken, the date the samples were received for testing and tested, calculations, and the initials or signatures of the staff that performs and verifies the test results.

Chapter 56

Artwork Development and Controls

The development of labeling artwork is a collaborative process involving both the commercial side of the organization (for example, Marketing) and the medical and regulatory side of the organization (for example, Medical Affairs, Regulatory Affairs). Often, competing demands for space occur as the groups negotiate how to incorporate all of the required safety and regulatory information while maintaining the look and feel or the corporate branding that is important to the company. This negotiation process ultimately results in the artwork (graphical representation of the proposed labeling) that is used by printing firms to produce the final printed labeling.

Like the drug product itself, the labeling that accompanies the product has a life cycle of its own. The collaborative development of labeling begins early in the product development phase and evolves as more information is learned about the drug, specifically its utility and safety profile. The labeling evolves after approval as more is learned about the drug product through its use in the general population. Product labeling needs to be current with all new information to ensure that medical practitioners and patients have the information that they need to make the best possible healthcare decisions.

A graphical representation of the product labeling is developed and is typically what is reviewed and approved internally before being sent to the printers for conversion to the actual labeling materials. These graphical files need to be controlled to ensure that what is submitted to the printers is current and contains the most accurate information regarding the safety and efficacy of the product. Version control is critical to this process, and procedures should be in place, both within the organization and at the labeling printers, to control current and obsolete versions of the graphical files.

PRINTING PROCESS

Regulatory agencies expect that there will be appropriate rigor in the printing process to ensure that labeling is accurate and that errors do not occur. Pharmaceutical companies should treat labeling vendors as they would any other vendor (that is, labeling vendors should be evaluated or audited and qualified in a manner similar to any other raw material or packaging component vendor).

Vendor Proof

Once the graphical representations are reviewed and approved internally, the files are forwarded to the labeling vendors to be printed. The labeling vendor should be expected to take the files and generate a vendor proof that is reviewed by the pharmaceutical company to ensure that the new or revised labeling is accurate and matches the internally approved artwork. If issues are noted, procedures should be in place to ensure that corrections are made and that preventive measures are implemented to preclude future problems.

Gang Printing

Gang printing is a practice that involves placing many different print projects on the same printing sheet in an effort to reduce printing costs and paper waste. The United States Food and Drug Administration (FDA) *good manufacturing practices* (GMP) regulations explicitly prohibit the use of gang printing of labeling for different drug products or different strengths or net contents of the same drug product unless the labeling from the gang-printed sheets is adequately differentiated by size, shape, or color. Because of the high potential for errors, pharmaceutical companies typically do not allow gang printing of drug product labeling.

Roll Label Splicing

Flexographic printing has become commonplace in the production of pharmaceutical labeling. After the labels are printed, they are typically die cut and, if necessary, wound onto master rolls. These master rolls are then slit into individual label widths and counted to provide the required number of labels per roll. It is not uncommon for the roll stock to break during the various steps of the process or for the process to require multiple rolls of label stock to complete the printing run. When this occurs, it may be necessary to splice the roll stock together. It is critical for the label vendor to clearly identify the presence of splices in each roll of labeling. The vendor should provide a report that demonstrates that they have verified that the labeling on each side of the splice is correct and that there are no issues with the printed copy on either side of the splice. Upon receipt of the labeling at the pharmaceutical company, verification of the spliced rolls should take place.

Off-Line Printing

The packaging and labeling of pharmaceutical products typically occurs together as a single operation. Labeling is applied to the packaged product, and a unique batch number and expiration date is printed on the labeling as part of this operation. In these cases, where the batch and expiration date are printed online, it is possible to return unused labeling to the secured storage area for use on another packaging run.

There are instances, however, where the labeling must be printed off-line with the batch-specific information. Equipment on the packaging lines may not be capable of printing the batch-specific information, or the type of product may preclude the ability to print this information online. In these instances, very tight controls over the use of this batch-specific labeling need to be in place. Any labeling that is printed off-line with batch-specific information should be stored separately from other labeling, and there should be very tight controls on reconciling the quantity used during the packaging run. Any labeling that is printed off-line with batch-specific information can not be returned to inventory and must be discarded and destroyed after completion of the packaging operation.

SECURE STORAGE OF LABELING

GMP regulations require that printed materials and labeling be stored in an area with limited access and in a manner that will prevent errors. According to FDA GMP regulations, the labels and labeling materials for each different drug product, strength, dosage form, or quantity of contents should be stored separately (that is, adequately segregated, either spatially or in separate containers) and with suitable identification to preclude errors. The regulations state that access to the labeling storage area should be limited to authorized personnel. Similarly, labeling that is returned to the labeling storage area (for example, after completion of a packaging operation) should be identified appropriately and stored in such a manner as to prevent errors.

Similar requirements are identified in the Canadian GMP regulations. Printed packaging materials need to be stored in an area that is restricted to designated personnel who are supervised by individuals with training and experience and who are directly responsible to the person in charge of the manufacturing, or a person having the same qualification.

DESTRUCTION OF LABELING

On a global basis, the GMP regulations are consistent when it comes to destruction of labeling. Any labeling that fails to meet specifications upon incoming receipt must be destroyed. Labeling that is superseded by new labeling, or is considered outdated, should be destroyed. Finally, any labeling that is not used, and that has been printed with lot (batch) number and expiration date (or any other batch-specific information) should be destroyed. No matter what destruction process is used, however, it should render the labeling materials unusable to prevent their unauthorized or mistaken use.

CONTROL OF GRAPHICAL FILES AND PRINTING PLATES

One of the major challenges in the area of label printing is the frequency with which product labeling changes in today's regulatory environment. Regulatory agencies want to ensure that healthcare providers and patients have access to current information related to the safety of pharmaceutical products, and, as a result, updates to the labeling are common. Version control and the handling of current and obsolete graphical files and printing plates is of critical importance to ensure that this current information is incorporated correctly and in a timely fashion.

Labeling vendors, like the pharmaceutical company itself, should have procedures in place to control current and obsolete versions. Current versions should be accessible for use, while obsolete versions should be archived or removed from an active file location. Printing plates for obsolete versions should be destroyed and documentation of their destruction provided to the pharmaceutical company for verification of the destruction process.

Part VIII

Product Development and Technology Transfer

Chapter 57

Quality by Design Concepts

To understand the most current thinking behind product development and regulatory expectations, it is important to understand the principles built into the International Conference on Harmonization (ICH) *Pharmaceutical Development* (ICH Q8) guidance. The concepts in ICH Q8 came about as a compromise of members of the ICH, which included the United States Food and Drug Administration (FDA) and Pharmaceutical Research and Manufacturers of America (PhRMA) with their counterparts from Europe and Japan. ICH Q8 describes the suggested contents for the 3.2.P.2 Pharmaceutical Development section of a regulatory submission in the ICH M4 *common technical document* (CTD) format. ICH Q8 was published in the Federal Register, May 22, 2006, as a guidance for pharmaceutical product development.

Before the ICH Q8 guidance, in the United States, the design and development information submitted in an application was variable; some information was submitted in the Investigational New Drug (IND) application, some information was submitted in European Union (EU) reports, and some information was distributed in New Drug Applications (NDAs) in inconsistent format. Europe had incorporated key elements of the ICH Q8 guidance, in that submissions described formulation development, the critical product attributes, and design of the manufacturing process. Japan had limited expectations, with more information for complex dosage forms. In general, though, there was limited (regulatory) incentive to truly understand processes and products, and to optimize them.

After implementation of the ICH Q8 guidance, product quality and performance may be achieved and assured by design of effective and efficient manufacturing processes, product specifications are based on mechanistic—mathematical relationship between input and output—understanding of how formulation and process factors impact product performance, and there is the ability to affect continuous improvement and continuous real-time assurance of quality.

In the United States, the ICH guideline is discretionary and nonbinding. It represents FDA's thinking on NDA submissions, and companies can offer alternative approaches. ICH, however, provides the preferred FDA format for submissions.

QUALITY BY DESIGN

Quality by design (QbD) designs quality into the product using knowledge of process. With QbD, a relationship exists between quality attributes and product efficacy and performance; with increased knowledge and control, decreased regulatory oversight is justified because all critical sources of variability are identified and explained, variability is controlled by the process, and product quality attributes can be accurately and reliably predicted over the design space established for materials used, process parameters, and environmental and other conditions.

ICH Q8 shows that pharmaceutical development is a learning process. Understanding is gained, for example, by knowledge, formal experimental designs, *process analytical technology* (PAT), and life cycle knowledge. Formal experimental design (*design of experiments* [DOE]) is a structured, organized method for determining the relationship between factors affecting a process and the output of that process. PAT is a system for designing, analyzing, and controlling manufacture through timely measurements (that is, during processing) of critical quality and performance attributes of raw and in-process materials and processes with the goal of ensuring final product quality. Both successes and failures are described as part of the life cycle story that demonstrates QbD.

CRITICAL PROCESS PARAMETER

The *critical process parameters* (CPPs) are the measured variables that are known to have an effect on one or more product quality attributes. All CPPs must be identified and controls established within a defined acceptable range. The ranges for these parameters may be typically obtained in later development studies (that is, full-scale, engineering studies, or technology transfer studies) aimed to optimize the process for commercialization, conducted in parallel with the human clinical trials. The process optimization efforts must ensure that the enhanced process remains equivalent to that used for the making of the clinical trials product.

CRITICAL QUALITY ATTRIBUTES

The *critical quality attributes* (CQA) are intrinsic quality characteristics that are desired or needed to ensure patient safety and benefit of the drug product. In ICH Q6A, some *active pharmaceutical ingredient* (API) attributes should be considered critical, regardless of the drug product end use. Identification, physicochemical properties, appearance, assay, and purity are applicable to all drug products. Particle size, microbial purity, and polymorphism depend on the drug product. The ICH Q6A decision trees can be used to determine the criticality of these quality attributes for solids, solutions, or sterile products. All CQA must be identified and have established acceptance criteria.

DESIGN SPACE

Information from pharmaceutical development studies is a basis for risk management (using ICH Q9). Critical parameters carry the risks, critical formulation and process parameters generally are identified through an assessment of the extent to which their variation can have an impact on the quality of the drug product, and this assessment helps define design space. Design space is therefore defined as the multidimensional combination and interaction of input variables (for example, material attributes) and process parameters that have been demonstrated to provide assurance of quality.

Within the regulatory framework, working within the design space submitted in an application is not considered a change. Movement out of the design space is considered to be a change and would normally initiate a regulatory post-approval change process, requiring regulatory notification. Therefore, ICH Q8 Section 2.4 "Design Space" facilitates regulatory flexibility. In the traditional submission process, there is limited knowledge, and any change needs new data and new approval. With the model after Q8 implementation, an influence of factors is explored, creating knowledge, and risk analysis of impact of change is possible; there is the ability to move within a defined area post-approval that gives flexibility for continuous improvement without the need for further approval. In addition, expanded design space facilitates flexible regulatory approaches. An increased understanding of the product life cycle, including material attributes—manufacturing process and process controls—facilitates the approval and submissions process.

VALIDATION PRINCIPLES WITH QUALITY BY DESIGN

Validation is evidence of a high degree of assurance that a specific process will consistently produce a product meeting its predetermined specifications and quality attributes. In ICH Q8, *continuous process verification* is defined as an alternative approach to process validation in which manufacturing process performance is continuously monitored and evaluated. Product quality and performance are achieved and assured by design of effective and efficient manufacturing processes.

Traditionally, validation has focused on system operations and testing the output of the system. In the ICH Q8 validation approach, validation focuses on system design, and on testing the quality that is being built into the process. The Q8 validation approach focuses on process design space and ongoing assessments. It uses DOE to define CQA, and design space to document the process used to verify CQA. The CQA and their interrelation are documented, and the CPP for each CQA is identified. The affect that CQA variability has on the process is identified. The design space for the process is formed based on findings.

The CQA and CPP are identified through experiments, risk analysis, and analyzer assessments. Validation is based on the range of control of the process within the design space rather than map testing to the frozen specification parameters.

PROCESS ANALYTICAL TECHNOLOGY TOOLS

FDA realized that changes were needed in its inspection approach: the perception was that the existing regulatory system was rigid and did not favor innovation. To encourage innovation, the FDA launched a new initiative in August 2002, Pharmaceutical cGMPs for the 21st Century: A Risk-Based Approach. This program included up-to-date concepts of risk management and quality systems, use of the latest scientific advances in technology, risk-based approaches that encouraged innovation, and a move to make FDA submissions and inspections more consistent. The Agency's resources addressed the most significant health risks. The desired state of pharmaceutical process is achieved when science and engineering principles are used effectively for assessing and mitigating risks related to poor product and process quality. This process should be accomplished with design of effective and efficient manufacturing processes, specifications that are based on understanding of how formulation and process factors affect product performance, continuous real-time quality assurance, and regulatory policies and procedures that accommodate the most current level of scientific knowledge. Together with the design space concept in QbD, the FDA envisioned *process analytical technology* (PAT) as part of the new initiatives that would reduce the risks associated with manufacturing uncertainty; risks would be fully contained and controlled.

PAT is a system for designing, analyzing, and controlling manufacturing through timely measurements during processing of critical quality and performance attributes of raw and in-process materials and processes, to ensure final product quality. Analytical requirements of PAT include chemical, physical, microbiological, mathematical, and risk analysis. PAT is not simply online/off-line, real-time analytical measurements. PAT combines multivariate tools for design, data acquisition, and analysis, process analyzers, process control tools, and continuous improvement and knowledge management tools.

MULTIVARIATE TOOLS

Multivariate tools include mathematical approaches, such as statistical DOE, response surface methodologies, process simulation, and pattern recognition tools, to increase understanding of the relevant multifactorial relationships (for example, between formulation, process, and quality attributes) and applicability of this knowledge in different scenarios (that is, generalization). These tools enable the identification and evaluation of product and process variables that may be critical to product quality and performance. They may identify potential failure modes and mechanisms and quantify their effects on product quality.

PROCESS ANALYTICAL TECHNOLOGY

PAT adds process analyzers for in-process multivariate (multiple variable) measurements, which are taken in one of three ways:

- *At-line*, where the sample is removed and analyzed close to the process stream

- *Online*, where the sample is diverted from the manufacturing process to an analyzer, and possibly returned to the stream

- *In-line*, which may be an invasive or noninvasive process that analyzes the sample while it is part of the process stream

PROCESS CONTROL TOOLS

We are most familiar with traditional in-process control tools used for monitoring such things as temperature, pH, pressure, flows, and other physical parameters (that is, univariate measurements). These measurements provide enough information to adjust equipment to more optimal settings for each variable as required, but do not typically provide enough information to learn more about the process as a whole. With PAT, rapid, dedicated in-/online testing is added to these traditional tools to monitor samples periodically and from targeted/strategic locations to actively manipulate the process to maintain a desired state. In the PAT framework, validation can be demonstrated through this continuous quality assurance, where a process is continuously monitored, evaluated, and adjusted using validated in-process measurements, tests, controls, and process end points.

CONTINUOUS IMPROVEMENT AND KNOWLEDGE MANAGEMENT TOOLS

Continuous learning through data collection and analysis over the life cycle of a product is important to increase the process knowledge base. A knowledge base can be of most benefit when it consists of scientific understanding of the relevant multifactorial relationships, for example, between formulation, process, and quality attributes. The desired state of pharmaceutical process gives the ability to effect continuous improvement and continuous real-time assurance of quality—continuously optimize the process within the design space—so that each batch is a new validation batch, and each batch provides the opportunity for a better process model. Continuous learning through data collection and analysis over the life cycle of a product is important to increase the process knowledge base.

Chapter 58

Phase-Appropriate GMP Requirements

The United States Food and Drug Administration (FDA) published a final rule in the Federal Register on "Current Good Manufacturing Practice and Investigational New Drugs Intended for Use in Clinical Trials," effective September 15, 2008. This guidance takes into consideration the nature of phase 1 clinical studies. It recognizes that the studies are of short duration, in well-controlled clinical settings with healthy subjects; therefore, it exempts most phase 1 investigational drugs and the *active pharmaceutical ingredients* (APIs) for the Investigational New Drug (IND) from compliance with 21 CFR 210 and 211. FDA is considering guidelines on investigational drugs used for phase 2 and phase 3 clinical trials; however, until they are published, 21 CFR 210 and 211 continue to apply.

In Europe, the Clinical Trials Application (CTA) requires *good manufacturing practices* (GMP) for all clinical trial phases and focus on the quality of the end product, and places emphasis on the *qualified person* (QP) for oversight of product quality.

CLINICAL TRIAL PHASES

FDA has five categories for describing the clinical trial of a drug based on the study's characteristics, such as the objective and number of participants. The five phases are:

- *Phase 0.* Exploratory study involving very limited human exposure to the drug, with no therapeutic or diagnostic goals (for example, screening studies, microdose studies).

- *Phase 1.* Studies that are usually conducted with healthy volunteers (20 to 80 people) and that emphasize safety. The goal is to discover the drug's most frequent and serious adverse events and, often, how the drug is metabolized and excreted.

- *Phase 2.* Studies that gather preliminary data (100 to 300 people) on effectiveness (that is, whether the drug works in people who have a certain disease or condition). For example, participants receiving the drug may be compared with similar participants receiving a different treatment, usually an inactive substance (called a *placebo*) or a different drug. Safety continues to be evaluated, and short-term adverse events are studied.

- *Phase 3.* Studies that gather more information about safety and effectiveness by studying different populations (1000 to 3000 people) and different dosages, and by using the drug in combination with other drugs.

- *Phase 4.* Studies occurring after FDA has approved a drug for marketing. These including post-market requirement and commitment studies that are required of or agreed to by the sponsor. These studies gather additional information about a drug's safety, efficacy, or both.

Chapter 59

Raw Materials, Packaging, and Infrastructure for Product Development

The United States Food and Drug Administration (FDA) provides guidance for raw materials, packaging, and infrastructure for product development within the guidance for industry *Process Analytical Technology—A Framework for Innovative Pharmaceutical Development, Manufacturing, and Quality Assurance.* The premise of this document is to ensure that the current concepts of risk management and quality systems approaches are incorporated into the design, development, and manufacture of pharmaceuticals while maintaining product quality.

Effective innovation in development, manufacturing, and quality assurance would be aided by answering several questions:

- What are the mechanisms of degradation, drug release, and absorption?

- What are the effects of product components on quality?

- What sources of variability are critical?

- How does the process manage variability?

- What are the packaging considerations?

The goal of *process analytical technology* (PAT) is to enhance understanding and control the manufacturing process, which is consistent with current drug quality system thought: quality can not be tested into products—it should be built in or should be by design.

Quality is built into pharmaceutical products through a comprehensive understanding of:

- The intended therapeutic objectives, patient population, route of administration, and pharmacological, toxicological, and pharmacokinetic characteristics of a drug

- The chemical, physical, and biopharmaceutic characteristics of a drug

- Design of a product and selection of product components and packaging based on drug attributes

- The design of manufacturing processes using principles of engineering, material science, and *quality assurance* (QA) to ensure acceptable and reproducible product quality and performance throughout a product's shelf life

Many tools are available that enable process understanding for scientific, risk-managed pharmaceutical development, manufacture, and QA. These tools, when used within a system, can provide effective and efficient means for acquiring information to facilitate process understanding, continuous improvement, and development of risk mitigation strategies. In the PAT framework, these tools can be categorized as:

- Multivariate tools for design, data acquisition, and analysis

- Process analyzers

- Process control

- Continuous improvement and knowledge management

Multivariate tools for design, data acquisition, and analysis from a physical, chemical, or biological perspective, and pharmaceutical products and processes, are complex multifactorial systems. Many development strategies can be used to identify optimal formulations and processes. The knowledge acquired in these development programs is the foundation for product and process design. Methodological experiments based on statistical principles of orthogonality, reference distribution, and randomization provide effective means for identifying and studying the effect and interaction of product and process variables. Traditional one-factor-at-a-time experiments do not address interactions between product and process variables. When used appropriately, these tools enable the identification and evaluation of product and process variables that may be critical to product quality and performance. The tools may identify potential failure modes and mechanisms and quantify their effects on product quality.

Some process analyzers provide nondestructive measurements that contain information related to biologic, physical, and chemical attributes of the materials being processed. These measurements can be:

- *At-line,* where the sample is removed and analyzed close to the process stream

- *Online,* where the sample is diverted from the manufacturing process to an analyzer, and possibly returned to the stream

- *In-line,* which may be an invasive or noninvasive process that analyzes the sample while it is part of the process stream

Process control tools used for the design and optimization of drug formulations and manufacturing processes within the PAT framework can include the following steps, although the sequence of steps can vary:

- Identify and measure critical material and process attributes relating to product quality.

- Design a process measurement system to allow real-time or near real-time (for example, on-, in-, or at-line) monitoring of all critical attributes.

- Design process controls that provide adjustments to ensure control of all critical attributes.

- Develop mathematical relationships between product quality attributes and measurements of critical material and process attributes.

Continuous improvement and knowledge management through data collection and analysis over the life cycle of a product are important. These data can contribute to justifying proposals for post-approval changes. Approaches and information technology systems that support knowledge acquisition from such databases are valuable for the manufacturers and can facilitate scientific communication.

Chapter 60

New Product Development Studies and Reports

Drug development is the process of taking a new chemical lead through the stages necessary to allow it to be tested in human clinical trials, and of identifying the process boundaries for realization of safe and effective products. Drug discovery is the first stage of drug development. At this stage, *new chemical entities* (NCEs) that have promising activity against a particular biologic target important in disease are discovered.

After discovery, the safety, toxicity, pharmacokinetics, and metabolism in humans, including dose and schedule, are assessed before human clinical trials. Studies are conducted to determine the major toxicities of the NCE, including an assessment of major organ toxicity (effects on the heart and lungs, brain, kidney, liver, and digestive system), and effects on other parts of the body that might be affected by the drug (for example, the skin if the new drug is to be delivered through the skin). These studies can be made either in vitro or by using experimental animals. The physicochemical properties of the NCE are established (that is, the chemical makeup, stability, and solubility, determination of the starting materials and their reaction paths, and basic specifications). The process to make the chemical is developed for suitability (for example, as capsules, tablets, aerosol, intramuscular injectable, subcutaneous injectable, or intravenous formulations). With the process of gathering human clinical trials data, long-term or chronic toxicities are determined, as well as effects on systems not previously monitored (that is, fertility, reproduction, immune system).

The process for realization of safe and effective products is identified after the discovery phase, and confirmed with the clinical study. The process may have started as small-scale experiments, and may have been increasingly scaled-up with appropriate *quality control* (QC) and manufacturing methods identified to ensure consistent product quality. The finalized process is summarized in a comprehensive development report, which should be approved by high-level company management. Technology transfer and other pre-validation activities should be considered part of the overall development report. The process of transfer includes verification of the parameters, controls, and associated supporting systems through formal studies, with implementation of any new required upgrades to ensure consistent quality product before moving into the process validation. The development report should include historical data, dosage form and formulation designs, design of manufacturing methods, specification and test method, and other information:

- *Historical data.* Information on the pharmaceutical development of new drug substances and drug products at stages from early development phase to final steps before process validation.

- *Dosage form and formula designs; design of manufacturing methods.* Successes and failures that contributed to learning more about the process, change histories of important processes and control parameters, and quality profiles of batches (including stability data).

- *Specifications and test methods.* Available for drug substances, intermediates, drug products, raw materials, and components, and their rationale (validity of specification range of critical tests such as assay, impurities, and dissolution; rationale for selection of test methods, reagents, and columns; and traceability of raw data).

- *Laboratory method development and validation.* Testing methods (for example, chemistry and microbial) are developed and validated before the human clinical trials, including, if applicable, successful transfer to the testing site.

- *Process model.* Brief description of the process, typically accompanied by a process flow diagram; each major step and equipment in the process are indicated, and, ideally, the batch record with all appropriate procedures and specifications should be finalized when the development report is finalized.

- *Active pharmaceutical ingredient* (API), *raw materials, and components.* APIs must be appropriately characterized, validated (manufacturing process), and identified as to source, and must satisfy quality specifications for manufacturing of drug product; critical excipients must be defined and well controlled.

- *Critical process parameter* (CPP). CPPs are the measured variables that are known to have an effect on one or more product quality attributes; all CPPs must be identified and controls established within a defined acceptable range, and the ranges for these parameters may be typically obtained in later development studies (that is, full-scale engineering studies, technology transfer studies aimed to optimize the process for commercialization, conducted in parallel with the human clinical trials); process optimization efforts must ensure that the enhanced process remains equivalent to that used for the making of the clinical trials product.

- *Critical quality attribute* (CQA). CQAs are intrinsic quality characteristics that are desired or needed to ensure patient safety and benefit of the drug product; in ICH Q6A, some API attributes should be considered critical, regardless of the drug product end use; identification, physicochemical properties, appearance, assay, and purity are applicable to all drug products; particle size, microbial purity, and polymorphism depend on the drug product; ICH Q6A decision trees can be used to determine the criticality of these quality attributes for solids, solutions, or sterile products; all CQAs must be identified and established acceptance criteria.

Chapter 61

Scale-up and Transfer Activities

DEVELOPMENT AND VALIDATION REPORTS

According to International Conference on Harmonization (ICH) Q8 (R2 *Pharmaceutical Development*), drug development studies contribute to scientific understanding that supports the establishment of product specifications, manufacturing *critical process parameters* (CPPs), and in-process *critical quality attributes* (CQAs). ICH Q8 (R2) provides guidance for the development studies that would be included in dossiers or New Drug Application (NDA) submissions to competent authorities. It describes a concept, known as *design space*, whereby and within which changes to a process may proceed with no regulatory resubmission of a dossier or NDA. Design space may be applicable to scale-up activities or to site changes.

Development studies and reports support specifications for the excipients, *active pharmaceutical ingredients* (APIs), intermediate, and drug product, and manufacturing process parameters. Process validation exercises and reports confirm the manufacturability at commercial scale of the drug substance or drug product in conjunction with transfer activities. Although the United States Food and Drug Administration (FDA) drug product submission process permits regulatory submissions before executing process validation, FDA expects that process validation will occur and be internally approved before any product is released to the market after an NDA or Biological License Application (BLA) approval.

The distinction between development studies and validation studies (or exercises) is that development studies may, in fact, result in unexpected negative results, disproven hypotheses, or novel responses, hence a new shape of the design space. Those development studies may be performed on any scale of equipment from laboratory, to pilot, to commercial scale of simulated manufacturing. Validation exercises, by definition, occur on commercial-scale equipment. Executed process validation protocols must neither subtract from nor add to anything in preapproved/signed-off protocol.

TECHNOLOGY TRANSFER TYPES

The only official regulatory guidance mentioning the term *technology transfer* is the ICH Q10 *Pharmaceutical Quality System*, and then only in relation to manufacturing processes and not analytical methods. Within a product's manufacturing life cycle, there exists drug development, technology transfer, commercial manufacturing, and product discontinuation. In Section 3.2.1, Table 1, technology transfer is described: "Monitoring during scale-up activities can provide a preliminary indication of process performance and the successful integration into manufacturing.

Knowledge obtained during transfer and scale-up activities can be useful in further developing the control strategy. "

For manufacturing, *technology transfer* serves as progressive scale-up at the final manufacturing site and by the actual personnel of that site. Included in the process transfer are relevant packaging and cleaning (residue) validation activities. No competent authority regulation mandates *research and development* (R&D) or the transferring site to assist in this transfer, but such collaboration improves the early success of *conformance batches*, as FDA terms commercial-scale pre-validation batches. Industry generally refers to these batches as *demonstration batches*.

Analytical technology transfer pertains to the transfer of analytical methods between laboratories for the testing of raw materials, finished product, or cleaning validation samples. It is a final location-specific exercise to acclimate the *quality control* (QC) personnel at the transfer receiving site in the applicable assays. Protocols are often written that contain statistical acceptance criteria for similarity of assay results between the transferring laboratory and the receiving laboratory (by blinded samples). The analytical test means and standard deviations must usually be compared or combined to arrive at an acceptably low difference (of means) and tight precision. A formal report is typically prepared to summarize the transfer activities. Although no competent authority regulation defines universally applicable or expected statistics, The United States Pharmacopeia (USP) Chapter <1224> is concerned with general requirements for the transfer of validated analytical methods. This chapter is scheduled to become official with the publication of USP 35.

PROCESS DEVELOPMENT AND CHARACTERIZATION STUDIES

To enable a successful manufacturing process transition and scale-up between R&D bench scale, R&D pilot scale, and commercial scale, numerous process development studies are undertaken. The term *unit operations*, coined by Arthur D. Little in 1915, is generally used to refer to distinct physical changes or unit actions (for example, pulverizing, mixing, and drying); unit operations involving chemical changes are sometimes referred to as *unit processes*. The physical changes comprising unit operations primarily involve contact, transfer of a physical property, and separation between phases or streams.

These studies do not require preapproved protocols as with formal validation; however, for process development study results to be able to contribute to a development report either included in a marketing application (for example, NDA, BLA) or available for competent authority inspection review, its raw data must adhere to record-keeping practices as rigorous as contained in 21 CFR 58 "Good Laboratory Practices."

Process Ranging Studies

Process ranging studies are experiments that, to achieve known CQAs of the intermediate or finished drug (or even the API and its precursors), establish allowable values of CPPs, which are equipment controls or controllable environmental conditions that influence in-process or finished product (or API) test results. In the language of statistical *design of experiments* (DOE), "factors" are the CPPs (for example, rotary tablet press speed), and "levels" are any allowable settings of those equipment controls or factors (for example, 100 rpm). Statistics books and readily purchasable software provide many choices in DOE methodology. DOE is the alternative to highly inefficient one-factor-at-a-time experimentation. DOE tells what factors have the most impact on resultant CQAs and tells how much variation around a nominal (target) value of a CPP is allowable. Any software packages used during process development studies contributing to a formal development report must be validated by the software provider or the drug or API manufacturer. See FDA guidance *General Principles of Software Validation; Final Guidance for Industry and FDA Staff.*

Process Capability Studies

Process capability studies are experiments intended to determine, for a particular process, how close to target specification a product output is running, as well as how widely dispersed that output is. The *process capability index* (C_{pk}) is a measurement of the process's ability to create product within specification limits.

In-Process Control Studies

In-process control (IPC) studies are experiments that determine and develop online or off-line measurement(s) that help predict acceptable API or finished drug release test results and enable tighter control over an adjustable process. Regardless of the dosage form (or API), IPC measurements, tests/inspections, or go/no-go attribute test results can be plotted/trended/interpreted via run charts or *statistical process control* (SPC) charts. In SPC, control limits for central tendency (that is, means or medians) and for variance (that is, range or standard deviation) can be calculated manually or using validated software. The main purpose of SPC is the use of unbiased statistics to decide when and when not to adjust a process parameter to maintain process control. Individual results or means of three or more consecutive points (subgroups) may be plotted versus time or versus lot number. A loss of statistical control (and a need for process adjustment) is indicated on a control chart by several factors (Figure 61.1).

- One or more points outside either control limit

- Run of seven or more successive points on one side of centerline

- Trend moving either up or down over seven successive points

- Cycle or pattern that repeats itself

- Absence of points near the centerline

- Stratification (points hugging the centerline, with few out near control limits)

- Clusters (grouping of points in particular areas of the chart)

Figure 61.1   Indicators of loss of statistical control.

Hold-Time Studies

As the name implies, a study must exist for every time lapse (that is, hold time) anticipated or intended to occur between any two API and drug manufacturing process steps. Tests used to judge the quality of the material in question after any hold time must be scientifically reliable and, ideally (but not necessarily), validated. Product and process design risk identification is expected to identify all hold times in API and drug manufacturing processes, and those risks assessed through hold-time studies. Cleaning processes have hold times that must be characterized and the maximum duration established. Bulk hold time represents the time lapse between completion of most of an API or drug manufacturing process and the primary packaging. For materials consisting of an emulsion, a suspension, or other multiple-phase combination, hold-time studies are most critical. Hold times are critical for cold-chain products (for example, proteins, vaccines, sensitive antibiotics) that undergo a primary or secondary packaging operation at ambient temperature.

Physico-Mechanical Simulations and Shipping Studies

In addition to ICH and any competent authority–mandated stability (and photostability) studies minimally required to be approved to ship and market a new drug product through and into various climatic zones, several studies are usually expected or mandated: physicomechanical simulations of vibration, shaking, package impact, and pressure changes, and shipping studies. The best reference for these physicomechanical and shipping studies is USP General Chapter <1079> "Good Storage and Shipping Practices." According to <1079>, a drug can take any number of routes to the ultimate consumer or patient, which may include a complex series of transfers outside the marketing owner's control.

It is usually expected in shipping studies for APIs and finished drugs that within the secondary or tertiary packaging will be judiciously placed (and calibrated) temperature and other indicators that may be inspected or downloaded at the receiving site. The API or drug product must undergo complete release testing at its destination. APIs and drug products with temperature sensitivities reflected in the labeling must use temperature cycling and shipping studies that greatly stress the insulating or refrigerating properties of the tertiary package. PDA Technical Report 39 provides strategies for cold-chain dominated shipping studies. Stability, physicomechanical, shipping, and cold-chain studies enable the product development team to conclude what excursions in labeled storage conditions are permitted and which necessitate material destruction or return. PDA Technical Report 53 provides guidance on the requirements for stability testing of new drug products to support distribution conditions.

Appendix

Body of Knowledge—
Pharmaceutical GMP Professional
Certification (CPGP)

This body of knowledge (BoK) covers compliance with good manufacturing practices (GMPs), as regulated and guided by national and international agencies for the pharmaceutical industry. It covers finished human and veterinary drugs and biologics, ectoparasitacides, and dietary supplements (alternatively called nutraceuticals) where regulated as drug products, as well as their component raw materials (including active pharmaceutical ingredients (APIs) and excipients), and packaging and labeling operations.

This BoK includes subtext explanations and corresponding cognitive levels for each topic or subtopic. These details will be used by the Examination Development Committee as guidelines for writing test questions and are designed to help candidates prepare for the exam by identifying specific content that can be tested. The subtext is not intended to limit the subject matter or be all-inclusive of what might be covered in an exam but is intended to clarify how topics relate to the role of the Certified Pharmaceutical GMP Professional (CPGP). The descriptor in parentheses at the end of each subtext entry refers to the highest cognitive level at which the topic will be tested. A more complete description of cognitive levels is provided at the end of this document.

I. Regulatory Agency Governance (15 Questions)

    A. *Global regulatory framework.* Identify the acts, statutes, directives, etc., that apply to pharmaceuticals. (Understand)

    B. *Regulations and guidances.* Interpret frequently used regulations and guidelines/guidances, including those published or administered by the Pharmaceutical Inspection Convention and Pharmaceutical Inspection Cooperation Scheme (PIC/S), Health Canada, the World Health Organization (WHO), the International Conference on Harmonization (ICH), the European Medicines Agency (EMEA), the Food & Drug Administration (FDA), the Therapeutic Goods Administration (TGA), USDA 9CFR, USDA Veterinary Service Memoranda and the International Pharmaceutical Excipients Council (IPEC). (Understand)

    C. *Mutual recognition agreements.* Interpret requirements that govern product registration, import or export of raw material or finished product, the sharing of inspection findings, etc. (Understand)

D. *Regulatory inspections.* Define and describe various types of inspections (pre-approval (PAI), system-based, for-cause, license renewal, etc.), including what triggers them, their frequency, and the inspection process used. (Understand)

E. *Enforcement actions.* Define and describe various enforcement actions and consequences (e.g., FDA 483s, warning letters, license withdrawals, product seizure). (Understand)

F. *Regulatory agency reporting*

1. *Post-marketing changes.* Describe how post-marketing changes to specifications, processes, methods, etc. are assessed for impact to determine the appropriate reporting method. (Understand)

2. *Regulatory reporting requirements.* Describe reporting requirements, including supplements, NDA Field Alerts, Biological Product Deviation Reports, annual reports, variations to dossiers and applications, etc. (Understand)

G. *Site master file (SMF) and drug master file (DMF).* Describe the purpose and content of these files. (Understand)

II. Quality Systems (30 Questions)

A. *Quality management system (QMS)*

1. *QMS elements.* Describe key elements of the structure of a QMS, identify their interrelationships, and develop and describe their hierarchical positions. (Create)

2. *QMS requirements.* Apply requirements related to QMS development and operations, as defined in ICH Q10, EU GMP, and other guidances. (Apply)

B. *Quality unit (site) management.* Describe quality management elements for individual sites or units, including responsibilities for company management, qualified persons, batch release requirements, the need for quality units to be independent from operations, etc. (Understand)

C. *Risk management.* Use various methods to apply risk management principles, as described in ICH Q9 and other guidance or regulatory documents. (Apply)

D. *Training and personnel qualification*

1. *Needs analysis.* Identify the requirements for determining the type of training needed by quality staff members, operations personnel and related functions. (Understand)

2. *Staff development requirements.* Determine proof of proficiency based on regulations, guidances, and directives and including documented evidence (job titles, job descriptions, etc.). (Apply)

E. *Change control and management*

1. *Pre-change analysis.* Assess the impact that proposed changes will have on products, processes, facilities, utilities, etc., to ensure risk minimization and ongoing regulatory compliance. (Analyze)

2. *Post-change analysis.* Analyze data and other inputs to determine the results of a change, and evaluate any new risk factors created by the change. (Analyze)

F. *Investigations and corrective and preventive action (CAPA)*

1. *Trigger events.* Identify trigger events that necessitate investigation and the implications of the event elsewhere, and determine the underlying cause for the event. (Evaluate)

2. *Response actions.* Define immediate action, corrective action, and preventive action, and explain their importance in terms of management responsibility, methods of implementing them, etc. (Evaluate)

3. *CAPA feedback and trending.* Describe how trending is used in relation to CAPA data. Use investigation feedback and CAPA results to modify appropriate quality system elements. (Create)

G. *Audits and self-inspections*

1. *Audits processes and results.* Differentiate between various audit types (systems, product, process) and analyze audit results to assess conformance to requirements. (Analyze)

2. *Audit follow-up.* Use various methods to evaluate and verify the adequacy of corrective actions taken. (Evaluate)

3. *Ineffective corrective actions.* Determine appropriate strategies to use when corrective actions are not implemented or are not effective. (Evaluate)

H. *Documents and records management*

1. *GMP document system.* Examine the GMP document system, including corporate standards, master plans, procedures, manufacturing and test instructions, etc., to determine compliance to regulatory requirements. (Analyze)

2. *GMP compliance records.* Review various records (log books, tags, training evidence, etc.) to confirm compliance to requirements. (Analyze)

3. *Record retention.* Identify regulatory requirements for GMP compliance in record retention. (Understand)

I. *Product quality complaints vs. adverse event reports*

   1. *Quality complaints.* Describe and distinguish between product complaints and adverse events, and evaluate complaint-handling processes. (Evaluate)

   2. *Adverse events and pharmacovigilance.* Describe adverse events and identify the regulatory reports for these events and pharmacovigilance. (Understand)

   3. *Problem response.* Evaluate the level of action that needs to be taken in response to these types of events, including corrections, product removal, etc. (Evaluate)

J. *Product trend requirements.* Describe and distinguish between components of the US annual product review (APR) and the European product quality review (PQR) with regard to data trends and other required review methods. (Understand)

K. *Supplier and contractor quality management*

   1. *Supplier quality systems.* Identify and interpret standards and regulations (e.g., ISO 17025) related to monitoring supplier and contractor quality management systems. (Analyze)

   2. *Supplier controls.* Assess the adequacy of controls over procurement and receipt of raw materials, components, and contract services. Determine the need for formal contracts. (Evaluate)

   3. *Supplier evaluation.* Assess the quality systems of suppliers and contractors using various methodologies, including supplier qualification, certification, evaluation, audit, as well as supplied product or service performance trending. (Evaluate)

III. Laboratory Systems (20 Questions)

A. *Compendia (US, Europe, and Japan)*

   1. *Required vs. informational compendia.* Describe and distinguish between required and informational ("general") compendial chapters. (Apply)

   2. *Marketing requirements vs. compendia.* Distinguish among the US Pharmacopoeia (USP), European Pharmacopoeia (PhEur or EP), and Japanese Pharmacopoeia (JP) in terms of requirements for marketing authorization. (Understand)

   3. *Compendial methods review.* Review compendial methods to ensure that they are verified as suitable for use in the testing lab. (Evaluate)

   4. *Compendial requirements review.* Review test methods, qualifications, and validations against required compendial general chapters as well as against informational general compendial chapters whenever

more specific tests are not prescribed in the product compendial monograph. (Analyze)

5. *Biological, microbiological, chemical, and physical test methods.* Identify and interpret results from compendia identification tests, quantitative analysis, qualitative analysis, and other tests or studies for biological, microbiological, and chemical, and physical tests. (Apply)

B. *Laboratory investigations of aberrant results*

1. *Test data.* Describe and distinguish among biological, microbiological, and chemical test data, and develop procedures for investigating each type. (Analyze)

2. *Aberrant results.* Identify, analyze, and interpret data on processes or products that are out-of-specification ("no test" in USDA) or out-of-trend, and determine the outcome of the laboratory portion of the investigation and the criteria for further investigation. (Evaluate)

C. *Instrument control and record-keeping*

1. *Instrument control.* Examine operating procedures for instrument identification, classification (e.g., GMP, for-information-only), and calibration, to meet requirements. (Apply)

2. *Instrument calibration.* Determine whether instruments are calibrated within the specified range of operation, and whether they are accurate and precise. (Apply) [Note: Calibration of facilities equipment is covered in IV.E.]

D. *Specifications*

1. *Types of specifications.* Determine whether approved specifications exist for raw materials, intermediates, packaging components, finished products, etc. (Analyze)

2. *Test data and specifications.* Compare test data with specifications to determine whether raw materials, intermediates, packaging, or products meet requirements. (Analyze)

3. *Specifications revision.* Review and update specifications when methods are revised or compendia are changed. (Evaluate)

E. *Laboratory record-keeping and data requirements*

1. *Record review.* Review laboratory records to detect errors or falsification and to prevent loss of data. (Apply)

2. *Record-keeping requirements.* Identify and review record-keeping requirements for data acquisition systems. (Apply)

3. *Certificates of analysis (COAs).* Review COAs to ensure they are complete, internally reviewed, and appropriately retained. (Apply)

F. *Laboratory handling controls*

1. *Sample identification.* Determine whether samples are identified and handled in accordance with requirements, including name, sample identification, chains of custody, etc. (Apply)

2. *Reagents, solutions, and standards identification.* Determine whether reagents, solutions, and standards are identified and labeled in accordance with requirements, including opened-on, expiry, (validated) use-by, or recertify-by dates. (Apply)

3. *Storage requirements.* Describe and use procedures to store samples, reagents, solutions, and standards in appropriate environmental conditions (e.g., temperature, humidity, light exposure, absence of oxygen, etc.) to maintain the material's characteristics for testing. (Apply)

G. *Stability programs*

1. *Release tests vs. stability-indicating tests.* Define and distinguish between these two types of tests. (Apply)

2. *Stability test data.* Review stability data and identify trends that can support or challenge an expiry date. (Evaluate)

3. *Stability-point failure.* Identify the stability-point failure of a product or material, and evaluate the implications for regulatory compliance. (Evaluate)

H. *Reserve samples and retains.* Describe the various regulatory requirements for retains and reserve samples. (Apply)

IV. Infrastructure: Facilities, Utilities, Equipment (18 Questions)

A. *Facilities*

1. *Buildings.* Determine requirements for appropriate size and construction of buildings and areas as well as location of control systems. Ensure that construction and location facilitate proper operation and minimize the risk of error and cross-contamination. (Apply)

2. *Manufacture and storage environment.* Identify requirements for appropriate lighting, ventilation, and drainage to avoid adversely affecting product (either directly or indirectly) during manufacture and storage. (Apply)

3. *Facilities change control.* Use various methods to verify that change control practices are in use to maintain the qualified state of the facilities. (Apply)

B. *Utilities*

1. *Water supply systems.* Identify and interpret regulatory requirements for design of water supply systems, including various unit

operations (e.g., dechlorination, reverse osmosis, deionization, distillation, etc.), delivery lines, back-flow or back-siphonage prevention, and drainage systems, as appropriate for the type of water (potable, purified, water for injection, etc.) needed in various processing steps. (Apply)

2. *Compressed air and gas systems.* Identify and apply regulatory requirements related to compressed air and gas systems, including storage, flow regulation, filtration, venting and purging, etc. (Apply)

3. *Utility design for production.* Identify and select utility designs related to production steps (e.g., washing, sterilizing, depyrogenation, etc.) for use with specific materials and processes. (Apply)

4. *Utilities design specifications.* Review operations of utilities to ensure that they meet design specifications. (Apply)

5. *Utilities change control.* Use various methods to verify that change control practices are in use to maintain the qualified state of affected utilities. (Apply)

C. *Equipment*

1. *Equipment planning.* Review equipment location, design, construction, installation, and maintenance based on the operations to be conducted. (Apply)

2. *Equipment layout.* Determine the layout of equipment to minimize the risk of errors, to facilitate effective cleaning and maintenance, and to avoid contamination or any other undesired effect on product quality. (Apply)

3. *Equipment cleaning and maintenance.* Review procedures and schedules for equipment cleaning, maintenance, and, where necessary, sanitization to ensure that they meet requirements. (Apply)

4. *Equipment cleaning validation or verification.* Evaluate the need and methodology for product-contact cleaning validation, verification, or both. (Evaluate)

5. *Equipment change control.* Use various methods to verify that change control has maintained the qualified state of equipment. (Apply)

D. *Qualification and validation.* Verify that the qualifications and validations of facilities, equipment, and utilities are conducted in accordance with various requirements, including factory and site acceptance testing (FAT/SAT), installation, operational, and performance qualification (IQ/OQ/PQ) prior to process validation. (Analyze)

E. *Maintenance and metrology systems*

1. *Maintenance procedures.* Verify that procedures are in use for routine and non-routine maintenance of heating, ventilation, air conditioning (HVAC) systems, air and water filters, and other GMP equipment and utilities, etc. (Analyze)

2. *Metrology change control.* Verify that appropriate calibration and engineering/equipment change control procedures are in use, and that a metrology program exists for the calibration of instruments that control manufacturing facilities, utilities, and equipment. (Analyze) [Note: Calibration of instrumentation is covered in III.D.3.]

F. *Cleaning, sanitization, and sterilization systems*

1. *Washing facilities.* Verify that washing facilities are adequate and properly located. (Apply)

2. *Cleaning procedures.* Review cleaning procedures in accordance with prior cleaning validation, whenever validation is required and performed. (Apply)

3. *Sanitization procedures.* Review sanitization procedures for facilities and equipment, including details on cleaning schedules, methods, equipment, materials, etc., and verify that sanitizers, disinfectants, sporicides, and sterilants are used in accordance with marketing authorization and any required validation studies. (Apply)

4. *Pest control.* Review and verify that a pest control program is in place and that it uses authorized rodenticides, insecticides, fungicides, fumigating agents, and appropriate traps for pest elimination, etc. (Apply)

5. *Sterilization processes.* Verify that appropriate sterilization processes are in place. (Apply)

G. *Automated or computerized systems*

1. *Validation procedures.* Review procedures for validation of these systems, including building maintenance systems, utilities and equipment. Verify that critical parameters for their operation and maintenance are controlled and monitored. (Evaluate)

2. *Open and closed computerized systems.* Distinguish between open and closed computerized systems. (Apply)

3. *Configuration control.* Verify that version control and configuration are maintained and monitored. (Evaluate)

4. *Security requirements.* Evaluate computerized systems to ensure they meet regulatory and guidance requirements for key elements, such as access control, data protection, change control, data archiving, maintenance, transcription, audit trail, periodic system monitoring, etc. (Evaluate)

H. *Business continuity and disaster recovery planning*

1. *Supply chain impact.* Review plans and verify procedures for disaster recovery and business continuity that will guard operations from interruption to the supply chain. (Evaluate)

2. *Contingency plan.* Verify the testing and effectiveness of contingency plans as required or proceduralized. (Apply)

V. Materials and Supply Chain Management (15 Questions)

A. *Receipt of materials*

1. *Incoming materials.* Describe and use processes to receive and store incoming materials, including raw materials, tank farm liquid chemicals or solvents, components, labels, etc., and take appropriate action on deviations, such as damaged materials, materials from unapproved suppliers, missing documentation, etc. (Apply)

2. *Inventory transactions.* Describe and use procedures for documenting inventory transactions, such as material selection and "stop shipments" for quality holds. (Apply)

B. *Sampling processes*

1. *Sampling plans.* Review sampling plans for representative sampling, appropriate sample size, and test or inspection criteria. (Apply)

2. *Sampling environment.* Differentiate and apply the requirements for sampling environment and utensils to the type of the material being sampled. (Apply)

3. *Cleaning.* Ensure that the sampling environment is appropriately cleaned and monitored and that sampling utensils are appropriately cleaned or are single-use. (Apply)

C. *Material storage, identification, and rotation*

1. *Storage suitability.* Confirm that the storage environment is suitable, controlled, and monitored as required for the type of materials. (Analyze)

2. *Storage labels.* Confirm that the identification label for stored materials contains the required information. (Analyze)

3. *Stock rotation.* Define and use stock rotation requirements, such as first-in/first-out (FIFO) and first-expired/first out (FEFO). (Apply)

4. *Retest dates vs. expiration dates.* Describe the difference between retest dates and expiration dates. (Understand)

5. *Mix-up risk.* Describe potential sources of mix-up and identify methods to minimize their risk, including material segregation, labeling, special storage for rejects, control of material returns, lot-control methods, special process for materials with similar names, etc. (Analyze)

D. *Shipping and distribution*

1. *Temperature-sensitive requirements.* Identify special requirements for temperature-sensitive products, including tertiary packaging design, monitoring devices, etc. (Analyze)

2. *Special requirements.* Determine specific product requirements and apply them to routine shipping processes. (Apply)

3. *Report requirements.* Analyze shipping reports and transportation requirements in accordance with good distribution practices. (Analyze)

4. *Supply chain security.* Identify and apply the various means to secure the supply chain, including tamper-evident seals, shipping manifests, verification of documentation, barcoding, radio frequency identification (RFID), etc. (Apply)

E. *Traceability and sourcing*

1. *Traceability requirements.* Define and differentiate the requirements for traceability of incoming materials, intermediates, and finished drugs. (Apply)

2. *Biological agent requirements.* Identify and apply the requirements related to biological agents such as bovine and transmissible spongiform encephalopathy (BSE and TSE). (Apply)

3. *Pedigree and sourcing requirements.* Identify and apply requirements for maintaining pedigree and sourcing details for active pharmaceutical ingredients (APIs), biological starting materials, excipients, intermediates, finished products, etc., and document the supply chain, from raw materials through wholesale or retail to end user. (Apply)

F. *Salvaged/returned goods and destruction*

1. *Disposition.* Review salvaged and returned goods and evaluate them for disposition. (Evaluate)

2. *Destruction facilities and processes.* Determine whether qualified facilities and processes need to be used to destroy materials. (Apply)

VI. Sterile and Nonsterile Manufacturing Systems (25 Questions)

A. *Master batch and completed batch records*

1. *Required elements.* Review batch records for required elements, including proper issuance, sections on yields, critical manufacturing step verification, processing instructions, hold times, etc. (Apply)

2. *Record processing requirements.* Confirm that batch records meet requirements for execution, review and disposition decisions. (Analyze)

B. *Production operations*

1. *Application factors.* Describe and differentiate the requirements for manufacturing processes according to their application: human or veterinary drugs or biologics. (Apply)

2. *Utility requirements.* Identify the facility and utility requirements that are appropriate for different production environments and product types, including sterile vs. nonsterile manufacturing, solid and semisolid dosage forms, liquids, creams, ointments, combination products, etc. (Analyze)

3. *Sanitization and protection.* Identify various production operations that require gowning, sanitization, hygiene, and other product-protective steps. (Apply)

C. *In-process controls*

1. *In-process testing.* Identify appropriate tests for each step in the manufacturing process and review results. (Analyze)

2. *Critical process parameters (CPPs).* Identify and select appropriate CPPs. (Analyze)

3. *Process capability studies.* Review process capability studies, and calculate C_p and C_{pk}. (Apply)

4. *Specification limits.* Assess specification limits in relation to registration or compendial requirements. (Evaluate)

D. *Dispensing and weighing controls*

1. *Staging areas.* Review product dispensing and after-dispensing staging areas to determine whether they meet requirements. (Analyze)

2. *Dispensing materials.* Identify the requirements for using weighing equipment and handling utensils for dispensing raw materials or intermediates, including proper cleaning, labeling, and environmental controls, based on the type of material and manufacturing process being used. (Apply)

E. *Requirements for critical unit processes*

1. *Parameters for sterilization.* Identify required CPPs for such unit processes as sterilization or sterilizing filtration, aseptic filling, depyrogenation, lyophilization, other drying processes, tablet granulation and compression, terminal sterilization, cream or ointment emulsification, etc. (Analyze)

2. *Validation studies.* Explain and evaluate the validation studies, specifically the methodologies and acceptance criteria—required before implementing critical unit processes. Explain and evaluate validation studies required for aseptic processes including process simulations ("media fills"). (Evaluate)

3. *Unit processes.* Assess unit processes or their validations for deviations requiring investigation. (Analyze)

4. *Operating procedures.* Review qualification and validation results and confirm that they are reflected in operating procedures. (Analyze)

5. *Reevaluation and revalidation.* Determine appropriate criteria and frequency for reevaluation and revalidation of unit processes. (Evaluate)

6. *Environmental monitoring requirements.* Differentiate between environmental monitoring requirements for different manufacturing area classifications. (Apply)

7. *Monitoring tools.* Describe and use various monitoring tools to measure viable and nonviable particulates, pressure differentials, temperature, humidity, etc. (Apply)

F. *Contamination and cross-contamination*

1. *Sources.* Identify potential sources for these events. (Apply)

2. *Risk mitigation.* Describe and apply various techniques for mitigating the risk of these events, including cleaning, facility and equipment design, qualified disinfectants, operator training, validation, monitoring, etc. (Apply)

G. *Reprocessed and reworked materials*

1. *Disposition process.* Distinguish reprocessing from reworking and apply appropriate documentation, approval, and disposition methods for these materials. (Apply)

2. *Storage.* Describe and apply requirements for segregation and secure storage of these materials. (Apply)

VII. Filling, Packaging, Labeling (17 Questions)

A. *Filling operations and controls*

1. *Materials control.* Develop and review procedures to ensure the identity, strength, and purity of specified materials (e.g., liquids, powders, ointments, tablets, capsules, suspensions, etc.) and to prevent them from being altered. (Create)

2. *Filling equipment control.* Analyze the controls needed for various types of production equipment and processes and ensure that the appropriate controls are in place to verify filling criteria. (Analyze)

3. *Contamination controls.* Identify controls to prevent microbial and other contamination at all stages of filling. (Apply)

4. *Staged materials.* Review staged materials and confirm that they are approved for use. (Apply)

5. *Status labeling.* Identify and apply proper status labeling throughout the process. (Apply)

B. *Environmental monitoring.* Use various monitoring techniques (active air sampling, settle plates, nonviable particle counting, contact plates for surfaces and people, etc.) to determine that appropriate environmental conditions are maintained in various operations. (Apply)

C. *In-process and finished goods inspections*

1. *Finished goods inspections.* Develop criteria for in-process and finished goods inspections of filled and packaged materials, including seal tests, torque testing, bottle rejection systems, etc. (Create)

2. *Vision and detection systems.* Ensure that vision and detection systems are qualified, calibrated, and challenged as required for the system. (Apply)

3. *Defect characterizations.* Ensure that defect characterizations are identified for each product and can be detected by inspection or test. (Apply)

4. *Equipment failure detection.* Confirm by inspection or test that equipment failures can be detected. (Apply)

D. *Parenteral product inspection*

1. *Staff evaluation.* Ensure that staff who perform manual inspections are properly trained and that their inspections meet reproducibility requirements. (Apply)

2. *Automated inspection processes.* Ensure that automated inspection processes are validated. (Apply)

3. *Defect library.* Ensure that a defect library is available to confirm proper manual and automated inspection processes. (Apply)

4. *Inspector requirements.* Establish requirements for inspectors to have periodic eye examinations. Confirm and document that they take frequent breaks from inspection. (Apply)

E. *Packaging operations and controls*

1. *Content protection.* Develop and apply procedures to prevent the environment or events from altering the identity, strength, and purity of the package content. (Create)

2. *Qualification and maintenance of equipment.* Ensure that equipment used in packaging operations is qualified and maintained. (Apply)

3. *Line clearance operations.* Determine that line clearance is performed and documented. (Apply)

4. *Quality check criteria.* Identify and apply specified criteria when quality checks are performed. (Apply)

     5. *Cut-label procedures.* Apply appropriate procedures for cut labels, splices, etc. (Apply)

     6. *Hand-applied label procedures.* Ensure that hand-applied labels are 100% inspected. (Apply)

     7. *Production process controls.* Distinguish between controls needed for different types of production processes. (Analyze)

     8. *Contamination controls.* Identify controls to prevent microbial and other contamination at all stages of packaging. (Apply)

     9. *Tamper-evident packaging.* Ensure that tamper-evident and child-proof packaging requirements are in place for required products. (Apply)

F. *Labeling operations and controls*

     1. *Label printing in packaging.* Confirm and document that any printing done separately or in the course of packaging is performed correctly. (Apply)

     2. *Quality of print used.* Ensure that any type of print information (engraved, embossed, etc.) on packaging materials is clear and resistant to fading, smudging, or erasure. (Apply)

     3. *Label reconciliation.* Confirm that label reconciliation is performed. (Apply)

     4. *Label changes.* Determine whether regulatory notification and approval is required for proposed label changes. (Apply)

     5. *Unused labels.* Confirm that procedures are in place and in use for destroying unused labels and labeling materials. (Apply)

G. *Filling and packaging records*

     1. *Terms.* Define terms related to these records, including evidence of line clearance, printed material reconciliation, yields, etc. (Understand)

     2. *Setup instructions.* Ensure that packaging line setup instructions are appropriate for all components. (Apply)

H. *Artwork development and controls*

     1. *Terms.* Define terms related to artwork/graphics, offline printing, roll label splicing, gang printing, secure storage and destruction, etc. (Understand)

     2. *Access control.* Ensure that controls are in place for the creation and use of artwork. (Apply)

VIII. Product Development and Technology Transfer (10 Questions)

A. *Quality by design concepts*

1. *Critical quality attributes (CQAs) and critical process parameters (CPPs).* Identify CQAs for products and CPPs for processes. (Understand)

2. *Design space.* Define the concept of design space as it is used throughout the product lifecycle. (Understand)

3. *Process analytical technology (PAT) tools.* Identify PAT tools, including multivariate data analysis, process analyzers, process and endpoint controls, etc., and describe their use in supporting the manufacture of quality products. (Remember)

B. *Phase-appropriate GMP requirements*

1. *ICH Q8.* Identify recommendations contained in the ICH Q8 guidance for pharmaceutical development. (Understand)

2. *Development phases.* Identify recommendations and requirements in relation to phases of development, including method qualification/validation, comparability protocols, adoption of critical process parameters and specifications, etc. (Understand)

3. *Combination products.* Identify various studies required for combination drug-device or drug-delivery products. (Understand)

4. *Clinical trials material.* Describe and apply requirements for packaging of clinical trials material/IMPs. (Apply)

C. *Raw materials, packaging, and infrastructure for product development.* Select appropriate development studies for raw material selection and evaluate the results to determine their critical quality attributes. (Analyze)

D. *New product development studies and reports.* Analyze studies and reports, including stability reports, material compatibility, method development, development reports, etc., to support product development and submissions. (Analyze)

E. *Scale-up and transfer activities*

1. *Development and validation reports.* Identify and distinguish development and validation studies. (Understand)

2. *Technology transfer types.* Define different types of technology transfer, including, manufacturing site change, analytical laboratory site change, etc., and analyze inter-site comparison of results. (Analyze)

3. *Transfer efficiency.* Define various studies, including ranging, capability, in-process control, hold times, shipping, etc., to improve transfer efficiency between development and commercial processes. (Apply)

SIX LEVELS OF COGNITION
BASED ON BLOOM'S TAXONOMY—REVISED (2001)

In addition to *content* specifics, the subtext detail also indicates the intended *complexity level* of the test questions for that topic. These levels are based on the Revised "Levels of Cognition" (from Bloom's Taxonomy, 2001) and are presented below in rank order, from least complex to most complex.

Remember

Recall or recognize terms, definitions, facts, ideas, materials, patterns, sequences, methods, principles, etc.

Understand

Read and understand descriptions, communications, reports, tables, diagrams, directions, regulations, etc.

Apply

Know when and how to use ideas, procedures, methods, formulas, principles, theories, etc.

Analyze

Break down information into its constituent parts and recognize their relationship to one another and how they are organized; identify sublevel factors or salient data from a complex scenario.

Evaluate

Make judgments about the value of proposed ideas, solutions, by comparing the proposal to specific criteria or standards.

Create

Put parts or elements together in such a way as to show a pattern or structure not clearly there before; identify which data or information from a complex set is appropriate to examine further or from which supported conclusions can be drawn.

Glossary

A

action level—Specification or limit (in fact, more correctly called an *action limit* rather than an action level) established in published regulation (or a guidance or guideline or standard that is regarded by competent authorities as de facto regulation) that, when exceeded, requires immediate intervention, including investigation of cause, immediate remediation, and/or corrective action.

adulterated (United States term)—Violative state of a drug or device as described in Section 501 "Adulterated Drugs and Devices" of the Food, Drug, and Cosmetic Act (FDCA). Any of the following are bases for adulteration: (i) if it is a drug or device containing a filthy, putrid, or decomposed substance (that is, an animal part or insect) or manufactured under unsanitary conditions, or if the drug or device may have been rendered injurious to health; (ii) if it is a drug and the methods used in, or the facilities or controls used for, its manufacture, processing, packing, or holding do not conform to current good manufacturing practice; (iii) if it is a drug recognized by the United States Pharmacopeia (USP) and its strength differs from, or its quality or purity falls below the standards set forth in the USP (unless exceptions are contained in the labeling); (iv) if it is a drug and any substance has been mixed or packed with it so as to reduce its quality or strength or substituted wholly or in part for the active pharmaceutical ingredient (API) (for example, oversulfated chondroitin sulfate for heparin).

aerosol generator—Instrument capable of producing particulate matter in an appropriate particle size (for example, 0.05 to 2 μm).

air exchange rate—Air changes per unit of time, which is calculated by dividing the volumetric flow rate of incoming air by the volume of the space/room.

alert level—Measurement magnitude set by an active pharmaceutical ingredient (API) or finished pharmaceutical manufacturer that gives early warning of a drift from normal conditions and that, when exceeded, should result in increased attention to the process.

annual review—An evaluation, conducted at least annually, that assesses the quality standards of each drug product to determine the need for changes in drug product specifications or manufacturing or control procedures.

antisepsis—Act or process of chemically reducing viable organisms on living tissue, including skin, oral cavities, and open wounds (*antiseptic* is the chemical agent).

as-built—Occupancy state in which the installation is complete with all services connected and functioning but with no production equipment, materials, or personnel present.

aseptic processing area (APA)—Controlled environments in which the air supply, materials, equipment, and personnel are regulated to control microbial and particulate numbers to acceptable levels. APA consists of "critical (processing) area" and "direct support area."

assay—Qualitative or quantitative analysis of a drug to determine its components.

at rest—Occupancy state in which the installation is complete with equipment installed and operating in a defined manner but with zero personnel present.

B

bioburden—The total quantity of recoverable microbes present on a defined surface, surface area, or within a nonsterile solid/powder or liquid drug, intermediate, or raw material.

bulk production batch—A batch of product, of a size described in the application for a marketing authorization, either ready for assembly into final containers or in individual containers ready for assembly into final packs. A bulk production batch may, for example, consist of a bulk quantity of liquid product, of solid dosage forms such as tablets or capsules, or of filled ampules.

C

certification of the finished product batch—Certification in a register or equivalent document by a European Union qualified person, as defined in Article 51 of Directive 2001/83/EC and Article 55 of Directive 2001/82/EC, before a batch is released for sale or distribution.

change control—A written procedure that describes the action to be taken if a change is proposed to facilities, materials, equipment, and/or processes used in the fabrication, packaging, and testing of drugs, or that may affect the operation of the quality or support system.

chiral—Not superimposable with its mirror image, as applied to molecules, conformations, and macroscopic objects, such as crystals. the term has been extended to samples of substances whose molecules are chiral, even if the macroscopic assembly of such molecules is racemic.

chromatogram—A graphical or other representation of detector response, effluent concentration, or other quantity used as a measure of effluent concentration, versus time, volume, or distance. Idealized chromatograms are represented as a sequence of Gaussian peaks on a baseline.

classification—Level (or process of specifying or determining the level) of airborne particulate cleanliness applicable to a cleanroom or clean zone, expressed in terms of an ISO Class N, which represents the maximum allowable concentrations (in particles per cubic meter of air) for considered sizes of particles (see ISO 14644-1).

classified area/cleanroom—Room or operating area designated by Grades A, B, C, or D as defined in *EU Guide to GMP* or designated Class 4.8, 5, 6, 7, or 8 per ISO cleanroom standards; a classified area is constructed (usually of durable walls as opposed to curtains) and used in a manner to minimize the introduction, generation, and retention of particles, and in which other relevant parameters, for example, temperature, humidity, and pressure, are controlled as necessary (see ISO 14644-1). A curtained area satisfying some of the definition of classified area, except its wall construction, is known as a *clean zone*, the distinction being necessary for purposes of the latter's moveable/flexible versus permanent nature and the degree of pre-use validation or qualification.

cleaning—Physical removal of soil, organic debris, and particulate from surfaces.

cleaning validation—Documented evidence with a high degree of assurance that a cleaning process will consistently yield product contact surfaces that meet predetermined acceptance criteria and critical quality attributes (visual and residual levels).

cleaning validation master plan—Overview document that describes, at a high level, the entire site's cleaning validation strategy, structure, content, and actual plan or schedule (latter may be an attachment or a stand-alone, referenced document).

competent authority—Country-specific agency or body designated to administer that country's laws/statutes governing marketing of safe and effective drugs, medical devices, foods, dietary supplements, cosmetics, and so on; competent authority fulfills this role by enacting regulations, guidelines, guidances, and so on, in line with those statutes/laws. Examples include the United States Food and Drug Administration (FDA), the United States Department of Agriculture (USDA), Health Canada, the United Kingdom's Medicines and Healthcare Products Regulatory Agency (MHRA) and Veterinary Medicines Directorate, Japan's Ministry of Health, Labor, and Welfare (MHLW), and Australia's Therapeutic Goods Administration (TGA).

confirmation—Signed statement that a process or test has been conducted in accordance with good manufacturing practices (GMP) and the relevant marketing authorization, as agreed in writing with the qualified person (QP) responsible for certifying the finished product batch before release. "Confirm" and "confirmed" have equivalent meanings.

contact plate (also touch plate)—A petri dish usually measuring 55 mm in diameter and containing convex-shaped agar that forms a dome above the dish to permit sampling flat surfaces for microorganisms. Note: RODAC is the brand name (Replicate Organism Detection and Counting Plate) of a contact plate the trademark of which is currently owned by Becton Dickinson.

contamination—The undesired introduction of impurities of a chemical or microbiological nature, or of foreign matter, into or onto a raw material intermediate, active pharmaceutical ingredient (API), finished drug, primary surface, or equipment. A *contaminant* is any particulate, molecular, and/or biologic entity that can adversely affect a material or process (*biocontaminant* is a bacterial, mycoplasma, fungal, or protozoa contaminant).

continual improvement—Ongoing activities to evaluate and positively change products, processes, and the quality system to increase effectiveness.

control strategy—Planned set of controls, derived from current product and process understanding, that assures process performance and product quality. The controls can include parameters and attributes related to drug substance and drug product materials and components, facility and equipment operating conditions, in-process controls, finished product specifications, and the associated methods and frequency of monitoring and control.

controlled area—A nonclassified room or operating area designed to control/minimize the presence, proliferation, and/or ingress of particulates, and in which specific environmental conditions (for examle, temperature, humidity, directional airflow, and viable and nonviable particulate limits) are defined and monitored to prevent contamination of exposed products.

correction—Repair, rework, or adjustment relating to the disposition of an existing discrepancy (also called *remedy, remediation*); usually the first step in a corrective action.

corrective action—Action taken to eliminate the causes of an existing discrepancy or other undesirable situation to prevent recurrence.

critical area—An area in which the sterilized drug product, containers, and closures are exposed to environmental conditions that must be designed to maintain product sterility.

critical process parameter (CPP)—Quantifiable equipment setting whose variability has an impact on a critical quality attribute and therefore should be monitored or controlled to ensure that the process produces the desired quality, purity, potency, and safety.

critical quality attribute (CQA)—Physical, chemical, biological, or microbiological property or characteristic that should be within an appropriate limit, range, or distribution to ensure the desired product quality.

customer—Person or organization (internal or external) that receives a product or service anywhere along the product's life cycle.

D

decision maker(s)—Person(s) with the competence and authority to make appropriate and timely quality risk management decisions.

design of experiments (DOE) or experimental design—Statistical technique used for planning, conducting, analyzing, and interpreting sets of experiments aimed at making sound decisions most efficiently.

design space—Multidimensional combination and interaction of input variables (for example, material attributes) and process parameters that have been demonstrated to provide assurance of quality. Note: Working within the design space is not considered as a change; however, movement out of the design space is considered to be a change and would normally initiate a regulatory post-approval change process.

detectability—Ability to discover or determine the existence, presence, or fact of a hazard.

discrepancy—Datum or result outside of the expected range; an unfulfilled requirement; may be called nonconformity, defect, deviation, out-of-specification, out-of-limit, out-of-trend.

disinfection—Act or process of chemically or physically destroying or removing vegetative pathogens on inanimate objects (a *disinfectant* is a chemical or physical agent that assists disinfection).

E

enantiomers—Compounds with the same molecular formula as the drug substance, which differ in the spatial arrangement of atoms within the molecule and are nonsuperimposable mirror images.

endotoxin—The lipopolysaccharide remnant of the outermost cell wall layer of a dead Gram-negative bacterium, which can be pyrogenic (fever-causing) to mammals, especially humans. Endotoxin is a potential contaminant of water, including pharmaceutical water. All pharmaceutical water for injection and pure steam have, among other specifications, an upper limit of not more than 0.25 endotoxin units/mL.

excipient—An inert substance used as a diluent or vehicle for a drug.

F

finished product—Batch of product in its final pack for release to the market.

flora—Identified microbes (to species level) found at a specific time in an operating area(s), room(s), or the collection of rooms used in manufacturing, testing, and warehousing (as in the whole facility); this includes microbes isolated from primary surfaces, air, as well as product, intermediates, and raw materials tested and determined to be contaminated after a specific area or suite exposure.

H

harm—Damage to health, including the damage that can occur from loss of product quality or availability.

hazard—Potential source of harm (ISO/IEC Guide 51).

housekeeping—General cleaning (including sweeping) and removal of accumulated process waste, dirty equipment, utensils, and other nonproduct materials resulting from normal manufacturing or warehousing activities.

I

importer—Holder of the marketing authorization required by Article 40.3 of Directive 2001/83/EC and Article 44.3 of Directive 2001/82/EC for importing medicinal products from countries outside the European Economic Community (EEC).

in vitro—outside the living body and in an artificial environment.

in vivo—within the living body.

in-process control—One of various control strategies that measures a critical quality attribute (CQA) at a particular point in an active pharmaceutical ingredient (API) or drug manufacturing process.

installation (vis-à-vis cleanrooms)—The ensemble that includes a cleanroom or one or more clean zones, together with all associated structures, air treatment systems, services, and utilities.

L

lyophilization—Freeze-drying process in which water is removed from a product after it is frozen and placed under a vacuum, allowing the ice to change directly from solid to vapor without passing through a liquid phase.

M

microbiological contamination—Presence of one or more various bacteria, yeasts, mold, protozoa, or their toxins/by-products (for example, endotoxins or exotoxins) that could adversely affect the product or a patient's health and safety.

microorganisms (or microbes)—Unicellular living creatures/organisms that include the bacteria, molds, yeasts, protozoa, mycoplasma, and archaea. Because viruses and prions do not satisfy the modern biology text definition of life, they are not organisms and, hence, not microorganisms.

mutual recognition agreement (MRA)—Appropriate arrangement between the European Economic Community (EEC) and an exporting third country mentioned in Article 51(2) of Directive 2001/83/EC and Article 55(2) of Directive 2001/82/EC.

mycobacterial—Of or relating to *Mycobacterium tuberculosis*.

N

nonconformity—Deficiency in a characteristic, product specification, process parameter, record, or procedure that renders the quality of a product unacceptable, indeterminate, or not according to specified requirements.

O

occupancy state—Status of a classified area with regard to the presence/absence of equipment and personnel and operation of the heating, ventilation, and air conditioning (HVAC).

official article—Term used by the United States Pharmacopeia (USP) to refer to any of the following materials: a drug substance, drug product, dietary ingredient, dietary substance, or excipient.

official compendium—Publication known as the United States Pharmacopeia (USP) according to Section 501(b) of the Federal Food, Drug, and Cosmetic Act (FDCA) (as amended) of the United States.

operational—Occupancy state in which the installation is functioning in a defined manner, with a specified number of personnel present and working in a defined manner.

P

particle/particulate matter—A minute piece of matter with defined physical boundaries; a solid or liquid object that, for purposes of classification of cleanrooms, falls within the size range of 0.1 to 5 micrometers (µm). A *viable* particle is one that consists of, or supports, one or more live microorganisms; a *nonviable* particle is one that consists of zero culturable microorganisms.

particle size—Diameter of a sphere that produces a response, by a given particle-sizing instrument, that is equivalent to the response produced by the particle being measured.

pathogenic—Regarding a microbe that is harmful to humans or animals.

pest control—System for preventing, evaluating, and eliminating infestation by rodents, insects, birds, and other vermin.

pilot scale—Manufacturing of drug product by a procedure fully representative of and simulating that used for full manufacturing scale.

polymorphism—The occurrence of different crystalline forms of the same drug substance. This may include solvation or hydration products (also known as pseudopolymorphs) and amorphous forms.

preventive action—Action taken to eliminate the cause of a potential discrepancy or other potential undesirable situation to make less probable such an occurrence.

primary surface—The first solid surface contacted in moving away from an exposed product. In a room, this includes the walls, floors, ceilings, and doors, the room side of air diffusers but not the duct side, and floor drain covers, but not the piping system. A primary surface is not a product contact surface.

prion—Infectious agent composed of protein, which can transmit its (mis-folded) configuration to native, similar proteins in an infected animal's central nervous system, causing transmissible spongiform encephalopathy.

process development studies—Experiments that help rule in or rule out the choice and sequence of specific unit operations and unit processes and their associated detailed choices of equipment models and critical process parameters for the manufacturing of an API or a finished drug.

product/service—Intended results of activities or processes; products/services can be tangible or intangible.

product life cycle—All phases in the life of the product, from the initial development through marketing and the product's discontinuation.

Q

qualified person (QP)—The person defined in Article 48 of Directive 2001/83/EC and Article 52 of Directive 2001/82/EC.

quality—A measure of a product's or service's ability to satisfy the customer's stated or implied needs; also, the degree to which a set of inherent properties of a product, system, or process fulfills requirements (see ICH Q6A definition specifically for quality of drug substance and drug products).

quality assurance (QA)—Proactive and retrospective activities that provide confidence that active pharmaceutical ingredient or drug product requirements are fulfilled.

quality by design (QbD)—A systematic approach to development that begins with predefined objectives and emphasizes product and process understanding and process control, based on sound science and quality risk management.

quality control (QC)—Steps taken during the generation of a product or service to ensure that it meets requirements and that the product or service is reproducible.

quality management—Accountability for the successful implementation of the quality system.

quality objectives—Specific, measurable activities or processes to meet the intentions and directions as defined in the quality policy.

quality plan—Documented result of quality planning that is disseminated to all relevant levels of the organization.

quality planning—Management activity that sets quality objectives and defines the operational and/or quality system processes and the resources needed to fulfill the objectives.

quality policy—Statement of intentions and direction issued by the highest level of the organization, related to satisfying customer needs. It is similar to a strategic direction that communicates quality expectations that the organization is striving to achieve.

quality system—Formalized business practices that define management responsibilities for organizational structure, processes, procedures, and resources needed to fulfill product/service requirements, customer satisfaction, and continual improvement.

quality unit (QU)—Group organized within an organization to promote quality in general practice.

R

reagent—A substance, other than a starting material or solvent, which is used in the manufacture of a new drug substance.

reprocessing—Subjecting all or part of a batch or lot of an in-process drug, a bulk process intermediate (final biological bulk intermediate), or a bulk drug of a single batch/lot to a previous step in the validated manufacturing process due to failure to meet predetermined specifications. Reprocessing procedures are foreseen as occasionally necessary, and are validated and preapproved by the quality control department or as part of the marketing authorization. Similarly, introducing an intermediate or active pharmaceutical ingredient, including one that does not conform to standards or specifications, back into the process and repeating a crystallization step or other appropriate chemical or physical manipulation steps (for example, distillation, filtration, chromatography, milling) that are part of the established manufacturing process. Continuation of a process step after an in-process control test has shown that the step is incomplete is considered to be part of the normal process, and not reprocessing.

requirements—Explicit or implicit needs or expectations of the patients or their surrogates (for example, healthcare professionals, regulators, and legislators). In this document, "requirements" refers not only to statutory, legislative, or regulatory requirements, but also to such needs and expectations.

reworking—Subjecting an in-process drug, a bulk process intermediate (final biological bulk intermediate), or final product of a single batch/lot to an alternate manufacturing process due to a failure to meet predetermined specifications. Reworking is an unexpected occurrence and is not preapproved as part of the marketing authorization.

risk—Combination of the probability of occurrence of harm and the severity of that harm.

risk acceptance—Decision to accept risk (ISO Guide 73).

risk analysis—Estimation of the risk associated with the identified hazards.

risk assessment—Systematic process for organizing information to support a risk decision that is made within a risk management process (the process consists of the identification of hazards and the analysis and evaluation of risks associated with exposure to those hazards).

risk communication—The sharing of information about risk and risk management between the decision maker and other stakeholders.

risk control—Actions implementing risk management decisions (ISO Guide 73).

risk evaluation—Comparison of the estimated risk to given risk criteria using a quantitative or qualitative scale to determine the significance of the risk.

risk identification—Systematic use of information to identify potential sources of harm (hazards) referring to the risk question or problem description.

risk management—Systematic application of quality management policies, procedures, and practices to the tasks of assessing, controlling, communicating, and reviewing risk.

risk reduction—Actions taken to lessen the probability of occurrence of harm and the severity of that harm.

risk review—Review or monitoring of output/results of the risk management process considering (if appropriate) new knowledge and experience about the risk.

run chart—Plot of process output over time without superimposed control limits.

S

sanitization—The act or process, physical or chemical, of reducing viable organisms on a surface to a defined acceptance level (a *sanitizer* is a physical or chemical agent that assists sanitization); *sterilization* is a subset of sanitization. Surface sanitization concerns product contact surfaces as well as durable surfaces not far removed from those that contact product (for example, outside surfaces of equipment, table tops, floors, walls, ceilings, exterior of drains, air registers).

senior management—Top management officials in a firm who have the authority and responsibility to mobilize resources.

settle plate—Suitable container (for example, Petri dish) of appropriate size, containing an appropriate, sterile, culture medium, which is left open for a defined period to collect viable particles depositing from the air.

severity—A measure of the possible consequences of a hazard.

sporicide—A chemical agent that destroys bacterial and fungal spores when used in sufficient concentration for a specified contact time. It is expected to kill all vegetative organisms. Health Canada prohibits a supplier from labeling a non-sporicidal disinfectant with claims against the vegetative cells of spore-forming bacteria whose spores may be the primary means of spread of healthcare-associated infections, which could mislead users into assuming that the disinfectant has sporicidal effectiveness.

stakeholder—An individual or organization having an ownership or interest in the delivery, results, and metrics of the quality system framework or business process improvements; also, any individual, group, or organization that can affect, be affected by, or perceive itself to be affected by a risk. Decision makers might also be stakeholders. The primary stakeholders are the patient, healthcare professional, regulatory authority, and industry.

statistical process control chart—Plot of process output over time with a superimposed central tendency line and upper and lower control limit lines.

sterilization—The act or process, physical or chemical, of destruction or elimination of all viable organisms (including bacterial and fungal spores, viruses, protozoa) in the inanimate environment; never being considered absolute, it is characterized by a probability of presence of one or more viable organisms and expressed as 10^{-n}. A *sterilant* is an agent that can assist sterilization; sterilants are liquid or vapor-phase agents. All sterilants are sporicides, but not all sporicides are sterilants.

stratified sampling—Process of collecting a representative sample by selecting units deliberately from various identified locations.

T

total organic (or oxidizable) carbon (TOC)—An indirect measure of organic molecules, measured as carbon, present in pharmaceutical (that is, compendial) waters.

U

unclassified area—A room or area not designated by grades but that needs to be designed and maintained such that its environment does not adversely impact the quality, purity, and integrity of the products. Unclassified areas may or may not be controlled areas.

unidirectional airflow—Controlled airflow through the entire cross-section of a clean zone with a steady velocity and approximately parallel streamlines.

unit operation—Distinct physical changes or unit actions (for example, micronizing, mixing, drying, filtration).

unit process—Unit operations involving chemical changes.

V

validation—Confirmation, through the provision of objective evidence, that the requirements for a specific intended use or application have been fulfilled.

validation life cycle—Process, equipment, and facility assurance that depends on the following stages (separated in time) being executed properly:

- *Stage 1—Process, equipment, and/or facility design.* The commercial manufacturing process is defined during this stage based on knowledge gained through development and scale-up activities.

- *Stage 2—Process, equipment, and/or facility qualification.* During this stage, the process design is evaluated (according to preapproved protocol) to determine if the process is capable of reproducible commercial manufacturing.

- *Stage 3—Process, equipment, and/or facility continued verification/ monitoring.* Ongoing assurance is gained during routine production that the process remains in a state of control.

- *Stage 4—Process, equipment, and/or facility retirement.* During this stage, any electronically stored data are transferred to replacement system(s) or simply preserved according to record retention policy. Also, to achieve "bookending," a final proving of proper calibration since the preceding set of calibrations is necessary to demonstrate that all instruments remained in a state of calibration prior to retirement.

verification—Confirmation, through the provision of objective evidence, that specified requirements have been fulfilled.

W

working shift—Scheduled period of work or production, usually no greater than 12 hours in length, during which operations are conducted by a single, defined group of workers.

References

21 CFR 11

21 CFR 11 Electronic Records; Electronic Signatures

21 CFR 210

21 CFR 210 Current Good Manufacturing Practice in Manufacturing, Processing, Packing, or Holding of Drugs; General

21 CFR 211

21 CFR 211 Current Good Manufacturing Practice for Finished Pharmaceuticals.
21 CFR 211 Subpart F Production and Process Controls
21 CFR 211.28 Personnel responsibilities
21 CFR 211.132 Tamper-Evident Packaging Requirements for Over-the-Counter (OTC) Human Drug Products
21 CFR 211.204 Returned Drug Products
21 CFR 211.208 Drug Product Salvaging

21 CFR 310

21 CFR 310 New drugs

21 CFR 314

21 CFR 314 Applications for FDA Approval to Market a New Drug

40 CFR 141

40 CFR 141 Subchapter D Water Programs, maximum contaminant levels for organic, inorganic and microbial agents.

21 CFR 829

21 CFR 829 Quality System Regulation

UNITED STATES FOOD AND DRUG ADMINISTRATION GUIDANCES AND OTHER DOCUMENTS

Administrative Procedure Act of 1946, 5 USC § 500 et seq.

Federal Food and Drugs Act of 1938, 21 USC § 301 et seq.

"Frequently Asked Questions About Therapeutic Biological Products." Dec 24, 2009.

"Grato Warning Letter." 2012. FDA Enforcement Action Page.

FDA Guidance for Industry: "Sterile Drug Products Produced by Aseptic Processing."

FDA Guidance for Industry: "Process Validation: General Principles and Practices."

Public Health Service Act of 1948, 42 USC § 262 Regulation of Biological Products, Subpart (j) "Application of the Federal Food, Drug, and Cosmetic Act."

Virus-Serum-Toxin Act of 1913, 21 USC § 151 et seq.

UNITED STATES PHARMACOPEIA

US Pharmacopeia General Notices and Requirements: "Preservation, Packaging, Storage, and Labeling."

US Pharmacopeia <1072> "Disinfectants and Antiseptics"

US Pharmacopeia <1079> "Good Storage and Shipping Practices"

US Pharmacopeia <1150> "Pharmaceutical Stability"

US Pharmacopeia <1118> "Monitoring Devices—Time, Temperature, and Humidity"

INTERNATIONAL CONFERENCE ON HARMONIZATION

ICH Q7A Section 7

ICH Q7 *Good Manufacturing Practice Guidance for Active Pharmaceutical Ingredients*

INTERNATIONAL ORGANIZATION FOR STANDARDIZATION (ISO) DOCUMENTS

ISO 19011:2011. 2011. *Guidelines for auditing management systems.* Milwaukee: ASQ Quality Press, 16.

WORLD HEALTH ORGANIZATION

WHO Good Manufacturing Practices: "Starting Materials."

WHO Good Manufacturing Practices: "Quality Assurance of Pharmaceuticals: A Compendium of Guidelines and Related Materials."

WHO "Guidelines for Sampling of Pharmaceutical Products and Related Materials."

WHO "Good Distribution Practices (GDP) for Pharmaceutical Products."

WHO "Expert Committee on Specifications for Pharmaceutical Preparations: Thirty-Seventh Report."

EUROPEAN AND OTHER NATIONAL GUIDELINES

European Directive 92/25/EEC Article 10 and Rules and Guidance for Pharmaceutical Distributors. 2007.

Final Version of Annex 15 to the EU Guide to Good Manufacturing Practice Qualification and Validation. July 2001.

EU GMP Guidelines, Eudralex Volume 4, Part I.

Health Products Food Branch (Health Canada) Guide-0069, "Guidelines for Temperature Control of Drug Products During Storage and Transportation."

Irish Medicines Board. "Guide to Control and Monitoring of Storage and Transportation Temperature Conditions for Medicinal Products and Active Substances." March 2006.

OTHER PUBLICATIONS

Anderson, P. F., and B. L. Wortman. 2004. *The Quality Auditor Primer*, 6th ed. West Terre Haute, IN: Quality Council of Indiana.

Arter, D. R. 2002. *Quality Audits for Improved Performance*, 3rd ed. Milwaukee: ASQ Quality Press.

Baker, G. 2010. "Only You Can Prevent Cross-Contamination: A Guide to Designing Cleaning Procedures for CMOs." Contract Pharma. Accessed 3/31/14. http://www.contractpharma.com/issues/2010-05/view_features/only-you-can-prevent-cross-contamination/.

Bossert, J. L., editor. 2004. *The Supplier Management Handbook*, 6th ed. Milwaukee: ASQ Quality Press.

Dean, D. A., E. R. Evans, and I. H. Hall, eds. 2000. *Pharmaceutical Packaging Technology*. London and New York: Taylor & Francis.

Fraise, A. P., P. A. Lambert, and J.-Y. Maillard, eds. 2004. *Principles and Practice of Disinfection, Preservation and Sterilization*. Oxford, UK and Malden, MA: Blackwell.

Pawar, H., N. Banerjee, S. Pawar, and P. Pawar. 2011. "Current Perspectives on Cleaning Validation in Pharmaceutical Industry: A Scientific and Risk Based Approach." *International Journal of Pharmaceutical and Phytopharmacological Research* 1 (August): 8–16.

PIC/S. 2007. P006-03 "Recommendations on Validation Master Plan Installation and Operational Qualification Non-Sterile Process Validation Cleaning Validation." September 25.

Pronovost D. 2000. *Internal Quality Auditing*. Milwaukee: ASQ Quality Press.

Russell, J.P., ed. 2013. *The ASQ Auditing Handbook: Principles, Implementation, and Use*, 4th ed. Milwaukee: ASQ Quality Press.

Russell, J.P., and T. L. Regel. 2000. *After the Quality Audit: Closing the Loop on the Audit Process*, 2nd ed. Milwaukee: ASQ Quality Press.

Shaw, A. B. 2007. "Drug Master Files." DIA webinar. March 19. Revised November 7, 2008.

Sinclair, U. 1906. *The Jungle*. New York: New American Library.

Whyte, W. 2010. *Cleanroom Technology: Fundamentals of Design, Testing and Operation*, 2nd ed. United Kingdom: John Wiley & Sons.

Wilkins, S. 2008. "Risk-Based Approaches to Cross Contamination." ISPE website. Accessed 3/31/14. http://www.ispe.org/knowledge-briefs/risk-based-approaches-to-cross-contamination.pdf.

United States Geological Survey. 2002. *Pharmaceuticals, Hormones, and Other Organic Wastewater Contaminants in U.S. Streams, 1999–2000: A National Reconnaissance*. Lincoln, NE: University of Nebraska.

Suggested Reading

CODE OF FEDERAL REGULATIONS 21 CFR (INCLUDING FDA PREAMBLE [FEDERAL REGISTER VOL. 43 NO. 190]) DOCUMENTS

210–211 Current Good Manufacturing Practice in Manufacture, Processing, Packing, or Holding Finished Pharmaceuticals

Section 7 Recalls (including Product Corrections)

Part 11 Electronic Records; Electronic Signatures

Part 58 Good Laboratory Practices for Non-Clinical Laboratory Studies

1308.11–1308.15 Schedules of Controlled Substances

205 Guidelines for State Licensing of Wholesale Prescription Drug Distributors

FOOD AND DRUG ADMINISTRATION GUIDANCES

Changes to an Approved NDA or ANDA

Container and Closure System Integrity Testing in Lieu of Sterility Testing as a Component of the Stability Protocol for Sterile Products

Container Closure Systems for Packaging Human Drugs and Biologics

Current Good Manufacturing Practice for Combination Products

Guidance for Industry for the Submission Documentation for Sterilization Process Validation in Applications for Human and Veterinary Drug Products

General Principles of Software Validation

Powder Blends and Finished Dosage Units—Stratified In-Process Dosage Unit Sampling and Assessment

Product Recalls, Including Removals and Corrections

Q1A (R2) Stability Testing of New Drug Substances and Products

Q1E Evaluation of Stability Data

Q3B (R) Impurities in New Drug Products

Quality Systems Approach to Pharmaceutical CGMP Regulations

Sterile Drug Products Produced by Aseptic Processing—Current Good Manufacturing Practice

FDA GUIDE TO INSPECTIONS

Investigations Operations Manual (IOM) 2008

Microbiological Pharmaceutical Quality Control Laboratories

Pharmaceutical Quality Control Laboratories

Topical Drug Products

Validation of Cleaning Processes
High Purity Water Systems
Biotechnology inspection guide reference materials and training aids

FDA GUIDELINES

Investigational New Drug Applications (INDs) for Phase 1 Studies of Drugs
Validation of the Limulus Amebocyte Lysate Test
Guide to Inspections of Sterile Drug Substance Manufacturers
Guide to Inspections of Oral Solid Dosage Forms Pre/Post Approval Issues for
    Development and Validation
Investigating Out-of-Specification Test Results for Pharmaceutical Production
Process Validation: General Principles and Practices

FDA POLICY GUIDES (COMPLIANCE POLICY GUIDES)

Preapproval Inspections 7346.832
Sterile Drug Process Inspections Program 7356.002A
Compliance Program Guidance Manual for FDA Staff: Drug Manufacturing Inspections
    Program 7356.002
Compliance Program Guidance Manual 7356.002F Active Pharmaceutical Ingredient
    (API) Process Inspection

PHARMACEUTICAL INSPECTION CONVENTION/ COOPERATION SCHEME

PE 008-2 Explanatory Notes for Industry on the Preparation of a Site Master File
PE 010-3 PIC/S Guide to Good Practices for the Preparation of Medicinal Products in
    Healthcare Establishments
PI 006-3 Recommendations on Validation Master Plan Installation and Operational
    Qualification Non-Sterile Process Validation Cleaning Validation
PI 007-4 Recommendation on the Validation of Aseptic Processes
PI 009-3 Aide-Memoire on Inspection of Utilities
PI 010-3 Procedure for Handling Rapid Alerts and Recalls Arising from Quality Defects
PI 011-3 Good Practices for Computerised Systems in Regulated "GXP" Environments
PI 012-3 Recommendation on Sterility Testing
PI 014-3 Recommendation on Isolators Used for Aseptic Processing and Sterility Testing

AMERICAN NATIONAL STANDARDS INSTITUTE

ISO 9001:2008 *Quality management systems—Requirements*
ISO 19011:2011 *Guidelines for auditing management systems*
ISO/IEC 17025:2005 *General requirements for the competence of testing and calibration
    laboratories*

DIRECTIVES

Directive 2001/82/EC on the Community Code Relating to Veterinary Medicinal
    Products

Directive 2003/94/EC Laying Down the Principles and Guidelines of Good
Manufacturing Practice in Respect of Medicinal Products for Human and
Investigational Medicinal Products for Human Use as Amended
Directive 2001/83/EC on the Community Code Relating to Human Medicinal
Products

EUROPEAN GOOD MANUFACTURING PRACTICE

Eudralex Volume 4, Parts I and II and Annexes

HEALTH CANADA GUIDELINES

0069 Guidelines for Temperature Control of Drug Products During Storage and
Transportation
Good Manufacturing Practices Guidelines

INTERNATIONAL CONFERENCE ON HARMONIZATION DOCUMENTS

ICH Q7 Good Manufacturing Practice Guide for Active Pharmaceutical Ingredients
ICH Q9 Quality Risk Management
ICH Q10 Pharmaceutical Quality System
ICH Q2A Text on Validation of Analytical Procedures
ICH Q2B Validation of Analytical Procedures: Methodology
ICH Q3A Impurities in New Drug Substances
ICH Q3C Impurities: Guideline for Residual Solvents
ICH Q6A Specifications: Test Procedures and Acceptance Criteria for New Drug
Substances and New Drug Products: Chemical Substances
ICH Q8 Pharmaceutical Development

INTERNATIONAL SOCIETY FOR PHARMACEUTICAL ENGINEERING GUIDELINES

ISPE GAMP IV and V (Good Automated Manufacturing Practice) Guide for
Validation of Automated Systems

US DRUG ENFORCEMENT AGENCY

21 USC § 812: L.91–513 Controlled substances act

PARENTERAL DRUG ASSOCIATION TECHNICAL REPORTS

Report No. 1 Validation of Steam Sterilization Cycles

JAPAN

Pharmaceutical Administration, Regulation, and Drug Development in Japan

EUROPEAN PHARMACOPEIA

2.2.44 Total Organic Carbon in Water for Pharmaceutical Use
2.2.46 Chromatographic Separation Techniques
2.6.7 Mycoplasmas

AUSTRALIAN GUIDELINES

TGA Guidelines for Sterility Testing of Therapeutic Goods
TGA Amended EU (EMEA/410/01) Guideline Note for Guidance on Minimizing the Risk of Transmitting Animal Spongiform Encephalopathy Agents via Human and Veterinary Medicinal Products

UNITED STATES PHARMACOPEIA

General chapters related to pharmaceutical analytical methods and practices
World Health Organization Documents
Good Manufacturing Practices (A Compendium of Guidelines and Related Materials Volume 2: Good Manufacturing Practices and Inspection)
QAS/04.068/Rev. 2 Good Distribution Practices for Pharmaceutical Products
Quality Assurance of Pharmaceuticals: A Compendium of Guidelines and Related Materials, 2004 (WHO)

FDA CENTER FOR BIOLOGICS EVALUATION AND RESEARCH GUIDANCES

Bioanalytical Method Validation
Biological Indicator (BI) Premarket Notification [510(k)] Submissions
Biological Product Deviation Reporting for Licensed Manufacturers of Biological Products Other than Blood and Blood Components
Characterization and Qualification of Cell Substrates and Other Biological Starting Materials Used in the Production of Viral Vaccines for Infectious Disease Indications
Points to Consider (PTC) in the Characterization of Cell Lines Used to Produce Biologicals
Q5A Viral Safety Evaluation of Biotechnology Products Derived from Cell Lines of Human or Animal Origin
Q5E Comparability of Biotechnological/Biological Product Subject to Changes in Their Manufacturing Process

9 CFR AND 21 CFR DOCUMENTS (RELATED TO BIOLOGICS)

9 CFR Parts related to animal biologics quality requirements in manufacturing
21 CFR 601 Licensing
21 CFR 600 Biological Products: General
21 CFR 610 Selected sections critical to biologic drugs

COMPLIANCE POLICY GUIDES

CPG 7345.848 Inspection of Biological Drug Products
Guide to Inspections of Lyophilization of Parenterals

Index

The Knowledge Center
www.asq.org/knowledge-center

Learn about quality. Apply it. Share it.

ASQ's online Knowledge Center is the place to:

- Stay on top of the latest in quality with Editor's Picks and Hot Topics.

- Search ASQ's collection of articles, books, tools, training, and more.

- Connect with ASQ staff for personalized help hunting down the knowledge you need, the networking opportunities that will keep your career and organization moving forward, and the publishing opportunities that are the best fit for you.

Use the Knowledge Center Search to quickly sort through hundreds of books, articles, and other software-related publications.

www.asq.org/knowledge-center

Ask a Librarian

Did you know?

- The ASQ Quality Information Center contains a wealth of knowledge and information available to ASQ members and non-members

- A librarian is available to answer research requests using ASQ's ever-expanding library of relevant, credible quality resources, including journals, conference proceedings, case studies and Quality Press publications

- ASQ members receive free internal information searches and reduced rates for article purchases

- You can also contact the Quality Information Center to request permission to reuse or reprint ASQ copyrighted material, including journal articles and book excerpts

- For more information or to submit a question, visit **http://asq.org/knowledge-center/ ask-a-librarian-index**

Visit www.asq.org/qic for more information.

ASQ®
The Global Voice of Quality™

Established in 1946, ASQ is a global community of quality experts in all fields and industries. ASQ is dedicated to the promotion and advancement of quality tools, principles, and practices in the workplace and in the community.

The Society also serves as an advocate for quality. Its members have informed and advised the U.S. Congress, government agencies, state legislatures, and other groups and individuals worldwide on quality-related topics.

Vision

By making quality a global priority, an organizational imperative, and a personal ethic, ASQ becomes the community of choice for everyone who seeks quality technology, concepts, or tools to improve themselves and their world.

ASQ is...

- More than 90,000 individuals and 700 companies in more than 100 countries

- The world's largest organization dedicated to promoting quality

- A community of professionals striving to bring quality to their work and their lives

- The administrator of the Malcolm Baldrige National Quality Award

- A supporter of quality in all sectors including manufacturing, service, healthcare, government, and education

- YOU

Visit www.asq.org for more information.

TRAINING   CERTIFICATION   CONFERENCES   MEMBERSHIP   **PUBLICATIONS**

The Global Voice of Quality™

Research shows that people who join associations experience increased job satisfaction, earn more, and are generally happier*. ASQ membership can help you achieve this while providing the tools you need to be successful in your industry and to distinguish yourself from your competition. So why wouldn't you want to be a part of ASQ?

Networking

Have the opportunity to meet, communicate, and collaborate with your peers within the quality community through conferences and local ASQ section meetings, ASQ forums or divisions, ASQ Communities of Quality discussion boards, and more.

Professional Development

Access a wide variety of professional development tools such as books, training, and certifications at a discounted price. Also, ASQ certifications and the ASQ Career Center help enhance your quality knowledge and take your career to the next level.

Solutions

Find answers to all your quality problems, big and small, with ASQ's Knowledge Center, mentoring program, various e-newsletters, *Quality Progress* magazine, and industry-specific products.

Access to Information

Learn classic and current quality principles and theories in ASQ's Quality Information Center (QIC), *ASQ Weekly* e-newsletter, and product offerings.

Advocacy Programs

ASQ helps create a better community, government, and world through initiatives that include social responsibility, Washington advocacy, and Community Good Works.

Visit www.asq.org/membership for more information on ASQ membership.

*2008, The William E. Smith Institute for Association Research

TRAINING   CERTIFICATION   CONFERENCES   **MEMBERSHIP**   PUBLICATIONS   The Global Voice of Quality™